MARGARET THATCHER
THE HONORARY JEW

MARGARET THATCHER

THE HONORARY JEW

HOW BRITAIN'S JEWS SHAPED THE IRON LADY AND HER BELIEFS

— ROBERT PHILPOT —

Biteback Publishing

First published in Great Britain in 2017 by
Biteback Publishing Ltd
Westminster Tower
3 Albert Embankment
London SE1 7SP
Copyright © Robert Philpot 2017

ISBN 978-1-78590-131-7

A CIP catalogue record for this book is available from the British Library.

Set in Adobe Garamond Pro

Printed and bound in Great Britain by
CPI Group (UK) Ltd, Croydon CR0 4YY

To my parents and Paul

'She is in some senses an honorary Jew herself'

– HUGO YOUNG, *THE GUARDIAN*, 27 MAY 1986

CONTENTS

PROLOGUE

VIENNA, JANUARY 1939

On 21 January 1939 Edith Mühlbauer received the letter from a Grantham grocer which would save her life.

Less than a year previously, the seventeen-year-old might have considered the notion that she would need rescuing by her English penfriend's father faintly ridiculous. The Mühlbauer family lived a comfortable existence on Schubertsgasse in Vienna's Alsergrund district. The area was home to the city's many medical institutions and to those Jewish professionals – doctors, lawyers, businessmen, bankers like Edith's father – who had escaped the poverty, immigrants, prostitutes and unassimilated orthodox Hasidic Jews of the old walled Leopoldstadt ghetto across the Danube. As the historian Marsha Rozenblit suggested, Vienna's ninth district was very much 'the proper address for a new breed of urban Jew'.[1]

It was an area rich with historical and Jewish association. Franz Schubert's birthplace was on a neighbouring street to Schubertsgasse. To the south stood the baroque Palais Lichtenstein with its art museum; the austere silver-grey Josephinum Palace founded by Emperor Joseph II to train the imperial army's doctors and surgeons; and the city's huge general hospital with the 'praying pavilion' synagogue for Jewish patients in its grounds. To the east, the disused Friedhof Rossau Jewish cemetery which dated back to 1540, bordered by the Jewish hospital and old people's home. Before he fled the city in June 1938, Sigmund Freud's practice lay on Berggasse. Besides

1

Schubert and Freud, the Alsergrund was at one time also home to Theodor Herzl, the father of modern Zionism; Wolfgang Amadeus Mozart; and Victor Adler, who founded the Social Democratic Party of Austria.

There seemed little that Edith needed, or wanted, to be rescued from. But when Alfred Roberts's letter, with the permit which allowed her to apply for a visa to travel to England, arrived on that winter morning, Edith took out her typewriter and wrote: 'I thank you very much for sending it. I will never in my whole live forgett [*sic*] it you.' With a hint at the mixture of pain and relief that their daughter's impending departure was causing them, Edith continued: 'Even my parents were happy that it is possible now for me to go to England.'

Edith also wanted to offer a sign of her appreciation: 'Please tell me what you and your dear family like for a present?' She had an idea that probably caused the Roberts family momentary confusion. Edith asked if Roberts's daughters, Muriel and Margaret, would like a 'pocket' – which, confusingly, is the word for handbag in German – and, if so, in what colour? And what would Roberts and his 'dear wife' like? 'Tell it to me,' she added neatly in her own hand at the end of the typed sentence. And then it was on to practicalities. 'How far it is from London to Grantham?' she asked. 'Have I to take the train from London to Grantham or the ship?'[2]

But, as she thanked Roberts once again for his help, Edith knew that she had to escape soon. The plight of her fellow Jews worsened by the day. The terror had begun a year previously, within hours of the Wehrmacht crossing the border into Austria on 12 March. No shots had been fired; it had not been necessary – there had been no resistance. They called it the Blumenkreig – the war of flowers. Cheering crowds greeted the German troops with Hitler salutes. Buildings were draped with swastika flags. Women threw flowers at smiling soldiers.

Some 70,000 people – many of them Jews – had been rounded up and arrested within days of the Germans' arrival. On 1 April, the first convoy set off for the Dachau concentration camp, across the former German border near Munich. Jewish-owned shops and businesses were seized or menacing

Brownshirts were stationed outside to enforce a boycott. Naturally, Jews were among the 400,000 people barred from voting in the plebiscite in which 99.7 per cent of Austrians endorsed the Anschluss.

The American reporter, William Shirer, recorded the 'unbelievable scenes' he witnessed in Edith's hometown:

> The Viennese, usually so soft and sentimental, were behaving worse than the Germans, especially toward the Jews. Every time you went out, you saw gangs of Jewish men and women, with jeering storm troopers standing over them and taunting crowds shouting insults, on their hands and knees scrubbing Schuschnigg [the former Austrian chancellor] slogans off the sidewalks and curbs. I had never seen quite such humiliating scenes in Berlin or Nuremberg.[3]

Shortly afterwards, the Nuremberg Laws – stripping Jews of their citizenship and making them mere subjects of the Nazi state, and forbidding intermarriage between Jews and Aryans – were applied to Austria. Jews were banished from most professions, the doors of schools and universities closed to them. By the summer, Jewish emigration had reached a monthly average of 8,600.

Worse was to come. On 9 November – Kristallnacht – plumes of smoke filled the night sky as all but one of Vienna's forty-two synagogues were burned to the ground. In the streets mobs attacked and looted 4,000 Jewish-owned shops as the police stood to one side. Eight thousand Jews were arrested and 5,000 were sent, in the following days, to Dachau.[4]

At some point during this unfolding tragedy, Edith's father realised he was powerless to protect his family. Edith wrote to her English penfriend, Muriel Roberts, asking whether she could come and stay. Muriel passed the letter to her father. Edith's father then wrote directly to Alfred Roberts. The Roberts had never met Edith and they could not accept such an undertaking alone. 'We had neither the time – having to run the shops – nor the money,' Roberts's younger daughter later recalled.[5] So Roberts turned to his fellow local Rotarians, reading out the plea from Edith's father at their next meeting. The Rotarians agreed that, together, they would support Edith.

They would pay for her travel, provide her with a guinea a week in pocket money and each take the teenager in for a month or so.[6]

With the promise of sanctuary and safety in England now on the horizon, Edith waited. On 23 March 1939, she replied to a further letter from Roberts in which she had enclosed a photograph. She had attempted to get her visa at the British Passport Office but there were about 200 people there and only twenty received visas. Therefore she had to send her passport to the consulate for a visa. 'Never mind,' she wrote, 'I'll wait patient [*sic*], for there are here a great number of applications to be dealt with.' Again, she expressed her gratitude to Roberts: 'I am ever so glad that you helped me and that there are various other people which want to help me too, and take me into their nice homes. I really hope to be happy there.'[7]

'The great spiritual and moral truths of Judaism'

Half a century after Alfred Roberts agreed to help Edith Mühlbauer escape the Nazis, his daughter delivered her most famous address on how her faith informed her politics. Nicknamed the Sermon on the Mound, Margaret Thatcher's May 1988 speech to the General Assembly of the Church of Scotland offered the then-Prime Minister the chance to defend her government's policies in the face of vociferous criticism from many leading churchmen.

But while she claimed to speak 'personally as a Christian as well as a politician',[8] the speech also hinted at the fact that, as the *Sunday Telegraph* had declared five months previously: 'Judaism is the new creed of Thatcherite Britain.'[9] The High Tory paper was not alone in its conclusion. From the other end of the political spectrum came a similar view: *The Guardian's* Hugo Young pronounced the Prime Minister 'in some senses an honorary Jew herself'.[10] In her speech, Mrs Thatcher referred twice to Britain's 'Judaic-Christian tradition', once to its 'Judaic-Christian inheritance' and pronounced: 'The Christian religion – which, of course, embodies many of the great spiritual and moral truths of Judaism – is a fundamental part of our national heritage.'

Neither was this praise for 'Judeo-Christian' values an isolated one. As Eliza

Filby suggested, Mrs Thatcher's repeated use of this term – which entered popular parlance in the United States in the aftermath of the Second World War – underlined 'her identification with the Jewish faith'.[11] Lady Thatcher confirmed this assertion: 'I believe in what are often called "Judeo-Christian" values: indeed, my whole political philosophy is based on them.' The former Prime Minister recognised the dangers of 'falling into the trap of equating in some way the Jewish and Christian faiths' – as a Christian, she did not 'believe that the Old Testament – the history of the Law – can be fully understood without the New Testament – the history of Mercy'. However, she also expressed her belief that Christians should pay more heed to 'the Jewish emphasis on self-help and acceptance of personal responsibility', while their bishops could learn from the teachings of her favourite religious leader, Chief Rabbi Immanuel Jakobovits.[12]

These sentiments were not simply another example of what critics saw as Mrs Thatcher's desire to drape her political project in the cloak of religious justification. Instead, the roots of her identification with Judaism – as with her political philosophy in general – are to be found in the Methodist upbringing and wider Protestant ethics imparted to her by her father, Alfred Roberts. For while Mrs Thatcher famously had little to say about her mother Beatrice, she frequently waxed lyrical about the impact of her father. 'I just owe almost everything to my father,' she declared on the steps of Downing Street after becoming Prime Minister in May 1979.[13]

Life in the Roberts household, in Lady Thatcher's words, 'revolved around Methodism'.[14] But there was, believed Charles Dellheim, 'a certain Hebraic tinge to the Methodist milieu' of her upbringing which contributed to her values and political outlook.[15] Alfred and Beatrice Roberts raised their daughters in a particular tradition of Methodism. It was those Methodist principles and her father's understanding of them, which, later in her life, Mrs Thatcher saw reflected in Judaism.

Nonconformism has historically had strong links with Liberalism and the left. In the nineteenth century, William Gladstone suggested it had 'formed the backbone of British Liberalism'.[16] Liberalism, in turn, had been the principal vehicle by which Nonconformists sought to advance the cause of civic and religious liberty and reduce the powers of the Established Church. At the same time, the Liberal Party advanced principles, such as support for free trade, with which many Nonconformists naturally sympathised, a reflection of their hostility to state interference in religious matters.[17] After its emergence, a strong bond also developed between the Labour Party and Nonconformism. Indeed, the party was often said to owe 'more to Methodism than Marx'.

But these associations were largely ones with Primitive Methodism, the strand of Methodism which split from Wesleyan Methodism in the middle of the nineteenth century. Primitive Methodism aligned itself with political progressivism and was strong in Wales, Cornwall, the Staffordshire Potteries, Yorkshire and the Durham and Northumberland coalfields.[18] Alfred Roberts and his family, however, were Wesleyan Methodists, who were altogether more conservative. In relation to other forms of Nonconformism, Wesleyan Methodism – which was usually associated with the middle classes and flourished in Lincolnshire, Bristol and parts of Manchester, Sheffield and Leeds – was, in the words of the Methodist leader Rupert Davies, 'almost "High Church"'.[19] The strong bonds between Liberalism and Methodism were far weaker among Wesleyans – John Wesley had been a Tory – and, wrote David Bebbington, 'only among Wesleyans were Conservatives to be found in any numbers'.[20]

The differing political dispositions of Primitive and Wesleyan Methodism were captured by a letter to the *Methodist Recorder* from one Reverend J. Ernest in 1922: 'Nothing has characterised Wesleyan Methodism more than its determination not to support a particular party ... can this really be claimed of Primitive Methodism?'[21] It was a sentiment which must have appealed to Roberts, who, throughout his career in local politics, always stood as an independent. Moreover, the interwar drift of lower-middle class Nonconformists away from the Liberal Party to the Tories – Stanley Baldwin assiduously wooed such voters – was echoed in Alfred Roberts's own political journey.[22]

While the two Methodist strands were reunited in 1932, Grantham waited another twelve years before accepting the reunion, maintaining a separate Wesleyan church, Primitive Methodist chapel and Free Methodist chapel. That Roberts chose to take his family not to the nearby Primitive or Free Methodist chapels but to Finkin Street in central Grantham was no doubt both a political and social statement, as much as it was a theological one.

Roberts's Methodism ran seamlessly through every aspect of his life. In his eyes, there were no distinctions between his time serving customers behind the mahogany counter in his shop on North Parade, preaching before the congregation in the pulpit beneath the giant organ in Finkin Street, or admonishing his over-spending fellow councillors across Grantham's council chamber and lamenting the fact that 'the people who don't pay the rates are sponging on those who do'.[23]

The homespun truths which Mrs Thatcher later used to deliver her political message – in which her father figured so frequently that, as Peter Hennessy suggested, it sometimes felt as if the country was ruled by him from beyond the grave – reflected this mixture of Roberts as lay preacher, grocer and civic leader.[24]

The beliefs which Roberts preached and which underpinned his daughter's worldview litter his sermon notes. 'The Kingdom of God is within you,' Margaret's father suggested, reflecting his belief in the individual's responsibility before God for their own actions.[25] Fifty years later in Downing Street, Mrs Thatcher recalled the impact of her parents' beliefs: 'All my upbringing was to instil into both my sister and I a fantastic sense of duty, a great sense of whatever you do you are personally responsible for it. You do not blame society. Society is not anyone.'[26]

Individual responsibility and the work ethic were closely tied. 'It is the responsibility of man ordained by the creator that he shall labour for the means of existence. It is a supreme act of faith,' Roberts told his congregants.[27] Just after she had won her third consecutive election victory in 1987, his daughter bemoaned the 'British guilt-complex' which traduced success. She pondered its cause and found the answer in 'a misplaced Nonconformist conscience – a misunderstanding of people like John Wesley'. No doubt with her father's teachings in mind, Mrs Thatcher attempted to correct this false impression of Methodism's founding father who, she was keen to point out, was 'of course a High Tory':

> He inculcated the work ethic, and duty. You worked hard, you got on by the result of your own efforts: then, as you prospered, it was your duty to help others to prosper also. The essence of Methodism is in Matthew 24 – the Parable of the Talents. You have a duty to make what you can out of your talents, and to assist others. All that helped to build up a middle class in this country – a middle class with a conscience. That conscience built churches, hospitals, schools, abolished slavery, founded Dr Barnardo's.[28]

That self-advancement was a moral obligation was also evident in Alfred Roberts's deep commitment to the value of education. It was a commitment seen not only in the manner in which he raised his daughter, but also in his somewhat more surprising, given its associations with trade unionism and the left, chairmanship of Grantham's Workers' Educational Association.

As Mrs Thatcher's comments in 1987 indicate, individual responsibility did not negate the importance of the community, public service or private charity. Roberts's belief in what his daughter later termed 'duties to the church, duties to your neighbour' was apparent in his household.[29] At Christmas, 150 parcels purchased by the Grantham Rotary Club and bound for poor families were made up in the shop. The beneficiaries of Beatrice's twice-weekly bakes were not simply her own family, but the sick, elderly and unemployed. Mrs Thatcher would later describe her parents' attitude: 'We were always encouraged to think in terms of *practical* help and to think very little of people who thought that their duty to the less well-off started and finished by getting up and protesting in the market place.'[30]

Methodism, of course, had a long tradition of such protesting: Wesley was involved in the anti-slavery movement and advocated prison reform, while his heirs fought against the privileges afforded to the Church of England, as well as for temperance and Sabbatarianism. By the 1930s, the Wesleyan Roberts

may have fought to retain 'our English Sunday' and, like his wife, been a tee-
totaller, but the causes to which many Methodists now gravitated – pacifism
and social reform – were not ones he shared. Involvement in 'social issues', he
believed, risked turning the church into a 'glorified discussion group', a sentiment which would be echoed in his daughter's assertion in her 1988 address
that 'Christianity is about spiritual redemption, not social reform.'[31]

Given his apparent aversion to protesting, it was unsurprising that Roberts had little sympathy for the unemployed Jarrow marchers as they passed
through Grantham in 1936.[32] His daughter did admire, however, 'how neatly
turned out' the children of the town's unemployed families were. 'Their parents were determined to make sacrifices for them,' she later wrote, before em-
phasising the link between individual responsibility, charity and community
which her father imparted: 'The spirit of self-reliance and independence was
very strong in even the poorest people ... It meant that they never dropped
out of the community and, because others quietly gave what they could, the
community remained together.'[33] Her upbringing thus led Mrs Thatcher to
believe in the moral superiority of private charity – where the individual
gave voluntarily – over tax-financed welfare, where he or she did not.[34] That
this may have felt paternalistic to the recipients, especially to those who felt
as citizens that they had certain 'rights', was not a concept for which either
father or daughter had much time.

While John Campbell described Roberts's preaching as 'fundamentalist
[and] Bible-based',[35] this appears to be a misreading of his beliefs. As Antonio
Weiss argued, Roberts's sermon notes indicate both a clear acceptance of evolutionary theory, a rejection of fundamentalism – 'Orthodoxy, tradition and
Fundamentalism may be a guide for some, but they must never become our
chains' – and, through his references to Charles Darwin, Herbert Spencer,
William Wordsworth, Aristotle and Alexander Pope, an openness to non-
religious influences.[36]

There are suggestions of limits to Roberts's ecumenism. Although he enjoyed a friendly relationship with the Catholic priest whose church stood
opposite his shop, Roberts refused an offer to view the pictures inside. 'No,

no, no,' he responded. 'I'll never put my foot inside a Catholic church.' However, as Charles Moore argued, such attitudes were not unusual at the time.[37] But there is also evidence to suggest that Roberts was not a bigot. Indeed, his sermon notes urged the congregation to 'avoid the presumptuous claim that any one way of any church has a special prerogative where the Holy Spirit of God is concerned'.[38]

Mrs Thatcher herself felt that no 'great theological divide had been crossed' when, after marrying in Wesley's Chapel in London, she began to worship with her husband at their local Anglican church. It helped, she later said, that the Farnborough parish church was low church, before adding slightly dismissively: 'Anyway, John Wesley considered himself a member of the Church of England to his dying day.'[39] Political and social factors may also have been at play. Given her political ambitions, joining the 'Tory Party at prayer', as it was then called, was not an unhelpful step, while worshipping at an Anglican church – she was never confirmed into the Church of England – signalled the rather firmer foothold in the ranks of the middle classes with which Mrs Thatcher's marriage had provided her. Perhaps unconsciously this little symbol of social mobility was her way of aping her father's attendance at a Wesleyan rather than a Primitive Methodist chapel.

That ecumenism may also, as Weiss noted, have manifested itself in Mrs Thatcher's later admiration for the Jews.[40] When ordaining her an 'honorary Jew', Young suggested that 'her interest in Jews and the Jewish cause has not been lifelong. In Methodist Grantham and on the Rotary circuit in Kent, where she was grounded in Tory politics, the bias, one imagines, might have been rather the other way'. Instead, he argued, the bond was forged in her future parliamentary seat of Finchley, where 'any novice politician becomes aware of the Jewish vote'. While twenty-five years of 'courting ... the synagogues' of her constituency had no doubt provided her with 'a long lesson in the Jewish virtues, which closely resemble her own'.[41]

It is true that for many in the small towns of England in the 1930s, the bias was, indeed, 'the other way'. As Dellheim suggested, 'a grocer's daughter from a classic lower-middle class background ... [would] more likely to have been an anti-Semite than a philo-Semite'. Margaret Roberts did not, however, fall prey to the prejudice that regarded Jews as 'capitalist usurpers undermining the "little man"'.[42]

Alfred Roberts certainly seems to have been free from such prejudices: apart from his efforts on behalf of Edith Mühlbauer, he subscribed to the *Picture Post*, with its liberal, anti-fascist bent, and encouraged his daughter to read books such as *Insanity Fair*, which recounted Nazi anti-Semitism. He appears as a man who was both aware of the perilous situation that Europe's Jews faced and prepared to answer a call for help. When, nearly sixty years later, Edith Nökelby (as she had become) was traced to Sao Paulo in Brazil, Lady Thatcher responded: 'What can one person do? That is the question that people so often ask. Never hesitate to do whatever you can, for you may save a life.'[43] These were words Alfred Roberts could easily have uttered.

Beyond this awareness of, and sympathy for, the victims of Nazi persecution, we see in Roberts's Methodism the religious and ethical foundations upon which his daughter's later relationship with the Jewish community would be built. The commitment to individual responsibility and self-reliance; the centrality of John Wesley's work ethic; the importance of education; and the belief in a moral obligation to better oneself and to give back to the community through good works. Mrs Thatcher recognised this herself. Three weeks after moving into No. 10, she met the Israeli Prime Minister, Menachem Begin, in Downing Street. She gushed about her admiration for Jews, offering a description which mixed religion with a paean to what she would later describe as the 'Jewish way of life':[44] 'It has to do with my Methodist upbringing,' she told Begin. 'Methodism, you see, means method. It means sticking to your guns, dedication, determination, triumph over adversity, reverence for education – the very qualities you Jews have always cherished.'[45] There was nothing hollow in the simple claim of Lord Young, one of her Jewish Cabinet ministers: 'She was a Judeophile.'[46]

In Finchley, Mrs Thatcher heard the values her father had preached expressed on the doorsteps of her Jewish constituents, as well as expounded in its synagogues. She may well have been unaware of these associations at the time, but she surely recognised them as they were expressed back to her in the streets of north London two decades later. 'In the thirty-three years I represented it [Finchley], I never had a Jew come in poverty and desperation to one of my constituency surgeries. They had always been looked after by their own community,' she wrote in her memoirs.[47]

Alone, however, this might not have been sufficient to turn her respect and admiration for Jewish values into an identification which was so close that it would lead her supporters to pronounce Judaism 'the new creed of Thatcherite Britain'. There were thus further bonds which went beyond the recognition of supposedly shared beliefs. As we shall see, Mrs Thatcher saw in her Jewish constituents' efforts to attain a place in the ranks of the middle classes – many of them had roots and family in distinctly non-suburban Spitalfields, Stepney Green and Whitechapel – echoes of her father's journey. And, of course, many years later, she would present herself as the champion of similarly upwardly mobile voters in the likes of Basildon, Welwyn Hatfield, Peterborough and Watford.

Still, though, there was something more. As Campbell wrote, Mrs Thatcher emerged onto the political stage in the early 1970s as the 'archetypal Tory lady in a hat and pearls, quintessentially southern and suburban'.[48] By then, this had become a very real part of her political persona: the persona which made her acceptable to, and accepted by, local Tory associations. But it rather disguised another crucial element of her make-up: the Nonconformist grocer's daughter from provincial England, the grammar school girl whose self-taught father had left school at thirteen.

The part of her that was acutely attuned to the snobberies and prejudices ingrained into the upper echelons of the Conservative Party and Britain's ruling classes recognised Jews as kindred spirits. Thanks to both her background and her gender, she, too, regarded herself as an outsider. But for her there was no shame, indeed, there was nobility in her father's trade as a shopkeeper. Having historically been excluded from so many occupations, few Jews would have considered joining in the sneering which sometimes accompanied references to 'the grocer's daughter'.

And when, through calculation and conviction, Mrs Thatcher began her assault on what she saw as the mushy, consensual and unprincipled form that the Conservative Party had taken in the post-war era, she found her staunchest allies among that distinct minority grouping: the Jewish Tory. Together, Sir Keith Joseph and Alfred Sherman would help provide the intellectual underpinning for what became the 'Thatcher revolution'.

The images which defined her election victories – encapsulated by their 1979 offering 'Labour isn't working' – were crafted by two brothers born into a family of Baghdadi Jews, Charles and Maurice Saatchi. They had never worked on a political account, weren't Conservatives and, suggested a colleague, feared they would be regarded by the Tories as 'upstart Jewboys'.[49] In those elections, as she did with millions of their fellow countrymen, Mrs Thatcher crafted an appeal which stripped the Conservative Party of the whiff of elitism which, as Sherman later suggested, had made it 'unsympathetic as a milieu, rather than as a political force' to many British Jews.[50] With power attained, she appointed more Jews than any previous Prime Minister to her Cabinets. There were, as one of her predecessors, Harold Macmillan, contemptuously and sniffily remarked, 'more Estonians in the Cabinet than Etonians'.[51] Their presence in the highest ranks of government was all the more remarkable given that in the twenty-five years after the Second World War, there had only been two Jewish Conservative MPs.[52] But in Sir Keith Joseph, Nigel Lawson, David Young, Leon Brittan, Malcolm Rifkind and Michael Howard, she found men who if not always sharing her views shared her impatience with the 'grousemoor' Conservatism of the party's old guard.

There would later be what she no doubt deemed as snobbish carping from such patricians. Of particular irritation to the Prime Minister was the moral censure of her policies by the Church of England, most famously in its 'Faith in the City' report. To her rescue, however, came the Chief Rabbi who had little time for the supposed obligations government owed to the poor and offered a rather different prescription for the nation's ills to that suggested by the bishops: 'Building up self-respect by encouraging ambition and enterprise through a more demanding and satisfying work-ethic, which is designed to eliminate idleness and to nurture pride in "eating the toil of one's hands" as the immediate targets.'[53] At times Jakobovits appeared to behave more like a traditional head of the Established Church. Rarely, suggested Hugo Young, did anything cross his lips which did not 'chime harmoniously with some aspect or other of the new Conservatism'.[54]

Not every Jew appreciated being the object of Margaret Thatcher's admiration – many would oppose her vigorously and baulk at the blessings the Chief Rabbi appeared to bestow on her project – but many more did. This, then, is the story of a very special relationship.

CHAPTER 1

IN THE BEGINNING

By mid-April 1939, Edith Mühlbauer was finally on her way to Britain, the anxiety of whether she would see her parents and family again mixed with the relief of escaping the Nazis' tightening grip on central Europe. There was little about Grantham that Edith found familiar. This provincial Middle England town was as far from Mitteleuropa as it was possible to imagine. Perhaps its reputation was best captured by a former town clerk: 'A narrow town, built on a narrow street and inhabited by narrow people.'[1]

Edith arrived at the Roberts's home bearing the gifts she had written about: red handbags, one for Muriel, the other for her penfriend's younger sister, Margaret. Seventeen-year-old Muriel was amiable and bright, had recently left school and was training to become a physiotherapist. It is not hard to see why she sometimes found Margaret, who was more academic and serious, irritating; constantly held up as a model pupil by her teachers at Kesteven and Grantham Girls' School, where Muriel had also attended and where their father was a governor.[2] Four years younger than her sister, Margaret was hard-working, diligent and invariably well-behaved.

Edith remembered Margaret's beautiful hair and thought her reserved.[3] That latter impression may have been misplaced. While others recalled that Margaret was quiet in class, there was nothing timid about her. She enjoyed public speaking, entering competitions where she recited the poetry of Longfellow, Tennyson, Whitman and Kipling. At Kesteven's debating club she invariably asked visiting speakers a question and, in debate, she exhibited greater self-confidence than many other pupils.[4]

Margaret was very much her father's daughter. Roberts cut an imposing figure: a tall, handsome man in his late forties with blond, almost albino, curly hair and striking blue eyes. His daughters' contemporaries would later recall him in a largely positive light: 'dignified', 'delightful', 'whenever his name was mentioned it was mentioned with great reverence'.[5] Despite his rather austere countenance – and surely the tale of Edith Mühlbauer confirms this – Roberts was also capable of acts of great personal kindness. In old age Edith recalled him as a 'serious and lovely man'.[6]

Edith's escape had been facilitated by Roberts's membership of the Rotary. For Margaret, her father, the local councillor, Methodist lay preacher, president of the Chamber of Trade, a governor of the local boys' and girls' grammar schools and a director of the Grantham Building Society, was truly committed to the Rotary's motto of 'Service above Self'. Rotarians called for their members to put partisanship to one side, raise money for charities and good causes, and become both informed about and involved in local, national and international affairs.[7]

But the foundations of this civic engagement, and the source of many of the homilies Margaret would later share with the nation, were her father's two shops. Within two years of marrying Beatrice Stephenson, a seamstress who lived at home with her 'very, very Victorian, very, very strict' mother,[8] Roberts had managed to acquire his first store: a small grocery at No. 1 North Parade. Over the next six years, he opened another shop half a mile away and then bought out his neighbour's newsagent in North Parade, thereby becoming a sub-postmaster.

Margaret's later claims that Alfred was a 'specialist grocer' may have been something of an exaggeration,[9] but it was a forgivable one. His daughter was justifiably proud of her self-made father who, hailing from a family of shoemakers, left school at thirteen and, by working and saving hard, had progressed from a series of odd jobs, including, as she joyfully related many years later at Prime Minister's Questions, working in the tuck shop at Oundle School, before becoming a grocer's apprentice and owner of two shops.[10]

For Margaret, her father was not simply a 'specialist grocer', he was also a 'self-taught scholar'.[11] While allowing again for daughterly pride, this description does capture Roberts's reverence for education. He had wanted to be a teacher but his vocation had been frustrated by the need for him to leave school in order to contribute to the family finances. He was, recalled Lady Thatcher, 'determined to make up for this and to see that I took advantage of every educational opportunity'.[12] Roberts was thus not simply a vociferous reader himself – the town librarian deemed him 'the best-read man in Grantham'[13] – but ensured through weekly library visits that his younger, more academic, daughter was, too. She may have struggled with his copy of the philosophical magazine, the *Hibbert Journal*, but Margaret dutifully read the Brontës, Charles Dickens and Jane Austen, and she came to share her father's love of poetry.[14]

Father and daughter also had a shared passion for politics. Two years after Margaret's birth, the local Chamber of Trade nominated Roberts to stand for election to the town council. As was the convention at the time, he ran as an independent. But this label was largely a guise: a Liberal who became a supporter of the National Government and actively supported the Conservative candidates in the 1935 and 1945 general elections, Roberts was part of the Chamber of Trade-backed anti-Labour grouping which controlled the council. It was a coalition welded together by a fear of socialism, disdain for the unions, and, especially for men like Roberts, the threat to their livelihoods posed by the Co-op.[15] As chairman of the finance and rating committee, Roberts was dubbed 'Grantham's Chancellor of the Exchequer' by the *Grantham Journal*,[16] and he was a fierce advocate of keeping the rates as low as possible. Lady Thatcher later described him as 'an old-fashioned liberal. Individual responsibility was his watchword and sound finance his passion'.[17]

Underlying these political principles were deep religious convictions. As Edith soon realised, Alfred and Beatrice's religious faith pervaded every aspect of family life. Grace was said before meals and their daughters' social lives revolved around church: concerts, sewing circles and the Methodist Guild.

On Sundays, Margaret and her sister attended up to two services a day at the Finkin Street Methodist Church, as well as a Sunday school at ten and a further Sunday school after lunch (where Margaret played the piano). Alfred would sometimes deliver the sermons, which was something of a privilege given Finkin Street's reputation as a 'powerhouse of good preaching'.[18] But he also spent many Sundays, often with Margaret in tow, preaching in the Methodist chapels throughout Lincolnshire's towns and villages that were part of the circuit for which he was responsible.

Roberts's daughters appeared to enjoy certain aspects of their religious upbringing. Margaret liked the music, singing Charles Wesley's hymns and listening to her parents' conversations with their fellow congregations, which often went beyond religion to national and international politics. But there were parts which they seem to have been less appreciative of. Lady Thatcher later wrote that she sometimes found the multiple church visits on a Sunday 'too much of a good thing' and would try to get out of going,[19] while Muriel complained that 'it was all church, church, church'.[20]

Some of the blame for the strictures imposed upon them – for instance, the bans on dancing, children's parties, or playing card and board games – Muriel appeared to lay at the door of her mother.[21] Margaret formed the view that 'it was rather a sin to enjoy yourself by entertainment … Life was not to enjoy yourself. Life was to work and do things.'[22]

Certainly, Beatrice shared her husband's thriftiness. The house in which Edith came to stay, above the shop in North Parade where the Roberts lived until their daughters were young adults, was one which Margaret remembered as 'very small … [with] no mod cons'.[23] It had no hot water and the toilet was outside, although the smell of spices, coffee and smoked hams that wafted up from the shop to the living quarters may have given the house a more exotic atmosphere than was first apparent. The lack of mod cons, believed Campbell, was more a reflection of Alfred's 'religious and temperamental' outlook – his 'puritanism and parsimony' – than straitened economic circumstances.[24] Margaret seems to have been aware of this: she dreamed of having 'a nice house … a house with more things than we had'.[25]

These explanations, although correct, fail to capture the insecurities and feelings of precariousness which may have been part of both Roberts's and his daughter's psyche. One historian noted that it was not a particularly 'heroic time' for shopkeepers and there was much 'gloom overhanging' the trade.[26] Roberts knew he had only climbed some way up the social ladder. But the fact that North Parade stood between the richer and more down at heel parts of town will have made him keenly aware of the potential fate awaiting his family if he hit hard times.[27]

It is not altogether unsurprising that the Roberts home – 'practical, serious and intensely religious' as Margaret later described it – was not one into which Edith settled easily.[28] She told Mary Wallace, whom she would later stay with for nearly a year, that it was a 'repressive household'.[29] It would certainly have seemed that way to Edith, who was described by another Grantham contemporary as a 'very grown-up seventeen-year-old'[30] who smoked Balkan Sobranie cigarettes, flirted with local boys and liked a night out.[31] Edith was 'very sophisticated', suggested a boyfriend she met in the town.[32]

Margaret's father, though, was less impressed by the family's visitor. Seeing Edith staring into the street from her bedroom window, Roberts, in the words of one of Lady Thatcher's friends, feared that she was behaving like 'one of these girls in Amsterdam'.[33] That fear was compounded by the fact that he viewed such time-wasting as, in and of itself, a sin.[34] His concern at the malign influence Edith's behaviour and appearance might have on young Margaret and Muriel is easy to discern.

Mary Wallace's brother, Kenneth, said she was 'patently unhappy' in the Roberts's home, while their father ended up arguing with Roberts about Edith: 'You asked this girl over, and you're not looking after her properly and she's very unhappy.' Muriel believes her father may have 'regretted having got her over' and 'refused to accept responsibility' for Edith, trying to persuade his fellow Rotarians to take her on.[35]

There are other reasons why Edith may have viewed this 'repressive household' unfavourably. 'We didn't have a proper bathroom in those days. She was used to better things,' recalled Lady Thatcher.[36] Muriel found her penfriend a 'nice girl' but suggested that 'her wonderful wardrobe' indicated they were 'well-breeched in Austria'.[37] Edith didn't take to the family's Sunday afternoon strolls in the countryside beyond Grantham, complaining: 'It'll ruin my shoes.'[38]

Edith's stay with her penfriend's family was thus a short one: Moore calculated that it was probably around a fortnight before she moved on to stay with another Rotarian. 'It seems to me as if I am a gypsy,' she wrote to Muriel on 16 May 1939, as she detailed the families she had lodged with. However, Edith seemed upbeat: she had been to the 'pictures' on a number of occasions, she reported, and signed off by telling Muriel she was off to see Shirley Temple in *Just Around the Corner*.[39]

But while her time in North Parade was by no means an unqualified success, Edith clearly retained an affection for Roberts, writing to her penfriend: 'I often go for a walk to see your dear father Mr Roberts and see if there are today any letters for me.'[40] Edith recognised that Roberts had saved her life: 'If Muriel had said: "I am sorry, my father says no," I would have stayed in Vienna and they would have killed me,' she later said.[41] While her parents had escaped, her aunts and uncles did not. As Moore suggested, Alfred Roberts emerges from the tale of Edith as 'a well-intentioned man, determined to live by his principles, genuinely kind, but also stern and forbidding. Perhaps it was easier to admire him than to live with him.'[42]

There is no evidence that Roberts's fears that Edith might lead his daughters astray were realised, but it is not hard to see how for thirteen-year-old Margaret Edith must have appeared impossibly glamorous. A contemporary photograph shows an attractive young woman with dark, styled hair wearing lipstick. It is also unlikely that Margaret had ever met a Jew before. In retirement, Lady Thatcher remembered Edith as 'tall, beautiful, well-dressed, [and] evidently from a well-to-do family'.[43] Thus a visitor from overseas, even one describing the horrific events in Vienna which Edith recounted to the Roberts, would surely have reinforced the desire to escape the confines of English provincial life that already appear to have been stirring in Margaret.

But Mrs Thatcher remembered much more about Edith than her so-phistication. 'She told us what it was like to live as a Jew under an anti-Semitic regime,' she recounted in her memoirs. 'One thing Edith reported particularly stuck in my mind: the Jews, she said, were being made to scrub the streets.'[44] Interviewed in Downing Street by Sir Laurens van der Post during the early years of her premiership, Mrs Thatcher further explained the impact of Edith's stay:[45]

> The shock that anyone could treat human beings in the way that they were being treated by Hitler. Total shock. That it could happen to someone we knew, because, you know, you hear of a lot of terrible things, but they never happen to you ... That it could happen in a Europe which had known the deepest feelings of religion, which had been the cradle of civilisation, which had known every culture. Then I remember someone saying 'But you know cruelty and culture can go together'. These things we didn't just read about. They came right into our house.

Edith's first-hand accounts of Jews scrubbing the streets remained etched in Mrs Thatcher's memory sixty years later and played no small part in her life-long abhorrence of anti-Semitism and self-professed 'enormous admiration for the Jewish people'.[46]

'We knew just what we thought of Hitler'

Hugo Young would claim during her premiership that, unlike some of her Westminster contemporaries, Mrs Thatcher had been too young for her polit-ical consciousness to have been shaped by the growth of fascism in the 1930s.[47] But, even beyond the story of Edith, this was untrue. While the Roberts household may have been deeply religious and provincial, it was not insular.

Roberts encouraged Margaret's precocious interest in politics, taking her to 'extension lectures' conducted by the University of Nottingham in Gran-tham about current and international affairs. Among the speakers was a local RAF pilot (and later wing commander), Ernest Millington, who with his wife and two daughters lived near one of Roberts's two shops.[48] Millington later went on to capture Chelmsford from the wartime coalition for the left-wing Common Wealth Party. After the death of his mother-in-law in 1935, Roberts also acquired a radio. Margaret recalled the excitement she felt anticipating its arrival and was not disappointed. Unsurprisingly, Alfred and Margaret avidly devoured talks about current affairs.[49]

But it was reading that Margaret and her father were most passionate about. Every week, they would visit the library together and borrow two books – a 'serious one' for Margaret and Alfred and a novel for Beatrice.[50] Roberts's choices rather belie Young's impression that the future Prime Minister acquired little knowledge about fascism and its consequences. Among the books which, she later claimed, made a deep impression was Douglas Reed's best-selling *Insanity Fair*. Reed's account of his travels through 1930s Germany and central Europe painted a vivid picture of the Nazis and of meeting Hitler himself: 'He addressed me as if I were the Sport Palast packed to bursting.'[51]

Reed also provided a graphic account of the persecution of the Jews. Margaret may well have appreciated his account of a young servant girl, whom Reed described as 'one of those buxom, strapping Berlin servant girls who work like bees for their Gnädige, keep the flat spotlessly clean, cook, look after the children, and still have neat hair and a smiling face'. The servant girl utters the word 'rubbish', pushes aside a storm trooper and shops in a Jewish-owned pharmacy on the day of the Nazis' nationwide boycott two months after Hitler became chancellor. Her 'courageous and hazardous' behaviour, wrote Reed, was 'one of the few things [that] happened that I remember with respect from this period in Germany'.[52]

At her father's urging, Margaret also read Robert Bruce-Lockhart's critique of appeasement, *Guns Or Butter*, in which a German newspaper editor tells the author: 'Germany wanted peace but she wanted it on her own terms.' In her memoirs, Lady Thatcher recalled the book's ending, with Bruce-Lockhart awakening at dawn on a misty morning to hear 'the tramp of two thousand feet in unison'. 'Nazi Germany was already at work,' he concluded.[53]

Roberts, however, forbade his daughter to read *Out of The Night*, written by the German communist Richard Krebs under the pseudonym Jan Veltin. When her father was out at meetings, though, Margaret would take the book from its hiding place and read its 'spine-chilling account of totalitarianism in action'. The authenticity of the book's scenes of sadistic violence, she wrote, made them 'still more horrifying'.[54]

Lady Thatcher's later suggestion that she suspected 'we were better informed than many families' was no idle boast.[55] But perhaps rather more interesting than his decision to take the *Daily Telegraph*, *John O'London's Weekly* and the *Methodist Recorder*, was Roberts's purchase of the pioneering photo-journalism weekly, *Picture Post*. Under the editorship of Hungarian-Jewish émigré Stefan Lorant, who had briefly been imprisoned by the Nazis, the mass-market magazine was robustly anti-fascist and opposed to appeasement, helping to keep Winston Churchill in the public eye during his time in the political wilderness. Its pages condemned and extensively reported the persecution of the Jews. Margaret may well have read its coverage of the aftermath of Kristallnacht. Entitled 'Back to the Middle Ages' above the strapline 'The four guardians of German culture today: they shield its purity from the "contaminated race"', the magazine featured mocking pen portraits of Hitler, Julius Streicher, Hermann Göring and Joseph Goebbels. As well as striking images of burning synagogues, anti-Semitic slogans daubed on shops and Jews scrubbing the streets, it detailed 'some of the world-famous Jews for whom there is no room in Nazi Germany today': Albert Einstein, Sigmund Freud, Luise Rainer and Elisabeth Bergner.[56]

Roberts's decision to take the *Picture Post* gives credence to his daughter's later claim that 'we had a deep distrust of the dictators … well before war was declared, we knew just what we thought of Hitler'.[57] She also suggested that, 'unlike many conservative-minded people', her father fiercely rejected the suggestion put forward by supporters of General Franco during the Spanish Civil War that fascist regimes must be backed to stop the spread of communism. 'He believed that the free society was the better alternative to both,' she wrote in her memoirs. 'This too was a conviction I quickly made my own.'[58]

Roberts's aversion to fascism and sympathy for the Jews was not a senti-ment which was necessarily universally shared in pre-war provincial England. This was evident at the Grantham Rotary's weekly lunches. In May 1934, for instance, Alfred Roberts may have been present to hear Professor H. Brose of Nottingham University return from Germany to report 'everybody was clothed and fed', there was no sign of 'unemployment about the streets' and that Britain should not be unduly concerned about Germany's 'defensive rearmament'. A reading of *Mein Kampf* showed that Hitler was 'extremely straightforward and sincere'.[59] A few months after Brose's talk, local cinema owner J. A. Campbell returned from a British Rotary delegation to Germany where he had heard Hitler speak. In September, he told Grantham members that fascism was preferable to communism and that while the Rotary's num-bers in Germany were diminished, thanks to the 'boycott of the Jew', Hitler looked favourably on the institution.[60] The *Grantham Journal* headlined its report on Campbell's talk: 'The Great Hitler'.[61] Local GP Dr Jauch also shared pamphlets favourable to Hitler with his fellow Rotarians, but Roberts was unimpressed.[62]

In the same month as Brose's talk, 1,000 people turned out to hear Oswald Mosley speak in Grantham. The leader of the British Union of Fascists was engaged in a five-month tour of agricultural counties across the country.[63] The tour illustrated that, while targeting poorer areas with large Jewish pop-ulations, such as the East End of London, Manchester and Leeds, Mosley also spent a high proportion of his time in market towns in rural areas. As Martin Pugh argued: 'There he tapped into the traditional conservatism of a farming community which had been suffering from apparently intractable economic problems since the end of the war.'[64]

Manifestations of anti-Semitism were not hard to come by, showing that hostility to Jews, if not rife, was not deemed socially unacceptable. The *Daily Despatch* reported in October 1932 that 'at least nine-tenths of the inhabit-ants of the British Isles think the worst of a man if they are told that he is a Jew'.[65] Advertisements commonly discriminated: 'No Jewess' demanded one in the *Daily Telegraph*; 'No Jews or men of colour' stated another in the

British Medical Journal. The official guide to Shanklin, Isle of Wight, had an advertisement which said: 'No Jews catered for', while builders in Ilford said that 'under no circumstances would they sell to a Hebrew'.[66] In Cardiff, as with similar bodies in Manchester and Harrogate, the credit traders association passed a resolution to say that membership 'to folk of alien origin, such as Jews, should not be encouraged'. Jews were also barred from golf, table tennis, motoring and country clubs.[67]

Anti-Semitism occasionally seeped into mainstream politics. In 1933, a Labour parliamentary candidate in Devon was forced to step down after making anti-Semitic remarks in an election address.[68] In the House of Commons, Edward Doran, the Conservative MP for Tottenham North, peppered his questions to ministers with references to 'alien Jews' and attempted to whip up outrage against the 'hundreds of thousands of Jews' allegedly 'scurrying' to Britain from Germany.[69] Encouragingly, his behaviour split the local Conservative association and the voters denied him re-election in 1935.

Margaret may have seen the advertisement barring Jews in her father's *Daily Telegraph*. She certainly encountered people willing to express positive views about Hitler. In the queue for fish and chips one Friday evening, she 'vigorously' argued with someone who had suggested that the Führer had given Germany some self-respect and made the trains run on time. In her memoirs, Lady Thatcher recalled 'the astonishment and doubtless irritation of [her] elders' and the reaction of the shop-owner, who laughingly told her customers: 'Oh, she's always debating.'[70]

Despite the assurances the Nazis had given to the British Rotarians, which Campbell had duly relayed to its Grantham members, Hitler went on to suppress the Rotary in Germany. Her father, Lady Thatcher suggested, believed this to be something of an honour for the organisation.[71] Together with her later recollection that this event first alerted the family to the nature of Hitler's rule, his daughter's recollections present Alfred in a somewhat Pooterish light.[72] However, it was perhaps the case that Roberts – with his Rotary lunches, Chamber of Trade meetings and school governor duties – might have shared her later explanation that 'dictators, we learned, could no more tolerate Burke's "little platoons" – the voluntary bodies which help make up civil society – than they could individual rights under the law'.[73]

A distaste for fascism and anti-Semitism did not necessarily equate into opposition to appeasement. With the Argentinian Junta, the Soviet Union and Saddam Hussein later providing the focus for her oft-repeated warnings about the perils of showing weakness to dictators, Lady Thatcher was no doubt tempted to provide a perhaps rather less nuanced recollection of her family's attitudes in the 1930s. Her memoirs indicate that 'like many people who were opposed to appeasement', the family had 'mixed feelings' about Munich and were ashamed of Britain's role in legitimising the dismemberment of Czechoslovakia, but also aware of its lack of preparedness to fight Hitler.[74]

Alfred Roberts's position on appeasement is not entirely clear. In January 1939, he delivered a somewhat opaque speech as chairman of Grantham Rotary's International Service Committee. Reflecting its international nature, the Rotary, he was reported as saying, 'took no sides as to whether there should be a dictatorship, monarchy or republic'. Nonetheless, he offered a thinly veiled defence of Prime Minister Neville Chamberlain who 'armed only with a neatly rolled umbrella, with his mind made up and his will intent on peace' had returned from Munich four months previously.[75] At the time, Roberts was expressing a widely held sentiment. Mrs Thatcher's predecessor as Prime Minister, James Callaghan, later recounted hearing of the news from Munich with 'mingled relief and shame', which led him and his wife Audrey to take into their home a young socialist Austrian journalist.[76]

But there is also evidence to suggest that Roberts's apparent support for appeasement was not unqualified. In addition to praise for Chamberlain, his 1939 speech also asserted that the Rotary's principles of 'justice, truth and liberty' meant that 'weak nations have sacred rights too, and ... they must be respected'.[77] Unlike most Methodists, Roberts also opposed the Peace Ballot of 1934–35, a nationwide referendum organised by supporters of the League of Nations to show public support for collective security, but widely seen as a way of voicing opposition to future rearmament. Backed by Labour, the

Liberals and leading churchmen, it was fiercely opposed by many on the right (the Conservative Party chose not to participate) for allegedly offering voters false and simplistic choices. Alfred Duff Cooper, who was soon to become an anti-appeasement Secretary of War, attacked it as 'poisonous propaganda' and such criticisms were fuelled by promotional materials headlined 'Peace or war?'[78] Lady Thatcher deemed it a 'loaded questionnaire' in her memoirs, in which the electorate was 'declared overwhelmingly to have "voted for peace"'. 'It was not recorded how far Hitler and Mussolini were moved by this result; we had our own views about that in the Roberts household.'[79]

While turning his back on what his daughter called the 'wrong-headed but decent impulses' of Grantham's pacifist Methodists who were campaigning for the Peace Ballot, Roberts instead turned his attentions to helping the re-election of Grantham's Conservative MP in the general election later that year.[80] Fought in 'the teeth of opposition from the enthusiasts of the Peace Ballot', as she later recalled, it was ten-year-old Margaret's first experience of an election campaign. She would go on to campaign in many more.[81]

CHAPTER 2

FINCHLEY AND BEYOND

In March 1958, Sir John Crowder announced his intention to stand down as the Conservative MP for Finchley. After two decades in Parliament, it appeared he would bequeath his successor a golden inheritance: a prosperous, north London suburban seat with a majority of nearly 13,000. Crowder had, moreover, a very strong view on the kind of person he thought befitting to succeed him. As the selection battle commenced, he raged at Lord Hailsham, the party chairman, that Conservative Central Office was trying to give his local association a choice between 'a bloody Jew and a bloody woman'.[1]

But the Conservatives' grip on Finchley was not as tight as it appeared – and, perhaps unsurprisingly given the attitudes of its current Member of Parliament, it had been loosened by allegations of anti-Semitism involving the local party.

Noting Liberal advances in the local elections in 1958, the party's area agent wrote to Central Office, asking that the constituency be reclassified as a marginal. While turning down the request, its response was hardly a ringing endorsement of Crowder's legacy: 'The whole place needs a shake up. Nevertheless I don't regard it as a supermarginal.'[2]

If anyone could provide a shakeup, it was the 32-year-old Margaret Thatcher. Once selected, she had no intention of treating the seat as anything other than a supermarginal. That she would do so was in no way surprising: Alfred Roberts's daughter had trodden a long path from Grantham and now, on the verge of achieving her dream of becoming an MP, she was determined not to stumble.

29

The road to Finchley

Politics and religion dominated Margaret Roberts's time at Oxford, a period which she later acknowledged as the foundation upon which her later successes were built.[3] But while Grantham may have been a world away from Oxford's dreaming spires, her university days did not fundamentally change the future Mrs Thatcher. Unlike many young people, her beliefs were neither seriously challenged nor shaped by leaving the parental home. 'I knew a great deal more about the world and particularly about the world of politics,' Lady Thatcher wrote in her memoirs, before adding tellingly: 'My character had not changed, nor had my beliefs.'[4] Instead, in Methodism, she said, she found 'an anchor of stability'.[5] A member of the John Wesley Society at Oxford, Margaret went out to preach in surrounding Oxfordshire villages, as she had done with her father back in Grantham. Her faith was described by one fellow student who became a Methodist minister as 'effervescent'.[6]

She quickly became subsumed by the activities of the Oxford University Conservative Association.[7] Her membership, together with other experiences at Oxford, helped shape a sense of herself as an outsider.[8] Despite becoming president of the OUCA, Margaret stood apart from its grandees. She was, recalled a fellow association officer, 'merely tolerated' by them, being seen as 'someone who could be relied upon to do the donkey work'.[9] Both her class and gender played a part. 'Politics was very difficult for Oxford women,' a male contemporary recalled, 'Margaret was excluded not only from the Union but from the select Canning Club.'[10] Perhaps conscious of how she was perceived – 'that rather humourless mouse' who 'hadn't got the style [to] make up' for her background[11] – Lady Thatcher later conceded that she would never have excelled in 'the kind of brilliant, brittle repartee' which the Union seemed to encourage.[12] Nonetheless, she did her best to fit in: her political outlook appeared in line with contemporary Oxford Toryism and her organisational skills when arranging social events were widely appreciated.[13]

But Margaret's Conservatism also set her apart from the prevailing mood of the student body as a whole and Somerville College's dons in particular.

It was not so much the fact that she and her politics were a source of mild amusement to her fellow students which was to shape Mrs Thatcher's later outlook and behaviour.[14] Rather, it was her first experience of the snobbery of the liberal establishment which was to prove searing. It was encapsulated by the principal of Somerville, Dame Janet Vaughan: 'She stood out. Somerville had always been a radical establishment and there weren't many Conserva-tives about then ... We used to entertain a good deal at the weekends, but she didn't get invited. She had nothing to contribute, you see.'[15]

Even after eleven years as Prime Minister, this perception that she was an outsider never left Mrs Thatcher. In the eyes of 'the "wet" Tory establish-ment', she believed she 'offended on many counts' because of her gender, class and respect for 'the values and virtues of middle England'.[16] This view would come to form an important element in her bond with Britain's Jews. Explaining her affinity for the community, former Chief Rabbi Jonathan Sacks – who, as an eager Finchley teenager went to question his local MP about an A-level project on electoral reform only to be asked: 'You're not a Liberal, are you?'[17] – suggested: 'She was an outsider herself.'[17] Lord Young, who served in her Cabinet for five years, agreed that Mrs Thatcher was not part of the 'inward-looking group of upper-middle-class people' who dominated the Tory Party prior to the 1970s.[18] While Israel's ambassador to Britain during the 1980s, Yehuda Avner, discovered that snobbery towards Mrs Thatcher and 'anti-Semitic hauteur' made comfortable bedfellows. At a reception at Hampton Court, a member of the House of Lords explained the number of Jews in the Prime Minister's Cabinet with the words: 'Margaret Thatcher is most comfortable among the lower middle class.'[19]

While some of her Jewish Cabinet ministers and advisers disputed this idea of a shared 'outsider' status between Jews and the Prime Minister, this perhaps reflected the fact that, by the time she left office in 1990, neither Thatcherites nor Jews were likely to see themselves as outsiders within the Tory Party.[20] But, before she triumphantly strode the Tory stage, that im-portant part of Mrs Thatcher which, from the onset of her student days, felt a distance from the traditional Conservative grandees – as well as, of course, from the liberal establishment – connected to those Jews who also

31

felt themselves outside the charmed circles of both. This was a perfectly natural response to the fact that the Tory Party appeared, if not overtly hostile, then certainly unwelcoming to many Jews, while, for many liberals, given the strong association between the community and the left, Jewish Conservatism seemed a strange and contradictory phenomenon.

Margaret Roberts may, with good reason, have left Oxford feeling herself to be an outsider, but the reality was a little more complex. While her future career was not directly assisted by those she came into contact with at the OUCA – either fellow students or eminent speakers such as Lord Dunglass (later Sir Alec Douglas-Home), Bob Boothby and Sir Anthony Eden, who she arranged to come and speak – having been its president gave her a certain cache with Central Office when it compiled the candidates' list.[21]

Nonetheless, early signs of her impatience with the prevailing character of the Conservative Party were also evident. This impatience was one she would later share with those upwardly mobile, meritocratic parts of the Jewish community who became her strongest supporters, initially in Finchley and then as leader of her party. Like many Tories, Margaret Roberts recognised that her party had an image problem after its defeat in 1945. In an OUCA policy subcommittee paper which she co-authored several months after Clement Attlee's election victory, Conservative policy was described as having come to be seen by many voters as 'correlated in certain fields by a few unreasoning prejudices and the selfish interests of the moneyed classes'.[22] The report represented, believed Charles Moore, a 'more rebellious and more socially mobile Conservatism'.[23]

Already, too, Margaret was showing a particular disdain for those patrician Tories who, in her eyes, appeared to show sympathy for left-wing ideas or who did not exhibit the seriousness which she brought to her politics.

She dispatched from the OUCA committee, for instance, Robert Runcie, the future Archbishop of Canterbury with whom she would have a famously strained relationship as Prime Minister. '[She] obviously associated me,' he later recounted, 'with those lordly characters who were giving Conservatism as a serious philosophy a bad name … She was trying to turn the

Conservative Association into a serious political force ... and I was nobody to have on board.'[24] Almost imperceptibly, she was drawing the lines of future battles, ones in which she would find Jewish Tories among her most stalwart allies.

Margaret Roberts left Oxford in the summer of 1947 as a qualified research chemist. Over the next decade, she utilised her degree – working for BX Plastics in Essex and J Lyons and Co. in Hammersmith – while also reading for the bar and qualifying as a barrister.[25] But all of this was simply treading water, albeit in intellectually testing areas, when ahead lay the truly desired end. By the time she went down from Oxford, she was determined to become an MP. Her appetite for politics was, she later wrote, 'insatiable'.[26]

In 1949, she was selected to fight the solidly Labour seat of Dartford in Kent. Her energy and hard work were rewarded in the 1950 general election, when she succeeded in reducing Labour's majority by one-third. Contesting the seat again eighteen months later, she knocked another 1,000 off of it. She did so by targeting the non-unionised working-class and women, and Nonconformists, speaking at chapels and recognising the potential rewards to be gained from a group that were, in the words of Eliza Filby, likely to be 'aspirational lower-middle-class voters and possibly wavering Liberals'.[27] Her upbringing made Margaret particularly adept at appealing to such voters – a group who would share many of the characteristics and values of her future Jewish Finchley constituents. Crucially, her efforts earned her good reports from the area agent to Central Office.[28]

Central Office was certainly keen to see a rising star selected in a winnable seat.[29] Over the next seven years, she attempted, unsuccessfully, to win selection in a string of seats – Canterbury, Orpington, Beckenham, Hemel Hempstead and Maidstone. All bar one were in Kent, the county to which, having married Denis Thatcher in 1951, the couple moved with their twins in 1957. But a seat there was not to be. Despite frequently impressing selection committees, she was invariably questioned about how she would balance her commitment as a mother of young twins with being an MP.[30]

She thus approached Finchley, in an area of London she did not know well, without high hopes. From a list of 150 applicants, Central Office sent the constituency eighty names. Mrs Thatcher fought her way through a preliminary interview, where she 'completely outshone' her competitors, reported the deputy area agent and made it onto a final shortlist of four.[31] Still, the deputy area agent did not appear to fancy her chances, suggesting that some of those who had voted to let her name go forward may have done so 'merely to include one woman'.[32]

Writing to her sister shortly before the final run-off on 14 July 1958, Mrs Thatcher glumly predicted: 'I expect the usual prejudice against women will prevail and that I shall probably come the inevitable "close second"'.[33] Later, some of those who attended the meeting suggested she was right to fear such attitudes. One Jewish member of the association, Derek Phillips, was the Young Conservative representative at the meeting. Leaving his mother's home before the meeting, he remembered saying: 'There's two men and one lady and I shan't be voting for a lady.' Mrs Thatcher's performance at the meeting – 'she was head and shoulders above the men' – changed his mind and Phillips voted for her.[34] Having narrowly topped the first ballot, she beat local businessman Thomas Langton by 46 to 43 votes in the run-off. Or so it seemed. In reality, it appears that she may have lost the second ballot. Bertie Blatch, the constituency chairman who counted the votes, told his son that evening: 'She didn't actually win. The man did, but I thought: "He's got a silver spoon in his mouth. He'll get another seat." So I "lost" two of his votes and gave them to her.'[35]

More legitimate assistance was provided to Mrs Thatcher by Marcus King, a local Jewish councillor, whom she had first met when he was a member of the Dartford Young Conservatives and she was the party's candidate. Impressed by her abilities, King persuaded Mrs Thatcher to stand for the nomination in Finchley. For his efforts, he came under considerable pressure from those who argued that Mrs Thatcher did not have the right background and had no hopes of winning the candidacy. 'I can remember seeing my father standing by the telephone for hours almost every evening with people ringing him up trying to dissuade him,' recalled his son.[36] King, however, was not deterred and Mrs Thatcher lent heavily on his support. 'If you want to know anything more about me ask Councillor Marcus King at the back of the hall,' she told her adoption meeting.[37] Mrs Thatcher never forgot King's crucial initial support, nor his later activism on her behalf. When he died in 1989, she wrote to his widow from Downing Street: 'Marcus had been part of our lives ever since I came into parliamentary politics ... We were proud to have [him] as a friend.'[38]

Mrs Thatcher's path to Westminster still faced obstacles, however. With an ironic understatement for which she was not generally noted, Lady Thatcher's memoirs recorded that Finchley had been 'run with a degree of gentlemanly disengagement that was neither my style nor warranted by political realities'.[39] Despite Crowder's sizeable majority, those political realities were none too comforting. It should have been otherwise. Bernard Donoughue, later head of the No. 10 Policy Unit under Harold Wilson and Jim Callaghan, covered the seat for the 1964 Nuffield Election Study. It was, he wrote, characterised by 'prosperity, femininity and intellect'. Over one-third of Finchley's adults, compared to a 14 per cent national average, were drawn from the AB managerial (executive and professional middle classes); twice as many were educated beyond the age of fifteen, then the school leaving age; and more than half owned their own homes.[40] Finchley was also around one-fifth Jewish – a significant proportion of whom might be expected to be Tory-inclined, middle-class voters. But, as Mrs Thatcher soon discovered, this key group had become alienated from her party. Although there were specific reasons for this, they compounded a historically strained relationship between Britain's Jews and the Conservative Party.

Suspicious minds: The Tories and Britain's Jews

Although it was the Liberal Party to which Britain's 50,000 Jews had looked for assistance in the struggle for political emancipation during the first half of the nineteenth century – and the first Jewish Members of Parliament, Sir David Salomons and Baron Lionel de Rothschild, were both Liberals – the Conservative Party had never been totally without Jewish support.[41] That support grew as the century progressed. Anti-Jewish innuendo directed at Benjamin Disraeli, a baptised Christian, rather than a professing Jew, by the Liberal press in 1868, and Liberal attacks on the first professing Jewish Conservative parliamentary candidate – Henry de Worms, selected in the general election of that year to fight Sandwich – coupled with later disagreements over Gladstone's 1870 Elementary Education Act, meant that, for the first time, in 1874 a significant portion of the Jewish vote went to the Tories.[42] 'Jews had discovered', wrote David Cesarani, 'that liberalism was at best ambivalent towards, and at worst intolerant of, their interests.'[43] This perception was added to by the dislike many Jewish businessmen, like their wealthy Gentile counterparts, felt for the Liberals' increasingly radical domestic agenda.[44]

At the same time, however, Anglo-Jewry, a small, largely assimilated middle-class community, began to undergo a massive transformation as a wave of Yiddish-speaking, poverty-stricken Polish and Russian Orthodox Jews hit Britain's shores.[45] In the two decades before the turn of the century, the Anglo-Jewish population tripled to an estimated 200,000.[46] Fleeing Tsarist persecution, many of the 150,000 or so new Jewish emigrants found a home in the East End of London, mostly in Whitechapel and Stepney, and in similar inner city parts of Leeds, Manchester and nearby Salford.

Concerned that the number of new arrivals might spark a revival in anti-Semitism, and troubled by their seeming sympathy for disturbing causes such as socialism and Zionism, the Anglo-Jewish establishment made little effort to oppose attempts by the Balfour government to stem the flow. But the Aliens Act of 1905 coupled with the discriminatory policies of the Conservative-allied Municipal Reform Party, which ran the London County Council between 1907 and 1934, was not so easily forgiven or forgotten by those whose targets they had been.[47] Nor was the party responsible for them.

Naturalisation, the coming of age of a generation born in Britain and the arrival of universal suffrage after the First World War established a new Jewish electorate that was naturally more supportive of the now ascendant Labour Party.[48] Labour, in turn, proved itself highly sympathetic to Zionism.

In December 1917, a special conference of the party and the Trades Union Congress approved the memorandum on war aims, which included a paragraph that was supportive of Jewish claims to settlement in Palestine. By the early 1920s, a substantial portion of the east London Jewish vote was backing Labour: in November 1922, Whitechapel and St Georges, with its substantial Jewish population, returned a Labour MP for the first time,[49] while in December 1923, the *East London Observer* reported that, aside from Bethnal Green South West, the East End constituencies were 'now solid for Labour, and so far as most people can see are likely to remain so'.[50] In 1935, four Jewish Labour MPs were returned to Parliament.

Labour, though, did not have all its own way. There was still Jewish support for the Liberals, especially in Manchester,[51] and the flame of Jewish Liberalism was kept alive by Sir Herbert Samuel, who led the party during the 1930s. In the East End, there was also, thanks to their willingness to resist Oswald Mosley's British Union of Fascists in the 1930s, a degree of Jewish support for the Communists.

Nonetheless, as Geoffrey Alderman argued, 'by the mid-1930s, the Labour Party had become the normal political home of the mass of poor working-class Jews in Great Britain and, one suspects, of a significant number of middle-class Jews'.[52] This support was cemented by Labour's apparently unbending commitment to the Zionist cause and its opposition to the Conservative government's White Paper of May 1939, which reneged on Britain's commitment, made in the Balfour Declaration two decades previously, to bring about a Jewish homeland in Palestine. In 1944, Labour declared the case for large-scale Jewish immigration to create such a homeland was 'irresistible' in the face of the 'unspeakable atrocities' perpetuated by the Nazis.[53]

The antagonism many Jews felt towards the Conservative Party was heartily reciprocated by many Tories, who obsessed about the community's size and power (both grossly overestimated); its supposed 'otherness' from their rigid view of 'Englishness'; and its alleged lack of loyalty to 'Crown and country'.[54] This mindset was captured by future Tory leader Austen Chamberlain in a letter in July 1920 which observed the anger aroused on his party's benches by Edwin Montagu, the Secretary of State for India, during a debate on the Amritsar massacre. 'All their English & racial feeling was stirred to passionate display,' Chamberlain wrote. 'A Jew may be a loyal Englishman & passionately patriotic, but he is intellectually apart from us & will never be purely & simply English.'[55]

The all too common mix of snobbery and anti-Semitism which dominated the Tory Party's upper echelons – one minister attributed the Conservatives' loss of the Hammersmith North by-election in 1926 to their candidate Samuel Gluckstein being 'a horrible Jew who could pay his own expenses' – was usually revealed only in trusted company.[56] However, examples of the Conservative Party's unseemly anti-Semitic underbelly occasionally burst forth: Edward Doran, the thankfully short-lived Tory MP for Tottenham North, who campaigned against refugees in the 1930s; Robert Tatton Bower who provoked an altercation in the Commons chamber when he told the East End-born Jewish Labour MP, Emmanuel Shinwell, to 'go back to Poland' during a debate on the Spanish Civil War; and the party's foremost anti-Semite, Captain Archibald Maule Ramsay, who, together with fellow backbencher, John Hamilton Mackie, formed the Right Club, to 'oppose and expose the activities of Organised Jewry' which was supposedly attempting to lead Britain into war against Germany to further their own interests.[57] A particular target of Ramsay's was Leslie Hore-Belisha, the Secretary of State for War. Understandably, when Hore-Belisha was removed by Neville Chamberlain from his post in 1940, this was viewed by many Jews as an example of Tories' indulgence of anti-Semitism in their own ranks.

But while there was, wrote Stuart Ball, an undercurrent of anti-Semitism in Conservative circles it stemmed more from class prejudice than from a political ideology. 'Conservatives,' he suggested, 'disliked, even despised, the openly paraded anti-Semitism of Fascism, and neither sympathized with it nor really understood its racial basis.'[58] As the decade wore on, this became evident, with many Tories openly condemning the Nazi persecution of the Jews, and some Conservative MPs, such as Oliver Locker-Lampson, going to great lengths to assist its victims.[59] The 1939 White Paper also provoked a revolt on the Tory benches, with two Cabinet ministers, Leslie Hore-Belisha and Walter Elliot, and 110 Conservative MPs abstaining from the vote, while twenty more, including Winston Churchill, joined Labour in voting against.

If the Conservative Party was not uniformly hostile towards Jews, it was also not the case that all Jews were uniformly hostile towards the Tories. Half of the Jewish MPs elected in the 1931 and 1935 general elections were Conservatives, including some prominent figures in the community, such as Louis Gluckstein and Sir Isidore Salmon.[60] Even beyond the ranks of the very wealthy, the Tories maintained a degree of Jewish support during the interwar period, some of it stemming from the Conservatives' support for denominational schools. There were also some Jews who backed restrictions on immigration, both at the turn of the century and in the 1930s, fearing that, without them, there would be a rise in anti-Semitism.[61] And there were some Jews, like Sir Herbert Samuel, the Home Secretary and Liberal Leader, who supported appeasement, and many prominent Jews, such as Claude Montefiore and Edwin Montagu, who opposed Zionism. Only in the aftermath of the Holocaust did opposition to Zionism within British Jewry collapse.[62]

Nonetheless, it is perhaps unsurprising that by 1945 most British Jews regarded the Conservative Party with a degree of unease.[63] It hardly helped that there were Tory candidates who would openly declare their desire to see Jewish refugees returned, in the words of Sir Wavell Wakefield, the MP for St Marylebone, 'to their own countries'.[64] The exact extent of Labour's support among Jewish voters in 1945 is unknown. However, in the majority of seats where Jewish voters were most heavily concentrated Labour was victorious, and twenty-six Jews returned to sit on the government benches.[65]

By contrast, the election saw just one Jewish Conservative, Daniel Lipson, retain his seat.[66] But Lipson's status as an independent Conservative was in itself telling: in 1937, the Cheltenham Conservative Association had refused to adopt the local mayor as its by-election candidate because he was Jewish. Standing as an independent, Lipson narrowly defeated the official Tory candidate. His estranged, solitary presence, starkly illustrated the antagonistic relationship which existed between British Jewry and the Tory Party in 1945.

Although, in rejecting the party, many Jews were simply sharing the more general public desire to punish the Conservatives for the 'hungry '30s' and appeasement. Not until the election of Sir Henry d'Avigdor-Goldsmid a decade later, would a Jew once again sit on the Conservative benches. Following a by-election, he was joined a year later by Sir Keith Joseph, who would later become the most significant Jewish Conservative in post-war Britain. The two men would remain, though, the only Jewish Tory MPs until 1970. Moreover, the fact that both were baronets, rather gave credence to the Jewish journalist Chaim Bermant's suggestion that 'to the local squires and colonels and grand dames in the boroughs and shires who actually selected candidates, Jewishness was a congenital defect which could be redeemed, if at all, only by good pedigree, a title and great wealth'.[67]

In opposition after 1945, the Tories were divided in their response to Churchill's avowed Zionism as the Attlee government struggled with the complexities and violence which accompanied the ending of the British Mandate for Palestine and the birth pangs of the state of Israel. Hostility towards Jews grew in some parts of the party, reflecting a strain of popular and press sentiment that was fuelled by the terrorism perpetrated against British forces. The Conservative leadership tried to dampen outright displays of it, such as when a delegate to the party's 1947 annual conference attempted to move an anti-Semitic motion which, in a traditional, barely coded reference to Jews, called for the rooting out of 'the ever-increasing foreign subversive influence within our own country and the Dominions overseas'. Despite considerable applause from the floor, the Tory hierarchy managed to forestall the debate until the next morning and pass an alternative motion deploring communist and fascist subversion. 'The party which still acknowledges the inspiration of Disraeli and is now led by Winston Churchill could not condone anti-Semitism without betraying its most cherished principles,' the *Jewish Chronicle* warned the Tories in response.[68]

However, the delegates' applause pointed to a blatant anti-Semitic sentiment which continued to fester in some local parties, and this became a problem which was recognised by Conservative Central Office throughout the 1950s.[69] In 1950, the party's Standing Advisory Committee on Candidates was forced to step in when Chorley Conservative Association attempted to adopt Andrew Fountaine, a right-wing anti-Semite, as its candidate. But the association refused to pick another candidate and Fountaine came within 400 votes of taking the seat from Labour.

Such prejudice also appeared in areas with large Jewish populations. Commander F. Ashe Lincoln, who had stood unsuccessfully for the Tories in 1945 in Harrow East, withdrew as a prospective candidate for the 1950 election due to what one member described as 'anti-Semitic feeling' in the local association.[70] When Lincoln failed to be adopted shortly afterwards in nearby Willesden East, the vice-president of the constituency association resigned, alleging anti-Semitism. 'By the end of the mandate,' believed Harry Defries, 'the relationship between the Jews and the Conservative Party had reached its nadir.'[71]

To the suburbs

However, even at its darkest hour, there was a glimmer of light for the Conservatives. Once heavily concentrated in the inner cities, Britain's Jews were socially, economically and geographically on the move. While two-thirds of London's Jews lived in the East End before the First World War, by 1930 that figure had fallen to one-third. As they joined the ranks of the lower-middle and middle classes, about one in ten of the capital's Jewish population had already moved out to London's north-west suburbs.[72]

The destruction of much of the East End by the Luftwaffe after 1940 simply quickened a process, driven by upward mobility, which was well underway prior to the outbreak of war. Hackney may have had London's largest and densest Jewish population in the 1950s, but many Jews had now found a home in Golders Green, Edgware, Finchley and Hendon to the north-west and Ilford and Woodford to the east.[73]

Whatever their origins, most suburban Jews considered themselves middle class. A study of Edgware Jewry in 1961 found that while just over half had been born in the East End, over 80 per cent now regarded themselves as belonging to the middle class, while only 8 per cent classed themselves as working class.[74] This was not simply a state of mind: in the same year over 40 per cent of British Jews could be found belonging to the top two social classes – the AB upper managerial and professional middle classes – double the figure for the population at large.[75]

It was clear that many Jews felt entirely at home with the True Blue political allegiances of the suburbs to which they had moved.[76] 'To the Toryism of the established Jewish gentry,' wrote Alderman, 'was added ... the Toryism of the Jewish nouveaux riches'.[77] Jews weren't only voting Conservative; some were also standing for the Tories too. While Jewish Toryism at Westminster was absent in the decade after 1945, blue shoots were emerging at the grass-roots level. Richmond-upon-Thames, Hendon and Finchley all had Jewish Conservative mayors at some point during the late 1940s and early 1950s.[78]

Crucially, however, the loosening of the ties many Jews felt to Labour wasn't simply the product of social mobility. Instead, it stemmed from Labour's attitude towards the Jewish state – an issue that has periodically soured relations between the party and the community ever since. Less than a year after Labour restated its commitment to a Jewish homeland in December 1944, it abruptly changed course. In November 1945, the new Foreign Secretary, Ernest Bevin, betrayed the Zionist cause which Labour had steadfastly advocated for nearly three decades and announced that the government was going to honour the terms of the 1939 White Paper. 'There cannot have been in twentieth-century British history,' Harold Wilson later wrote, 'a greater contrast between promise and performance than was shown by the incoming Government over Middle East issues.'[79] The anger many British Jews felt at Bevin's announcement was compounded by the rejection of a proposal to outlaw anti-Semitism by Labour's annual conference in 1946, the failure in 1948 of a parliamentary Bill along similar lines, and the government's decision, following the ending of the Mandate in May 1948, to withhold de facto recognition from Israel until February 1949, and de jure recognition for a further year.

Nonetheless, back in opposition after 1951 and with Bevin now dead, Labour's support for the new Israeli state was evident once again. At its annual conference in 1955, the party demanded a military pact with Israel. Speaking for the National Executive Committee, Sam Watson saluted the fledgling socialist state which contained 'some of the finest creative impulses mankind has ever seen'.[80]

Within a year, however, the Suez Crisis provoked a serious deterioration in relations between Labour and the many Jews who felt that – whatever the rights and wrongs of Britain and France's actions – Israel's invasion of Sinai had been more than justified by Egypt's use of the Gaza Strip as a base to launch raids by Palestinian fedayeen, most of which targeted Israeli civilians. Labour leader Hugh Gaitskell's likening of Anthony Eden to a policeman who had decided to 'go in and help the burglar [Israel] shoot the householder [Egypt]' provoked dismay.[81] Indeed, the defeat in 1959 of the Jewish Labour MP Maurice Orbach, whose East Willesden constituency contained a sizeable number of Jews, was attributed to his failure to support Israel at the time of the Suez Crisis.[82] Harold Lever, later a Jewish Cabinet minister under Wilson and James Callaghan, believed that, alongside growing affluence, Suez was the factor which shifted traditional Jewish allegiances from right to left.[83] Despite the fact that Eden's actions had been guided more by his dislike of Nasser than by a desire to assist Israel, Labour's response had provided the Tories with an opening to persuade Jewish voters to look at them anew.[84]

It was, perhaps, with this in mind that Mrs Thatcher chose, alongside the 'despotism' of the trade unions, to focus on the Middle East in her adoption speech. 'Nasser had stated he would never be satisfied until the Arabs had destroyed the State of Israel.' The *Finchley Times* reported her telling the meeting before declaring: 'In any discussion on the Middle East we must take into consideration the State of Israel, because we were mainly responsible for its existence.'[85] But, as she was soon to discover, the new-found allegiances of suburban Jews to the Tories were fragile and liable to snap at the first hint of anti-Semitism.

A little local difficulty

For the descendants of Jews who had fled pogroms in East European *shtetls*, a detached, mock Tudor home in north-west London may have signalled that they had finally made it into the ranks of the English middle classes, but their arrival brought with it new challenges. While their parents and grandparents may have suffered anti-Semitism at the hands of the East End working class, elements of the middle classes practised a perhaps subtler, but no less pernicious, form of the oldest hatred.

Manifestations of middle-class anti-Semitism were evident in housing, employment and the *numerus clausus* which operated in legal and medical schools. But it was symbolised by its prevalence in that quintessentially English middle-class pursuit, golf. From the moment in the late nineteenth century when golf courses began to open in suburban areas, attempts to exclude Jews were widespread.[86] Some clubs simply told those applying for membership that it was 'a tradition that no Jews are accepted'; others were more circumspect but, ultimately, no less discriminatory, allowing existing members to anonymously 'blackball' new applicants or operating a formal quota system to allow only limited numbers of Jews to join.

In early 1957, the year before Finchley's Tories selected Mrs Thatcher as their candidate, a number of Jews applied to join Finchley Golf Club. In the section marked religion, each had written 'Jewish' and each had had their membership refused.[87] Among the unsuccessful applicants was Shirley Porter, daughter of Sir Jack Cohen, the founder of the Tesco supermarket chain, who had recently joined the Liberal Party in Finchley after failing to be selected as a Conservative parliamentary candidate.[88] 'We got people with a good handicap to apply, therefore there was no reason to reject them,' recalled Alan Cohen, who would later become the Liberal leader of Finchley borough council.[89] Thus, as Anthony Howard reported in the *New Statesman*, the antics of Porter and her fellow campaigners were 'deliberately intended to blow the gaffe on a local scandal'.[90]

But what gave the story its political edge was the fact that the club leased the land which formed its links from the Conservative-dominated borough council and the officers of the club included prominent local Tories. In elections in May 1957, Cohen and a fellow Jewish Liberal activist, Frank Davis, unseated the Tories from two of Finchley's wealthiest and most Jewish wards,

Manor and the Bishop's. The golf club dominated the campaign as the Liberals distributed leaflets highlighting the blasé responses received by Jews who had applied to join it – 'since the formation of the club, there had always been a bar against Jewish members' – together with calls for an investigation and an end to its discriminatory practices.[91] A 'feature of the polling', commented the *Finchley Times* after the elections, 'was the enthusiasm of the young Jewish element for the Liberal cause', rather ignoring the issue that had been central to the Liberal campaign.[92] It was only a start, but as a later account of the party's rise related, 'a gap had been made through which the Liberals were later to pour, and swamp their opponents'.[93]

At their first council meeting, Davis and Cohen returned to the fray: in what the *Finchley Press* termed an 'acid debate', they accused fellow councillors of effectively condoning the golf club's 'despicable' anti-Semitism and sought to block the reappointment of the council's nominee on its committee, proposing instead Cecil Altman, a Jewish solicitor.[94] In return, the Tories and Labour accused the two Liberals of 'a cheap electioneering stunt' and excluded Cohen and Davis from council committees which met in secret, and where much of the authority's real business was conducted.[95] Such behaviour, however, simply allowed the Liberals to open a new front, attacking the cosy manner in which the town hall was run.

In reality, the golf club issue was swiftly resolved. By the end of May 1957, the club had deleted from its membership form the question relating to applicants' religion.[96] But, as the newly selected Conservative candidate for Finchley soon discovered, the row rumbled on and the anger it engendered was to last much longer.

Further Liberal gains in the May 1958 local elections soon caught Mrs Thatcher's attention. Two months after her adoption, she alerted Central Office to her little local difficulty. Reporting Finchley's electorate to be 25 per cent Jewish, she warned:

For reasons with which I need not bother you, the Jewish faith have allied themselves to Liberalism and at the last local election won five seats from the

Conservatives on our council. We are now finding great difficulty in making headway in these particular areas, particularly in Hampstead Garden Suburb. As Finchley has had a Liberal MP in the past we are naturally apprehensive and are now making great efforts to further the Conservative cause.

She concluded with a swipe at her predecessor: 'I fear the division as a whole has not been very dynamic in the past.'[97]

Mrs Thatcher's call for help was a little alarmist: the Liberals had held the parliamentary seat for just eleven months after the 1923 general election, but she was right to be concerned that the Tories were in danger of alienating a group of voters who they might otherwise expect to capture. The golf club furore symbolised a cloud of anti-Semitism which appeared to hang over the local Conservative association at the time of her selection. As we have seen, her predecessor, Sir John Crowder, had already denounced Central Office for attempting to impose a choice between 'a bloody Jew and a bloody woman' on the local association. While the party had defied his wishes in picking Mrs Thatcher, it may have connived in his desire the Tories not be represented by a Jew. With the Liberals having chosen a Jewish candidate, Ivan Spence, the selection committee, alleged Campbell, decided to rule out Jewish applicants.[98]

Moreover, John Tiplady, later chair of the Finchley party, recalled that Mrs Thatcher's selection meeting was held on a Friday in order to prevent Orthodox Jews from attending. This was not, in fact, the case: the meeting was held on a Monday, but the fact that Tiplady remembered it as such indicates, noted Moore, that 'some sort of ill feeling did, indeed, exist'.[99] While Lady Thatcher suggested there was something rather cynical in her opponents' campaigning on the golf club issue – 'the Liberals never missed an opportunity to remind people of it' – she recognised the damage it had done. As she recalled: 'I simply did not understand anti-Semitism myself, and I was upset that the Party should have been tainted by it. I also thought that the potential Conservative vote was not being fully mobilized because of this.'[100]

Ridding the party of this taint thus became her priority. Locally, she made it clear that she wanted new members, 'especially Jewish Conservatives'.[101] She established a new branch of the Young Conservatives in Hampstead Garden Suburb which recruited eighty new members.[102] In a further effort to reach out to Finchley's Jews, Sir Keith Joseph was one of the first speakers Mrs Thatcher invited to the constituency after her adoption.[103] We do not know whether they discussed the rift between the Finchley Tories and the local Jewish community, but it would be surprising – given that she had asked him to address the two ward parties, Manor and the Bishop's, where the Liberals had triumphed – if she did not brief him on the controversy. If she did, Joseph may, as we will see in Chapter 3, have been able to offer some advice based on his recent first-hand experience of being selected in Leeds North East.

The *Finchley Press* gave Mrs Thatcher's visitor front-page billing. 'Life is a private affair, it is a government's job to remove some of the obstacles – not to force the individual to conform to a pattern,' Joseph told the meeting, no doubt to his host's approval, before warning the 100 assembled local Tories of the various threats to individual freedom: 'Russian ambition, Russian fear, the loss by the West of the neutral world.' On a rather more mundane level, Joseph said he approved of hire purchase if it brought a higher standard of living, provided that families also saved for the future.[104] For Alderman Roberts's daughter that would no doubt have been a crucial caveat. Un-impressed by his putative successor's activities, Crowder wrote to Central Office to protest that Mrs Thatcher was inviting speakers to his seat without informing him.[105]

Although she was never really in danger, Mrs Thatcher was determined to campaign as if Finchley were a marginal: in the eight months after her adoption, she attended 130 speaking engagements.[106] With the Tories under Harold Macmillan experiencing a political recovery after the disaster of Suez, and the country, in the new Prime Minister's words, seemingly never having had it so good, her little slice of middle-class suburbia was unlikely to turn its back on the Tories or the energetic young woman that the Finchley Con-servative Association had chosen to represent the party.

Mrs Thatcher was on holiday in the Isle of Wight when Macmillan fired the starting gun on the general election in September 1959. She hurried back to London and launched her campaign. Her Liberal opponent attempted to suggest that the race was between him and Mrs Thatcher. Despite the party's local election advances, the claim was hardly justified by the result in the constituency at the previous general election and Mrs Thatcher was having none of it, framing the debate solely in terms of the national contest between Labour and the Conservatives.[107]

When the result was declared shortly after 12.30 a.m. on Friday 9 October 1959, Mrs Thatcher's efforts had clearly paid off: she increased the Tory majority to 16,260, nearly 3,500 more than that she had inherited. However, in part reflecting the national picture, the Liberals had also made progress: winning nearly 5,000 more votes, they had come close to pushing Labour into third place. The Tories' fortunes, however, had reached a post-war peak, as Mrs Thatcher was about to discover.

The honourable member for Finchley

Thanks, quite literally, to the luck of the draw, soon after entering Parliament the new member for Finchley found herself with an opportunity to continue rebuilding bridges with her Jewish constituents and to forge a relationship which would later prove one of the most important of her political life. Despite never having previously 'so much as won a raffle' – given the Methodists' dislike of gambling, she may have entered rather fewer than the population at large – Mrs Thatcher was drawn second in the House of Commons ballot for Private Member's Bills.[108] She opted to pursue legislation which sought to close a loophole in the law that had allowed Labour local authorities in a recent print dispute to effectively bar strike-breaking journalists from their town halls. While declaring that it would enhance scrutiny and ensure ratepayers knew how their money was being spent, Mrs Thatcher also relished the opportunity to attack what she viewed as 'socialist connivance with trade union power'.[109]

Mrs Thatcher's first piece of legislation, the Public Bodies (Admissions to

Meetings) Act, was rather weaker than she had hoped for. However, it won her press support and attention – the *Yorkshire Post* deemed it 'a safeguard for local democracy'[110] – and led to her first real, practical dealings with Joseph, who, as a junior minister in the Ministry of Housing and Local Government, had been given responsibility for liaising with her on technical matters. At the Bill's third reading in May 1960, Joseph told the House he was confident it would pass because of the 'cogent, charming, lucid and composed manner' of its author. Mrs Thatcher would not forget his visible support for her first parliamentary venture.[111]

But while her memoirs present her first legislative foray as a defence of the ratepayer against the dark forces of municipal socialism, her targets were perhaps closer to home. As we have seen, her Liberal opponents in Finchley had repeatedly attacked the Tories for conducting town hall business in secret committee meetings. Mrs Thatcher was, therefore, probably unsurprised when, a couple of weeks after she introduced the Bill, Cohen moved a motion that the council 'congratulates [Mrs Thatcher] on the introduction of the Admission of the Press Bill and assures her of our utmost support for that measure'. In the ensuing debate, Reginald Norman, the council's Tory leader, made clear the ruling group would not support the motion.[112] 'It will serve the Tories right if Mrs Thatcher doesn't open their next bazaar,' quipped *The Star* in response.[113] None of this caused Mrs Thatcher much concern. Seeing it as part of her 'long campaign to recover Jewish support', Moore believed: 'It did no harm for Finchley's new Member of Parliament to put herself on the side of openness, and thus head off Liberal attack.'[114]

Nonetheless, perhaps sensing a degree of lingering hostility, Mrs Thatcher moved cautiously as she sought to win over her Jewish constituents. In November 1960, a year after she was elected and more than two years after first being picked to fight the seat, she was a panellist at Finchley Zionist Society's 'brains trust' event. Mrs Thatcher was, reported the *Jewish Chronicle*, attending a 'local Jewish function' for the first time.[115] It was to be the first of many and she soon appeared to feel on firmer ground: in February 1962 she was elected vice-president of the newly formed Finchley Council of

Christians and Jews, which, according to its founding chairman, sought to eliminate 'anti-Jewish or anti-Christian feeling' locally: there was, of course, rather more of the former than of the latter.[116] A few months later she accepted the presidency of the newly formed Finchley Anglo-Israel Friendship League, the first association of its kind in the country.[117] Her diary was soon filled with such engagements, as it would be for the next three decades. Over the course of a few months, she could, for instance, be found speaking at meetings of the Friends of Hebrew University (she was delighted, she said, to be involved with any organisation which 'gave women equality in education');[118] attending the dedication of Finchley's first Liberal Jewish synagogue; visiting the homes and offices of the Finchley Jewish Board of Guardians; and travelling to Manchester to open the Israel Trade Fair, part of the city's celebrations of the Jewish state's Independence Day. 'She liked being with Jewish people,' recalled Tessa Phillips, who later became secretary to Mrs Thatcher's agent in Finchley, 'not to the exclusion of anybody else, but she felt the warmth.'[119] References to her admiration for Jewish values peppered her speeches, as they would do frequently after she entered Downing Street. At the Kinloss synagogue, she spoke of the importance of religion sustaining 'the moral sense of the people',[120] while, on another occasion, the words of Rabbi Frank Hellner of the Finchley Progressive Synagogue warning of the dangers of compromising principles caught her attention. Listening to the rabbi on numerous occasions, Mrs Thatcher said, she had 'never failed to pick up a phrase that subsequently proved useful in her political life'.[121]

But Mrs Thatcher's difficulties in Finchley were not over. Following sweeping gains in the 1962 local elections, the Liberals finally achieved the breakthrough they had long predicted and took control of Finchley town hall a year later. Six of the Liberals' nineteen councillors were Jewish,[122] including Alan Cohen, the new leader of the council, his deputy, Leonard Sattin and Frank Davis, the mayor. With his Flying Officer Kite moustache, Davis, who came to be seen as Finchley's 'Mr Liberal', was an extrovert with a magnetic personality. He did not suffer fools gladly.

There was no single cause of the Liberals' victory. After more than a decade in power, the Conservative government, of which Mrs Thatcher had become a member as a junior minister in October 1961, was showing signs of decay: having 'never had it so good', many voters were now feeling the pinch as economic difficulties mounted. In March 1962, the Liberals dramatically overturned the Tories' 15,000 majority and won suburban Orpington in a by-election. The Tory candidate, Peter Goldman, was the 'bloody Jew' who Crowder had feared Central Office was seeking to impose upon Finchley, but who had failed to make that constituency's shortlist.[123] Four months later, a panicky Macmillan fired one-third of his Cabinet, including his Chancellor of the Exchequer, on what became known as the 'Night of the Long Knives'. The move did little to revive the government's fortunes, which were further damaged when, the following year, the Profumo scandal broke.

Coming just two months after their by-election triumph, the press inevitably dubbed the Liberals' victory in Finchley 'the Orpington of North London'.[124] In part their success was an early demonstration of the 'pavement politics' which would power their dramatic resurgence in the mid-1970s, but it was also backed by a formidable campaign organisation. 'You've got to hand it to them,' an impressed Bertie Blatch told Anthony Howard, 'they've got a first-class political machine.'[125] Perhaps more reflective of the true feelings of their opponents was one Labour Party worker's description of the Liberals as a 'lot of bastards and bandwagoners'.[126] The power behind that machine was Sattin, under whose direction intensive canvassing had been undertaken and membership of the party in the seat had quadrupled to 4,000 by 1964.[127]

As she prepared to defend her seat in 1964, Mrs Thatcher appeared under threat, with the *Evening Standard* predicting that 'if the Liberals gain any seats in London at the General Election, their strongest hope is at Finchley'.[128] Donoughue was dispatched there by the psephologists David Butler and Anthony King precisely for this reason. On the basis of the 1963 local election results, he later noted, the Liberals looked set to evict Finchley's Tory MP.[129]

Bringing in a new agent to help rebuild her organisation and fend off the

Liberal challenge, Mrs Thatcher thought she knew exactly why she was now imperilled. 'It's the golf club, you know,' she told Howard. 'That's where it all started and where the whole thing has come from.'[130] Three decades later, she had not changed her assessment. Acknowledging the press speculation that she might have been defeated, Lady Thatcher wrote simply: 'The Golf Club scandal kept rumbling on.'[131] While disputing that it represented the whole explanation, Howard believed that 'the Jewish discrimination question has run like a tape worm through the whole fantastic Liberal success in Finchley'.[132] And, knowing that it was a winning card, the Liberals kept playing it: in 1962, five years after the initial scandal broke, the party publicly charged that, by letting the golf club have a new lease at the old rent, the Tories were 'implying that the land is now worth less because the club has had to admit Jews'.[133] The Liberals, remembered Laurence Brass, who later contested Finchley for the party, 'weren't shy about mentioning the Conservative Party golf club connection'. However, many Jews in the seat were also 'progressive' in their politics, he believed, disliking both the Tories and the Labour alternative and finding in the Liberals a 'natural home'.[134] For Alan Cohen, the golf club issue was less important in the Liberals' establishment of a Finchley foothold than the fact that many newly middle-class Jews combined an antipathy to socialism with a lingering resentment of the Conservatives' attitude towards Jewish immigration at the turn of the century and in the 1930s.[135]

A survey of Jewish voters in Finchley conducted for the Nuffield Election Study underlined the strength of support for the Liberals. In recent local elections, six out of ten had backed the party, with the Tories winning the support of 30 per cent and Labour trailing on 10 per cent. Two-thirds of Jews believed the Liberals in Finchley had more support among Jewish voters than the other two parties did and the fact that the party had many Jewish candidates and members led many to believe that it was 'particularly sympathetic' to them. Seven years after it had occurred, two-thirds had also heard of the golf club scandal.[136]

Against this backdrop, Mrs Thatcher sometimes appeared to possess a somewhat cavalier attitude as, for instance, during the summer of 1962 when Jewish community groups protested about far-right rallies planned in Trafalgar Square, including by former blackshirt leader Sir Oswald Mosley's Union Movement.[137] While the government initially resisted calls to ban the meetings, some Tory MPs representing seats with large Jewish populations joined Labour in calling for action.[138] In Finchley, Mrs Thatcher was deluged by protests from Jewish constituents. In private, she was scathing, writing to her father that 'the constituency correspondence continues unabated with every Jew in the area demanding more curbs on freedom of speech'.[139] In public, even as the government announced a U-turn and banned the forthcoming fascist meetings in Trafalgar Square, Mrs Thatcher was barely more sympathetic. 'Since 1959 Mosley has held eight meetings in Trafalgar Square which have all gone off like damp squibs,' she told a meeting in Finchley. 'It is only since the Communists started a campaign that there has been trouble. If Mosley's meetings are banned it means any meeting which the Communists do not like could be banned.'[140] Given the feeling of many of her constituents, and the heavy losses the Tories had sustained in the local elections only a few months previously, it was either a bravely principled or foolhardy stance. Certainly, her lack of empathy towards why many of her Jewish constituents might have felt as they did at the sight of fascists spouting anti-Semitism on the streets of central London was surprising.

But, as the general election approached, there were some signs that Liberal support might have peaked too early. Elections for the newly created Greater London Council and London Borough of Barnet in the spring of 1964 saw a strong performance by the Conservatives. 'Liberals In Eclipse,' declared the *Finchley Press* gleefully.[141] Mrs Thatcher's Liberal opponents were not easily deterred, however, and their energetic candidate, John Pardoe, who would later become a prominent MP, made clear his belief that 'the Jewish vote will be the key to this Finchley election' and predicted that he would win over half of it.[142] Pardoe had worked hard to build his credentials: becoming an executive member of the Finchley Anglo-Israel Friendship League and, as the general election campaign commenced, using a speech to the Liberal Party conference to call for both greater economic aid and military assistance if Israel was threatened.[143]

Warning Labour voters that only by backing him could they defeat Mrs Thatcher, while attempting to reassure Tories that a Liberal vote could not let Labour slip through the middle, Pardoe confidently predicted victory.[144] That the Liberals might unseat Mrs Thatcher certainly seemed plausible. On the eve of the election, Donoughue later wrote, Finchley was 'blooming with orange posters' while on polling day it was flooded with party campaigners. An observer could thus easily have concluded that 'the Liberal miracle was about to happen'.[145] Nationally, the party did its best to boost Pardoe's chances: he was selected to appear in party political broadcasts, while the Liberal leader, Jo Grimond, visited the constituency.[146]

Outwardly confident, Mrs Thatcher dismissed Grimond's visit by suggesting that, given the seat was in no way a marginal, she wouldn't be bringing in big guns to campaign for her.[147] However, she had, in fact, secured Central Office's agreement that, although now a minister, she should do only a small number of visits outside the constituency and concentrate her efforts on holding Finchley.[148] The Tories were able to draw on the reputation, name recognition and high profile Mrs Thatcher had built up since her original selection in 1958.[149] She also had the unswerving support of the *Finchley Press*, whose cheerleading bordered on sycophancy: as polling day approached it described the Conservative candidate as 'genuinely loved by the people'.[150] As she always did, Mrs Thatcher threw her energies into the fight for re-election, addressing ten public meetings, which each drew audiences of nearly 200 people as the campaign drew to a close.[151] And, as she had done in 1959, she was determined to make the election about the choice between whether Labour or the Conservatives ruled at Westminster.[152]

On polling day, Mrs Thatcher publicly accepted her majority would fall but predicted she would win by 13,000 votes, while, a little more cautiously, Pardoe suggested he would 'scrape home'.[153] When the votes were counted, Mrs Thatcher's prediction proved to have been overly optimistic: she won but her majority was nearly halved, falling to just under 9,000. Although

Pardoe had failed to unseat her, he had scored the highest Liberal vote of any seat in the south-east – except for Orpington.[154]

The Tories had also arrested the loss of Jewish voters to the Liberals. Mrs Thatcher and Pardoe each took 40 per cent of the Jewish vote in Finchley, while Labour won the support of just one in five.[155] Some Finchley Tories were unsurprised: they had long expected that many local Jews would bridle against too close association with one political party, and, reported Donoughue, feared that such an association might provoke prejudice in members of the opposing parties.[156] Perhaps most importantly, however, Mrs Thatcher had put sufficient clear blue water between herself and the Finchley Tory association's old guard not to be punished for the taint of anti-Semitism which she recognised had attached itself to the party.

Nonetheless, it is also clear that there was a distinct 'Jewish vote' in Finchley, and that while it may not have succeeded in electing Pardoe, Jews had voted Liberal in the seat in a considerably higher proportion than non-Jews. Indeed, had Finchley's Jews had their way in 1964, Mrs Thatcher might have been narrowly defeated. Britain would have taken a very different course, and the future Prime Minister's relationship with its Jews would have had a rather different, and, for her, altogether less happy conclusion.

Yom Kippur fallout

Mrs Thatcher hung on in Finchley but the government of which she was a member did not. With the Tories now in opposition, Mrs Thatcher flitted swiftly through a series of frontbench posts. Over the next six years, she held six different portfolios: three as junior spokeswoman – on pensions, housing and economic policy – and three in the shadow Cabinet, covering power, transport and education. As we shall see in the next chapter, she loyally served her party's leadership, while beginning to cut a national profile.

Locally, her political position strengthened. The Liberal wave of the early 1960s had crested and fallen. In 1966, Labour's wafer-thin parliamentary majority provoked Harold Wilson to call a general election. The Liberals picked Frank Davis, their former mayor, to stand against Mrs Thatcher. Despite a poll in the *Finchley Times* during the campaign showing him only six points behind, Davis now represented little threat.[157] With Wilson winning the landslide denied him in 1964, and the third-party vote nationally dipping, Liberal support fell back. Labour – represented by a Jewish candidate, Yvonne Sieve – regained second place and, despite a small fall in her vote, Mrs Thatcher's majority edged back up. By now, memories of the golf club incident had finally begun to fade: Finchley Borough Council, the target of many local Jews' anger, had itself disappeared in 1965 with the local government reorganisation. Mrs Thatcher's little local difficulty appeared finally to be behind her. In 1970, as Ted Heath, much to her surprise and that of much of the rest of the nation, led the Tories to victory, Mrs Thatcher was comfortably re-elected in Finchley.

But when Heath called a snap election less than four years later, Mrs Thatcher found her position in Finchley rather less secure. As had been the case a decade previously, her Jewish constituents were to be at the forefront of that challenge. This time, however, it wasn't discrimination on the putting greens of Finchley, but a conflict in the Middle East which triggered the threat.

Mrs Thatcher's strong support for Israel, though entirely genuine, had been one of the ways she had reached out to Jewish voters.[158] She visited the country for the first time in 1965, had found much to admire and was full-throated in her support for it during the Six Day War two years later.[159] At a rally in the constituency shortly after Israel's victory, Mrs Thatcher made clear her belief that it 'should not withdraw from her new territories until she has her borders guaranteed. You cannot ask a nation to withdraw from the only bargaining point she has'.[160]

Six years later, at Yom Kippur on 6 October 1973, Egypt and Syria launched a surprise attack on Israel aimed at retaking lost territory, and avenging the psychological humiliation suffered in 1967. For a few days, the Jewish state appeared genuinely endangered. On the doorsteps of Finchley, the politics of this conflict were to prove rather less comfortable for Mrs Thatcher than those of 1967. Although the backdrop against which the February 1974 election was fought – a miners' strike, the three-day week and soaring inflation – was hardly propitious, Mrs Thatcher's biggest problem came from decisions taken by the Heath government in response to the Arab assault on Israel, decisions which, behind closed doors, she had vigorously opposed.

Behind the cloak of official neutrality, Wilson had staunchly backed Israel in 1967.[161] However, his successor in Downing Street had an altogether less sympathetic view of the Jewish state, as would become all too obvious in 1973.[162] Fearing that an interruption in supplies would blow a further hole in his already teetering economic policy, Heath sought to appease the oil-producing Arab states. While the United States offered Israel its support, Britain joined with its new EEC partners – Holland proving an honourable exception – in attempting to keep its head down. Seemingly ignoring the aggression perpetrated against Israel, Heath affected a policy that, he claimed, was 'genuinely even-handed', calling for a ceasefire and a return to the 1967 frontiers, imposing an arms embargo on both sides and refusing to allow the US to resupply Israel from British bases.[163] Although presented as affecting both sides, the arms embargo hit the Jewish state hardest, with Britain denying Israel spare parts for weapons, including shells for Centurion tanks that it had previously sold to it. It was, suggested the future Labour Foreign Secretary David Owen, 'the most cynical act of British foreign policy since Suez'.[164] At the same time, Egyptian pilots were continuing to be trained by Britain.

The government's words were little better than its deeds. Addressing the Conservative Party conference a week after the attack, Foreign Secretary Sir Alec Douglas-Home adopted a tone of sympathy for Israel's enemies, declaring that he had been certain 'it would not be psychologically possible for the Arabs to go on gazing indefinitely at their own lands without the eruption of war', thereby rather forgetting that those 'own lands' had been lost to Israel only because, six years previously, they had planned to annihilate her.[165]

Heath's approach immediately drew condemnation from the Labour opposition. At the urging of the Israelis, with whom he was in daily contact, Wilson pressured the government to lift the arms embargo, on the basis that the Arab states were being resupplied by their allies. In a highly charged debate in Parliament, Wilson accused the government of 'dishonouring contractual obligations [to supply arms and spare parts] at the very moment of Israel's greatest need', likened its stance to Britain's policy of non-intervention during the Spanish Civil War, and, raising the spectre of appeasement, warned that Britain must not give in to blackmail by 'oil-rich monarchs and presidents'.[166]

In a vote following the debate, fifteen Labour MPs backed Heath, while seventeen Tories followed Labour and the Liberals into the opposition lobby. All but two of the Tories' nine Jewish MPs – Sir Keith Joseph and Robert Adley[167] – rebelled against the government. Although most of the Tory rebels had no such interest, six, including: Hendon North's John Gorst, Tom Iremonger in Ilford North, Andrew Bowden in Brighton Kemptown, Michael Fidler in Bury and Radcliffe, Geoffrey Finsberg in Hampstead and Sir Stephen McAdden in Southend East, represented marginal seats with Jewish constituents.[168] A further thirty to forty Tory MPs abstained.

Conspicuously absent from those opposing the government's policy was the honourable member for Finchley, who found herself caught between Cabinet collective responsibility, on the one hand, and her own feelings and political interests on the other. Recognising that, in the early days of the war, Israel's situation was far more perilous than in 1967, Lady Thatcher later recalled anxiously following the news hour by hour. As MP for Finchley, she wrote, 'I knew at first hand what the Jewish community in Britain felt about our policies.'[169] It could hardly have been otherwise: in north London, feelings ran high. There were concerted attempts to assist Israel as it fought for its life and righteous anger rained down on the government's seeming indifference to it from charismatic rabbis such as Leslie Hardman in Hendon and Saul Amias in Edgware.[170] Thousands of posters of Golda Meir appeared in the windows of Jewish homes; money poured in to fundraising appeals; and synagogues set up blood banks to provide Israel with urgently needed supplies.[171] Public support for Israel was strong: two weeks into the war, the Joint Israel Appeal announced that 90,000 Britons had donated money and 300 meetings had been attended by 20,000 people.[172] Polls showed backing for Israel at ten times the level of support for the Arab states.[173]

Within the ranks of the Finchley Conservative Party there were public signs of deep unease with the government's position. Eight Jewish Tory councillors on Barnet council, including some from Mrs Thatcher's constituency, issued a statement making clear their 'unanimous and united stand against the uneven-handed embargo detrimental to the State of Israel enacted by the Government ... an action we cannot defend since we hold that nothing is politically right which is morally wrong'.[174] One of their number, Leslie Sussman, the chair of Barnet's Tory councillors, publicly admitted he was considering resigning from the council over the government's policy.[175]

Adding to Mrs Thatcher's discomfort, the charge against the government was led by one of her neighbouring MPs, John Gorst. In the Commons he accused the government of attempting to 'creep off the pages of history into frightened neutrality' and bowing to 'the oily blackmail of the Arab states'.[176] Writing to Douglas-Home, Gorst said that his Jewish constituents found the government's position difficult to 'understand or tolerate'. In words that would surely have stung Mrs Thatcher deeply, he said the government's 'ignominious neutrality' had turned Britain into 'a latter-day Sweden or Switzerland in world affairs'.[177]

Gorst's stance, and that of his fellow Tory rebels, commented the *Finchley Times*, might not make him popular with the government, but would meet with 'almost 100 per cent approval' from local voters.[178] Gorst urged them to put his Tory colleagues under pressure. 'If you want my advice,' he told a public meeting, 'you should be getting those people who don't join me in the lobbies involved in this affair.'[179]

Mrs Thatcher's woes deepened when the chair of Finchley's Young Conservatives, Ray Tomecki, wrote to the *Finchley Times*, attacking Gorst and the other Tory rebels for supposedly putting the interests of the Jewish state above their own country. Suggesting that Jewish MPs would 'put Britain first only where Israel is not directly affected', he went on to liken the latter – 'an expansionist and imperialist nation' – to Nazi Germany.[180] The letter caused a storm, with Mrs Thatcher's local association moving swiftly to shut the row down and effectively forcing Tomecki's resignation.[181]

As a member of the government, Mrs Thatcher did not have Gorst's luxury to vote as she liked. But while her fellow Cabinet minister and north London constituency neighbour, Welsh secretary Peter Thomas, parroted the government's line,[182] Mrs Thatcher made clear locally her disapproval of it.[183]

On the day Douglas-Home delivered a statement in Parliament on the issue, 200 people attended a protest meeting of the Finchley Anglo-Israel Friendship League and unanimously passed a resolution deploring 'the failure of the Government to denounce the aggressors' and urging it to give 'political and diplomatic support to Israel'.[184] Unable to attend because of an emergency Cabinet meeting to discuss the situation, Mrs Thatcher instead sent a message which was read out to loud applause in which she pledged 'to oppose the ban'.[185]

Although she loyally trooped through the division lobbies in support of the government, she honoured her pledge around the Cabinet table. The discussions, Lady Thatcher remembered, were difficult and not helped by the fact that while Douglas-Home defended his policy 'courteously', the same could not be said for the Prime Minister. 'Ted [exercised] a rigid determination to control an issue which – as he saw it – would determine the success or failure of our whole economic strategy.' She and Joseph were, in turn, 'intensely irritated' by the government's policy.[186]

In Cabinet, the dissenting ministers – the Lord Chancellor, Lord Hailsham, Joseph and Mrs Thatcher – made their case. The supply of ammunition to Israel was becoming a 'crucial problem'. It was not in Britain's national interests to see Israel's ability weakened and the Arab countries 'which were Soviet clients' strengthened. If Britain was willing to sell arms in times of peace and contracted to supply spare parts in ammunition, 'we were in honour committed to continue that supply if war broke out'. Whatever Israel's faults, there was 'no justification' for the Arabs' breach of the ceasefire and it was 'wrong that we should appear to be tolerant of it'.[187]

Mrs Thatcher addressed both the politics and morality of the government's policy. Public opinion, she said, was 'uneasy' and there was sympathy, not confined to the Jewish community, for Israel, especially as the arms embargo was seen as 'particularly damaging' to the Israelis and imposed simply because we were afraid for 'our oil supplies'. And then, in a clear reference to the mood in Finchley, she reported that 'acute problems' were likely to arise in some areas: local councillors were threatening to resign and this risked creating 'a separateness on the part of the Jewish community which would have very serious long-term consequences'.[188]

Heath was characteristically dismissive. Yes, the government was faced with a complex domestic and international situation, but it was also important to 'keep the matter in proportion'. Any supplies from the UK would be minimal compared to those now flowing from the US and fears that Israel would be destroyed were 'exaggerated'. The Prime Minister's only concession was to ask Douglas-Home to make it clear in his statement to Parliament that the government would keep the situation under review.[189] It was not a message Mrs Thatcher could easily relate to her Finchley constituents, nor did it appeal to her tendency to see matters in black and white rather than shades of grey.

She was not, however, to be deterred. Two days later when the Cabinet met again, Mrs Thatcher warned, minuted the Cabinet Secretary, that Britain's policy had 'lost [the] support of everyone, especially [the] young. Must say no question of Israel being wiped off [the] face of the earth'. Referring, as is practice in the Cabinet, to Mrs Thatcher's ministerial department, Heath responded: 'Don't accept Educ's view of public opinion. It's a Jewish-inspired press campaign.'[190] Heath finally told his Cabinet bluntly that he was having a note circulated telling them the public line they must take.[191]

Although the war was over in less than three weeks, its political ramifications at home were longer-lasting. They were felt almost immediately in a by-election in Hove. The rock-solid Tory seat, which the party had held with a majority of over 18,000 in 1970, had a sizeable Jewish population of around 5,000.[192] With the Conservatives' majority already threatened by the government's mounting economic problems, and a series of Liberal by-election victories over the previous year indicating a revival in the party's support, it was clear that the Jewish vote in the seat – normally reliably Tory – could be critical. A strong supporter of Israel, the Liberal leader, Jeremy Thorpe, sensed an opening and used a speech in Hove to attack the government's Middle East policy as 'all too reminiscent of Munich'. The Tories hit back by attempting to link his party's candidate, Des Wilson, to the Young Liberals' anti-Israeli stance.[193] In desperation, the Tory candidate, Tim Sainsbury, branded the government's policy 'not even-handed and actually prejudicial to the security of Israel'.[194] On polling day, the Liberals, who had not even stood a candidate in 1970, came within 5,000 votes of winning the seat. Sainsbury's words appeared to have shored up enough of the Jewish vote to stave off disaster.[195]

The Zionist Federation (ZF) ramped up the pressure, publishing a pamphlet, 'Why Did They Ignore Israel?' which listed all the MPs who had backed Heath or abstained in the arms embargo vote. An accompanying letter by the ZF's chairman, the Labour MP Eric Moonman, urged that MPs who had 'voted for the Alec Douglas-Home line' should be made to explain their votes.[196]

One of the MPs on the ZF list was, of course, Mrs Thatcher, who now faced the most difficult election she would ever fight in Finchley. Once again, the Liberals targeted Finchley's Jewish voters, adopting a young, Jewish candidate, Laurence Brass, who was a founder member of the Liberal Friends of Israel.[197] He immediately served notice that he intended to make Mrs Thatcher's 'betrayal of Israel' an issue. Since being chosen as his party's candidate, he told the *Finchley Press*, he had received far more correspondence about that than the miners' strike. 'I know a lot of people want to tell Mrs Thatcher how they feel about the role she played personally over the government's moves on the Middle East war. I will certainly be reminding people of that record,' he warned as the three-week campaign got underway.[198] 'I felt she was a bit two-faced in reality,' recalled Brass, 'going around to all the synagogues and Jewish organisations in Finchley saying how much she loved them all and then ... not publicly opposing the arms embargo, which to the Jewish community was a treacherous thing to do.'[199] However, as in Hove, the anti-Israel fanaticism of the Young Liberals – which had already caused ructions in the local party and the defection to Labour of Finchley's former 'Mr Liberal', Frank Davis – somewhat hampered Brass's attack, especially among the more politically savvy members of the electorate.[200]

Publicly, Mrs Thatcher's team shrugged off concerns about her support among Jewish voters. 'She has done so much personal work with the Jewish community here,' her agent told one journalist. 'She goes to their functions; she knows the rabbis by their first names and a lot of Jewish people are active members of our association.'[201] Despite the party's support rising sharply in the opinion polls, Mrs Thatcher attempted to ignore the Liberals, and focused her attack instead on the striking miners and their allies in the Labour Party.[202] Nonetheless, Mrs Thatcher's behaviour in the campaign, most of which she spent in Finchley, betrayed signs of anxiety. She refused to take part in a joint meeting of candidates and opted not to be interviewed on local radio so that her less well-known opponents would be denied valuable airtime thanks to rules governing broadcasters' political neutrality during an election campaign.[203]

By polling day, both the opinion polls and the evidence in Finchley indicated, Lady Thatcher later wrote, that the 'Liberals were posing a serious threat'. Her initial optimism had 'been replaced by unease'. On election day itself, a high turnout on the Labour-voting council estates in the constituency fuelled her fears.[204] With 'tremendous momentum' building, Brass believed he would pull off a famous victory. So, too, did his party and the media. ITV called the young Liberal candidate on polling day asking him to appear the following day. They were expecting him to be one of the night's shock victors, a producer explained.[205]

When the results were declared, Mrs Thatcher had survived, but, falling below 6,000, her majority was the lowest it had yet been. She had suffered to a degree from unhelpful boundary changes but, as it had across the country, the Liberal vote in Finchley had risen sharply. Although in third place, Brass won 27 per cent of the vote: the best result since Pardoe had threatened to make Finchley the 'Orpington of North London' ten years previously.[206]

But to what degree had Mrs Thatcher's Jewish constituents punished her for the government's stance towards Israel the previous autumn? Brass remained convinced that 'the small success in Finchley that I had in the first election of 1974 was due to the big Jewish following that I had', itself a consequence, he believed, of Heath's policy.[207] Certainly, other results appeared to bear out that assessment. In Hendon North, Gorst was richly rewarded by his Jewish constituents for his outspoken criticism of the government's supposedly pro-Arab line. A poll of Jewish voters in the seat carried out by Geoffrey Alderman showed that, despite Labour attacking the Tories for failing to stand by Israel, 16 per cent of those who had not voted Conservative in 1970 intended to switch to help re-elect Gorst. In a tight contest, that 16 per cent was a not insignificant 2,000 votes.[208] Among them were Saul Amias, the minister of Edgware Synagogue and a lifelong socialist, who publicly endorsed Gorst and – citing his support for Israel – signed his nomination papers.[209]

Gorst thus emerged largely unscathed: despite predictions of his demise, he held the seat with a majority of 2,612, publicly acknowledging that the Jewish vote had helped him hang on.[210] Significantly, at 1.1 per cent, the anti-Conservative swing in Hendon North was half that in Greater London as a whole. By contrast, in Finchley, Mrs Thatcher saw an above average swing against her of 3.2 per cent.[211] From across the country there were signs that, where their votes counted, Britain's Jews punished Tory MPs who had failed to oppose the government over the arms embargo, while rewarding those who had. In Leeds North East, Joseph, who like Mrs Thatcher had argued against the government line in Cabinet but could also only signal public dissent, suffered a swing against him more than three times higher than that which hit the Tories in the city as a whole.[212] In Ilford South and Middleton & Prestwich, Conservatives who had abstained in the vote on the embargo were defeated,[213] while in Ilford North Tom Iremonger, trumpeting his willingness to stand up to the government in defence of Israel, managed to survive in February 1974, even faced with a strong Jewish Labour opponent, Millie Miller.[214] In marginal Paddington, Marc Wolfson blamed his defeat on Jewish anger at the arms embargo.[215]

But even as, losing thirty-three seats and its parliamentary majority, their party headed for defeat, the February 1974 general election marked another step forward for Jewish Conservatives. In the twenty-five years since 1945, only two Jews had sat on the Tory benches in the House of Commons. That number rose to nine when Heath won in 1970. In February 1974, even as it shrunk in size, the Tory parliamentary party saw twelve Jews elected. Among them were three men – Nigel Lawson, Leon Brittan and Malcolm Rifkind – whose future fortunes were to be inextricably bound up with the member for Finchley.

Mrs Thatcher had survived in Finchley but Heath had not. Ousted from Downing Street after the inconclusive result of February 1974, the Tories' poor performance when Wilson went back to the country six months later in an attempt to win a majority for his government sealed Heath's fate. In October 1973, Mrs Thatcher had formed an alliance with Sir Keith Joseph over their shared opposition to Heath's policy towards Israel. But this issue, it would turn out, was not the only thing that they agreed Heath had got badly wrong.

CHAPTER 3

THE JUNIOR PARTNER

Sir Keith Joseph was an improbable revolutionary. Born into an affluent, well-established Anglo-Jewish family as the Great War entered its final year, his upbringing, Joseph later suggested, had certain parallels with the wealthy London Jewish family described by C. P. Snow in one of his favourite books, *The Conscience of the Rich*.[1]

Joseph's father, Sir Samuel, was not simply a successful businessman, he had also reached the summit of the arcane world of the City of London's politics, becoming Lord Mayor of London in 1942. It was, though, not just his baronetcy or his stake in the Bovis construction business that Joseph inherited on his father's death in 1944. Less than eighteen months later, he was invited to represent his father's old City of London ward, Portsoken. Joseph had his feet on the first rungs of the political ladder. He climbed it swiftly: despite his lack of party activism, he was selected to fight the winnable seat of Barons Court at the 1955 general election. Joseph's narrow loss to Labour proved a blessing in disguise: instead of having to spend years nursing a marginal seat, his strong performance ensured that, when, less than a year later, a by-election was called in solidly Tory Leeds North East, Joseph was well placed to win his party's selection. On 9 February 1956, the 38-year-old became only the second Jewish Conservative candidate elected to the House of Commons since 1945.

If Joseph appeared not to be a revolutionary by background, nor was he was one by temperament. Sir Alfred Sherman, a fellow Jew who would play a critical role in both Sir Keith's political journey and Margaret Thatcher's rise to power, later noted Joseph's 'tendency to wilt under pressure' and his aversion to conflict.[2] Recalling Joseph in the chamber of the House after the controversial speech in Birmingham in 1974 which ended his prospects of becoming Tory leader, Enoch Powell – no stranger to controversy himself – believed he was seeing 'a man who didn't like the heat in the kitchen'.[3] Perhaps most importantly, Joseph appeared to lack the revolutionary's sense of the absolute rectitude of their cause. One former Cabinet colleague, John Biffen, found him 'indecisive and given to public agonising'[4] while another, Sir Geoffrey Howe, deemed Joseph 'hugely intelligent' but 'immensely unsure of himself'.[5]

And yet Joseph was to be the man who lit the touchpaper which, as Sherman put it, 'sparked off the Thatcher revolution'.[6] In *The Path to Power*, which she dedicated to Joseph's memory, Margaret Thatcher wrote simply: 'I could not have become Leader of the Opposition, or achieved what I did as Prime Minister, without Keith.'[7] Her debt to him, she suggested, could 'never be repaid'.[8] Biographers of both concurred. Hugo Young deemed the relationship between Mrs Thatcher and Joseph 'one of the most formative' in modern British political history, while Morrison Halcrow questioned whether, without him, Thatcherism would have occurred in the manner that it did.[9]

In both their background and temperament Mrs Thatcher and Joseph were proof of the attraction of opposites. Hers was lower-middle-class, Methodist and provincial. His was upper-middle-class, Jewish and metropolitan. Keith's childhood memories were happy ones; his parents indulged their only child. The Roberts home was altogether chillier and more austere.

Alfred Roberts may, like Sir Samuel Joseph, have made a name for himself in local politics, but Grantham and the City of London were rather different ponds in which to swim. Joseph may have chosen not to exploit his connections when he decided to stand for Parliament,[10] but Margaret Roberts had no strings on which to pull had she so desired. Nor did politics appear to infuse Joseph's upbringing or thrill him, in the way that it did Margaret. Instead, he eschewed it for cricket at university. He chose not to engage in the great debates about war and peace to which the Oxford Union echoed in the late 1930s, although in the famous by-election of September 1938, in which the issue of appeasement was fought out on the streets and in the meeting halls of the city, he privately supported A. D. Lindsay, the independent, anti-appeasement, if ultimately unsuccessful, candidate to whom Labour and the Liberals gave a free run.[11] Whatever qualms Mrs Thatcher later professed about the policy of appeasement, it is hard to imagine her supporting a non-Conservative candidate. This points to another crucial difference between the two: unlike Mrs Thatcher, who wrote in her memoirs that 'by instinct and upbringing, I was always a "true blue" Conservative',[12] Joseph lacked what his biographers, Andrew Denham and Mark Garnett, termed that same 'instinctive, almost "tribal" loyalty'.[13]

It was not, in fact, until he was thirty, in 1948, that Joseph decided to join the Young Conservatives. By this time, Margaret Roberts, despite being seven years his junior, had already been an active member of the Oxford University Conservative Association, been 'entranced' by her first Conservative Party conference and was just months away from being selected to fight Dartford. Once Joseph had decided to pursue a political career, his repeatedly expressed reasons for doing so were not ones which Mrs Thatcher ever claimed were her primary motivation. 'I had arrived anxious to eliminate poverty,' Joseph later recalled.[14] There was nothing false or pious about Joseph's claim: as a student, he had participated in a Quaker project and stayed with a miner's family in Yorkshire.[15] His experiences in Portsoken, his charitable work in East London and nationally, and his interest in the social services both as a new MP and minister were all further testament to that. Pointedly, Lady Thatcher later wrote that, 'Keith had gone into politics *for the same reason many on the left had done so* – he wanted to improve the lot of ordinary people, particularly those he saw living deprived, stunted, unfulfilled lives [author emphasis].'[16] By contrast, fighting her first parliamentary campaign in Dartford, Margaret

Roberts viewed herself as the champion of the lower-middle classes: echoing their concerns about the Labour government's alleged high taxes, wasteful spending and the shackling of private enterprise, and calling for a rediscovery of the value of individual responsibility.[17]

Their public personas, too, were very different. Whatever her attributes, compassion and gentleness were rarely words associated with Mrs Thatcher. However, she considered Joseph 'the most sensitive human being I have ever met in forty years of politics',[18] while Biffen believed he was 'too kind to have the butcher instincts required of a party leader'.[19] She appeared to thrive on confrontation; he would often seek to avoid it. And the certainty Joseph seemed to lack, she, at least publicly, made up for in spades.

The outsiders

Yet, for all their seeming differences, Margaret Thatcher and Keith Joseph shared a common attribute: the sense that they were both outsiders. The origins of this feeling were very different. Hers stemmed from her upbringing in Grantham, the snobbery and disdain she encountered in both the OUCA and liberal intelligentsia at Oxford, and later, her gender, as she sought a safe Tory seat willing to adopt her as its candidate. His originated from his Judaism. In later life, Joseph suggested that the advantage of being Jewish was that to be successful 'you have to spark on all four cylinders'.[20] Or, to put it less positively, Jews faced greater barriers to achievement than others.

Joseph was first made aware of this at an early age. At his prep school, Lockers Park, he was the victim of verbal bullying for being Jewish.[21] Unlike the Jewish working-class of the East End, Joseph's family may not have encountered the most violent manifestations of interwar anti-Semitism, but they were not unaffected. When Samuel Joseph stood for one of the two Sheriff of London posts in June 1933, he and a fellow Jewish candidate were subjected to an anti-Semitic campaign by their opponent, the Tory MP Arthur Leonard Bateman. After his defeat, Bateman suggested the City of London had been 'lost' to the Jews and it would soon be necessary to 'declare war on them as they have done in Germany'.[22] By 1937, with the nature of the Nazi regime no longer in any doubt, and its Mosleyite supporters attracting support in the East End, the family's fears were all too apparent and a number of them attempted to Anglicise their names. Samuel changed his middle name from Gluckstein to George. Whatever his seeming lack of interest in politics, Joseph was an intelligent and informed enough young man to have sensed the mood of the times.

Despite his seemingly effortless rise, Joseph was also not totally immune from the subtle anti-Semitism which lingered on in the Conservative Party after the Second World War, as the response of one of those who interviewed him for inclusion on the party's candidates list demonstrated. 'As a Jew,' he commented, 'I suppose he is not every constituency's man and, therefore, his placing would need care.'[23] Although Halcrow suggested that being Jewish had not counted against Joseph in the by-election which brought him into Parliament, this was only partially true.[24] Leeds North East had a sizeable Jewish vote and Labour had also picked a Jewish candidate. However, that was not the whole story. A family friend on the constituency executive suggested to Joseph that the local association would never pick a Jew. 'Just get me an interview,' he responded.[25] The association then bridled at a shortlist which forced it to choose between 'a Jew and a woman', while Central Office noted 'anti-Semitic prejudice' was strong in the seat and many Tory voters would not turn out for Joseph.[26]

Once he arrived in Westminster, Joseph's career was hardly hampered by anti-Semitism and it would be wrong to overplay his outsider status. Within a year of his election, Joseph was appointed a parliamentary private secretary; after the Tories were re-elected in 1959, he became a minister for the first time at the Ministry of Housing and Local Government. Impressing his fellow ministers,[27] he unsurprisingly caught the eye of the Prime Minister and, only six years after he was first elected to parliament, Joseph entered the Cabinet as Minister of Housing and Local Government. Young modernising Tories were soon gushing to the media that the dashing housing minister could become 'the Tory Jack Kennedy'.[28]

Beneath the surface, however, a sense that Joseph was somehow different lurked. One Tory who knew him during his early years in parliament later confessed that, while he liked Joseph, he nevertheless always found him somewhat mysterious and 'almost alien'.[29] Looking back on Joseph's career, John Ranelagh, who worked at the Conservative Research Department in the late 1970s, suggested: 'For all his having been to Harrow and to Oxford there is still something of the outsider about Joseph. The average Conservative, confronted by this highly strung, brilliant Jewish millionaire Fellow of All Souls College, Oxford, doubtless finds him a bit rich for the diet.' For a party which preferred the 'less able, unimaginative, steady types', Joseph represented 'something lamentably exotic'.[30] Even Macmillan couldn't help a condescending aside about the man whose early career he had done so much to promote. Joseph, the former Prime Minister later remarked, was 'the only boring Jew I've ever met'.[31]

This sense of Joseph standing slightly apart from the Conservative Parliamentary Party of the 1960s stemmed from a number of factors. Aside from his intellect, his interest in the social services was as, he himself recognised, if not unique, then certainly somewhat unusual on the Tory backbenches.[32] Nonetheless, the feeling that Joseph – the first Jew to sit in a Tory Cabinet since the fall of Leslie Hore-Belisha in 1940, and, for fifteen years, one of only two Jews in the parliamentary party – was somehow 'exotic' and 'alien' no doubt also reflected the wider uneasy relationship between the Conservative Party and the Jewish community.

Joseph was in some regards also something of an outsider twice over. With his Harrow and Oxford background, Joseph, like his fellow Jewish Tory MP, Sir Henry d'Avigdor-Goldsmid, was not 'remotely typical of the Anglo-Jewish community,' believed Geoffrey Alderman.[33] At the same time, *The Observer*'s description of him in the 1970s as 'probably the most committed Jew ever to serve in a Cabinet' fails to capture the complexities of Joseph's Judaism.[34] His family, he suggested, were best characterised as 'minimally observing, but maximally acknowledging' Jews.[35] Minimal observance may not have been unusual, but the fact that, as Joseph later put it, his father 'denied him' a bar mitzvah – the overprotective response, Denham and Garnett speculated, of a man well aware of the anti-Semitism of the period – most certainly was.[36] As a child, believed his fellow Jewish MP, Leo Abse, Joseph therefore lacked 'any sense of belonging to his own people'.[37]

'I am not what an observing Jew would call an Orthodox Jew in any way, nor do I claim to be,' Joseph suggested in 1973, 'but I am a confessing Jew and a proud Jew.'[38] A member of both the Liberal Jewish Synagogue in St John's Wood and an Orthodox synagogue near his home in Chelsea, he attended neither regularly and chose not to abide by Judaism's dietary laws. However, he worshipped on what he termed 'the imperative days', observed the Day of Atonement (Yom Kippur),[39] and was an active supporter of a number of communal organisations, most notably the Friends of Hebrew University and the Institute of Jewish Affairs. At the same time, Joseph's Zionism was less pronounced: while joining Mrs Thatcher in urging support for Israel in 1973, he had opposed Suez in 1956 and showed little interest in the activities of the Conservative Friends of Israel after it was formed in 1975.[40] Joseph's feelings were, perhaps, best encapsulated by his dismissal of those who were 'guilty, either of being too obviously Jewish or of trying too obviously not to be'.[41]

But, as Sherman suggested, Joseph's Jewishness was 'unmistakable' and 'extended far beyond his synagogue membership and association with Jewish causes'. Despite his privileged upbringing, he 'exemplified the insecurity and self-questioning that most diaspora Jews take with them through life'; qualities, Sherman believed, that were both 'a spur and a handicap'. 'Quite apart from his looks,' his old ally suggested, 'he could never have been mistaken for an Englishman of his social class.' This was because Joseph 'worried about everything, particularly the suffering of the poor and inadequate, as his gentile colleagues atop the Conservative summit did not'.[42] Many patrician Conservatives would, of course, have bridled at such an assertion about their concerns, or alleged lack of them.

No hint of a sign?

Despite the revolution they would go on to lead, there were only sporadic signs during the first decade they shared together in parliament that Margaret Thatcher and Sir Keith Joseph would go on to upend the post-war consensus.

A member of the progressive One Nation Group of Tory MPs, Joseph pursued an ambitious ministerial agenda of slum clearance, housebuilding and high-rise flat construction, thereby fitting in effortlessly in what Sherman termed 'the Age of Macmillan'.[43] As James Callaghan mockingly suggested from Labour's front bench in 1963: 'The right Hon. Gentleman is not fully a Socialist yet, but he is coming along.'[44] Marching very much in lockstep with the Tory mainstream, Joseph backed the winning candidates – Macmillan, Alec Douglas-Home and Ted Heath – on each occasion the party leadership became vacant and, in declaring himself a 'Heath man' in 1965, chose not to support Enoch Powell, the Conservatives' foremost proponent of much of the economic agenda which he would come to espouse.[45]

But Joseph's later self-proclaimed 'conversion' to Conservatism – in reality, as Brian Harrison suggested, a 'radical variant of free-market Liberalism'[46] – was hardly Damascene. Alongside his liberal social outlook – he opposed capital punishment, supported prison reform and backed race relations legislation[47] – and concern for the poor, sat a long-standing belief in the importance of entrepreneurship. As a profile in the *Jewish Chronicle* in 1974 suggested, Joseph's 'major asset' had long been 'his ability to strike a balance between efficiency and social concern'. 'He has always stood for those decent values which might be termed "the acceptable face of Toryism".'[48]

After the Tories lost power in 1964, there were fleeting public glimpses of the revolutionary who would emerge when the party was ejected from office once again a decade later. In a speech in Reading in 1967, for instance, Joseph complained that when the Conservatives had entered government in 1951 'we found private enterprise totally shackled by the socialists. Our error was that we only half freed it.'[49] With Sherman playing the role of self-described 'mentor, familiar, moving spirit'[50] – and, more mundanely, wordsmith – Joseph provided a further foretaste of what was to come in a series of speeches on the eve of the 1970 general election. The first saw Joseph levelling his criticisms not only at Labour, but also at the last Conservative government. 'We Conservatives may not have gone far enough in getting taxes down,' he suggested, before raising the prospect of what, a decade later, would become one of the defining policies of the Thatcher years: privatisation.[51] As the *Sunday Times* noted, the speeches marked 'a fundamental change, not only from the policies of the present Government, but from those of previous Tory administrations as well'.[52]

But despite his public rhetoric, behind closed doors at the south London hotel where the Tory shadow Cabinet had gathered to agree its radical proto-Thatcherite agenda for government, Joseph was hardly the 'Selsdon Man' of Labour lore, determined to unleash the chill winds of the free market on the British people.

Instead, he fretted about those low earners who wouldn't be compensated for planned benefit cuts by reductions in income tax. 'There are so many employments,' he told his colleagues, 'in which these people cannot … earn more; many are people who are working very hard.' By contrast, Mrs Thatcher's concerns about benefits which allowed people to 'go on having large families which they cannot afford' were altogether rather different.[53]

The mentor

One of those whom Joseph persuaded to support Heath in 1965 was Margaret Thatcher. When the Tories went into opposition in 1964, she continued to shadow her old pensions' portfolio. With Joseph assuming responsibility for social services, the two now worked closely together. She considered him a 'friend, not just a senior colleague, whom I liked', but she considered Joseph 'very much … the senior partner'.[54] That was not always how the relationship appeared to others. 'Most of his colleagues would have bridled at being corrected by a bossy younger woman who had only been in Parliament for five years. He revelled in it,' remembered Ferdinand Mount, who at the time was responsible for health and pensions policy at the Conservative Research Department.[55]

Like Joseph, Mrs Thatcher was very much part of the Conservative mainstream during the 1960s. Fighting unwinnable Dartford in 1950, she had been careful not to disavow the emerging post-war consensus, but had sounded her reservations about both the moral and economic dangers of socialism – she framed the choice at the election as between two very different futures:

'one which leads inevitably to slavery and the other to freedom' – with a starkness which was both uncommon at the time and, in retrospect, telling.[56]

Once the Conservatives had lost power five years after she entered parliament, Mrs Thatcher showed little inclination to exploit the greater freedoms of opposition to offer insights about the direction the Tories should now move in, perhaps understandably, given that she would not make it into the shadow Cabinet until 1967. However, in 1968, Heath gave her limited licence to range a little wider and set out some of her own thinking when she was chosen to deliver the prestigious Conservative Political Centre lecture at the party's annual conference.

Poring over books on philosophy, politics and history, the speech was her own work. Her ostensible subject: 'What's wrong with politics?' provided her with a broad enough canvas on which, albeit studiously loyally, to sketch a position which had a distinctive character.[57] As a precursor to the clashes which would occur six years later, three things stand out. First, she showed her distaste for what she termed in her memoirs 'the fraudulent appeal of consensus',[58] declaring: 'There are dangers in consensus: it could be an attempt to satisfy people holding no particular views about anything.' Instead, she insisted, it was more important to have 'a philosophy and policy which because they are good appeal to sufficient people to secure a majority'. In the battle for the heart and soul of the Tory Party which would be fought during the next decade, Joseph and Mrs Thatcher would mount the barricades steeled by a conviction that, when provided with an alternative to 'Buskellite' politics of the 1950s and 1960s, the British people would take it.

Second, she proclaimed that the state had grown too big and fretted that this sapped the virtues of personal responsibility and self-advancement. Wealth creation was both the responsibility of individuals, not the state, and a moral imperative: conjuring up a biblical image she would return to repeatedly, she announced: 'Even the Good Samaritan had to have the money to help, otherwise he too would have had to pass on the other side.' Not for the first time, or the last, Alfred Roberts's homilies were being proclaimed from a stage far larger than Grantham town hall.

Finally, she indicated her sympathy for the then nascent theory of monetarism: 'The essential role of government' she declared, was the *control of money supply* and [the] management of demand [author emphasis]'. This would mean, she sarcastically noted, that the government would have 'to exercise itself some of the disciplines on expenditure it is so anxious to impose on others'.[59] Mrs Thatcher may, as she later wrote, have lacked a 'guide' for her speech, but, on this final point, she had had a helping hand. Around this time, Joseph met Alan Walters, who he introduced to Mrs Thatcher. Joseph took her with him on visits to the young economist's flat where Walters taught them about the virtues of monetarism. Much later, he would become Mrs Thatcher's economic adviser in Downing Street and his presence the source of Nigel Lawson's resignation as Chancellor of the Exchequer in 1989.

When the Tories found themselves back in power eighteen months later, Heath sent Mrs Thatcher to the Department for Education while dispatching Joseph to the Department for Health and Social Services (DHSS). 'By chance or calculation,' Lady Thatcher later suggested, the new Prime Minister had managed to keep his two most economically conservative Cabinet members 'well out of economic decision-making'. There was, she recognised, 'a natural opposition' between what each wanted for their own programmes and 'the requirements of tight public expenditure control'.[60] Neither, however, appeared to struggle much with their philosophical consciences. Having been cast as 'Selsdon Man' incarnate, Joseph was to disappoint both Labour and his friends. Sherman felt that he had been able 'turn him' in 1969–70, but that, upon arriving at the DHSS, Joseph 'promptly returned to the bosom of Party orthodoxy'.[61] Recalling his earlier spells as a One Nation pamphleteer and slum-clearing housing minister, Joseph happily trumpeted his high-spending record. Indeed, such was the growth of spending that even some on the left who supported social services expansion came to regard this as 'uncontrolled'.[62]

While Lady Thatcher suggested that his spell at the DHSS meant that Joseph's 'compassionate, social reforming side had become uppermost as the expense of his more conservative economic convictions', this is too fine a distinction.[63] Joseph may have believed that government intervention in industry was stifling competition and growth, but – at this time, at least – he saw no contradiction between using the proceeds of that prosperity to invest in the welfare state.

Joseph emerged largely unscathed from the wreckage of the Heath government. For the *Sunday Mirror*, Joseph was 'a man of strange contradictions. The Tory Minister who really cares',[64] while in Downing Street, he was allegedly referred to as 'our statutory humane minister'.[65]

Few would have said the same for Mrs Thatcher. As Education Secretary, she chalked up a pragmatic, centrist record. Despite her later claims of misgivings, she did little to arrest the rush to abolish grammar schools, approving more schemes for comprehensive schools than any of her predecessors or successors. In the face of opposition from most of the Cabinet, she fought off attempts to scrap the Open University – declaring: 'We can't make education our first sacrifice'[66] – and pursued ambitious plans to massively expand nursery education and build new primary schools.

However, none of this was to define her time at Curzon Street. As the Treasury searched for savings, Mrs Thatcher fatally agreed to cuts in the provision of free school milk to primary school children. The reputation she developed as 'Thatcher the Milk Snatcher' would never desert her. In contrast to the praise heaped on Joseph's compassion, she became, as one newspaper put it, 'the Lady Nobody Loves'.[67] The cuts to school milk were, however, a rare, albeit bruising, defeat for Mrs Thatcher at the hands of the Treasury. Philosophically, she may have believed that government had got too big, but, like Joseph, she showed little inclination to prune her own ministry's spending. As a strong supporter of Ted Heath, Jim Prior no doubt had an axe to grind, but his description a decade later of his former Cabinet colleagues contains a strong element of truth: 'She and Keith Joseph were the big spenders in the Heath administration. It wasn't that they were saying the whole time "we must cut back". They were actually always asking for more.'[68]

Less than two years into office, the Heath government executed its famous

U-turn: caving into the miners in the face of a strike and rolling back some of its own restrictions on the unions; ditching fiscal caution in an ill-fated 'dash for growth'; and, with the introduction of wage and price controls and an Industry Act which Tony Benn cheerfully labelled 'spadework for socialism', abandoning the free-market principles to which it had committed at Selsdon Park.[69]

Privately, both Mrs Thatcher and Joseph were deeply unsettled by this turn of events, although neither felt so distressed as to leave Heath's Cabinet. With typical self-deprecation, Joseph later claimed that he had 'never been a very effective Cabinet member' and suggested that he had been too distracted with the affairs of his own department. 'I failed to lift up my eyes,' he remarked woefully.[70] Sherman was characteristically scathing. Joseph who had been 'a lion in opposition' had proven himself 'a lamb in government'.[71]

Like Joseph, Mrs Thatcher was also immersed in the affairs of her department and far removed from economic decision-making. She was also aware of her own comparative lack of political importance. 'I was not senior enough,' she wrote in her memoirs as to whether she should have resigned, 'for it to be other than the littlest "local difficulty"'.[72] She offered occasional signals to those outside the Cabinet of her true sympathies, telling one junior minister who had quit the government: 'I wish I could join you in your battle'.[73] But, publicly, Mrs Thatcher, like Joseph, loyally defended the government's new direction.[74]

Sounding the cry

Lunching with Dirk Gleysteen of the US embassy at the Connaught Hotel in May 1973, Mrs Thatcher offered her opinions on her Cabinet colleagues. One, above all, stood out. She had, reported Gleysteen, 'tremendous admiration' for Joseph, considering him 'brilliant, versatile and full of further promise'. He could, she proudly boasted, 'handle any ministry' and she was 'confident he has been marked for higher responsibility'.[75] In the wake of the Conservatives' defeat and ejection from office ten months later, her admiration for Joseph would grow further. Moreover, while it would be her who was to ultimately assume that 'higher responsibility', Mrs Thatcher could almost certainly not have achieved it without him.

When the Cabinet met as the results of the general election were still coming in on Friday 1 March 1974, future fault lines were already becoming apparent. During the early hours of the morning, Heath had lost his majority after a hapless bid to prove that he, not the striking miners, ruled the country. But, having narrowly edged in front of Labour in the popular vote, the Prime Minister was keen to open negotiations with the Liberal leader, Jeremy Thorpe. Both Mrs Thatcher and Joseph were adamantly opposed. He voiced concerns about constitutional propriety; her take was typically more partisan.[76] Many of those who had backed the Liberals, she claimed, were disgruntled Tory voters. 'They are ours,' Mrs Thatcher declared stridently to the Cabinet. 'If we coalesce [with the Liberals], we lose them for ever.'[77]

The talks between Heath and Thorpe soon collapsed, forcing the Tories back into opposition. For Heath, however, it was clear that without a majority Harold Wilson would soon be forced to return to the country to secure a stronger mandate. The Conservatives should thus avoid a potentially divisive navel-gazing examination of their record in office and instead stick firmly to the centre ground to woo back supporters they had lost to the Liberals. But in his determination to hold to a steady course, Heath now made a potentially fatal political miscalculation. Unexpectedly, he opted not to appoint Joseph as his shadow Chancellor, instead offering the post to the former Home Secretary, Robert Carr. A disappointed Joseph asked for a roving policy role in the new shadow Cabinet. It is impossible to know whether, as Sherman later claimed, if Joseph had been given the job of shadow Chancellor 'there would have been no "Thatcher revolution"'.[78] What is clear is that, after apparently being granted the opportunity to roam freely, Joseph now began a very public reassessment of the Tories' time in power. It was one that would have far-reaching consequences and one in which Sherman – persuading, cajoling and hectoring – would be at his side every step of the way.

'Zealot of the right'[79]

Alfred Sherman was born in the East End of London in November 1919 into a family of poor Jewish immigrants who had escaped Tsarist Russia. It was an environment in which, he recalled, 'you were born a socialist, you didn't have to become one'.[80] Against a backdrop of barely disguised official anti-Semitism (see Chapter 2), many Jews attempted to assimilate. Sherman's way of doing so was to become a communist. As he recognised, for Jews like himself there was a certain quasi-religious fervour to their attachment to communism. 'When we deserted the God of our fathers,' he wrote, 'we were bound to go whoring after strange gods, of which socialism in its various forms was a prominent choice.'[81]

'Appalled by fascism', seventeen-year-old Alfred abandoned his studies and, without telling his parents where he was going, boarded a train from London determined to join the nearest fight against its growing menace.[82] Thus, while Mrs Thatcher was watching her father preaching in the villages around Grantham, and Keith Joseph was playing cricket at Oxford, Sherman became a machine-gunner in the International Brigade during the Spanish Civil War. Far from home, he fitted in: over one-third of the members of the Brigade were estimated to be Jews. Sherman felt 'a sense of belonging' which British society had denied him.[83]

Although he recognised in retrospect that Stalin had betrayed the Republican cause, his experiences in Spain did not shake Sherman's Marxism. That was to come later when studying at the LSE after the war. He later suggested that reading F. A. Hayek's *The Road to Serfdom* had 'set him thinking'.[84] But thinking for oneself was not encouraged by the Communists and in 1948 Sherman was expelled from the party, after his support for Yugoslavia was deemed an act of 'Titoist deviationism'. Sherman's political journey from the extreme left to the right was by no means a unique one for many Jews; instead, it was a reflection of the uneasy relationship between the Jewish left and the increasingly anti-Semitic Soviet regime.

Sherman may have lost one faith, but he had discovered another. In the unpromising terrain of 1950s socialist Israel, he developed his fervent support for the free market while working as an economic adviser. Returning to Britain in 1965, Sherman joined the *Daily Telegraph* as local government correspondent and later became a leader writer. In 1971, he became a Conservative councillor. For a polemicist of Sherman's bent, wrote Halcrow, 'bumbling municipal socialism' was the perfect target.[85] So, too, was the 'Buskellite' Toryism of the party's ruling class.

The two future collaborators in the Thatcher project first met when Sherman came to interview Joseph shortly after he had become a Cabinet minister. They stayed in touch after the Tories went into opposition, with Joseph, knowing that Sherman occasionally wrote for *Haaretz* and spoke both Hebrew and Arabic, sometimes turning to him for advice in the face of concerns raised by his Jewish friends and constituents about British policy in the Middle East.

But it was during the period when Joseph was preparing the series of controversial speeches he would deliver in early 1970 that the partnership between the two men was first forged. Ironically, it may have stemmed from a well-intended suggestion by James Douglas of the Conservative Research Department, who was concerned that some of the former Cabinet minister's proposed comments might be open to misinterpretation, that Joseph ought to find someone to help him with speeches.[86] Sherman, who, as one journalist noted in 1978, 'pushes his convictions until he starts to antagonise', was probably not the kind of helper Douglas had in mind.[87] Joseph was, his new collaborator recalled, 'disproportionately impressed' by the 'standard journalistic techniques' he employed to knock the speeches into shape.[88] It was a somewhat unexceptional beginning to a relationship that would reshape British political history.

His 'lamb-like' behaviour in the Heath government had caused Joseph and Sherman to drift apart. When they did speak, the conversations were strained. On one occasion, the sensitive Joseph even told Sherman that he had found one of his *Daily Telegraph* articles, which attacked the new towns and their ministerial architects, so upsetting that it had ruined his holiday.[89] Nonetheless, as Joseph's private doubts about the government's direction grew, their relationship began to recover. In early 1974, Joseph invited Sherman to his home, ostensibly to discuss the political fallout from the Yom Kippur War (see Chapter 2), but, predictably, their conversation ranged more widely around the growing crisis enveloping the government.

'Both you and Keith are Jews,' Mrs Thatcher later remarked to Sherman, 'but your Jewishness is very different.'[90] In fact, Sherman and Joseph were different in just about every way possible. Mrs Thatcher, as Charles Moore suggested, 'linked [Sherman's] Jewishness with that of Joseph as part of their combined virtue'. But while anointing Sherman a 'genius', Lady Thatcher admitted that he could be 'very difficult to get on with'.[91] Until one saw how effectively he and Joseph worked together, she remembered, 'it was difficult to believe how they could cooperate at all'.[92]

Sherman lacked Joseph's urbane polish, his political connections and standing, and his elevated views about the manner in which political debate should be conducted. None would have said of Joseph, as Halcrow wrote of Sherman, that his debating style was in the 'knockabout tradition of shouting matches' in the 'boulevard cafes of central Europe'.[93] For Mrs Thatcher the 'force and clarity of his mind' meant that he had a 'complete disregard for other people's feelings or opinion of him'.[94] 'He was brilliant, funny, terribly rude,' recalled Norman Strauss, who worked closely with him during the opposition years.[95] Lord Young, a future Cabinet minister who would also work with Sherman at the CPS, believed he was a man of 'unbelievable extremes … He was amusing, he was intelligent, but he had zero common sense'.[96]

Sherman was to nonetheless prove Joseph's invaluable partner. The former Cabinet minister may have lacked the revolutionary's disposition but his comrade-in-arms had no such weakness: an unshakeable certainty about the righteousness of his ideas; a turn of phrase which popularised complex subjects; and a relish for taking the fight to the enemy. Indeed, Sherman would draw on much of what he had learned in his 'communist decade', regarding it as 'an essential ingredient in the mix which prepared me to take a hand in key political events in the 1970s'. Communism had taught him 'to think big, to believe that, aligned with the forces of history, a handful of people with sufficient faith could move mountains'.[97] Others, too, detected and were disturbed by these qualities. When Joseph introduced Sherman to his close friends, the political scientist Bill Letwin and philosopher Shirley Letwin, they sensed the sectarian mindset of some of their ex-Marxist academic colleagues.[98] 'I never liked Sherman,' suggested one Thatcher intimate, 'he was a convert from the Communists, and they are always a bit dangerous. He was like a Moonie.'[99]

Most important of all, Sherman steeled Joseph for the coming fight. 'Keith,' he bluntly told him over lunch one day, 'the trouble is that you agree with me but you haven't got the backbone to say so.'[100] This was no isolated incident. 'You do not understand,' he berated Joseph shortly after the 1974 election, 'Keynes is dead. Dead.'[101] 'You have to do something about the state of the country,' Sherman commanded.[102] Later, visitors would be surprised on visiting the Centre for Policy Studies (CPS) to find Joseph, head in hands, being harangued by his junior officer.[103] Sherman thus provided Joseph with the courage of his convictions, forcing the former minister to turn thought and contemplation into bold action.

Joseph did not need convincing that things had gone badly wrong: he had been, albeit unenthusiastically, an accomplice in the Heath government's abandonment of its free-market principles and then, along with his colleagues, had undergone the humiliation of the three-day week and defeat by the miners, rejection at the ballot box, and ejection from office. Sherman, however, wanted more than penitence. While a Conservative, his disdain for 'the Establishment' did not recognise party labels. The Tories, he believed, appeared to judge virtue by the measure of whether it won them elections.[104] Shocked by its defeat in 1945, the party had adopted 'the Labour Party version of state-socialism', not out of conviction but out of desperation.[105] For Sherman, the free-market revolution that he wanted Joseph to lead was designed not simply to sweep away socialism, but to cleanse the Conservative Party of its post-war sins.

And so it was that, with Sherman acting as his confessor, Joseph underwent his very public recantation and conversion to Conservatism. It was, he wrote a year later, 'only in April 1974 that I was converted to Conservatism. I had thought I was a Conservative but I now see that I was not one at all'.[106] The phraseology may have been Shermanesque hyperbole, but it signalled a new determination to speak out and to chart a course very different from the one Heath and the majority of his colleagues were set upon. Sherman's role, Joseph acknowledged, was critical: his 'conversion' could never have happened without him.[107] Lady Thatcher concurred; she might not have been able to achieve what she did without Joseph, but nor, she believed, could he have done so without Sherman.[108]

The assault on Jericho

Having failed to offer Joseph the shadow Chancellorship, Heath now erred again, agreeing that his party's increasingly turbulent priest could establish his own think tank. Cunningly but not disingenuously, Joseph proposed to Heath that it should conduct comparative analyses to inform party thinking about the lessons from Europe's social market economies.[109] But, as Lady Thatcher diplomatically suggested, the Centre for Policy Studies was to find that the social market approach 'did not prove particularly fruitful and was eventually quietly forgotten'.[110] Instead, it would soon become the engine room of Thatcherism.

The idea that the Tories needed a place, as he later put it, to 'question the unquestioned, think the unthinkable [and] blaze a trail' was Sherman's.[111] Privately, he spoke of the CPS launching an intellectual assault upon the orthodoxies of post-war Britain. The 'objective of its work', Sherman wrote in an early memo, should be to 'batter down the walls of Jericho'. These, he reminded his CPS colleagues, 'include Conservative Central Office and the shadow Cabinet among their bastions together with the Treasury, a good part of the universities and the "new establishment" which includes much of the communications media'.[112] Sherman's ambition was for the CPS to be much more than simply a Tory think tank, its work written and consumed by policy wonks. Instead, he wanted it to reshape public opinion by highlighting the failures of the post-war settlement and thereby widening the 'options open to a Conservative government which dared take them'.[113] The CPS would be nothing less than 'an animator, agent of change, and political enzyme'.[114] Part research institute, part political campaign, the CPS wooed journalists, academics, businessmen and politicians, inviting them to lunches and dinners: 'eating our way to victory', as Sherman called it.[115] Attempting to change the climate of opinion, the CPS – like its fellow combatants at the free-market Institute for Economic Affairs (IEA) – thus targeted what Ben Jackson termed the 'small metropolitan media and political elite that shaped policy debate in Britain'.[116] It was a strategy which would bear rich political fruits.

Adopting the title of chairman, Joseph offered Sherman the job as the CPS's director. Typically, he swiftly changed his mind. Joseph, Sherman believed, 'had a thing about our mutual Jewishness' and felt that Jews could not occupy the posts of both director and chairman. Swallowing his pride, and fighting off attempts by others to force him out altogether, Sherman ploughed on, eventually accepting the position of director of studies, but initially working part-time for the healthy sum of £5,000 per year at a desk in the basement of the CPS's new Wilfred Street offices.[117] But Sherman's closeness to the chairman and his skill at writing the speeches which Joseph believed to be the CPS's '*raision d' être*'[118] – as well as his ability to write lines which would attract media attention – made him indispensable as the battle for the Tory Party commenced.

The 'London Spring'

What Sherman would later dub the 'London Spring' began on 22 June 1974, when Joseph finally took the plunge, announced the launch of the CPS, and delivered the speech which he and Sherman had been batting back and forth for several weeks.[119] It was the first of a series of speeches delivered throughout the summer which were to provide the political, economic and moral underpinnings of Thatcherism. During this period, recalled one journalist, Joseph compared himself to a 'prophet come down from the mountain ... There was an Old Testament ring to his cries of woe ... [as he] beat his breast in immolation for his own part in the betrayal of the ark of the Conservative covenant'.[120]

Joseph's speech in Upminster thus represented the opening volley in what was to become a five-year assault on the post-war settlement. No aspect of that settlement, including its alleged attachment to a failing Keynesian mix of high taxes and excessive spending, indulgence of abusive trade union power, the creation of an over-mighty state and cosseting of flabby, unprofitable public and private industries, would be spared, as Joseph showed from the outset:

> This is no time to be mealy-mouthed. Since the end of the Second World War we have had altogether too much Socialism. There is no point in my trying to evade what everybody knows. For half of that 30 years Conservative Governments, for understandable reasons, did not consider it practicable to reverse the vast bulk of the accumulating detritus of Socialism which on each occasion they found when they returned to office.

Accepting his own share of the blame, Joseph nonetheless charged that the Tories' actions had contributed to the disastrous results which lay all around them. Albeit with the best of intentions, he declared, they had 'overburdened the economy ... [and] overestimated the power of government to do more and more for more and more people'. In comparison with its European neighbours, Britain had ended up with a noxious cocktail of longer hours, lower pay, higher taxes and less prosperity. Having attempted to 'make semi-socialism work', it was now time for the Tories to give free enterprise a chance.[121]

The speech represented a repudiation of almost everything the Heath government, which Joseph had been a member of just weeks before, had stood for. Its vision also stood in stark contrast to the one presented by the former Prime Minister just four days later when he implicitly evoked the spirit of the post-war consensus and argued that 'what we need right now and before all else is a programme for national unity'.[122] Unsurprisingly, Heath and the Tory old guard were aghast at Joseph's actions.[123]

But encouraged by his new heroic status on the Tory right, Joseph was not for turning. At the Bull & Royal Hotel in Preston in early September, Joseph upped the ante once more. The timing was even less propitious than in June. Just two days previously, with a second election looming, Heath had inserted into the draft Tory manifesto a pledge that, even should his party win a majority, it would bring non-Conservatives into the newly formed government.[124] In the shadow Cabinet, Joseph was asked not to deliver his speech. When he refused, the Tory leader gave way, saying only that he wanted Mrs Thatcher and Sir Geoffrey Howe to take a look at what Joseph had to say. It was an odd vetting committee, given that, by this time, both were known to be sympathetic to Joseph's thinking. Unsurprisingly, neither made substantive suggestions for changes – Mrs Thatcher judging it: 'one of the most powerful and persuasive analyses' she had ever read.[125]

Heath was right to be concerned. As he had done at Upminster, Joseph accepted his 'full share of collective responsibility' – and then proceeded to carry out a post-mortem on the Tory government's economic misman-agement and the U-turn in which it abandoned 'sound money policies'.[126] Declaring that inflation, then running at 17 per cent, was 'threatening to destroy our society', he laid the blame squarely at Heath's door. Inflation was, Joseph argued, less the result of rising wages or 'rocketing world prices' but of 'trying to do too much, too quickly' and allowing the 'creation of new money'.

Aside from his endorsement of monetarism, it was his attack on the sup-posedly debilitating effects of the 'fear of unemployment' – the false belief that the 'gaunt, tight-lipped men in caps and mufflers' of the 1930s were just 'round the corner' – which was most significant, given the primacy afforded to keeping the dole queues down by both Labour and the Conservatives for the previous three decades. For many in a party which had spent much of the last thirty years attempting to shake off the images seared into the public consciousness by the 1930s, this was truly shocking talk.

Having offered his diagnosis, Joseph's prescription for the ailing British economy, which he admitted would be neither 'easy nor enjoyable', was no less controversial. He believed governments should tackle inflation by cutting deficits, gradually bearing down on the money supply, and accepting that there was a resultant risk of a temporary increase in unemployment. However, Joseph was adamant that, after a period of three to four years, the economy would be on the path to sustainable full employment. Joseph concluded by showing his barely disguised contempt for Heath's 'national unity' strategy. 'We, the Conservatives, are not without blemish, I freely admit,' he suggested, 'but how much of this derives from bi-partisanship, from middle-of-the-road policies, from confusing a distinctive Conservative approach with dogmatism.'

The speech gained widespread coverage across the tabloids and broadsheets: while *The Times* reprinted it in full, *The Sun* was barely less generous, devoting two pages to Joseph's words. Judging that 'what Sir Keith Joseph has done may ... prove good for his party', *The Times* said that 'it will certainly be good for his country'.[127] Not everyone was so impressed. The former Tory Chancellor of the Exchequer, Reginald Maudling, declared Joseph to be 'totally divorced from reality'. In private, he pronounced his former Cabinet colleague 'nutty as a fruitcake'.[128]

The significance of the Preston speech, undoubtedly the most important of Joseph's career, is hard to overestimate. This was the moment at which the Tories began to break with the principal tenet of Keynesianism – that government's overriding goal should be to secure full employment – which had shaped the thinking of both parties when they held office.[129] As Lady Thatcher argued in her memoirs, it was 'one of the very few speeches which have fundamentally affected a political generation's way of thinking'.[130] Indeed, as Sherman suggested nearly two decades after he wrote it, 'much of what then seemed revolutionary in the speech is now commonplace, and would hardly seem worth saying'.[131]

But the power of the speech stemmed less from the novelty of its content – free-market and monetarist thinking was already attracting much attention in response to the economic difficulties afflicting many Western economies – and more from the reputation of the man who delivered it. Joseph could not easily be dismissed in the manner of the country's other leading political proponent of free-market economics, Enoch Powell. Hitherto studiously loyal and mainstream, Joseph was 'the acceptable face of Toryism'; a description that few would have applied to Powell, the man who six years previously had predicted that mass immigration would lead to blood on the streets, and whose Europhobia had led him to abandon the Tory Party in February 1974 and instead urge the electorate to vote Labour. Moreover, what Howe termed Joseph's 'engaging blend of naivety and intelligence' and his willingness to accept his share of responsibility, apparent lack of personal ambition and insistence that the mistakes had stemmed from the very best of motivations added further power to his indictment.[132]

A decade later, when Mrs Thatcher had been in Downing Street for five years, the import of Joseph's words in Preston were clearer still. By this stage, Britain was led by a woman whose government had broken decisively with the policies of its predecessors, placed the defeat of inflation above that of unemployment, turned monetarism into its economic lodestar, and had determined that she would not, as Joseph had cautioned against at Preston, 'be stampeded again' into a change of course. By that time, though, as unemployment reached a post-war high of over 3 million it would be all too apparent that Joseph's time frame of 'three or four years' was wildly over-optimistic.

A supporting role

As Joseph took centre stage throughout the summer of 1974, Mrs Thatcher's role was very much a supporting one, and a barely public one at that. Despite his ill-concealed dislike of her, Heath had promoted Mrs Thatcher in the reshuffle following the Tories' election defeat, making her shadow Environment Secretary. But at the very time Joseph was suggesting the party needed to offer a thin gruel of higher unemployment and spending restraint to control inflation, Mrs Thatcher was – at her leader's insistent behest – preparing to shower the voters with electoral gifts. When the party's manifesto for the October election was published three days after Joseph's Preston speech it contained a number of eye-catching initiatives from Mrs Thatcher, including a pledge that the Tories would protect homeowners by not allowing mort-gage rates to rise above a certain level. Instinctively, Mrs Thatcher agreed with Nigel Lawson, the newly elected Tory MP who had been appointed to her housing group, that a subsidy for mortgages was a counterproductive piece of interventionism. However, she managed to convince herself that, whatever the merits of the 'purist view', the middle classes, hit by inflation and under assault from Labour, deserved some 'modest temporary' relief.[133] Their differing views on the competing merits of intellectual consistency and political necessity would later become a hallmark of the relationship between the future Prime Minister and her Second Lord of the Treasury.

Despite her private doubts and the ignominy of having *The Times* report shadow Cabinet concerns that her policy 'leans towards socialism',[134] Mrs Thatcher defended the policy robustly during the election campaign. It was, as Moore suggested, a mark of Mrs Thatcher's 'political professionalism' that she behaved in the manner which she did.[135] It was also a sign of the caution – again in contrast to Joseph – with which she began to detach herself from the orthodoxies of the Tory leadership.

Unlike Joseph, Mrs Thatcher rarely ventured in public on subjects outside of her shadow Cabinet brief. Her thoughts on the causes of the Tories' loss and the party's performance in government verged on the inane. 'I do hope that we shall return to being the party which I believe can get the economy right,' she suggested during a radio interview in May 1974, before offering the briefest of glimpses into her own view: 'I think we shall finish up being the more radical party.'[136] Even in the shadow Cabinet, recalled their col-league, Peter Walker, her support for Joseph was far from vocal: 'Margaret did not openly side with Keith, except to say that we should pay careful attention to what he was saying.'[137]

Nonetheless, she was the only member of the shadow Cabinet to put her head above the parapet and associate herself with the CPS. She later wrote that she 'jumped at the chance' to become Joseph's vice-chairman,[138] and attended her first board meeting on 25 June, three days after the Upminster speech. Sherman believed that Joseph later exaggerated Mrs Thatcher's role in the CPS's early days. Certainly, she didn't write anything for it or make any speeches under its banner. Perhaps she preferred a more practical, if less high-profile, role: when the CPS moved into its Wilfred Street offices she turned up and helped wire plugs. It was clearly not a task she performed regularly. Holding up the wires, she announced: 'The brown one is supposed to be the live wire. That is absolutely ridiculous. Brown is for earth.'[139]

While the suggestion that Mrs Thatcher vet the Preston speech indicated a failure by Heath to recognise how close she was to Joseph's thinking, others in the Tory leader's close entourage sensed just where she stood. Asked to approach Mrs Thatcher to persuade Joseph not to make the speech, Jim Prior recalled her reaction:

> Margaret said: 'Oh, I don't know … I think Alfred' – and that I thought was significant, because it wasn't even Sherman, it was Alfred – 'I think Alfred has written it for Keith, and I think you'll find that Keith is now determined to make it, and I don't think I can influence him.'[140]

Mrs Thatcher went on to confide in Prior that she believed Joseph 'did not always understand the political impact of arguments'.[141]

The remark was probably not intended to disparage Joseph or his arguments but was an indication of Mrs Thatcher's more sensitive political antennae and greater willingness to adjust to political realities, even if only temporarily and for tactical reasons. In the wake of the Preston speech, she recorded in her memoirs, she determined that, in the short term, she would 'fight as hard as I could for the policies which it was now my responsibility to defend'. In the longer term, however, she was 'convinced that we must turn the Party around to towards Keith's way of thinking, preferably under Keith's leadership'.[142]

In Finchley, her Labour opponent in October 1974 attempted to taunt Mrs Thatcher for the political company she kept. 'Is she a follower of Sir Keith Joseph and his ideas which every commentator has explained must lead to enormous unemployment?' Martin O'Connor asked.[143] At her adoption meeting, she gave a clue as to the answer: assuming the same language as Joseph had used in Upminster and Preston she declared: 'The central issue is do we continue the free society with its emphasis on individual freedom and responsibility or do we become the most state-controlled society in the world outside the Iron Curtain?'[144] Despite her public silence between 1974's two elections on the Tories' great internal debate, that Mrs Thatcher was a 'follower' of Sir Keith Joseph was beyond doubt.

Beliefs and ideas

Mrs Thatcher's caution was not simply a matter of calculation or an unwillingness to tie herself publicly to the banner Joseph had hoisted aloft. Her political journey differed from his. While Joseph's 'conversion' was accompanied by a period of very public agonising and recantation for past sins, she felt no need to do likewise. Mrs Thatcher had always been what she termed 'an instinctive Conservative'.[145] Thus, as Joseph later recalled, she had arrived at 'by her own commonsense [sic] and instinct' the same conclusions as he had about the dangers of the ruinous road the Tory Party and the country had travelled along over the past three decades. Far from influencing her, he insisted, the pair had reached the same destination 'along parallel lines'.[146]

Drawing on the distinction made by the Spanish philosopher José Ortega y Gasset, Sherman believed that she was 'a woman of beliefs, and not of ideas', but this fails to capture Mrs Thatcher's recognition of the importance of the latter.[147] 'We must have an ideology,' she declared to the Conservative Philosophy Group which was formed in the year she became party leader. 'The other side have got an ideology they can test their policies against.'[148]

Although, as Oliver Letwin, who worked for her in the No. 10 Policy Unit and later served in David Cameron's Cabinet, recalled, Mrs Thatcher had 'absolutely no interest in ideas for their own sake', she nonetheless regarded politics as a clash of opposing philosophies.[149] She thus looked to Joseph and Sherman, as the former suggested, to articulate her 'beliefs, feelings, instincts and intuitions into ideas, strategies and policies'.[150] However, Mrs Thatcher was to show an ability to sell those ideas and policies to the country in a manner that Joseph could never have matched. She intuitively shared, understood and articulated in a way that he did not the values, hopes and, indeed, prejudices of middle England. A politician to her fingertips, Mrs Thatcher displayed – at least until near the end of her time in Downing Street – a caution, an acute sense of timing and an ability to judge those ideas which contained electoral bear traps. Their partnership – while still not one of equals in the autumn of 1974 – was one to which each brought something distinctive.

In the immediate aftermath of the February 1974 election, Joseph invited Mrs Thatcher to his Mulberry Walk home to hear Sherman and Walters's forceful critique of the government in which they had both served recently. In the ensuing months, as she later acknowledged, Mrs Thatcher 'learned a great deal' from Joseph and Sherman.[151] It was, said Lord Harris of High Cross, the co-founder of the Institute of Economic Affairs, 'entirely through Keith Joseph' that Mrs Thatcher began to attend lunches and seminars at the free-market think tank and 'ponder our writing and our authors' publications'.[152] Joseph had become interested in its work after the 1964 election. In March 1974, he gingerly made another approach. 'I'll understand if you think it's a waste of time. I came to see you 10 years ago, and we've been discredited in between,'[153] he told Harris and Arthur Seldon, its co-founder and long-standing editorial director, as he asked for their help in launching 'a new "crusade" for private enterprise'.[154] Seldon, who, like Sherman, was born into an East End family of Russian-Jewish immigrants had, together with Harris, kept the flame of free-market economics from being completely extinguished in the late 1950s and 1960s. They provided, Mrs Thatcher acknowledged after her victory in 1979, 'the foundation work' upon which the philosophical reinvigoration of the Conservative Party had been constructed.[155] More dramatically, she proclaimed towards the end of her time in office, the 'lonely' duo had 'saved Britain'.[156] A frequent contributor to the *Daily Telegraph*'s editorial pages, Seldon was a supporter of the Liberal Party, an arch-critic of the post-war consensus and a vociferous advocate of rolling back the frontiers of the state who hoped to return his party to the path of Gladstonian Liberalism from which it had long strayed.

After he had overcome Harris and Seldon's initial scepticism, Joseph became a regular visitor to the IEA's Lord North Street offices, departing with reading lists or the names of people he should talk to, as well as tips on businesses that might help him fund the CPS. The relationship wasn't all one-way: Joseph agreed to help, too, with the IEA's fundraising. Mrs Thatcher's intellectual appetite was rather more modest than Joseph's. She had read *The Road to Serfdom* while at university. Thirty years later, she renewed her reading of what she called 'the seminal works of liberal economics and conservative thought'.[157] Some of these books came from Sherman's library; many of these loans, he grumpily complained, Mrs Thatcher failed to return.[158]

The candidacy that never was

In October 1974, the Conservatives were defeated at the polls for the third time under Ted Heath's leadership. This weak electoral record, the failure of the government which had resulted from his sole victory over Harold Wilson, and the aloof, tactless and stubborn manner in which he led his party, meant that many backbench Conservative MPs – if not his shadow Cabinet – now concluded that their leader had to go.

The picture was complicated by Heath's adamant refusal to stand aside gracefully and thus free his supporters from the bonds of loyalty which tied them to him. No such bonds, though, constrained Joseph or Mrs Thatcher. Having begun to set out an alternative course to Heath's over the summer of 1974, Joseph was seen by many of the party's backbenches as the most plausible potential challenger. The notion was treated with hilarity by Heath's camp. 'When Keith's name was mooted, we all roared with laughter. If that's the person who's going to challenge Ted, then we're all right.'[159]

Not everybody found the notion of Joseph standing so comical. Within days of the Tories' defeat, Airey Neave, a member of the 1922 Committee executive who was desperately seeking a candidate who could supplant Heath, recorded in his diary that Joseph was 'the favourite' to take on the Tory leader.[160] While Neave's desire to replace Heath was largely unideological, Joseph was naturally seen as a potential standard-bearer by the Tory right. As

Ian Gow, later Mrs Thatcher's loyal parliamentary private secretary, recalled: 'Keith was our man.'[161]

Joseph was certainly Mrs Thatcher's man. While her later claim that, by the weekend after the election, she had 'virtually become Keith's informal campaign manager' was somewhat exaggerated, she fully intended to support Joseph.[162] Since the February defeat, as Hugo Young suggested, he had led and she had 'almost invisibly followed'.[163] She had no intention of their changing places now. In public, she repeatedly batted away suggestions that she might stand. 'You can cross my name off the list,' she told the *London Evening News* the day after the general election. Her actions, she recalled, 'had little to do with keeping Ted in his present position … [and] everything to do with seeing Keith take over from him'.[164] In private, Mrs Thatcher was having none of the overtures from journalists at *The Spectator* that she stand: firmly instructing them to back Joseph, recalled the magazine's political editor, Patrick Cosgrave.[165]

But would Joseph take up the baton that some were keen to thrust into his hand? Later, he claimed merely to have 'flirted' with the notion of standing.[166] 'I know my own capacities,' he remarked in 1987, 'adequate for some jobs, but not for others.'[167] While a few people had suggested he might stand, he explained, he had not thought it 'sensible or likely' and did not start laying plans to do so.[168] Joseph was no doubt conflicted but his recollections were partial, for the former Cabinet minister also indicated to some supportive MPs that he would throw his hat into the ring.[169] Sherman certainly believed that he intended to. The reception to his speeches over the summer, especially that at Preston, he believed, meant that Joseph no longer 'shuddered away from the suggestion with something approaching genuine horror' as he had done earlier in the year.[170]

All that would change barely a week after the Conservatives' defeat. Just as, in 1968, Enoch Powell's future ministerial career had ended in Birmingham on the pyre of the 'Rivers of Blood' speech, so Joseph chose the same city to dig the grave of his leadership ambitions. After his forays into economics at Preston, Joseph's speech to the Edgbaston Conservative Association on

19 October returned to what might have appeared safer terrain: the field of social policy that had long been his area of expertise and greatest concern.[171] Harder-hitting than his previous speeches, he launched into a searing indictment of the 'new establishment' – an amorphous group encompassing the left, the BBC, teachers and other assorted 'false shepherds' – who advocated both the 'permissive society', and the 'collectivised society'. The resulting 'new utopia' had stripped people of their sense of personal responsibility and led to 'delinquency, truancy, vandalism, hooliganism, illiteracy' and falling educational standards.

In the face of such a threat, Joseph issued a rallying cry to the Tory Party. He urged it to take a leaf out of the book of Mary Whitehouse, who, through her National Viewers' and Listeners' Association, had become the self-anointed guardian of the nation's morals, and her campaign against alleged permissiveness. The party needed to fight 'the battle of ideas' – words that Mrs Thatcher would soon echo – in 'every school, university, publication, committee, [and] TV studio'. It needed to rethink both its economic outlook as well as its attitude towards the welfare state. The poor needed to be helped to help themselves. The alternative was simply more welfare dependency, which would destroy the poor 'morally', while placing an 'unfair burden on society'.

The force of Joseph's argument reflected the power of Sherman's polemical writing. However, it was a line that did not come from Sherman's pen[172] which immediately triggered controversy and for which the speech was to be remembered. It came towards the end of the speech as Joseph discussed what he termed one of the 'dilemmas inherent in the remoralisation of public life'. Citing research from the Child Poverty Action Group, Joseph claimed that, 'the balance of our population, our human stock is threatened'. More and more children, he claimed, were being born to mothers who were least suited 'to bring children into the world and [to] bring them up'. Picking up the theme of earlier speeches he had made on what he termed the 'cycle of deprivation', Joseph suggested that these women, 'some of low intelligence, most of low education attainment', were 'producing problem children'. The future would be a world populated by 'unmarried mothers, delinquents, denizens of our borstals, sub-normal educational establishments [and] prisons'. The dilemma Joseph intended to illustrate was whether it was 'condoning immorality' to extend birth control facilities to these young women, or whether this might be the 'lesser evil until we are able to remoralise whole groups and classes of people'.

Breaking the embargo on the speech and splashing the story before Joseph had uttered a word, the *London Evening Standard*'s headline: 'Sir Keith In "Stop Babies" Sensation', provided the narrative for much of the media reporting which followed.[173] Joseph, in the words of Mrs Thatcher, soon found himself under fire as a 'mad eugenicist' by an unholy alliance of 'bishops, novelists, academics, socialist politicians and commentators'.[174] As Labour MPs suggested that Joseph was ordering the poor to 'castrate or conform' and was planning to build a 'master race',[175] the *Sunday Times* produced evidence undermining a number of Joseph's claims, including his central contention that the birth rate among working-class women was rising.[176] Their enemies in the Conservative Party remembered Mrs Thatcher could 'barely contain their glee'.[177]

The unfortunate echoes of the Third Reich contained in Joseph's 'human stock' phrase guaranteed that the speech was extensively debated within the Jewish community. The *Jewish Chronicle*, while conceding that the concluding section of Joseph's speech might have been better 'left unsaid', gave it a warm reception. His words, it argued, 'exude the spirit of Judaism in proclaiming the vital importance of moral issues'. Amid the need to make progress towards a 'more just and more humane society', it was important that 'enduring civilising values' were not corroded.[178]

Judging by its letters page, however, not all of the paper's readers were so impressed. To 'read Judaism' into Joseph's words was 'bizarre', wrote one, while another drew a parallel with the decree the Nazis had issued in occupied Poland in October 1941 as they sought to 'lower the fertility' of conquered and 'inferior' races and concluded that, while Joseph had 'no such inhuman intention', the attitude and philosophy behind his thinking appeared 'frighteningly similar'.[179] Others, however, rushed to Joseph's defence, wondering how 'any Jew with a grain of Jewish feeling' could cast such aspersions on such a 'highly intelligent, able, compassionate and perceptive man' who had simply been attempting to defend those least able to cope with 'unwanted children'.[180]

The speech was to have a deep significance in terms of Joseph's relationship with Mrs Thatcher, the development of Thatcherism and, ultimately, Britain's future direction. Unusually, Joseph had not shown his closest ally a draft of the speech in advance. History may have been very different had he done so, as her sharper political judgement may have spotted the dangers the offending 'human stock' phrase portended. However, while she remembered that her 'heart sank' when she saw the *Evening Standard*'s front page, Mrs Thatcher nonetheless believed that, as he had begun to do with its economic policy, Joseph was inserting some much-needed 'backbone' into Conservative social policy.[181] Talk of the 'human stock' may have been unfortunate, but she had no qualms about the rest of the speech with its warnings about the 'decline of the family, the subversion of moral values and the dangers of the permissive society'. More mindful of such matters than Joseph, it was the politics and the presentation about which she had concerns.[182]

There was, Mrs Thatcher believed, a growing constituency for Joseph's 'larger moral message' in 1970s Britain.[183] Mixed in with and intimately connected to its concerns about inflation and the nation's economic travails, the Conservative-voting middle class was, as Eliza Filby argued, awash with 'a sense of paranoia and frustration'. At its root lay a fear that middle-class values – of personal responsibility, discipline and hard work – were under assault. Moreover, while the working class had the unions and the Labour Party to fight its corner, the middle classes had no such champion. In neither word nor, after it had capitulated to the unions, deed could Ted Heath's Conservative Party be said to fulfil such a role.[184] Before he busied himself with the dilemmas of birth control, Joseph had told the middle classes at Edgbaston they were right to be paranoid and implicitly admitted that the Tories had failed to provide them with the protection they deserved.

For Mrs Thatcher, the significance of Joseph's speech lay in its attempt both to show the Conservatives shared these middle-class concerns, and to link the perils of the permissive society with 'socialism and egalitarianism'.[185] The response to the speech – she spoke admiringly not simply of the polls but of Joseph's 'five bulging mail bags'[186] – showed the rich seam of untapped public support that the party could garner from such a message, albeit shorn of some of her mentor's 'unfortunate' phraseology.[187] A few days later Mrs Thatcher pronounced that the Conservatives needed to win back their support among the middle classes. Being middle class, she declared, 'has never been simply a matter of income, but a whole attitude to life, a will to take responsibility for oneself'.[188] Asked about Joseph's speech, she responded: 'Keith is perfectly right. This is the twilight of the middle class', although she was careful to concede that Edgbaston had not helped their cause.[189]

Together, Joseph's speeches in Preston and Edgbaston prefigured the mix of free-market economics and social conservatism – the attempt to 'marry Adam Smith to ... Mary Whitehouse' – which was to define Thatcherism. After she won the leadership, Mrs Thatcher thus began to speak, Filby wrote, of 'moral revival as necessary for economic revival'.[190] Electorally, the combination was to be a potent one, although, at the time, many were unconvinced. Within days of Edgbaston, Peter Walker delivered a speech warning the Tories about the dangers of 'hard-line economic policies' and 'retreating into the bunkers and bolt-holes of narrow middle-class politics'. His targets were not hard to discern.[191]

Intellectually, it was arguably more questionable. Samuel Brittan, the *Financial Times* economic commentator and brother of Mrs Thatcher's recently elected Tory colleague, Leon, had helped write the Preston speech, but had little time for the language or arguments of Edgbaston. The child of a Jewish home in the north-west London suburbs, he identified, he later suggested, with 'the permissive values' of the 1960s; his argument was with those among its adherents who failed to recognise that the free market 'embodied their emphasis on "doing your own thing"'.[192] There was indeed a contradiction in Joseph's social and economic outlook: he appeared to believe that the state should cease interfering in the nation's boardrooms while concerning itself with scrutinising its bedrooms.

The hostility the speech aroused, however, hurt Joseph deeply. He rarely questioned the motives of others and thus could not understand why what he believed to be his self-evident concern for the plight of the poor could have been so misconstrued. He then began to flail himself publicly for the damage he had done to the things in which, he lamented to one interviewer, he 'rather deeply believed'.[193] For Sherman, the fact that Joseph's 'nerve broke' and he began to 'backtrack and apologise' was simply further proof that the former Cabinet minister lacked the 'robustness and fighting spirit' of which true leaders are made.[194] It was not the speech which sank him, Sherman believed, but his 'reaction to the subsequent attacks on him'. [195] He would now be relegated from the role of 'Conservative Messiah to that of John the Baptist'.[196] For others, however, it was the speech itself which indicated Joseph's unsuitability as a replacement for Heath. Howe, who had urged Joseph to stand, now concluded that 'Keith's judgment was too erratic for him to be entrusted with the leadership.'[197]

Mrs Thatcher hoped, probably with little expectation that this would be the case, that the furore surrounding the speech would simply die down. Despite what she dismissively termed the 'brouhaha' caused by the speech, she remained convinced that 'Keith must be our candidate.'[198] Joseph, however, had other ideas. Characteristically, he simply decided that he was not up to the job of leading the Tory Party. Edgbaston had exposed not that he lacked the stomach for the fight, but his own weaknesses as a politician. While Mrs Thatcher had plenty of 'instinct and flair', Joseph later reflected when discussing the events of autumn 1974, he did not.[199]

More positively, it was a measure of the manner in which the Tory Party had already changed that Joseph's Jewishness hardly seemed to figure in discussions around any potential leadership bid. There was the occasional muttering: The Spectator's Patrick Cosgrave reported the 'contemptible' view of one Tory that he could not become Prime Minister because he was a Jew and 'might offend the oil companies',[200] while the ambassador of one Arab state later claimed to have been consulted by the Tories as to how countries in the region might react to a Joseph leadership.[201] However, these seem to have been isolated incidents. Instead, Sherman later suggested, 'true blue Tories' had told him that 'since Disraeli was the best Tory Prime Minister ever, Keith Joseph should be given a chance'.[202]

Having made his decision, Joseph now had to tell his loyal lieutenant that he was departing the battlefield. On the afternoon of Thursday 21 November Mrs Thatcher was working in her room in the House of Commons when Joseph came to see her. 'As soon as he entered, I could see it was serious,' she recalled. 'I am sorry,' Mrs Thatcher recounted Joseph telling her, 'I just can't run. Ever since I made that speech the press have been outside the house. They have been merciless.' Mrs Thatcher admitted that she felt 'on the edge of despair' at the news. Then, she later remembered, she heard herself saying: 'Look, Keith, if you're not going to stand, I will, because someone who represents our viewpoint has to stand.'[203]

Mrs Thatcher would tell Charles Moore towards the end of her life that she was 'really rather shocked' by this turn of events because Joseph 'really was the leader'.[204] She was, in fact, too astute a politician not to sense the damage that Edgbaston had inflicted on her friend's chances and the prospect that it might now be her that took up the cause of the Tory rebels. While she had attempted to dampen speculation that she might stand, a number of Tory MPs had already encouraged her to throw her hat into the ring.[205] Having now informed Heath that she planned to challenge him – 'If you must,' he coldly responded – Mrs Thatcher attended shadow Cabinet. 'I felt that apart from Keith I would find few supporters here,' she wrote in her memoirs. Her colleagues' lack of open hostility simply reflected the fact, she suspected, that they regarded her decision as 'ridiculous'.[206]

First among equals

Just over two months later, however, Mrs Thatcher entered the shadow Cabinet room as the Conservative Party's new leader, having sensationally displaced Heath in the first ballot, and then dispatched those – Willie

Whitelaw, Geoffrey Howe, Jim Prior and the relatively unknown John Peyton – who had entered the contest on the second ballot once the humiliated former Prime Minister had finally stood aside. The reason for her unexpected victory was clear to Howe: Mrs Thatcher had won because 'like all the others, she wasn't Ted – and, like none of the others, she had had the guts to offer her colleagues the choice'.[207] However, by electing Mrs Thatcher, Conservative MPs had not delivered a decisive ideological verdict on the past or the future. The Tory backbenches had not, Hugo Young argued, suddenly been converted to 'Josephite attitudes'.[208] Instead, as the MP Julian Critchley suggested, Mrs Thatcher's election represented a 'peasants' revolt' against a leader who had either ignored or insulted far too many of those in whose hands his fate now lay.[209]

If Mrs Thatcher's election owed much to Heath's own shortcomings, she also had a debt to Joseph which extended far beyond the fact that he had stumbled along the away, freeing her to run in his stead. During the leadership campaign itself, Joseph attended Sunday-night strategy sessions at Mrs Thatcher's home, even if he had neither the ability, nor desire, to compete with campaign manager Airey Neave's backroom machinations. On the first ballot, he was the only member of the shadow Cabinet to vote for Mrs Thatcher. But, more importantly, while the Tory Party may not have shown its endorsement of 'Josephite attitudes' in choosing Mrs Thatcher, her mentor had helped clear some of the obstacles on her path to power. Sherman, who had now begun helping write Mrs Thatcher's speeches, was convinced of the centrality of Joseph's role: 'If it hadn't been for Keith, Heath's position would not have been shaken, and Margaret would not have become leader.'[210] In the 1980s, the Thatcherite mantra was that 'there is no alterative'; in 1974, in the wake of the disasters which had befallen it in office, Joseph had begun to open the eyes of many in the Tory Party to the possibility of an alternative to the manner in which it had sought to govern over the previous three decades.

With the Tory establishment warning, in the words of the former Cabinet minister Ian Gilmour, that the party must not 'retreat behind the privet hedge into a world of narrow class interests and selfish concerns', Mrs Thatcher sought to exploit the case which Joseph had advanced over the previous summer and autumn.[211] Her message was more prosaic and less theoretical than his; however, her central charges against Heathite Toryism were the ones which Joseph had rehearsed already. The party had been insufficiently stout in its defence of 'middle-class values'. Its failure at the polls stemmed from the fact that 'people believe too many Conservatives have become socialists already'. Britain was moving inexorably in the direction of socialism, taking 'two steps forward' under Labour, but only 'half a step back' under the Tories.[212] That said, Mrs Thatcher's attack would have sounded much more novel – and potentially unsettling – had Joseph not already 'blazed the trail' as Howe put it.[213]

At Joseph's memorial service in 1995, Mrs Thatcher lamented the events of twenty years previously that had seen her become leader. 'Keith should have become Prime Minister. So many of us felt that was his destiny. All those who believed in him were ready to serve him with loyalty and devotion. In 1975 we wanted him to become Leader of the Opposition.' Implicitly referring to Edgbaston, she continued: 'If only in the course of one day fate had flowed through different channels, if only.'[214]

But were it not for the events of that 'one day' might Joseph have become leader with Mrs Thatcher perhaps later occupying No. 11 Downing Street as his neighbour? It is impossible to say. If others had not come forward, Joseph, too, would have benefited from the desire of Tory MPs to rid themselves of their leader and the skills of Neave in delivering that result. But, as Denham and Garnett noted, the Edgbaston speech also confirmed the doubts that many already had about Joseph's unsuitability as leader. They may have regarded a vote for Mrs Thatcher as 'a leap in the dark', but many would have viewed a Joseph leadership as 'a plunge from the cliffs'.[215]

One thing, however, is certain: Mrs Thatcher was neither weighed down by doubts about her own capabilities nor did she have his tendency to indecision. Bloodied by the 'milk snatcher' controversy, she did not have, or, at least, display, Joseph's sensitivity in the face of attacks, either. 'I saw how they destroyed Keith. Well, they're not going to destroy me,' she declared steelily.[216] She kept to her word, striking back during the leadership contest to good effect against her critics.[217] Thus while Mrs Thatcher confessed to feeling Joseph's hurt over Edgbaston 'as if it were my own', she also suggested that she would not have allowed herself to be tossed around on the waves of the ensuing media storm in the manner that he was. 'Keith,' she remembered, 'did not help his cause by constantly explaining, qualifying and apologising.'[218] No such criticism was ever levelled against her. Indeed, as Moore wrote, while she 'genuinely loved and admired Joseph both for his kindness to her and for the intellectual power he brought to the attack on socialism', she was aware of his frailties. It was a 'tragedy' that he had not become Prime Minister, Lady Thatcher told her biographer, before conceding: 'He would have agonised over every decision.'[219] Nonetheless, the improbable revolutionary had helped Mrs Thatcher to her first victory over the forces of conservatism in the Tory Party. But they were not done yet.

CHAPTER 4

THE SENIOR PARTNER

In the upper echelons of the Conservative Party, the first woman to lead them was widely viewed as an inexperienced, narrow-minded lightweight – 'a corporal ... not a cavalry officer', as one of her shadow Cabinet condescendingly put it[1] – who could potentially lead them down a right-wing electoral cul-de-sac. Moreover, the reign of Mrs Thatcher and her ideological soulmate, Sir Keith Joseph, was seen as merely a temporary interruption to the natural order of things. As a member of the Tory Reform Group put it: 'An unfortunate although possibly necessary interlude which allows the party to get the bile out of its system.'[2]

However, while Mrs Thatcher frequently struggled in parliament against both of the Prime Ministers – Harold Wilson and James Callaghan – whom she faced across the dispatch box, the country's dire economic straits, the government's precarious position in parliament, and the public's mounting unease and frustration with Britain's condition in the mid-1970s made the ground more fertile for the kind of radical break with the past she and Joseph believed necessary.

In her first shadow Cabinet, the pair were virtually isolated: Mrs Thatcher had received the second ballot support of a mere four of its twenty-four members.[3] A suitable prize for Joseph's loyalty might have been the post of shadow Chancellor denied to him the previous year by Ted Heath. While Lady Thatcher later claimed that she did not offer, and Joseph did not ask for, the position, this is probably untrue.[4] Rather, as he had done a year previously, Joseph told the new leader that he wanted the shadow Chancellorship or nothing. His aspirations were, however, blocked by Willie Whitelaw, who apparently agreed to Mrs Thatcher's offer to become the party's deputy leader on condition that Joseph was not appointed to the opposition's top economic role.[5] Showing both her willingness to accommodate political reality and her ruthlessness, Mrs Thatcher acceded to Whitelaw's request, appointing the economically dry but socially liberal Sir Geoffrey Howe to the post. In reality, Mrs Thatcher needed both Whitelaw and Joseph and, correctly calculating that the latter would be more amenable to her wishes, asked him to retain the roving responsibility for policy and research he had held under Heath. The position was, of course, a more attractive one than it had previously been; Joseph was now serving a leader with whom he had a personal and ideological bond. Moreover, through his membership of Howe's Economic Reconstruction Group, and presence at informal meetings at the shadow Chancellor's Vauxhall home, Joseph was hardly locked out of the party's economic debate. Indeed, in February 1977, Mrs Thatcher handed Joseph the then-key economic portfolio of shadow industry spokesman. Thus, wrote Lady Thatcher, in Whitelaw and Joseph she had her 'two key figures, one providing the political brawn and the other the policy-making brains of the team'.[6]

'You always need a first-class mind to coordinate the thinking out of new policies,' she suggested on *The Jimmy Young Programme* a few days later, before going on to draw a comparison with the man who had redefined the Tories' agenda after their defeat in 1945: 'Keith in a way is the new Rab Butler.'[7] The compliment, no doubt well intended, was hardly apt: Butler was one of the principal architects of the post-war consensus that Joseph had spent the previous year railing against.

Mrs Thatcher had no doubt about the direction in which she wished to lead her party. 'Don't tell me what. I know what. Tell me how,' she would admonish advisers who attempted to tell her what she should do.[8] Nonetheless, she had no illusion that her victory in the leadership election represented a 'wholesale conversion' by the party to her and Joseph's way of thinking.[9] 'Instead, she believed our ability to change Party policy, as the first step toward making changes in government, depended upon using our position to change minds.' Thus she dispatched Joseph to continue his 'intellectual crusade' for free-market economics, while noting caustically that Joseph often founded a 'readier hearing' from left-wing audiences on campuses than he did from 'the cynical tendency among his colleagues'.[10]

The pair were mutually dependent. For Joseph, Mrs Thatcher was now the 'standard-bearer' of the cause to which he had so agonisingly converted.[11] Having stumbled himself in his attempt to lead it, he could not let her fail. At the same time, Joseph was Mrs Thatcher's ideological outrider – 'the licensed thinker scouting ahead in Indian country,' as Chris Patten, the liberal-minded director of the Conservative Research Department (CRD), put it[12] – helping to open up new territory which she would decide to occupy when she judged it politically prudent to lead her divided party into it. It was what President Mitterrand would later admiringly call 'her inimitable mixture of firmness and tactical flexibility' which was to thus provide the crucial ingredient in their joint enterprise.[13] Moreover to be, as the *New Statesman* put it in 1976, 'the intellectual gadfly at the side of the leader, but to be free of painful necessities like decision-taking' was a role to which Joseph was, by temperament, well suited.[14]

But being the outrider meant that Joseph performed another important function: as Alfred Sherman suggested, during the time she led the opposition, Mrs Thatcher's critics within the Conservative Party 'found it easier to attack Keith Joseph than to turn their fire on the real target'.[15] It was not a duty from which Joseph shied. Indeed, when the punches were aimed at her, he was only too keen to help deflect them. 'I do not listen to the radio very much and I do not have a television set,' he wrote her on one occasion, 'I am not, therefore, aware immediately when you are attacked.' But, he continued, 'I am always ready to pick up any attack that is made upon you and to speak in your defence.'[16]

The battle of ideas

For the woman who had declared on the day she was elected leader, 'you don't exist as a party unless you have a clear philosophy and a clear message',

Joseph's role as the Tories' new philosopher-in-chief was central.[17] Just over a month later, Mrs Thatcher adopted martial language to serve notice that the philosophical contest was about to begin. 'This Party of ours has been on the defensive for too long,' she told a gathering of Conservative students. 'If we can win the battle of ideas, then the war will already be half won.'[18] But while Joseph was preparing to go over the top once again, some of her generals were determined to remain in their trenches. Jim Prior, the Heathite whom she had reluctantly decided to keep as shadow Employment Secretary, believed that the Tories had no business getting involved in such a fight. It was, he told the academic David Butler in 1978, 'wrong to speak of winning an intellectual argument because that implied you had a body of doctrine'.[19] Even, Patten who, as director of the Tories' in-house think tank, might have been expected to relish such a contest, was unimpressed by his new leader's call to arms. Used to an approach to politics which 'saw things in a less intel-lectually confrontational way', he recalled initially thinking Mrs Thatcher's talk of a 'battle of ideas' was 'a bit rum'.[20]

Joseph, by contrast, ran towards the sound of battle: like Mrs Thatcher he believed passionately in the necessity of the intellectual crusade which she had launched. 'Strategy matters. Policies matter. But behind them all stands the vision,' he declared to the Conservative Party conference in 1976, 'Scorn not the vision; scorn not the idea. Man [Mao: *sic*] said that power grows out of the barrel of a gun. A gun is certainly powerful, but who controls the man with a gun? A man with an idea.'[21] And so the 'battle of ideas' commenced: waged in the shadow Cabinet; between the Conservative Party's own estab-lished policy-making machinery and the insurgents at the Centre for Policy Studies; and in print, before the television cameras, and on campuses across the country. While he may have missed out on the leadership, this was the moment when Joseph truly showed his mettle.

The first skirmish occurred barely two months after Mrs Thatcher's election on 11 April 1975 when Joseph presented the shadow Cabinet with a paper entitled 'Notes Towards the Definition of Policy'.[22] The tone was dark – its opening line spoke of the 'shadow of electoral defeat and national decline' – although its analysis and prescriptions were familiar to those who had followed Joseph's pronouncements over the previous year. As he had done before, Joseph laid the blame for the Tories' travails squarely on their decision to embark upon the 'path of consensus' after the war.

Joseph's denunciation of the policies he and his colleagues had supposedly promoted in office barely a year previously was unsparing. They had tried to deliver full employment without regard to 'wage-levels, productivity and the state of the economy', while the party's failure to reward 'talent and effort' and reluctance to impose 'sanctions against irresponsibility' had led to 'the economic morality of the pig trough'. The Tories had gone along with education policies which had led to a decline in standards and behaviour; liberal views which had led to crime, the destruction of communities and the erosion of the role of the family; mass immigration which had been imposed against the wishes of the public; and had 'subordinated the rule of law to the avoidance of conflict' thereby encouraging mass defiance of the law by every sectional interest from miners and dockers to farmers and fishermen. Fearing accusations of intolerance and being old-fashioned, the party had allowed the values and morals which underpinned society to come under attack and failed to resist communism abroad and domestic subversion at home.

So how might the Tories seek redemption for their sins? Joseph called for radical change. They should ignore the siren voices which warned of electoral catastrophe and instead reach out to all those with whom they could find 'common ground', sure in the knowledge that a majority of the British public shared the Conservatives' 'fundamental aims and values ... what some intellectuals disparagingly call "middle class suburban values" – a desire to enjoy economic independence, to be well thought of, patriotism'.

With this in mind, Joseph advocated the party should face the communist threat abroad and at home head on, prioritise defence spending – because 'if we lose independence, we lose all' – and adopt a tougher approach to domestic subversion, especially in the trade unions. The Tories should steel themselves for a battle with the unions and remove benefits from strikers' families. On the economy, Joseph advocated a determinedly free-market approach: prices should be allowed to rise to release pent-up inflation, the money supply controlled, and public spending cut. 'Lame duck' industries should be propped up by public money only on condition that they showed they would soon be able to stand on their own two feet, and direct taxes on income and investment should be cut sharply.

Joseph also advanced a robust social conservatism. It was time to shut the door gently on mass immigration and to bolster the family – 'the sole reliable transmitter of attitudes and culture' – by using the tax system to encourage mothers with young children to stay at home, protecting the public from 'gratuitous pornography' and introducing education and health vouchers. In a section on the 'climate of opinion', Joseph railed against teachers who propagated 'alien values ... based on variants of tyranny and anarchy'; questioned why schools failed to teach about the system of free enterprise; called for a bias on television to be systematically monitored; and demanded a big reduction in the number of postgraduates to reduce the number of politically motivated eternal students.

As Charles Moore argued, 'this startling paper furnished the main elements of what came to be called Thatcherism, both in specific policy and in general psychological terms'. But, he continued, while its approach was 'deliberately at odds with prevailing views', on one area which would later define Thatcherism, even Joseph could not foresee what was to come. Of what would become known as privatisation, he timidly asked: 'Presumably, we do not think that denationalisation is practicable ... Can we go half-way?'[23]

The official minutes of the meeting diplomatically noted that Mrs Thatcher and Joseph's shadow Cabinet opponents had questioned whether the paper was 'too critical of the recent past', urged the party not abandon the political centre ground and suggested that Tory policy should be 'evolutionary, and build upon the past, not revolutionary'.[24] But this record failed to capture the 'battle of ideas' which raged around the shadow Cabinet table. As Lord Hailsham's notes of the meeting revealed, there was, as he drolly put it, 'hardly a dull moment'. Reginald Maudling, the newly appointed shadow Foreign Secretary, declared: 'I do not agree with one little bit.' Ian Gilmour, the shadow Home Secretary, asserted that the 'consensus' up until 1970 which Joseph appeared to deride had been a Conservative one. 'Ian, do you believe in capitalism?' asked Mrs Thatcher sharply in response. The shadow Agriculture Secretary, Francis Pym, directly contradicted his analysis. 'Society is moving left,' he argued. Joseph's paper was thus 'a recipe for disaster'. To those who argued that the Tories had simply failed to explain themselves properly, Mrs Thatcher sarcastically responded: 'All our policies were right. All your presentation was wrong.'[25]

Behind Joseph's back, his shadow Cabinet critics were even less polite. After one meeting, Hailsham, Whitelaw, and the shadow Leader of the House of Lords, Lord Carrington, discussed their tiresome colleague. 'Keith is an albatross,' Hailsham noted afterwards in his diary. The three men had agreed, no doubt in reference to the Preston speech, that Joseph had caused the party to lose the October 1974 election by more than was necessary. 'May bring us down. Clever-silly. Attracts barmies,' Hailsham scrawled.[26] On another occasion, Carrington confided to Hailsham his fear that the Tories were giving 'the impression of an extreme right wing party'. Joseph, the pair agreed, was 'largely to blame'. While 'clever, even brilliant', recorded Hailsham, he was also 'dotty & lacks moral fibre for high office'.[27]

The third man of Thatcherism

While they may have been outgunned at the shadow Cabinet, Mrs Thatcher and Joseph were marshalling their forces elsewhere. Soon after her victory, the CPS's director, Nigel Vinson, wrote to Joseph asking whether, now the Tory Party was 'in the hands of true believers', the organisation needed to continue to exist.[28] Sherman was adamant that it did. The CRD, he wrote Joseph, 'is still staffed by a group of low calibre opportunists whose ideas are fundamentally at variance with our own'. Indeed, with Heath's replacement, its work was 'more urgent [and] more necessary' given that the new leadership 'is more likely to press against constraints than its predecessors'.[29] Mrs Thatcher and Joseph agreed. 'There was nobody in the room with a single idea that was worth having,' she complained of the CRD, which she deigned to visit just once.[30] It was thus the CPS and Sherman to which Mrs Thatcher and Joseph continued to turn for the ammunition to wage the battle of ideas.

As they wrestled for control of the Tories' intellectual direction, the antipathy between the CPS and CRD, in which formal control of policy-making within the party still rested, came to be seen, as *The Times* reported, as 'a symbol of Conservative Party differences'.[31] Sherman unsuccessfully recommended a purge of Patten and his colleagues. 'They were actively working to undermine her,' he later wrote, with Patten using his influence over policy to 'exclude or restrain radical thinking'.[32] While there was no personal antipathy between Patten and Joseph, the CRD had little regard for the CPS; its director viewed the young think tank's very existence as a 'provocation'.[33] At its offices in Old Queen Street overlooking St James' Park, the CRD viewed its rival, *The Economist* suggested, as 'a band of fanatical heresy hunters'.[34] Joseph was, in the term first coined by *Private Eye*, known simply as 'the mad monk'. A flavour of the dislike some Tories felt for the CPS was hinted at in a slightly defensive note Sherman wrote marking the organisation's second birthday in 1976, which dismissed suggestions that it was 'a party within a party or private army'.[35]

Perhaps most unsettling of all for his enemies, Sherman himself was now firmly established in the new leader's court: frequently visiting Mrs Thatcher's Flood Street home in the evenings or weekends to work with her and her favourite wordsmith, the playwright Ronnie Millar, on major speeches. As she pottered about in the kitchen preparing food for them, Mrs Thatcher would insist on working through 'every phrase [and] every word', recalled Sherman.[36] Given Mrs Thatcher's propensity to side-step shadow Cabinet opposition by making policy through public pronouncements, Sherman's role assumed added importance.[37]

There in Chelsea, away from the old guard in Westminster, there was 'a meeting of minds'. Contrary to the popular image of her as 'shrill and unfeeling', Sherman found the new Tory leader 'warm and an attentive listener'.[38] His antagonists fumed: Prior did not know whether it was more irritating to be kept waiting outside Mrs Thatcher's office while the leader consulted her adviser or, when ushered into her presence, to find suggestions met with the words: 'But Alfred says ...'[39] Hugo Young recorded Patten's off-the-record thoughts in September 1977: 'Whatever else may be said about KJ [Keith Joseph], he has some nasty people around him. Alfred Sherman is a pretty bad man: obsessed with race and immigration, very far to the right on economic issues.'[40] Even some of the free-market economists sympathetic to Mrs Thatcher regarded Sherman as nothing more than a 'hack' who 'didn't know enough of ... [the] substance'.[41]

While *The Times* noted in 1978 that Sherman had become 'a particular focus' for the Tory old guard's wider uneasiness about Mrs Thatcher, his influence – 'at least equivalent to that of Sir Keith Joseph', believed Mark Garnett[42] – was such as to make him a legitimate target. The relationship between the working-class, former Communist Jew and the daughter of a Grantham shopkeeper was, argued Young, 'most intimate and fruitful' and pivotal to the development of Thatcherism.[43] Sherman himself later liked to boast that he invented Thatcherism and Thatcher in that order.[44]

While Joseph famously spoke of his 'conversion' to Conservatism, both he and Mrs Thatcher had spent all of their adult lives in the Conservative Party; neither were, in any sense, converts to it. Sherman, of course, very much was and, with the enthusiastic backing of Mrs Thatcher, both he and Joseph determined to use the CPS to reach out to potential new converts. This exercise was not, however, to be conducted by attempting to occupy the political 'middle ground' but by pitching the Tory tent on what Sherman termed the 'common ground'. Whereas the former represented a centrist midpoint between the two main parties' positions, the latter, Sherman argued, was the territory on which 'the majority of the British people finds itself on the opposite side to the political establishment'.[45] In a memo to Joseph in the summer of 1975, Sherman argued that the Tories' problems resulted from the party's abandonment of the 'common ground' and 'move towards the "middle ground", which encouraged the Labour left to pull its party leftward'.[46]

Three months later, in a speech delivered at Mrs Thatcher's first Tory Party conference as leader, Joseph made the argument his own. Penned by Sherman, the address warned that 'the trouble with the middle ground is that we do not choose it … It is shaped for us by extremists. The more extreme the left, the more to the left is the middle ground.' The middle ground was thus a 'will-o'-the-wisp'.[47] In what was to become one of Sherman's most famous phrases,[48] Joseph went on to outline the dynamics of what he termed the 'ratchet' effect: every Labour government, he claimed, had left office having moved the country to the left, forcing the Tories to engage in an unending scramble to get back to where they had been before. Rather than the tick of the 'mild pendulum' between the two main parties, the Conservatives faced a 'savage and destructive … Labour ratchet'.[49]

But, as Sherman later explained to Mrs Thatcher, the 'middle ground hankering' of the Tory establishment was also electorally disastrous for the party, leading it ever-further from the public mood. Jumping on 'every trendy band-waggon' as it sought to compete with Labour, the Tories had abandoned precisely those things which most voters supposedly supported: 'patriotism, the puritan ethic, Christianity, conventional family-based morality'.[50] Although it provoked the ire of the left and the 'Heathites', Mrs Thatcher should continue to speak out on issues such as 'national identity, law and order and scrounging', Sherman advised her. 'We prefer the wisdom of the people to the fashions of the parties,' he self-righteously concluded.[51] In the notion of the 'common ground', Sherman thus provided Mrs Thatcher with an electoral and moral justification for pursuing a populist political strategy, one which chimed very much with her own instinctive convictions and appalled her critics within the party.

Converts and heretics

In the months that followed, the CPS staged a series of seminars, inviting 'thinking people in or associated with the Labour movement' to join them in the search for 'common ground'.[52] Winning converts from the left to the new Conservatism became Sherman's obsession. As Labour lurched to embrace Marxism, he wrote to Mrs Thatcher, telling her the Tories should seek to proclaim themselves 'heirs to the [party's] Social-democratic Heritage ... incorporating its best features into a synthesis suited to our times'. Keir Hardie, George Lansbury and Ernest Bevin, he claimed, would find much more in common with the direction in which Mrs Thatcher was leading her party than with 'Benn, Mikardo and the Tribunites'. By adopting such a position, the Tories thus opened a door to those who could no longer stomach Labour. But, he warned her, disenchanted former Labour supporters such as ex-editor of the *New Statesman* Paul Johnson and historian of the Spanish Civil War Hugh Thomas would have no truck with a Tory Party pitching its tent on the 'middle ground'. Instead, they had 'forcefully pointed out that they do not want a Conservative Party which is being dragged along leftward behind Labour; for that, there would be no point in the trouble of leaving Labour'.[53] As Sherman told her on another occasion, many potential recruits were 'if anything, already more militant and radical in our sense than many Tories, who still have one foot in Butskellism'.[54]

Joseph wined and dined potential left-wing converts to the Tory cause, but it was Sherman who grasped the need to present Thatcherism as an anti-establishment radical force. Some were indeed attracted simply by the sense that, with the CPS at its vanguard, the Tories were, unlike Labour, showing some signs of intellectual life. Mrs Thatcher's outreach to academics was led by the recently elected Tory MP, Leon Brittan. Aside from Thomas and Johnson, the roll call of intellectuals who would be won over to Mrs Thatcher included the novelist Kingsley Amis and the academic John Vaizey. Among the academics whom Mrs Thatcher consulted were also a number of prominent Jews including the Sovietologist Leonard Schapiro; philosopher Sir Isaiah Berlin; and the historian Max Beloff.

While Schapiro and Berlin also advised the Liberal Party at this time, Beloff – the son of Russian-speaking Jews who migrated to Britain at the turn of the century – had already turned his back upon it. In 1978, he was showcased as one of the Tories' converts in a collection of essays entitled *Right Turn: Eight Men Who Changed Their Minds*. Beloff had been a student socialist before becoming a self-declared 'mildly active' supporter of the Liberals after the war.[55] His break with the Liberal Party in 1971, prefiguring the later disillusion many Jews came to feel with the Labour Party, came when the Young Liberals provided a platform to the Palestinian Liberation Organization (PLO) (see Chapter 6). Beloff wrote to Jeremy Thorpe suggesting that the party could 'choose between retaining my services ... and retaining those of Peter Hain', the then-chair of the Liberals' youth wing.[56] Having received no response, he resigned from the party. But Beloff's reasons for becoming a Conservative under Mrs Thatcher ranged far wider than his former party's antagonism towards Israel. He believed that the Liberals had abandoned their commitment to 'traditional liberalism' and become 'merely an appendage' of a Labour Party which was increasingly committed to a 'particularly dogmatic and insular' form of socialism.[57]

However, like a rabbi testing the commitment of a would-be convert, Joseph could be exacting. David Young, a formerly Labour-supporting businessman, was chairman of the Jewish charity British ORT and chaired a dinner in May 1975 at which the former Cabinet minister was the guest speaker. Impressed by Joseph, he made an appointment to see him shortly afterwards. When he offered his help, though, he was initially rebuffed. 'Why?' Joseph responded 'You don't believe.' Surprised, Young replied: 'Why not try me?'[58] Young subsequently became involved with the CPS, both helping to raise money for it and contributing to policy papers. Despite the inauspicious beginnings, the meeting was the beginning of a lifelong relationship between Young and Joseph, as well as the former's entry into politics which would eventually see him joining his one-time interrogator at Mrs Thatcher's Cabinet table.

If Sherman was keen to win new converts to the Thatcherite cause, he was equally determined to winkle out potential heretics. As he warned Joseph within months of Mrs Thatcher becoming leader: 'We must fight back, particularly with the enemies in the wings, ready to exploit, and in some cases actually initiate or instigate these attacks.'[59] Sherman was also on guard for any signs of backsliding on Joseph's part. The Conservatives' attitude on one issue, he wrote him, was 'tantamount to unconditional surrender'. Alluding to Joseph's regret over his own record in Ted Heath's government, Sherman continued: 'I can only beseech you … to recall our conversations over the past ten years, and reflect whether you might not be mistaken.'[60]

His messages to the leader herself were equally nerve-jangling. The year 1978 was, Lady Thatcher later wrote, 'a politically difficult year' as inflation and unemployment began to fall and, with them, the Conservatives' lead in the polls.[61] Sherman was ever-alert for signs of betrayal. In July 1978, for instance, he wrote to warn her of 'misbriefing' of the press by her colleagues. It fell into two categories: 'denigration and "disinformation"'. On this occasion, Sherman bothered himself only with the latter, providing Mrs Thatcher with examples of 'deliberate attempts to create the belief that things are moving in a certain direction, in order to create a band-waggon in that direction'. Her critics, Sherman warned the leader, were thus attempting to suggest that she was backtracking on immigration, spending cuts and tackling the power of the unions in order to force her to do so.[62] Still worse than efforts to force her into retreat, he also sniffed collaboration in the air. There was a real risk, Sherman wrote Mrs Thatcher, of a run on the pound which would be accompanied by an attempt by Callaghan to 'dragoon the Conservatives into a coalition'. Some on her own side – 'the inveterate anti-Margareteers and those who hanker after a party of the centre' – would be all-too-ready to accept such a poisoned chalice, he cautioned her.[63]

After a difficult party conference Sherman wrote again, urging that she not appease their internal critics. There was, he maintained, 'little point in saying that we must unite the party, if what we do plays into the hands of those whose whole aim is to destabilise the party, e.g. Heath, et al. Party unity, like anything else, has terms and a price'.[64] But, in Sherman's eyes, Mrs Thatcher was not the only potential victim of the 'inveterate anti-Margareteers'. He himself was feeling the heat, writing to her on one occasion requesting a face-to-face meeting to discuss 'the implications of the witch-hunt'. There were, he suggested conspiratorially, 'loose ends difficult to tie up over the phone'.[65]

To counter the 'enemies in the wings', Sherman proposed an audacious plan to create a Thatcherite Praetorian Guard. This 'territorial army of advisers' would, he wrote to Joseph, be several hundred strong.[66] Its loyalty was to be less to the Conservative Party than to the impending revolution. Appointed in opposition, the advisers would neither report to shadow ministers nor be restrained by the party machine or policy-making processes.[67] After meeting Arthur Seldon, who shared his enthusiasm for the project, Sherman wrote to Joseph that the two men had agreed that recruits to their army need not show a commitment to the Conservative Party, but to 'certain shared principles'. They also agreed that its recruitment would reassure businessmen and academics sympathetic to the unfolding Thatcherite cause that 'the next government would break with the approach exemplified by Heath and Barber, with such disastrous results'.[68]

Once the Conservatives came to power, Sherman envisaged his 'territorial army' occupying not simply Whitehall, but also the commanding heights of the state: the BBC, the Bank of England, Inland Revenue, the nationalised industries, and all other 'nominally dependent institutions which can virtually impose policy on governments'.[69]

In the end, Sherman's territorial army was confined to the barracks of his imagination. In a covering letter attaching a series of papers on advisers, Joseph wrote drily to Mrs Thatcher of Sherman's: 'It is, as you would expect, bolder than mine.' He continued unenthusiastically: 'You may wish to go some way along the route it sketches.'[70] Joseph, surmised Morrison Halcrow, probably believed that internal resistance to a new Tory government's agenda could be overcome by 'rational persuasion and argument', while Mrs Thatcher would no doubt have baulked at any suggestion that a party committed to cutting the size of government would, at its outset, bring several hundred advisers into it.[71] But, despite Joseph's evident lack of enthusiasm, Sherman continued to press his case with Mrs Thatcher. Sending her his earlier memos in late 1978, he added a forlorn note: 'KJ advised me that he would be dealing with the matter and that I should withdraw, which I have done.'[72]

The intellectual development of Thatcherism in the 1970s was, of course, the work of many hands. While not by any means exclusively so, many were Jewish. The academics Bill Letwin and Shirley Robin Letwin, who had clashed with Sherman when Joseph introduced them, began to offer advice and assistance with Mrs Thatcher's speeches. Samuel Brittan, who found her marriage of market economics to a belief in 'national reassertion abroad ... and Victorian values at home' so jarring that he could never fully subscribe to being 'one of us', was nonetheless an influential exponent of monetarism.[73] His economic commentary in the *Financial Times* was the only newspaper article Mrs Thatcher never missed reading.[74]

Brittan had initially viewed Milton Friedman as a 'far out Republican' when the latter was his Cambridge tutor.[75] By the mid-1970s, however, the University of Chicago professor's ideas no longer seemed 'far out' but instead had begun to represent a potent challenge to Keynesian orthodoxy. The only son of Jewish immigrants from Carpatho-Ruthenia, then part of the Austro-Hungarian Empire, Friedman stood apart from many of the other Jewish intellectuals who shaped modern American conservatism. He shared neither the metropolitan New York upbringing (he grew up in Rahway, New Jersey), nor the previous background in left-wing politics (although he had been an admirer of Franklin Roosevelt) of many prominent neoconservatives such as Irving Kristol and Daniel Bell. Nonetheless, while Friedman may arguably have been the most famous example, many other leading post-war proponents of free-market economics – such as Ludwig von Mises, Gary Becker, Murray Weidenbaum and Israel Kirzner – were also Jewish. As the historian Murray Friedman wrote in his examination of American Jewish conservatism, this reflected the 'ever-present Jewish distrust of authority and power ... whether linked to collectivist political models or not'.[76]

Alongside his Chicago colleague, F. A. Hayek – whose book, *The Constitution of Liberty*, Mrs Thatcher would famously produce from her handbag and pronounce 'This is what we believe'[77] – Milton Friedman had fought a lonely battle in favour of free-market economics during the 1950s and 1960s, challenging conventional thinking about the causes of the Great Depression and highlighting the alleged failings of the welfare state and government intervention in the economy.[78] Although his 1967 presidential address to the American Economic Association represented the key moment in the development of monetarism, Friedman himself recognised that the 'watershed in the abandonment of Keynesian doctrine' arose not from academic debates, but the experience of the 'stagflation' of the 1970s.[79] With both growth stalled and inflation rising in contravention of Keynesian thinking, the levers with which governments of left and right had sought to manage the economy for the previous three decades appeared to have jammed.

While *The Times* had published Friedman for the first time in 1968, it was Arthur Seldon who helped introduce his ideas to Britain. In 1970, Seldon – who, as Charles Robinson argued, 'was always quick to recognise promising areas of research before their significance was widely recognised' – brought Friedman to London to deliver a lecture at the IEA on monetary economics.[80] It was thus through the IEA that Joseph first became familiar with Friedman's theories. Friedman had advised Richard Nixon during the president's 1968 campaign and had continued to offer advice once he reached the White House. But there was to be no such interest from the newly elected Ted Heath.[81]

The political tide was, however, turning as the economic storm clouds darkened. The shift in thinking on both sides of the Atlantic was readily apparent, provoking curious conversions. In 1971, a Republican President, Richard Nixon, had declared: 'I am now a Keynesian in economics'. Just five years later, a Labour Prime Minister, James Callaghan, warned his party it was 'now impossible to spend your way out of a recession'. It would be unfair to suggest that Mrs Thatcher simply rode that right-ward tide; even within her own party, she had to battle the opponents of monetarism. However, the adoption by the Labour Party of monetarist policies weakened the intellectual defences of the Keynesians.

Mrs Thatcher herself did not meet Friedman until 1978. When she did, recorded John Campbell, she showed uncharacteristic deference. She was, once again, the diligent Kesteven and Grantham Girls' School student, making notes as she quizzed him on his ideas.[82] As for Friedman, he was not yet convinced of Mrs Thatcher's resolve. She was, he wrote to the IEA's Ralph Harris who had hosted the dinner, 'a very attractive and interesting lady', but, he continued: 'Whether she really has the capacities that Britain so badly needs at this time, I must confess, seems to me still a very open question.'[83] While she would no doubt have disputed this assessment, Mrs Thatcher continued to display her sharp sense of political realities. After meeting Friedman, she, too, wrote to Harris. She agreed with Friedman's view that an incoming Tory government should abolish exchange controls, but fretted: 'But how can I carry my party?'[84] Nonetheless, the lifting of exchange controls, thus allowing the pound to float freely and large-scale investment in and out of the country to commence, was introduced in the Conservatives' first Budget in 1979. It was, Friedman later suggested, 'the most important thing which Margaret Thatcher did ... That was a precondition for other measures'.[85]

After leaving office, Lady Thatcher dropped the act of adoring pupil. Writing of the Keynesian approach which dominated economic thinking for almost all of the period she was in parliament before becoming Prime Minister, she pronounced: 'Before I ever read a page of Milton Friedman or Alan Walters, I just knew that these assertions could not be true.' The biggest single change which had occurred during her time as Tory Party leader, she continued, was that 'the great majority of policy-makers (and even economists) came around to the view which I held'.[86] There was, beneath the vainglorious tone, a degree of truth to her assertion. As Sherman suggested: 'Keith and Margaret turned to ... Friedman to justify what they already thought.'[87] Thus, like others, Friedman provided the intellectual edifice for instincts – that 'thrift was a virtue and profligacy a vice' and that governments should live within their means like any prudent household – that she had long harboured.[88] That edifice was, however, crucial in giving Mrs Thatcher's homespun economics – which had been learned, she proudly declared, from 'the world in which I grew up – Grantham, Methodism, the grocer's shop'[89] – philosophical credibility.

But whatever sustenance and support she drew from others, it was Joseph who remained Mrs Thatcher's principal warrior in the battle of ideas. In his seminal Stockton Lecture in 1976 – the credit for which he later refused to take, saying 'Oh no, that was Alfred'[90] – Joseph argued that Britain was 'over-governed, over-spent, over-taxed, over-borrowed and over-manned'. Squeezing the money supply to bring down inflation would need to be accompanied by 'substantial cuts in tax and public spending and bold incentives and encouragements to the wealth creators, without whose renewed efforts we shall all grow poorer'.[91] As Mrs Thatcher recalled, however, given that most members of the shadow Cabinet were unconvinced by monetarism, the very title of Joseph's speech – 'Monetarism Is Not Enough' – was 'a deliberately bold way of expressing an important truth'.[92] Fifty years after Keynes had argued 'we have to invent new wisdom for a new age' Joseph sought to do likewise.[93] Speeches and lectures poured out, many of which were then published in the series of books and pamphlets – *Freedom Under the Law*, *Stranded on the Middle Ground*, *Reversing the Trend*, *Conditions for Fuller Employment* and *Solving the Union Problem is the Key to Britain's Recovery* – which rolled off the printing presses.

Like a modern-day Daniel, Joseph determined to take what he called the 'moral case for capitalism' into the lion's den of the campuses. In just over three years, he made 150 speeches at universities and polytechnics. They were, he later told Halcrow, 'self-inflicted misery', before adding: 'It was lovely.' In reality, it was anything but. Joseph would speak for thirty minutes, expounding on the virtues of the free market and then take an hour of questions.[94] He was invariably heckled; but on other occasions, eggs and flour bombs were thrown at him. 'I was frightened in some cases,' he admitted near the end of his life.[95] On a number of occasions, most famously at the LSE in April 1978, he was prevented from speaking altogether. Joseph may not have won many converts in the lecture halls in which he spoke – although he inspired young Tories such as the future Cabinet ministers Peter Lilley and William Hague[96] – but, argued Brian Harrison, his 'nationwide public tutorial … [sought] to draw lay people into a complex economic debate':[97] one which damned the multiple failings of government, excoriated the 'socialist anti-enterprise climate' and lauded wealth-creation and entrepreneurship.[98]

For Mrs Thatcher, what Joseph termed 'my mission' was critical.[99] He had restored the right's 'intellectual self-confidence,' she said later[100] and turned the 'intellectual tide' against socialism through his efforts to reach out to students, academics and the media. If Joseph had not been doing 'all that work with the intellectuals,' she suggested as she approached a decade as Prime Minister, 'all the rest of our work would probably never have resulted in success'.[101] As Hugo Young argued, Joseph's speeches during this period were remarkably prophetic, containing as they did 'everything that is distinctive about the economic and political philosophy which later became known as Thatcherism'.[102]

Like Joseph, Mrs Thatcher was also keen to make the 'moral case for capitalism'. In March 1977, she delivered a speech at the Zurich Economic Society written for her by Sherman. Socialism had failed economically and politically, she argued, before going on to sing the praises of capitalism and 'the free society'. As 'an engine of mass production', it had demonstrated its 'material superiority', giving its 'main benefits to the very people the Socialists claim to cherish'. But, she suggested, the economic results were superior because the moral philosophy was superior, too. Capitalism's great virtue rested on the fact that it starts with 'the individual, with his uniqueness, his responsibility, and his capacity to choose'. Choice, she proclaimed, 'is the essence of ethics'. Without choice, there could be no ethics, no good or evil. The concept of good and evil, she suggested, only had meaning to the extent that man was free to choose between the two. Her Methodism and Sherman's Judaism were plainly on display: 'The sense of being self-reliant, of playing a role within the family, of owning one's own property, of paying one's way,' Mrs Thatcher declared, 'are all part of the spiritual ballast which maintains responsible citizenship.'[103]

Sherman was on hand a few months later to help draft Mrs Thatcher's Macleod Lecture. This son of Jewish immigrants disliked the term 'Judeo-Christian values' and believed it was important to root her message explicitly in Christianity.[104] Mrs Thatcher was not, however, prepared to go quite as far as her speechwriter suggested. His first draft had her arguing that the Tories were 'more than just a British party, we are also a Christian Party … We are a Christian party in the broadest sense of the word.' The references to a 'Christian Party' were swiftly excised. So, too, was his suggestion that she proclaim that 'our Christianity gives us not only values … but also our historical nexus'. In its place, came a rather more ecumenical reference to those values stemming from 'religion'.[105]

A year later, Sherman helped again with a speech focused on her religious beliefs at St Lawrence Jewry in the City of London. He was concerned about the 'de-theologisation of British politics' and urged 'a restatement of Christian culture and the Protestant ethic within a Conservative framework'.[106] This time – perhaps more comfortable because she was addressing her own personal beliefs rather than making claims for the Tory Party as whole – Mrs Thatcher spoke more explicitly about Christianity. She challenged the notion that 'Man is perfectible'. Christianity teaches us, she preached, that 'there is some evil in everyone and that it cannot be banished by sound policies and institutional reforms; that we cannot eliminate crime simply by making people rich, or achieve a compassionate society simply by passing new laws'. While the relief of poverty and suffering was 'a duty' of the state, it must never become exclusively its responsibility. 'Once you give people the idea that all this can be done by the State,' she argued, 'and that it is somehow second-best or even degrading to leave it to private people … then you will begin to deprive human beings of one of the essential ingredients of humanity—personal moral responsibility'. The impact of this would be to drain individuals of 'the milk of human kindness'.[107] As we shall see, seven years later, with the Chief Rabbi as her principal ally, Mrs Thatcher and the Established Church would fight their own battle of ideas over these very questions.

Setting the agenda

If Joseph's contribution to the battle of ideas was undeniable, the part he played in turning their ideas into the policies Mrs Thatcher hoped to implement as Prime Minister was altogether more mixed. As she gently conceded in her memoirs, the operation which Joseph headed had a 'somewhat ramshackle feel to it'.[108] The management of such an operation did not play to his strengths: policy groups mushroomed – by 1977, there were over eighty – and their work was poorly coordinated. 'Here we go again!' Chris Patten scribbled to a colleague on one of Joseph's letters; 'Do you know anything about this waste of time?' he appended to another.[109]

In the critical field of economic policy, out of Joseph's chaos, the shadow Chancellor, Sir Geoffrey Howe – patient, deliberate and consensual – helped to create some sense of order. But Hugo Young's formulation which saw Joseph waging a lofty intellectual battle, Howe making policy and Mrs Thatcher acting as the 'essential conduit' between the two[110] – is rather too neat for it downplays Joseph's essential role in helping to open up the policy debate.

On the two interrelated issues which had bedevilled Heath's government – how to control inflation and the unions – Mrs Thatcher's shadow Cabinet was deeply divided. Party policy documents such as 'The Right Approach' and 'The Right Approach to the Economy' simply attempted to smooth over these differences. 'Strings of homilies which were chosen because they would not provoke trouble among Mrs Thatcher's colleagues,' remembered Sherman dismissively, noting that he had been excluded from the preparation of the latter.[111] Joseph, while publicly praising 'The Right Approach', rather ruined the effect by publishing a collection of his speeches, provocatively entitled *Stranded on the Middle Ground?*, the day before its publication.[112] More sensitive to the need to move cautiously, Mrs Thatcher labelled the document 'a fudge – but temporarily palatable'.[113] A year later, however, her patience was waning. 'The Right Approach to the Economy', which blandly attempted to paper over what she termed the party's 'policy cracks', was refused any official status. Joseph, who had failed in his attempt to toughen its wording, allowed his name to appear as one of the five authors. Despite sharing her doubts, Mrs Thatcher recalled that he was 'more prepared to compromise' on the document than she was.[114]

This was not the usual dynamic between the two. Aware of the need to maintain party unity and concerned about anything that might frighten off floating voters, Mrs Thatcher trod with caution. Joseph, by contrast, raced ahead preparing the ground. Nowhere was this more evident than on the subject which had split Harold Wilson's government in 1969, brought down Ted Heath's in 1974, and would shortly prove fatal to James Callaghan's: how to clip the wings of the mighty trade unions. Throughout her parliamentary career, Mrs Thatcher had done little to disguise her lack of sympathy for the labour movement: her 1960 Private Member's Bill, which had brought her together with Joseph for the first time, was an early shot across its collective bows. As she was well aware when she put him in charge of shaping the Tories' approach to the unions, Jim Prior did not share her hostility. 'We … must convince the public (and as far as possible the trade unions),' he suggested to the shadow Cabinet in the summer of 1976, 'that we are not antipathetic towards trade unions and do not seek a major confrontation.'[115]

Mrs Thatcher was highly sceptical about such an approach and recognised that, given their links to Labour, there was 'a basic incompatibility between their economic approach and ours, and indeed between their political allegiance and ours'. Nonetheless, fearing the perception that the Tories wished to provoke industrial unrest and plunge the country back into power cuts and another three-day week, she bit her tongue and chose her own words on the subject with care.[116] Joseph, however, lacked Mrs Thatcher's patience. In December 1976, he circulated a paper to the shadow Cabinet suggesting a very different strategy to Prior's. Joseph regarded the unions as Luddites, who were frustrating the modernisation of the economy and the creation of new jobs, and had an insatiable appetite for more political and economic power. It was 'fanciful' to think the Tories could govern the country in the way they believed was in its best interests with the unions 'so entrenched and so expansionist'. A Conservative government needed to both adopt a tough economic approach which would 'encourage self-discipline and the recognition of realities' and show a willingness to fight and defeat strikes ('the cost of winning them may be high, the cost of losing them will be higher still'). In the meantime, the Tory opposition needed to put the union leaders on the defensive. By not denouncing their 'misuse of power' or systematically explaining the damage they were doing to living standards, the party was failing to legitimise the public's 'instinctive distaste for what is going on'.[117]

The tensions in Mrs Thatcher's team exploded into public view six months later over an increasingly violent, year-long dispute at the small Grunwick photo-processing laboratory in north London. With the right-wing National Association for Freedom determined to help keep the plant working and huge numbers of pickets – including, on occasion, moderate Labour Cabinet ministers like Shirley Williams – determined to bring it to a halt, it came to symbolise increasingly competing, and irreconcilable, views about the rights of workers, trade unions and management, and the government's role in upholding them.

Prior wanted the Conservatives to steer clear of the issue and the party limited itself to formulaic condemnations of the violence. In private, Mrs Thatcher was rooting for the strike-breakers: referring to the Israelis' freeing of hostages from Idi Amin's Uganda, she confided to the National Association for Freedom that its smuggling of 80,000 items of post out of the plant to beat the pickets was 'the best thing since Entebbe'.[118] Joseph wanted an altogether tougher public stand. At Sherman's urging, he delivered a blistering speech in which he attacked Labour moderates for allowing themselves to become fellow travellers of the hard left. 'The Battle of Grunwick sorts out the democrats on the one hand from the red fascists and time-servers on the other,' he announced. 'The Labour democrats have yet to stand up and be counted.'[119] The speech, believed Sherman, was important: 'The feeling that "something could be done" about the unions,' he recalled, 'gained momentum.'[120]

When Lord Scarman, who had been appointed by the government to examine the issue, published his report and recommended the striking workers sacked by management the previous year be reinstated, Joseph was enraged, attacked the judge, and called for the 'closed shop' to be outlawed. With her employment and industry spokesmen publicly at odds, Mrs Thatcher, who was visiting Washington, was called upon to pronounce. Admitting later that she could afford neither to move nor to sack Prior, and that the time was 'not right to try to harden our policy', she was forced to publicly back him and, somewhat feebly, announce that, although she did not like the closed shop, an incoming Conservative government could not legislate against it. 'Mrs Thatcher appears to be aligning herself with Mr Prior and other voices in the Conservative Party urging moderation rather than "union bashing",' reported *The Times*.[121] 'In retrospect,' Lady Thatcher wrote in her memoirs, 'Jim and I were wrong and Keith was right.' Her party's 'careful avoidance of any kind of commitment to changing the law on industrial relations,' the dispute had proved, 'would be weak and unsustainable in a crisis'.[122]

Despite the private protests of Hailsham and Prior to Mrs Thatcher and public condemnations by *The Spectator* of his remarks as 'maladroit', neither Joseph nor Sherman were deterred.[123] Instead, in John Hoskyns, a former army captain turned businessman, and Norman Strauss, an executive for Unilever who had met Joseph when the former Cabinet minister came to lunch with senior managers at the company, they found two men capable of plotting a much longer-term approach.

Tough and argumentative, Strauss, suggested Halcrow, had something of the air of Alfred Sherman about him.[124] Unable to make him out at first – he appeared 'typecast as the mad Jewish professor' – Hoskyns soon came to re-alise that Strauss had 'a mind of great originality [and] a burning impatience with what was happening to the country'. Still, it was not just the 'conven-tional apparatchiks' at Conservative Central Office who viewed Strauss as 'mad, bad and professionally dangerous to know'.[125] Sherman was not even sure how Mrs Thatcher would react to him when, her interest piqued by a paper Strauss had prepared on how the Tories might shape the public debate and make voters more amenable to their policies, she asked to see him. Sherman advised Strauss: 'You'll scare her; you'll need to take along John Hoskyns with you.'[126]

Sherman was right to be wary. Although their first meeting went well – enjoying the discussion so much Mrs Thatcher cancelled a lunch – the relationship was not without tensions. At a second meeting where they presented some ideas for her party conference speech, Mrs Thatcher 'just got into nit-picking about punctuation'. The atmosphere was not improved by the fact that, 'looking at me with absolute horror', Mrs Thatcher mistook the family cat stroking her leg for Strauss doing so.[127] Moreover, she found the concept of systems analysis – the importance of which Strauss and Hoskyns attempted to impress upon her – both baffling and irrelevant. She had cooked them a whole joint of roast beef, Mrs Thatcher declared after Sunday lunch at Flood Street, and she was not sure what she had received in return.[128] With gritted teeth, she later wrote that the two had 'a refreshingly if sometimes irritatingly undisguised scorn for the ad hoc nature of political decision-making in general and the decision-making of the Shadow Cabinet in particular'.[129]

Soon, however, Hoskyns and Strauss brought Mrs Thatcher something she was unquestioningly impressed by. The 'Stepping Stones' document – the title came from Joseph – was to become, believed John Ranelagh, 'the effective blueprint' for her first term in Downing Street.[130] It outlined a series of 'turnaround policies' – controlling public spending, beating public sector strikes, tackling inflation, deregulation, and cutting direct taxation – which were to be the government's principal objectives.[131] But most important, 'Stepping Stones' reinforced Joseph's view that tackling the power of the unions was critical to the success of any future Conservative government. 'There is one major obstacle – the negative role of the trade unions,' Hoskyns and Strauss wrote. 'Any strategy which does not address this problem of the trades union role from the outset,' they suggested, 'ensures failure in office, even though it might, at first sight, appear to make electoral success more likely.' The Tories thus needed to capitalise on growing public unease about the power wielded by the unions and win the argument for radical reform. If handed skilfully, they could turn the unions from Labour's 'secret weapon into its major electoral liability'.

When the ideas were presented to her at a small dinner also attended by Joseph, Mrs Thatcher 'liked it immediately', recalled Strauss.[132] That view was not, however, shared by much of her shadow Cabinet. At a meeting of the

Leader's Steering Committee at the end of January 'we argued ourselves to a standstill,' Mrs Thatcher later recalled.[133] Lord Thorneycroft, the party chairman, was concerned by the tone of 'extreme antagonism' towards the unions in the report and urged caution; Gilmour believed it 'over-ambitious', while Pym warned against anything 'too insensitive and controversial'. Only Joseph and Howe backed Hoskyns and Strauss's strategy. Frustrated, Mrs Thatcher ordered the minutes of the meeting locked in the safe.[134]

Instead of a bang, 'Stepping Stones' initially produced only a whimper: in the coming months what Mrs Thatcher described as 'some of the more solid Shadows', including Joseph and Nigel Lawson, worked in small policy groups to try to develop further its ideas.[135] But, by the summer of 1978, despite Strauss urging Mrs Thatcher to fire him, Prior's approach remained intact.[136] Had Callaghan, as was widely expected, called an election in October, the Tories would have fought it offering 'no significant measures' on union reform, Lady Thatcher later admitted.[137] All that was changed, however, by the Prime Minister's decision not to go to the polls early and the ensuing industrial chaos of the Winter of Discontent which destroyed Labour's chances of re-election. Sherman urged her to seize the moment. 'The people of this country are in advance of the politicians in that they know that "something must be done about the unions",' he wrote her in December 1978, 'The Unions' moral ascendancy has been eroded, they are no longer seen as valient [sic] fighters for the underdog but as selfish and often ruthless operators.'[138]

Urged on by Sherman and Joseph – whose earlier suggestion on curtailing benefits to strikers' families she had initially given 'short shrift' but now agreed should be re-examined – this was a crisis that Mrs Thatcher was determined not to let go to waste.[139] She now succeeded in breaking free from the shadow Cabinet doves and indicated her party's willingness to take a tougher approach. The Winter of Discontent had, she argued later, 'rejuvenated the Stepping Stones initiative'.[140] With the help of Joseph and Howe, Mrs Thatcher thus succeeded in making significant revisions to the manifesto which had originally been drafted for an election in autumn 1978. Out went pledges to be 'even-handed in our approach to industrial problems' and not to undertake 'any sweeping changes in the law on industrial relations'. In came a vow to strike 'a fair balance between the rights and duties of the trade union movement', and proposals to crack down on secondary picketing, introduce secret ballots in union elections, and restrict the closed shop.[141]

As with the shift in the Tories' economic policy, where Labour's adoption of monetarism smoothed the path, events beyond Mrs Thatcher's control had played a big part in allowing her to move her party in a new direction in its approach to the unions. In both cases, Joseph – assisted by Sherman and, in the case of the unions, Strauss – had played the leading role. During this critical period, his normal penchant for indecision gave way to a revolutionary fervour. Alone, it would probably not have been enough to begin the process of transforming the Tory Party and reshaping British politics. But once combined with Mrs Thatcher's political cunning and sense of timing, it was to have consequences that few in the country could yet begin to imagine.

CHAPTER 5

CHANGING THE EQUATION: THE 'JEWISH VOTE' AND THE SHIFT TO THE RIGHT

T he closely fought general election of February 1974, which rescued Harold Wilson's political career and effectively ended that of Ted Heath, turned on a handful of seats. One of them was Ilford North, where suburban north-east London, with its post-war council estates and solidly lower-middle-class homeowners, meets the Essex countryside. This was an area to which aspirational voters, including many Jews who left the East End in search of a better life moved; 'full of people going slightly up in the world, with a mortgage round their necks and a long haul on the Central Line to work every morning,' as one reporter put it.[1] The fortunes of such voters and those of Margaret Thatcher were to become closely intertwined.

When the country, beset by economic woes, went to the polls in the winter of 1974, the Tories retained the seat by just 258 votes. Paradoxically, while the oil crisis following the Yom Kippur War had torpedoed the Conservative government, Tom Iremonger's decision to rebel against Heath's arms embargo on Israel during the conflict had rescued him from defeat by the narrowest of margins. Eight months later, when Wilson returned to the country in an ill-fated bid to secure a working majority in parliament, Iremonger – a populist right winger known for what one profile termed his 'salty remarks' – was not so lucky.[2] Once again, he faced Millie Miller, a Jewish Labour candidate who had previously served as mayor of both Stoke

Newington and Camden. This time, though, she unseated him, snatching Ilford North by 778 votes. If Iremonger's staunch Zionism had saved him in February 1974, it was his other great crusade – opposition to immigration – which would dominate the by-election caused by Miller's untimely death three years later. Moreover, it was the seat's 6,000 Jewish voters who would find themselves dragged into the centre of that debate. When the votes were counted, the result indicated the changed relationship between Margaret Thatcher's Conservative Party and many of Britain's Jews.

With Labour defending so narrow a majority, the Tories should have been able to seize Ilford North with ease in early 1978. Nationally, however, the Conservatives' once-solid opinion poll lead had collapsed, provoking speculation that Wilson's successor as Prime Minister, James Callaghan, might call an early general election. Locally, the picture was equally confused by a feud between Iremonger and his former constituency association. Ilford Tories chose not to readopt him as their candidate in favour of an estate agent, Vivian Bendall. Their decision – the result of his rebellion in the October 1973 vote, Iremonger publicly alleged – and the former MP's consequent decision to contest the seat as an independent, thus risked a split in the Conservative vote.[3] At the same time, in Tessa Jowell, Labour had picked a candidate who, though publicly sympathetic to Israel's cause, was not herself Jewish.[4]

In such a potentially close contest, the votes of Ilford's Jews were likely to play a key role in deciding the outcome. Iremonger's much-trumpeted support for Israel, and his vigorous campaigning on the plight of Soviet Jewry, had made him a popular figure in the community. Indeed, when twenty-four years previously, he had been picked to defend the seat for the Tories in another by-election, Iremonger had recruited Joe Emden, a prominent East End Jewish Tory, to help him woo Jewish voters. But, as the tight battles between them in 1974 showed, Miller – a former chair of the North London Progressive Synagogue, who was also active in the Jewish Welfare Board, Labour Friends of Israel (LFI) and Pioneer Women – also had an appeal to many Jews. She was estimated to have attracted a personal vote from several hundred of them.[5]

As campaigning for the by-election was about to commence, however, Mrs Thatcher gave one of her most controversial interviews, lobbing the highly incendiary question of immigration into this precarious mix. Appearing on *World in Action*, she predicted that, at current rates, Britain would have 4 million Pakistani and Commonwealth immigrants by the turn of the century, and went on to declare: 'Now, that is an awful lot and I think it means that people are really rather afraid that this country might be rather swamped by people with a different culture.'[6]

There was undoubtedly a degree of political calculation to her remarks. Private polling suggested that, with the economy recovering, social issues such as crime and immigration might prove fertile terrain for the Tories.[7] As was frequently the case with Mrs Thatcher, however, her actions reflected a convenient blend of politics and principle. When she decided to reject the urgings of some of her staff to at least avoid the emotive term 'swamped' – in fact, just to make sure there was no misunderstanding, she used it twice – she was not saying anything that she did not herself believe.[8] In private, for instance, she sympathised with some of the sentiments Enoch Powell had voiced in his 'Rivers of Blood' speech ten years previously.[9] With Labour's relaxation of some immigration controls after it returned to power in 1974, and signs in by-elections and local government elections that support for the racist and anti-immigration National Front might be stirring, Mrs Thatcher was also convinced that it was the duty of mainstream politicians to tackle the public's concerns head on. Support for the Front, she thought, reflected less agreement with its objectives than a feeling on the part of some that 'at least they are talking about some of the problems'.[10]

On immigration, as on so much else, Sir Keith Joseph was her most reliable shadow Cabinet ally. Unlike Mrs Thatcher, Joseph had been pained by Powell's speech. Nonetheless, his views on immigration had shifted. In July 1976, he had nominated immigration as one of the themes that Mrs Thatcher and her colleagues should 'hammer away' on over the next few months.[11] Five months later, he circulated a shadow Cabinet paper urging that the party be 'ready to disappoint the expectations of immigrants if the only alternative is to disappoint the expectations of the English. The English have rights too.'[12] And, in a speech in the somewhat unpromising terrain of Hampstead, he ventured the thought that: 'In the 1950s, we opened the doors to immigrants – we didn't realise then that perhaps we should have shut them. But when we tried to shut them in the early 1960s the Liberals and Socialists made such a fuss that we couldn't.'[13]

Immigration, of course, represented a key element of the wider populist 'common ground' strategy that Sherman had been urging on the Tory leader. In a memo to Mrs Thatcher, barely a week after her *World in Action* appearance, Sherman suggested that, on immigration the 'establishment' had overruled 'the popular instinct' – which, in his eyes, had proven to be right – resulting in 'terrible problems'.[14] As he well knew, legitimising Mrs Thatcher's instincts by suggesting they were in tune with a public mood, which was frustrated by a liberal-leaning establishment, would often elicit a positive response. Immigration was not an issue of race, he wrote, 'but one of nationhood' – a phrase which she approvingly underlined twice – 'compounded by that of third-world migration into an advanced urban country'.

Taking aim at the policy of multiculturalism which was then guiding Britain's response to mass immigration, Sherman argued that it was necessary not merely to control numbers but to reassert 'the relationship between immigrant communities and the host nation'. Britons were being asked to give up their own identity, history and traditions and instead become simply 'a microcosm of the wider world'. Nothing could more have terrified Mrs Thatcher, who believed throughout her life that her country and its inhabitants had certain unique virtues.

Sherman went on to paint a bleak picture of the manner in which the interests of working-class whites were being neglected in favour of those of 'mainly poor backward' immigrants. Perhaps with his native East End in mind he described how local people had been 'deliberately "decanted"' from their homes and now found that 'in the name of racial equality and racial harmony, priority is given to immigrants … making the immigrant more equal than others'. It was time, he declared, 'to deal with this cancer before it grows larger and more intractable'.

Mrs Thatcher's appearance on *World in Action* provoked an immediate furore. Callaghan, whose whips were privately urging him to 'steal [her] clothes' on immigration, publicly suggested she was attempting to appeal to what he euphemistically termed 'certain elements of the electorate'.[15] The *Sunday Times* charged her with giving 'aid and comfort to the National Front', while *The Economist* accused the Tory leader of 'genteel demagoguery'.[16] Among many of her colleagues, there was dismay. The shadow Home Secretary, Willie Whitelaw, whom she had not consulted, talked privately of resigning.[17] At the Conservative Research Department, a horrified Chris Patten confided to his then colleague, Michael Portillo: 'Just imagine if she'd said we were being swamped by Jewish people.'[18] The finger of blame was soon pointed at Sherman.[19]

Despite the outcry her interview had caused, Mrs Thatcher had no intention of backing down. With a postbag of 10,000 letters of support and an immediate jump in the opinion polls to reassure her, she gave no ground. But one of the principal defences of the stance she had taken – that addressing popular worries about immigration was the best way to fend off the threat from the far right – was now about to be put dramatically to the test in north-east London.

The National Front had not fielded a candidate in Ilford North in either of the 1974 elections. But having pushed the Liberals into fourth place in one-third of Greater London's constituencies in the previous summer's GLC elections, it was now determined to make its presence felt, both on the streets and at the ballot box. A planned march by the Front in the constituency on the Friday before polling had helped to raise temperatures, with the Board of Deputies of British Jews and the Zionist Federation appealing to the Home Secretary to step in amid fears for the safety of Jews planning to attend synagogue while it was taking place. In the end, the police banned the march but, with immigration dominating the campaign, the fascists' performance on polling day was awaited with trepidation.[20]

But how would the Jewish voters of Ilford North react to Mrs Thatcher's talk of Britons being 'swamped'? Conventional wisdom suggested she was taking a risk. 'One tricky problem with playing the immigrant card is that Ilford has, at 12 per cent, one of the largest Jewish votes in the country,' recorded one reporter from the by-election trail.[21] Sherman, however, advised Mrs Thatcher to ignore such predictions in a memo written the day before she taped the *World in Action* interview.[22] Noting the seat's significant Jewish vote, he provided her with a guide as to how and why it differed from that of Finchley. Ilford's Jews had, he wrote, 'changed less' than those Mrs Thatcher was more familiar with in north-west London, representing 'later waves of exodus from the East End to suburbia, the deuxieme cru, the late starters'. These 'late starters' may once have been more inclined to vote Labour than Mrs Thatcher's Jewish constituents, but they were now ripe for the picking. Relative affluence, the Soviets' persecution of the Jews and the 'bitter experience' of Labour policies had combined to erode many of the 'socialist certainties' which had accompanied the life in the East End many had left behind. Most were now homeowners, many self-employed taxi drivers ('a Jewish trade par excellence'). Their belief that personal achievement stemmed from education – the 'spring-board for economic opportunity' – and hard work heightened resentments against those who allegedly abused welfare.

Sherman then turned to immigration and its supposed political consequences, a rise in activity by the National Front. There was a genuine concern among many Jews in the mid-1970s that large-scale immigration was threatening, in the words of Alderman, to 'waken the dead' forces of the fascist right.[23] But Sherman also recognised another factor at work. Attempts by the left, in tandem with Jewish communal organisations, to co-opt Jews into 'anti-racist anti-fascist popular front style organisations' to oppose the far right, he wrote, had not gone down well in Ilford and were resented. Many Jews did not like the way politicians and anti-racist campaigners sought to lump them together with 'blacks and other third world migrants, both from practical considerations and pride'. Some Jews believed that they should deal with anti-Semitism if and when it arose and 'not go out looking for trouble'. For others, there was a principle at stake. Sherman reported the words of one leading local Jewish figure who had told him: 'We came as refugees from persecution, a few thousand a year, we did not automatically receive citizenship, we did not place a burden on the state; we earned our place in the sun by our behaviour and contribution.' In this regard, Asian immigrants, with their 'aspirations and strong family links', were similar to Jews; black, West Indian immigrants, he implied, were rather less so.

These were, without doubt, words to warm Mrs Thatcher's heart, and, as we will see, they prefigured the clash in the Jewish community eight years later about its attitude towards criticism of her government's approach to the inner cities and some of those who dwelled in them. Moreover, although their principal focus was attitudes towards immigration, those words touched on the wider themes – rights and responsibilities and the nature of the welfare state – which she would go on to utilise in order to persuade those who had never or rarely voted Conservative before to support her. Just as Sherman had previously advised Mrs Thatcher to reach out to disenchanted Labour-supporting intellectuals, now he was urging her to fish for converts among a pool of voters who some Tories might still regard as the preserve of the left. She needed little persuading.

However, as was so often the case with Sherman's ideas, his plans for the Tories to make a direct play for Jewish votes challenged prevailing, if largely unspoken, orthodoxies within the party. Nationally, the Conservatives, with the backing of Jewish Tories, had always avoided any such tactics. Indeed, when Samuel Landman, the former secretary of the World Zionist Organisation's London Bureau, had proposed a strategy to Conservative Central Office in 1962 to 'enrol British Jews into the ranks of the Conservative Party and to popularise Conservative principles among Jewish voters in preparation for the General Election' it was swiftly dismissed.[24]

Sherman believed that Mrs Thatcher's election as Tory Party leader had changed the equation. Her sympathies for Jews and for Israel, he wrote to Alan Howarth at Conservative Central Office in December 1977, 'are felt to be warm and genuine'.[25] 'A majority of Jews in this country are now conservative with a small "c". They are not socialists. They are now overwhelmingly middle class and they suffer from socialism together with their gentile fellow-citizens.' However, many Jews found the Conservative Party 'unsympathetic as a milieu, rather than as a political force'. At the same time, the Tories had been slow to reach out to Jews, a problem compounded by the fact that some Jewish Conservatives – perhaps Sherman had Joseph in mind – had 'tended to treat their own Jewishness with ambivalence, fearing consciously or otherwise that to wear it too prominently might compromise their standing as Englishmen'. Sherman thus proposed the formation of a 'Jewish Advisory Committee', consisting of businessmen, academics and others who were both 'prominent in their own field of activity' and 'committed Conservatives [and] committed Jews'. The industrialist Justin Kornberg; the chairman of Ladbrokes, Cyril Stein; the academic Julius Gould, who the previous year had produced a controversial report alleging Marxists were infiltrating the teaching of sociology; and the leader of Leeds City Council, Irwin Bellow, who had come to Mrs Thatcher's attention by cutting the rates and selling 3,000 council homes, had all been approached about membership and were prepared to join, he wrote.

Now, under the full glare of the national media spotlight which had fallen upon Ilford North, Sherman had the opportunity to put his theory to the test. He pushed for an appeal to the seat's Jewish voters, knowing that it would likely antagonise not simply left-leaning Jews but the communal leadership. The gambit had a logic: Tom Iremonger's slim victory in February 1974 and equally narrow defeat in October 1974 encapsulated the inconclusive results of the two general elections of that year which, the polls now suggested, might well be repeated whenever Callaghan went to the country. Nor was Ilford unique. In a handful of seats with sizeable Jewish populations, MPs – mainly Conservative, including Mrs Thatcher herself – perched upon perilously small majorities. Knowing that, as in 1974, the overall outcome of a tightly fought general election could well be decided in such constituencies, wrote Geoffrey Alderman, 'seems to have concentrated the minds of the party leaders on winning seats by appealing to local and sectional as well as national interests'.[26]

As campaigning entered its final stretch, Sherman had the ever-loyal Joseph join the fray and travel to Ilford to make a pitch to the constituency's Jews to back Mrs Thatcher.[27] The speech was written by Sherman and drew heavily on the analysis he had provided her with three weeks previously; indeed, it is unlikely that Joseph would have made it without the persuasion of his trusted adviser.[28] The positive response to Mrs Thatcher's *World in Action* interview, Joseph argued, showed that most people viewed immigration as a 'mistake'. Britain was not a country of immigrants like America, but the 'homeland of its indigenous peoples' who had no other home. It would always offer sanctuary to those escaping persecution, as it had it to Jews in the past, but, he went on, it was important to remember that previous generations of immigrants had not been given automatic citizenship. Instead, 'they asked for nothing except the chance to make their own way'. 'The immigration problem is not so much one of colour as of numbers and culture,' Joseph suggested. 'There is a limit to the number of people from different cultures that this country can digest. We ignore this at our peril, everyone's peril.' He concluded: 'Therefore, I say that the electors of Ilford North, including the Jews – who are just like everyone else, as the saying goes, only more so – have good reason for supporting Margaret Thatcher and the Conservative Party on immigration.'

Joseph's words simply fanned the flames Mrs Thatcher had already ignited. *The Times* branded them 'most un-British',[29] while the *Daily Mirror* labelled the speech the 'politics of hate'. Recalling attacks on Jewish immigrants in the early twentieth century, Joe Haines, Harold Wilson's former press secretary, wrote: 'My God! A Jew saying stop immigration!' His words were blown up across the paper's front page. The *Daily Telegraph*, where Sherman worked as a leader writer, struck back in Joseph's defence, saying that Haines and others were displaying a 'conditional acceptance of the Jew, provided only that he accepts their Left-wing religions'. The paper was confident that 'a majority of Jews, not only in Ilford, will identify more readily with their English hosts than with their would-be guests'. As the *Jewish Chronicle*'s media correspondent argued, that formulation appeared somewhat conditional itself.[30]

In the Jewish community the debate was equally fierce. Some disliked the very impression that there was a distinct 'Jewish vote' to appeal to. 'There is no such thing as a Jewish vote,' thundered the *Jewish Chronicle*, 'and it will be a wretched day if ever one emerges, since it could only be a negative vote against such a party as the National Front.' Joseph's speech was 'inept and misguided and a great disservice to the community'.[31] The long-standing nervousness about this subject was reflected in the advertising policy of the *Jewish Chronicle* which in 1950 had – in 'the best interests of the community' – barred election adverts from the paper.[32]

But, as the paper's editorial condemning Joseph also indicated, many Jews also objected to the notion that they should be asked to support Mrs Thatcher's message on immigration. Jewish Labour MPs took up the cudgels. Arnold Shaw, the MP for Ilford South, found Joseph's words 'nauseating', addressed as they were to the 'children and grandchildren' of immigrants who had suffered at the hands of the Aliens Acts passed by a Conservative government at the turn of the century. His colleague, Ian Mikardo, drew a similar parallel and argued that 'a Jew, appealing to Jews in Sir Keith's terms, degrades himself, degrades the ethical traditions of the Jewish community and degrades the decent standards of British political behaviour'.[33] In an open letter to Joseph, Gerald Kaufman, a government minister and Manchester Labour MP, called the speech 'suicidal'. 'Do not imagine,' he wrote, 'that a culture campaign would stop short at this country's coloured population. Such a campaign has an irresistible momentum. We would be next – you, I, and every other Jew.'[34]

As the argument dragged on, Joseph, who had privately panicked at the hostile reaction to the speech,[35] hit back at his critics, charging the Board of Deputies with being 'left-wing dominated' and unrepresentative, and asking whether the subject of immigration was a taboo for all Jewish MPs or only those, such as himself, who did not agree with the views of the left.[36] Malcolm Rifkind, a fellow Jewish Tory MP, echoed this point, accusing Labour MPs of double-standards.[37]

It was, though, Jewish voters in Ilford North who would ultimately decide the argument. When the *Jewish Chronicle* went out onto the streets of the seat, it appeared to find few Jews willing to support Joseph. Voters labelled his speech 'totally disgusting', 'foolish and ridiculous', and 'derisive'. 'Keith Joseph has never been associated with the Jewish community,' suggested one, 'so how he has the gall to turn up periodically as the Tory Jew, I do not know.'[38] But the paper's letters pages showed opinion within the community to be more finely balanced. 'I believe we owe the people of this country a debt for admitting the aliens, who were our grandparents, in their hour of need,' wrote one reader. Parroting the language adopted by the *Daily Telegraph*, he continued: 'It is a strange way of repaying hospitality by inviting other guests. As the Talmud puts it, "One guest does not invite another".'[39] Another correspondent urged that immigrants 'be encouraged to pull themselves up by their own bootstraps, as the Jewish people here have done'. Those Jews lucky or skilled enough to make money had lent a helping hand to those less fortunate. 'No one ever asked for a penny from the public purse.'[40]

On 2 March, voters in the outer London seat delivered their verdict. Iremonger's presence turned out to be inconsequential: the Tories easily overturned Labour's 778 majority, capturing the seat by 4,497 votes. At just under 7 per cent, the swing to the Tories was not as high as the Conservatives, by now eleven points ahead in the opinion polls, had hoped for, and lower than some Labour MPs feared it might be.[41] Similarly, the National Front's performance was not as strong as it had wished for, but it had polled over 2,000 votes and come close to pushing the Liberals into fourth place. Mrs Thatcher's talk of Britons being 'swamped' had, moreover, appeared to have registered. An ITN poll indicated that immigration had been crucial to her party's victory: almost half of those who switched from Labour to the Tories said they had done so on the basis of the issue.[42]

In the immediate aftermath of the by-election, some suggested that Mrs Thatcher's immigration rhetoric and Joseph's play for the 'Jewish vote' had been ill-judged. The *Jewish Chronicle* commented that Jewish voters in the seat seemed to have been 'deterred rather than attracted by the Conservative emphasis on coloured immigration', while *The Times*'s Fred Emery reported: 'Mrs Thatcher's remarks about preserving "British" culture certainly offended some Jews I met more than she or Sir Keith Joseph or his lieutenant, Mr Alfred Sherman, seem to imagine.'[43]

But these snap analyses proved incorrect. In fact, as Sherman had publicly predicted in advance of the vote, and polling by Geoffrey Alderman later revealed, the most remarkable aspect of the result appeared to be the surge in support for the Conservatives among Ilford North's Jews.[44] Thus, while the overall swing to the Tories was 6.9 per cent, it was 11.2 per cent among Jewish voters.[45] What Alderman termed the 'ethnic differential' – the difference between the actual result and Jewish support for each candidate – was nearly nine points, and it continued to grow over the next year. The swing to the Tories between Millie Miller's narrow victory in October 1974 and the 1979 general election was 7.8 per cent, but it was 12.4 per cent among Jewish voters.[46]

Five years later, on reading about Alderman's recently published polling, a self-satisfied Sherman sent Mrs Thatcher a note. 'Keith's intervention won us the by-election.' 'I feel vindicated,' he concluded.[47]

In fact, Sherman did not await the vindication of Alderman's research. Three weeks after the by-election he wrote to Richard Ryder, the head of Mrs Thatcher's private office. In an attached memo labelled 'highly confidential' and entitled 'The Jewish Dimension', he advocated a renewed effort to 'end the quasi-monopoly enjoyed by Labour and Liberal [*sic*] of Jewish support'. Joseph's Ilford speech – 'the first shot across the bows' – had sparked opposition, but the feedback Sherman claimed to have received was positive. Now was the time for 'second and third strikes'.

One such strike was, of course, the Conservative Jewish Advisory Committee Sherman had suggested three months previously. This, he wrote, could be capable of 'mobilising substantial financial and human resources for the Party'. There could be, Sherman claimed with characteristic exaggeration, 'something of the order of hundreds of millions a year in new Jewish money for party', as well as 'dozens of first-rate intellectuals in universities, publishing etc and political aid'. The Tories needed to break the left's hold on Jewish communal organisations and publications by encouraging greater participation by 'our people' as well as better organising those who were already involved. But, he suggested, his initiative had hit opposition, not least from the 'vested interests' of the recently formed Conservative Friends of Israel (CFI). But, despite the inevitable 'tactical problems', he concluded, the task of winning Jewish support for the Tories 'cannot be shirked'.[48]

Ultimately, like those of Samuel Landman, Sherman's grand designs would come to nothing; frustrated, perhaps, by his own party's 'vested interests' but also by a feeling, that with the creation of CFI, Mrs Thatcher's own high sensitivity to Jewish concerns and Joseph's prominence it was already doing 'more or less enough' on this score.[49] However, as Ilford had proved, stripped of its occasional propensity to paranoia, Sherman's underlying analysis of shifting attitudes on the part of many Jews, and the opportunities this presented to Mrs Thatcher, was largely correct. While it was not the case that either immigration or Joseph's intervention alone had won the Ilford by-election, they had clearly struck a chord with a significant segment of the constituency's Jewish voters. More importantly, the result would also indicate the appeal that 'common ground' populism might have to the kind of previously Labour-inclined, aspirational white working-class who would defect to Mrs Thatcher in the 1980s. It also symbolised the opening of a new chapter in the relationship between British Jewry and the Conservative Party: in their voting behaviour, Jews were becoming, as Joseph had suggested, just like everyone else, only more so.

Of course, as in the country at large, the issue of immigration was one which sharply divided the community. There was plenty of evidence of concern among many Jews about the rise in support for far-right parties at this time and some, though by no means all, blamed this phenomenon on immigration. 'To show sympathy to the Black community may be a principle but is this principle so pure and important that it is worth jeopardising the security of the Jewish public?' asked the *Jewish Tribune*, which was widely read in north London's ultra-Orthodox communities.[50]

Moreover, although many Jewish Labour MPs were heavily involved in the fight for the first race relations legislation in the 1960s and the Board of Deputies had condemned Enoch Powell's speech in 1968, Sherman was correct in identifying a strain of thinking in the community which bridled at the suggestion that the situation of Jews and blacks was comparable and warranted a common response. There were occasional indications – sometimes brutally expressed – of such sentiments. In 1977, for instance, a Conservative local election candidate and synagogue teacher reportedly told a meeting of Edgware Conservatives that immigration had to be stopped and Britain could 'no longer be the "dustbin" of the world'.[51] David Sassoon, the head teacher of the Jewish Hillel House school, wrote to the *Jewish Chronicle* in response to Joseph's speech lamenting the fact that he heard Jewish parents – 'who only a couple of generations ago were themselves immigrants' – refusing to 'send their children to this or that school simply on the grounds that they don't want their children to mix with those of coloured immigrants'.[52]

But Jewish attitudes towards immigration were complex as Dr Yona Ginzberg discovered when she conducted a study of fifty elderly Jewish residents in Hackney.[53] Many of them blamed the area's decline on black immigration. 'I hate to say it,' suggested one, 'but when coloured people come to a place the area goes down.' The Hackney Jews suggested local blacks were responsible for rising crime and violence, and disapproved of their family lives. Despite what Ginzberg termed 'a general empathy to the black immigrants based upon mutual experience' of prejudice, there was also bitter resentment about welfare payments. 'The Jews were also immigrants,' argued an interviewee, 'but they didn't ask for anything when they came. The blacks come here and get welfare cheques.' Nonetheless, wrote Ginzberg, while some of their sentiments occasionally seemed to parrot those of the National Front, their animosity toward the far-right was evident. Any reference to the National Front, indeed, 'evoked strong emotional reactions' and comparisons with the battles against the blackshirts in the 1930s. As Ginzberg concluded: 'Although in many respects their reactions to blacks were similar to that of non-Jewish inner-city residents, they felt uneasy about their own anti-black sentiments.'

Support for the National Front among Jews in areas like Hackney was, unsurprisingly, well below the local average.[54] The Board of Deputies, the Chief Rabbi and the Association of Jewish Ex-Servicemen all repeatedly called on Jews to turn out and vote both in local elections and in May 1979, explicitly linking this to the danger posed by the high number of National Front candidates standing.[55] However, as Lord Fisher, the president of the Board of Deputies, outlined in response to Joseph's speech, while it campaigned against race discrimination, 'we do not campaign against restraint in immigration'.[56]

The appeal of Mrs Thatcher's Tory Party, evident among Jewish voters in Ilford North, was driven, as it was for many other Britons, by issues beyond concerns about immigration.[57] What was clear, moreover, was that the by-election result was by no means unique.[58] In local elections two months later in both inner and outer London boroughs, 'Jewish' wards were more likely to return Conservative councillors.[59] In May 1979's general election, inner-city and heavily Labour Hackney and Stoke Newington saw Jews more likely to vote Conservative and less likely to vote Labour than voters across the constituency as a whole.[60] In suburban Finchley, a similar pattern emerged. Mrs Thatcher won the support of nearly 56 per cent of Jewish voters, against barely 30 per cent of Jewish voters who backed Labour. As in Hackney, the Tory vote among Jews was higher, and the Labour vote lower, than among all voters in the seat.[61]

The growing presence of Jews on the Tory benches at Westminster was another sign of the increasing warmth between the party and the community. The lopsided imbalance between the number of Jews elected to parliament for the Conservatives and Labour in the twenty-five years after the Second World War – there were only two Jewish Tory MPs during this period versus, at its peak in 1966, thirty-eight Jewish Labour MPs – did not accurately reflect Jewish sympathies in the country as a whole.[62] Most Jewish MPs were not, after all, elected to represent seats with a large Jewish population.[63] Nor was there anything monolithic about the manner in which Jewish MPs voted in parliament, even on conscience issues, such as capital punishment, which are not subject to the whip.[64]

It was, however, telling that the number of Jewish Tory MPs during the 1980s outstripped the number of Jewish Labour MPs. In each of the elections between February 1974 and 1992, more Jews were elected as Tory MPs than had ever been the case before (the highest level had been nine in 1924). In 1983, the year of Mrs Thatcher's greatest landslide, seventeen Jewish Tory MPs were elected, the largest contingent ever. That number fell by one in 1987, but this was also the year in which, despite Labour improving its overall electoral performance from the nadir of 1983, the number of Jewish Labour MPs fell to its lowest level since 1935.[65] The number of Jewish candidates for each party was also revealing: twenty-five Tories, twenty-one for the Alliance and only fifteen (down from twenty in 1983) for Labour.[66]

This shift preceded Margaret Thatcher's election as Tory leader, and it continued apace both before and after she arrived in Downing Street. The 'Jewish vote' in Britain is nowhere near as homogeneous as in the United States, where Jewish support for the Democrats in presidential elections has, with the exception of 1980, ranged between 60 and 90 per cent of the vote. Thus, even at the height of her election-winning streak, large numbers of British Jews rejected Mrs Thatcher and all that she stood for.

However, as Alderman's polling indicated, in north-east and north-west London Jewish electoral behaviour was different to that of other voters in these areas: almost always, Jews were more likely to vote Conservative and less likely to vote Labour.[67] In two of the most heavily Jewish areas of London – Barnet in the north-west of the capital and Redbridge in the north-east – somewhere between a half and two-thirds of Jewish voters backed the Tories.[68] Mrs Thatcher's own constituency, Finchley, was proof of this. In 1987, her overall share of the vote in the seat increased by nearly 3 per cent; among Jewish voters, however, it rose by nearly three times that amount to just over 60 per cent. Overall, she suffered a swing of 1 per cent against her, but the swing towards her among Jewish voters was 5 per cent.[69] There was thus a certain symbolism to the defection to the Tories of Finchley's one-time 'Mr Liberal', Frank Davis, who was elected a Barnet councillor towards the end of Mrs Thatcher's tenure in Downing Street.

As was already apparent when Mrs Thatcher first entered parliament in 1959, some of this trend both was long-term and reflected the demographics of the Jewish community. In London – home to two-thirds of Britain's Jews – but also in cities with significant Jewish populations, such as Manchester and Leeds, the move to the Tory-leaning suburbs, which was underway by the interwar and immediate post-war years, continued. Two-thirds of Jews once lived in the East End; by the mid-1970s, that figure had dropped to one-quarter, with over 70 per cent living in outer London.[70] This reflected the fact that more Jews had joined the ranks of the middle classes. A survey conducted in Redbridge around the time of the Ilford North by-election found that 70 per cent of Jews (as against 50 per cent of economically active males in the borough as whole) were members of the top two profession-al, managerial and skilled non-manual social classes. Over-representation of Jews in these socio-economic groups was evident not only throughout Greater London, but in other parts of the country, too.[71] Jews were also much more likely to be self-employed and to own their own homes: in Red-bridge, the borough which contained Ilford North, 90 per cent of Jews were owner-occupiers.[72]

As Barry Kosmin suggested, therefore, 'by any socio-economic criteria British Jewry in the 1970s should have been oriented towards the Conserv-ative Party'.[73] But, even allowing for this, Mrs Thatcher's Tories appeared to have a special attraction for many of the nation's Jews, with Jewish voters leaning more heavily towards the Conservative Party than voters in the top social classes as a whole. Thus while she won the backing of 60 per cent of Finchley's Jews in 1987, Mrs Thatcher's support among middle-class ABC1 voters was six points lower at 54 per cent.[74]

Mrs Thatcher's Jewish opponents were contemptuous of these develop-ments. 'The essence of Thatcherism is selfishness and self-seeking,' Gerald Kaufman, Labour's shadow Home Secretary suggested on the eve of the 1987 election. 'But the whole ethos of Judaism is that you don't just care about yourself. I'm horrified that there are Jews who are so seduced by the materialistic philosophy in this country that they should forget what really being a Jew is all about.' Nor did Kaufman, later a virulent critic of the Jewish state, believe Israel's security was safe in Mrs Thatcher's hands. 'How any Jew can have faith in the Conservative Party when it was the Heath Government that cut off the flow of arms to Israel when the Yom Kippur War broke out, I don't know,' he charged.[75] Others were even more scathing of what Kaufman's fellow Jewish Labour MP, Leo Abse, termed 'yuppie Jews' for whom 'the only battles that can command their attention are the takeover struggles of the company boardroom'. Most of these voters, he derisively noted, had reached North London from the East End, abandoned their grandparents' sense of principle and instead were 'possessed of a vulgar materialism' – they yearned for 'BMWs, minks, diamonds, cruises, or holidays in Cannes, Florida or Bali' – and shared the Prime Minister's 'sickly pious celebration of the work ethic'. Their charitable giving was simply to salve their consciences, freeing them from the commitment to societal change their grandparents had fought for.[76] It was not, perhaps, a description likely to charm wavering Jewish voters, although it exemplified the left's wider ill-disguised distaste for the country it sought to govern.

Suburban middle-class homeowners were at the heart of the electoral coalition which brought Margaret Thatcher three consecutive general election victories in the 1980s. But for Britain's Jews, something else had changed, too. The Conservative Party had, even in the first decades after the war, seemed somewhat inhospitable to many of them. By the time Ted Heath became Prime Minister in 1970, old suspicions had lessened: in the election which brought him to power, the number of Jewish Tory MPs quadrupled (from an admittedly low threshold) to nine – the highest level in four decades. Heath's business-friendly, meritocratic managerialism was a world away from the patrician Conservatism – with its waft of exclusivity – of his predecessors.

However, in Heath's last months in office his government's handling of the Yom Kippur War had outraged many Jews. Assuming the party's leadership eighteen months later, Margaret Thatcher was perhaps uniquely placed to repair the damage. In opposition, she had done much to do so. But the real test would come once she entered Downing Street. From the outset, she would have the invaluable assistance of the Labour Party.

CHAPTER 6

DAVID BECOMES GOLIATH: HOW THE LEFT TURNED ON ISRAEL

A middle-class profession and a home in suburbia may have opened the door to more Jews voting Conservative, but, for many others, there was a strong feeling that the Labour Party was slamming it hard behind them.

Alone, 'moving up and moving out'[1] did not necessarily equate to the adoption of new political allegiances. The children and grandchildren of the huddled East European masses who arrived on America's shores in the late nineteenth and early twentieth centuries became faithful members of Franklin D. Roosevelt's New Deal coalition and then joined the ranks of the American middle classes in the post-war years. But, unlike Anglo-Jewry, America's Jews did not then go on to desert the left, instead remaining, alongside African-Americans, one of the Democratic party's most loyal constituencies.[2] This American exceptionalism reflected, in part, the fact that the Democrats did not join in the hostility to Israel which became fashionable among sections of the Western left in the 1970s.

The same, though, could not be said for the Labour Party. Instead, Harold Wilson's defence of 'democratic socialist' Israel in October 1973 – and the marked drop in Tory support in many heavily Jewish areas in February 1974 – turned out to be the last hurrah of Labour Zionism, at least until the emergence of New Labour two decades later.

The steadfast support for Israel much of the left had previously displayed had, in fact, already begun to splinter six years previously.[3] In the wake of the Six Day War, perceptions of the Jewish state began to shift. In the eyes of the youthful activists of the New Left, who were already engaged in battling the Vietnam War and the South African apartheid regime, Israel was now viewed less as the plucky socialist underdog, surrounded by reactionary Arab states set on its annihilation, but instead as an imperialist 'occupier' of the lands of the stateless Palestinian people. Thus, as Joshua Muravchik wrote, 'David had become Goliath.'[4]

Some of the change in attitudes simply reflected the passing of time. A generation whose views were forged by the battles against fascism and the horror of the Holocaust, and who marvelled at the social democrats who made the deserts of Israel bloom, was being supplanted by one for whom the struggles against colonialism had been formative in their youth.[5] With the launch of *Free Palestine* magazine in 1968, the Palestine Solidarity Campaign in 1969 and the British Anti-Zionist Organisation in 1975, left-wing activism on behalf of the Palestinians and against Israel finally found its voice. It would grow louder and, arguably, more extreme over time.

Of course, for most Jews in Britain, as around the world, it was Israel – threatened, once again, with destruction by its neighbours – which had emerged from the 1967 war as the true heir to David. By this point, the young state had already become, in the words of the historian Robert Wistrich, 'an undeniable core of Jewish identity, cohesion and continuity in the post-war world'.[6]

An early taste of how these tensions might play out was provided by the assault upon Israel from within the ranks of the party with which many Jews – including those living in Mrs Thatcher's Finchley – had historically felt some affinity, the Liberal Party. While the party's leader, Jeremy Thorpe, was, like his predecessor Jo Grimond, a strong supporter of Israel, the Young Liberals placed themselves at the vanguard of anti-Israel, pro-Palestinian activism with near-fatal results for Jewish support for the Liberal Party.[7]

The Young Liberals' hostility towards Israel was epitomised by its chair, the party's parliamentary candidate for Hackney Central, Louis Eaks. Not content with deploying incendiary language about the conflict – he accused Israel of 'brutal atrocities against humanity' and compared it to both Nazi Germany and the apartheid regime in South Africa – Eaks provoked further anger by suggesting that 'Jews see themselves as a master race'.[8] At their annual conference in March 1970, the Young Liberals passed a motion which, in line with the policy of the PLO's political wing, Fatah, called for Israel's replacement with a 'secular Palestinian state'.[9] The following month, Eaks further embarrassed the party leadership by praising the PLO and calling for the destruction of Israel at a time when Thorpe was receiving a fraternal visit from Moshe Kol, a leading Israeli Liberal.[10]

As we have seen, the behaviour of Eaks and his Young Liberal comrades, dubbed the 'Red Guard' by the press, had led Frank Davis to quit the Liberal Party. It was shortly after this that Max Beloff resigned, too. Thorpe attempted to repair the damage, apologising for the fact that the 'foolish and offensive words of a few inexperienced and unrepresentative people ... should have wounded the feelings of the Jewish Community'.[11] The following year, a special commission established by Thorpe charged that the Young Liberals' attacks on Israel – 'in terms totally at variance with the policy of the party' – had been calculated to upset Jewish voters and had done so.[12] The words largely fell on deaf ears. One of Eaks's successors as chair and later president of the Young Liberals, Peter Hain, invited PLO representatives to attend a fringe meeting at the party's annual conference and called for 'radicals and the Left wing in Britain' to fight for the Palestinian cause.[13] From his new home in the Labour Party, Davis accused the Liberal Party leadership of 'lack[ing] the guts to kick the Hainites out'.[14]

At the same time, the defection to the Liberals of the fiercely anti-Israel Labour MP and former defence minister, Christopher Mayhew, in July 1974 also unsettled many Jewish Liberals. Both Mrs Thatcher's Liberal opponent in the two 1974 elections, Laurence Brass, and his fellow candidate in Hendon South, Michael Colne, suggested that it had alienated potential Jewish supporters, while Hendon North saw Jewish support for the Liberals fall much more sharply than among voters as a whole between the February and October elections.[15] Thus polling indicated that while, after February 1974, Jewish support for the Tories generally outstripped that of voters in the upper social classes, the Liberals did worse among Jews than they did with these middle-class voters as a whole.[16]

The activities of the Young Liberals was just one facet of a wider attack on Zionism – the Jewish people's right to self-determination – and Israel's very right to exist which began to surface in the 1970s. Zionism, argued Dave Rich, was presented as 'a racist, colonialist ideology, and Israel an illegitimate remnant of Western colonialism in the Middle East'.[17] Nowhere was the attack more virulent than on Britain's campuses. Its opening came in 1974 when the National Union of Students passed a resolution, aimed principally at the National Front, barring assistance to 'openly racist and fascist organisations' and calling for members of them to be prevented from speaking at universities 'by whatever means are necessary'. When the United Nations General Assembly passed its infamous resolution labelling Zionism 'a form of racism and racial discrimination' the following year, left-wing activists began to attempt to apply the NUS's 'no platform' policy to Zionist speakers and Jewish student groups which supported Israel.

In just two terms, students at more than twenty universities and colleges debated, and eleven passed, resolutions calling for the destruction of Israel, labelling Zionism as racism and offering support to the PLO. The atmosphere on some campuses where the resolutions were successful became toxic for many Jewish students: at York, the student union attempted to strike the Jewish Society from its register; at Salford, a 43-point 'indictment' declared that 'the South African fascists, the Zionists and fascists' shared a common belief in 'race superiority' and a rabbi was told by the student union president he could talk about the differences between Judaism and Zionism 'but not about the links'; and at the University College of Wales, Swansea, the student newspaper warned of the 'Zionists' plot to conquer the world'. The unholy alliance between hard left and far right was evident when the National Front began distributing anti-Semitic leaflets praising the York and Salford student unions.[18]

While the leadership of the NUS sought to end such activities and the Federation of Conservative Students, Union of Liberal Students, National Organisation of Labour Students and Communist Students Committee issued a joint statement condemning all attempts to ban Zionism from student unions, anti-Zionism had already begun to seep into the wider body politic. The shift in attitudes was evidenced by the increasing, at best disenchantment with, or, at worst, hostility towards, Israel in the pages of those stalwart house journals of the British left, *The Guardian*[19] and the *New Statesman.*

The anti-Zionist histrionics of the Young Liberals and Trotskyite students were to prove, however, simply the curtain-raiser for those of the Labour left – behaviour which would have far greater significance for Mrs Thatcher's relationship with Britain's Jews. The schism between Labour and large sections of British Jewry was all the greater because of the warmth which had existed under the party's hitherto most electorally successful leader, Harold Wilson. His philo-Semitism had helped to repair much of the damage done to the party's reputation among Jews by the Attlee government's handling of the creation of the state of Israel and the Suez crisis (see Chapter 2). In many ways, Wilson's relationship with, and admiration for, the community was akin to that of Mrs Thatcher. As his biographer, Philip Ziegler, facetiously suggested, the Labour leader was 'abnormally free of racial prejudice except in so far as it was a racial prejudice to find Jews generally more attractive than the rest of mankind'.[20]

Like Mrs Thatcher's, Wilson's 'court' was a welcoming one for Jews. The lawyer Arnold Goodman was a close confidant and political adviser. The economists Thomas Balogh and Nicholas Kaldor, who Denis Healey nicknamed the 'terrible twins from Hungary',[21] helped shape Wilson's economic thinking, while the journalist Geoffrey Goodman was brought in to head the No. 10 counter-inflation unit in the mid-1970s. Wilson had long been close to George Weidenfeld, who had published the new MP's first book in 1945: he would go on to publish many of his others.

Early in his political career, Wilson had also forged close bonds with a number of Jewish businessmen, such as Tom Montague Meyer of the timber merchants Montague Meyer, the commodity trader Harry Kissin, industrialist Frank Schon, and, most controversially, the raincoat manufacturer Joseph Kagan. On occasion, such as with Kagan, there were mutual financial interests at stake, but these relationships were much more than transactional. Many of these self-made men, who had fled their homes in Central and Eastern Europe in order to escape the Nazis, continued to see Labour as their natural political home. With good reason, they viewed the Tory Party and the business establishment which supported it with suspicion. In return, like Mrs Thatcher, Wilson was drawn to those who he saw as fellow outsiders. Like her, too, he admired the energies of the immigrant entrepreneur, contrasting it favourably with the complacent conservatism which plagued British corporate life.

Over the years, Wilson sent many of his Jewish friends and advisers to the House of Lords. His controversial resignation honours list in 1976 was to include not just Kagan, Weidenfeld and Schon, but also the media proprietor Lew Grade and his brother the theatre impresario Bernard Delfont. Wilson's political secretary, Marcia Falkender, believed that much of the criticism which accompanied it was simply ill-concealed anti-Semitism.[22]

Wilson's staunch support for Israel was in many ways at odds with the rest of his famously pragmatic political persona. As the left-wing, but strongly Zionist Labour MP, Ian Mikardo, later commented: 'I don't think Harold … [had] any doctrinal beliefs at all. Except for one, which I find utterly incomprehensible, which is his devotion to the cause of Israel.'[23] Wilson's sympathy for Israel and his determination to 'expiate Bevin's sins' was one that was shared by leading Labour politicians of the 1960s and 1970s such as Richard Crossman, Ted Short and Barbara Castle.[24] In both 1967 and 1973 Wilson had angrily slapped down those in his own party who did not share his determination to stand with the imperilled Jewish state in its hour of need. In part, his attitude towards Israel was, as Falkender suggested, 'a romantic one', seeing as he did the fledgling state as 'a wonderful experiment in socialist politics'.[25]

But, perhaps like Mrs Thatcher's philo-Semitism, it also reflected their shared non-conformist upbringing. In *The Chariot of Israel*, Wilson's post-premiership work on the tangled history of the Jewish state's creation, he noted the strong public support for Israel on both sides of the Atlantic. He attributed it in part to admiration for the 'courage and tenacity of the Israelis'. But, he continued, as in his own case, it also stemmed from 'the teaching of religious history in our day schools and Sunday schools, chapels, churches, kirk and conventicles'.[26] He may have been less openly confronta-tional than Mrs Thatcher, but Wilson was also no less concerned about the plight of Soviet Jewry. Using his close contacts with the Soviet leadership, he tried to improve their lot, and win exit visas for those who wished to leave.[27]

It was not, though, simply Wilson's evident warmth towards the commu-nity or his approach towards Israel or Soviet Jewry which ensured the support of many British Jews. 'Growing up in the 1960s it was natural to assume that anybody with a social conscience supported Labour,' wrote Stephen Brook in his account of modern Anglo-Jewry. 'Jews of my age were attracted almost en masse to the ... Labour Party, largely because of its enlightened views on social matters.'[28]

Not only were Jews such as Joel Barnett, Edmund Dell, John Diamond, Gerald Kaufman, Harold Lever and John and Sam Silkin prominent on the government benches of the Wilson-Callaghan governments, but, from the party's backbenches, they were also at the forefront of pushing the liberal reforms which were to be their legacy. Sidney Silverman led the campaign to abolish capital punishment, while Leo Abse was a major player in that to decriminalise homosexuality and change the law on illegitimacy. For Abse, this was no accident. 'I could address ... those issues to do with family rela-tionships because I wasn't burdened by the Christian view, which would tend to accept existing laws, nor was I burdened by the ghetto Orthodoxy,' he later suggested. 'The confident sense of identity which comes from belonging to an older culture meant that you were not intimidated by the prevailing ambience.'[29]

While Wilson and his successor, James Callaghan, held Labour's reins, the party remained largely immune from anti-Zionism. In June 1975, the Labour Middle East Council, which had been formed by Mayhew six years previously, launched a renewed bid to bring about what it called 'a revision of Labour's pro-Zionist attitude' and to free the party from 'Zionist infiltration'. But at the time LMEC had just twenty-six supporters in the parliamentary party; one quarter of the strength of Labour Friends of Israel.[30]

However, ten years after the 1967 war began to alter the contours of the left's relationship with Israel, and a year after Wilson had left office for the final time, the election of the Jewish state's first right-wing government was to herald the onset of new tensions. The image of Israel as an experiment in the building of socialism – symbolised by the kibbutzim – was replaced by that of Menachem Begin. Despite the signing of the Camp David Accords, the face of Israel which Begin presented to the world – his commitment to Eretz Israel, the expansion of settlements in the occupied territories and, perhaps most controversially of all, the invasion of Lebanon in 1982 – was wholly unattractive to many on the left. Begin's policies led to deep divisions within Israel and among Jews around the world. But, for many British Jews, the left's concern for the plight of the Palestinian underdog, which many indeed shared, also contained some altogether more unsettling undercurrents.

This noxious mix was captured by Paul Rose, a Jewish former Labour MP, shortly after the party's defeat in 1979. There had been, wrote Rose, a 'slow but discernible erosion of sympathy with Israel' in the party during the fifteen years he had sat in parliament.[31] Some of this, he recognised, was an understandable reaction to the election of an Israeli government which many viewed as one of 'religious zealots and narrow nationalists' and its 'blinkered and self-destructive' attitude towards the aspirations of the Palestinians. But, Rose argued, much of the declining support for Israel had deeper roots: namely, his party's growing 'identification with the Third World' and Arab nationalism which had served to cast Israel in a 'quasi-imperialist role'. Rose may have been correct about the 'slow but discernible' decline in support for Israel, but his conclusion that it would be 'wrong to exaggerate the move-ment of opinion' was to prove misplaced.

The hard left, which Wilson and Callaghan had variously sought to both ignore and contain, burst forth after Labour's defeat: using the power it had stealthily amassed at the grassroots level to attempt to seize control of the party nationally. Labour's lurch to the left in the early 1980s extended well beyond the arena of foreign policy in general and Israel in particular. Given the overwhelmingly middle-class nature of the Jewish electorate, the party's new-found radicalism would anyway have alienated many Jews who had previously supported it, as it did with millions of other Britons. Such a development had been predicted by Milton Friedman nearly a decade before. In a 1972 lecture to the Mont Pelerin Society, he had puzzled over why Jews – who had 'seldom benefited from governmental intervention' – had historically been drawn to the left. But, with the memory of Senator George McGovern's presidential candidacy fresh in his mind, Friedman noted the manner in which the Democratic standard-bearer's left-wing economic agenda had produced a strong reaction among many Jews. They had realised, Friedman suggested, that it 'would greatly hamper the upward social and economic mobility of which they had been great beneficiaries'.[32]

A comparable sentiment no doubt took its toll on Jewish support for a Labour Party similarly intent on electoral suicide. But, for many of Britain's Jews, Labour's unattractiveness was compounded by the fact that virulent opposition to Israel had become one of the hallmarks of the hard left, while attacks on the Jewish state became the mainstay of debates in many local parties. For the new generation of young activists who were reshaping Labour's identity, support for the Palestinian cause, wrote Rich, was 'a natural fit with their broader anti-American sentiment and anti-racist politics'.[33]

The first signs of the strains which would soon threaten to destroy the once close bond between Jews and the Labour Party came just a month after Mrs Thatcher became Prime Minister, when the Labour Party in Hackney North and Stoke Newington – a constituency with a historically large but now much-depleted Jewish population – passed resolutions in two successive years declaring their opposition to the 'Zionist State of Israel', endorsing the 'struggle of the Palestinian people for the liberation of their homeland'

and seeking recognition of the PLO. Arthur Super, the Jewish former mayor of Hackney, declared that the founders of the Hackney North and Stoke Newington Labour Party would 'turn in their graves' at the actions of a 'small, but virulent, anti-Semitic element'.[34] The resolution provoked anger in Hackney's Jewish community and resignations from the local party, and was bitterly attacked by Stanley Clinton-Davis, a former minister and the MP for neighbouring Hackney Central.[35] In response, at a meeting of the Hackney Council for Racial Equality, Rudy Narayan, a black barrister and Lambeth Labour Party activist, labelled Clinton-Davis a 'racist'.[36] Narayan's very presence was controversial. Three years previously, he had claimed that British Jews had 'learnt only too well from Adolph [sic] Hitler', controlling not just business but the media and politics where 'their infiltration has been secret and overwhelming'.[37] By 1981, attempts to oust Clinton-Davis and replace him with a hard-left Hackney councillor were under way.[38]

The rows in Hackney were, however, to be simply the opening salvo in a ferocious anti-Zionist campaign within the Labour Party. The tensions between the Jewish community and Labour in some parts of London became intense. As the hard left attempted to wrest control of the party in Brent, for instance, John Lebor, the former leader of the council and a member of National Executive of Labour Friends of Israel, was – alongside seven other moderate councillors – deselected as a candidate for the May 1982 local elections.[39] As a result, in Jewish areas of the borough, support for Labour fell by almost twice the amount as elsewhere.[40] At the other end of the country, a young Scottish Labour activist, George Galloway, encouraged Dundee City Council to fly the Palestinian flag from the town hall and twin the city with Nablus. And at Labour's 1981 conference, only one resolution on the Middle East was submitted by constituency parties – a call by East Dumbartonshire CLP to effectively disband the Jewish state and instead 'pursue the creation of a newly constituted and democratic multi-racial State of Palestine in which all Palestinian Arabs and all citizens of the present State of Israel would be full members'.[41]

Israel's invasion of Lebanon in 1982 and the massacre at the Sabra and

Shatila refugee camps – carried out by Lebanese Christians but for which Israeli forces bore indirect responsibility – raised the temperature still further. The Labour Party's annual conference passed resolutions (including one proposed by the hard-left leader of Lambeth council, Ted Knight) recognising the PLO and endorsing the establishment of 'a democratic secular State' – words that were widely viewed as challenging Israel's right to exist.[42] The 'extremist formulations from constituency parties', noted the *Jewish Chronicle*, had 'ugly implications'.[43]

Delegates at the TUC conference overruled the leadership and – for the first time ever – overwhelmingly passed a motion attacking Israel. One major union, the Transport and General Workers' Union, urged an air and sea boycott of the Jewish state.[44] At the grassroots, the attacks on Israel were, if anything, even more violent. At a meeting of the Paddington Constituency Labour Party, loud applause greeted the remarks of a local councillor who argued that Israel – a 'racist, theocratic state' – had 'no right to exist' and had come about because of the world's 'guilty conscience' about the Holocaust.[45] Even from the party's front bench, inflammatory language was to be heard: the most senior figure on the party's right, the shadow Foreign Secretary Denis Healey, suggesting that until the Palestinians had their own homeland, they would 'like the Jews in an earlier diaspora … be subject to persecution and pogrom'.[46]

The controversial 1982 conference resolutions did not gain the two-thirds majority needed to become party policy. By the time of the general election, Labour had scrambled to repair the damage, ditching references to the PLO and the proposed 'secular democratic state', and backing a two-state solution.[47] Nonetheless, the row rumbled on and the harm had been done: just before Mrs Thatcher fired the starting gun on the general election campaign, sixty Labour candidates and thirty-nine sitting MPs signed a statement which 'warmly welcomed' the stand taken by delegates at the previous year's conference.[48] On election day, Philip Kleinman, a columnist for the *Jewish Chronicle* and a Labour Party member, wrote a piece for the *London Evening Standard* saying that, thanks to his local Labour candidate's continuing support for a conference motion which effectively called for 'the destruction of Israel', he would be voting Social Democratic Party (SDP). Jeremy Corbyn nonetheless won Islington North comfortably.[49]

However, as they would continue to do for the next three decades, it was the actions and pronouncements of Ken Livingstone which would probably do most to sour relations between Labour and the Jewish community. Having unseated the Labour group's moderate leader, Andrew McIntosh, the day after the party won control of County Hall in 1981, Livingstone's five-year leadership of the Greater London Council (GLC) provoked anger in the community and dismay among Jewish Labour supporters. Moreover, even after Mrs Thatcher abolished the GLC in 1986 (a policy which, Geoffrey Alderman believed, got her 'a great deal of Jewish applause'),[50] Livingstone's legacy – and his continuing presence in London Labour politics – would tarnish the party's reputation among Jews and non-Jews alike long after Neil Kinnock had begun to haul Labour back to the centre-ground.

Livingstone appeared to embody all that many Jews feared and disliked most about the hard left. In 1982, for instance, the newspaper of which he was an editor, the *Labour Herald*, published a cartoon of Menachem Begin dressed in a Gestapo uniform amid the skulls and corpses of Palestinians with the caption 'The Final Solution'. Such a caricature was straight out of the pages of Soviet anti-Israeli propaganda[51] and the Board of Deputies attempted, unsuccessfully, to persuade the Attorney General to prosecute under the Race Relations Act. Nor was this an isolated incident. Elsewhere in its pages, Israel was labelled 'a State entirely built on the blood of Europe's Jews, whom the Zionists deserted in their hour of greatest need'.[52]

Two years later, Livingstone caused further uproar when, in an interview with the Israeli magazine *Davar*, he suggested that the Board of Deputies has been 'taken over by Jews who hold extreme right-wing views' and offered the bizarre pronouncement that Jews 'have been organising here in London, and throughout Britain, into paramilitary groups which resemble fascist organisations'.[53] The GLC Labour group went into open revolt against its leader, passing a resolution demanding Livingstone withdraw these 'outrageous accusations'.[54]

The *Jewish Chronicle* suggested that Livingstone's characterisation of Anglo-Jewry was 'a gift to antisemites' and warned that his 'sweeping vilification of the community at large' threatened to make 'Labour-supporting movements "judenrein"'. The party, it argued, should be alert to the 'negative impact he is having on what has not been an unimportant segment of its Metropolitan support and vote', and called on 'a few more powerful voices' among its leaders to distance themselves from Livingstone's 'distorted opinions'.[55]

It was not only Livingstone's words, however, which angered much of the community. In 1984, the GLC's 'Anti-Racist Year' swiftly descended into a platform for the hard left to attack Israel. The council's Ethnic Minorities Unit, for instance, provided a grant to the Palestine Solidarity Campaign (a far-left organisation which worked to replace Israel with a 'democratic secular state') to hold a conference on 'Anti-Arab Racism', with the chairman of the Arts and Recreation Committee explaining that 'since the philosophy of Zionism has been condemned along with apartheid by the United Nations as racist, it is perfectly in order to place Palestinian solidarity on this anti-racist platform'.[56] At a public meeting where Livingstone was present, Laurence Brass, Mrs Thatcher's opponent in 1974 and now a member of the Board of Deputies, labelled it 'a conference of hate' which had caused great offence to the Jewish community.[57]

As Geoffrey Alderman argued, the events of 1984 'marked a watershed of devastating dimensions' in the relationship between London's Labour Party and the capital's Jewish citizens.[58] Shortly afterwards, Gerry Ross resigned as the Labour assistant chief whip on the GLC in protest at the 'long line of attacks made against the Jewish people' by Livingstone.[59] By October 1985 relations between the community and Livingstone were, in fact, so bad that an attempt to organise a lunch to celebrate the Jewish contribution to London was abandoned when both the Chief Rabbi, the planned guest of honour, and the Board of Deputies indicated that they would not attend if the GLC leader was also present.[60]

Under Neil Kinnock's leadership, Labour made efforts to reassure the Jewish community. At its 1983 conference, the party's new deputy leader,

Roy Hattersley, acknowledged the 'creeping antisemitism operating in the Labour Party'[61] and shortly after pledged that Labour's 'affection for the State of Israel will be maintained'.[62] Warm words were matched by action to rid Labour of hard-left entryists, thus quietening the anti-Zionist rhetoric and allowing a more balanced position on the conflict between Israel and the Palestinians.

Kinnock strove to avoid a repetition of the events of 1982. Motions on the Middle East did not figure in debates on the party's conference floor again until the outbreak of the Intifada in late 1987 made them impossible to resist.[63] In 1985, the party's National Executive Committee, on which moderates had mounted a fightback against the hard left, rejected a proposal that representatives of the PLO be invited to attend its annual conference in Bournemouth.[64] It subsequently rejected the pro-Palestinian resolutions passed by the party's 1988 and 1989 conferences and ditched Labour's previous commitment to Palestinian statehood in favour of a vaguer-sounding promise to support a 'homeland'. Hard-left resolutions proposed by Tony Benn and Ken Livingstone were overwhelmingly defeated.[65] Kinnock himself attended LFI events and developed links with Israeli politicians such as Shimon Peres. Reflecting his wider strategy towards modernising the party, Kinnock attempted to drive a wedge between the pro-Palestinian soft left, which nonetheless accepted Israel's right to exist, and an anti-Zionist hard left which did not. Unlike Livingtone's GLC, whose interest in highlighting victims of human rights abuses never extended to Soviet Jewry, Kinnock publicly aligned himself with the plight of the refuseniks and took up individual cases with the Soviet leadership.[66]

However, the tide of hard-left anti-Zionism was only slowly turned. Two years after Hattersley's pledge, Labour's general secretary, Larry Whitty, was forced to condemn local moves to disaffiliate Poale Zion, the Jewish socialist society affiliated to the Labour Party, and admit that 'in some areas of the party, any apparent support for Israel gets attacked and there is a dangerous spillover from legitimate criticism into anti-Zionism, which in some cases comes pretty close to antisemitism'.[67] Thus Labour's efforts at reassurance were constantly undermined and drowned out by new instances of hard-left grassroots' anti-Zionism, each of which was dutifully reported in the Jewish media. In June 1985, for instance, Valerie Cocks, the director of Labour Friends of Israel, proposed a motion at the party's women's conference congratulating Israel on 'Operation Moses', its recent airlift of thousands of Ethiopian Jews from their famine-ravaged homes. It was overwhelmingly defeated, as delegates chose to protest instead at Israel's alleged 'massacre' of Palestinians.[68] Moreover, in Gerald Kaufman, Kinnock opted for a foreign affairs spokesman after 1987 who increasingly provoked the ire of many of his fellow Jews. His book *Inside the Promised Land* charted Kaufman's increasingly hostile attitude towards the policies of the Jewish state, an attitude which was evident in some of his strikingly anti-Israel rhetoric.[69]

Crucially, the abolition of the GLC failed to remove Livingstone's long shadow from the London Labour Party. Instead, it now fell on Brent East, the constituency which the GLC leader coveted as his route into Westminster politics. Blocking that path was the seat's long-serving MP, Reg Freeson. The grandson of Jewish immigrants who had fled the Russian pogroms of the 1890s, Freeson was elected to Parliament in 1964, avenging the defeat of Maurice Orbach five years previously and helping to provide Harold Wilson with his wafer-thin parliamentary majority. Freeson was no right-winger: after entering parliament, he had attacked his own government over Vietnam, South Africa and immigration. However, Freeson was also a committed Zionist and co-chair of Poale Zion. In 1983, there was an attempt to displace him in favour of Livingstone. The minister of Willesden Synagogue, Rabbi Dr Harry Rabinowicz, stepped into the row, pleading with the local Labour Party not to adopt Livingstone: 'To remain silent in the face of evil,' he suggested, 'is to abdicate one's moral responsibilities.'[70] Freeson, a vocal critic of the GLC leader, survived on that occasion, but in 1985 he eventually abandoned his uphill struggle to fend off deselection. 'It was a lot of other things, but there was a bit of "Jew-boy" mixed in it,' he said of his ousting. His public support for Israel, he argued, meant that some had branded him 'that bloody Zionist and Jew'.[71]

Livingstone's difficult relationship with the Jewish community inevitably intruded into the 1987 general election campaign. Some Tories harboured hopes that the tensions between local Jews and the new Labour candidate might, as they had done in 1959 when the seat was called Willesden East, allow them to pull off a surprise win. Harriet Crawley, Livingstone's Conservative opponent, boldly proclaimed: 'If I were Jewish, over my dead body would I vote for Livingstone. It would be a total betrayal of being Jewish in the most fundamental sense.'[72] Many Jews felt the same way: Daniel Finkelstein, the SDP–Liberal Alliance's Jewish candidate in the seat, believed that Livingstone had a polarising effect. 'There's a genuine aversion to him among Jewish people,' he argued, 'even among those of quite solidly Labour persuasion, because of his record and reputation on Israel and the community.'[73] Livingstone managed to hold on, although that aversion – shared by Jews and non-Jews alike – saw Freeson's 1983 majority slashed.

Remnants of the traditional bonds between Jews and the Labour Party, however, survived both inside and outside parliament; a symbol of the hostility many Jews felt to Mrs Thatcher and her government. At the 1979 general election, nearly twice as many Jews were elected as Labour MPs than were elected to sit on the Tory benches. They included the president of the Board of Deputies during the early 1980s, Greville Janner. Nor were Jewish Labour MPs staked out solely on the party's beleaguered right fringe. Among both veteran MPs, such as Ian Mikardo, Frank Allaun, John Silkin, and Renée Short, as well as newcomers such as Harry Cohen and Mildred Gordon (Mikardo's replacement in Bow and Poplar whom Fleet Street christened 'the biggest red menace this side of the Urals')[74] there were some whose sympathies were very much on the left. But Jewish Labour parliamentarians were a diminishing breed. In 1983 the number of Jewish Labour MPs fell to eleven, while seventeen Jewish Tories were elected. Prominent among the Jewish Labour MPs leaving the Commons were Joel Barnett, the former Chief Secretary to the Treasury who had been a sharp critic of Tony Benn and found himself the victim of boundary changes in 1983; Sam Silkin, Harold Wilson's Attorney General; and Stanley Clinton Davis who, like Barnett, found himself without a constituency when the number of Hackney seats was reduced. In 1987, alongside Freeson, his fellow co-chair of Poale Zion, Maurice Miller, and the veteran Zionist, Mikardo, also left the House of Commons.

Elsewhere, a Jewish Labour presence in London local government was maintained. That tradition was encapsulated by Ellis Hillman. Hillman hailed from a famed rabbinic family – his uncle, Dr Isaac Herzog, was Chief Rabbi of Ireland, Palestine and later Israel, father of former Israeli President Chaim Herzog and grandfather of the current leader of the Israeli Labor Party, Isaac Herzog – and spent thirty-five years in London local government on the London County Council and later the GLC. 'He greeted everyone with "shalom" as if they were on the set of Fiddler on the Roof', his fellow GLC Labour councillor, Illtyd Harrington, later recalled.[75] Although very much on the Labour left, he was written off by the Livingstone new left. Geoffrey Alderman recalled his close friend being 'horrified' by the GLC leader, of whom he became a fierce critic.[76] After standing down he became a councillor in Mrs Thatcher's home turf of Barnet. Less than four years after she left office, he became the authority's first ever Labour mayor. One of his first acts was to remove a bust of the former Prime Minister from the town hall.

A new generation of young Jewish Labour activists who would enter parliament in the 1990s was also beginning to emerge. In 1982, Margaret Hodge became leader of Islington Council, a post she would hold for the next decade, before entering parliament in 1994 and later serving as a minister under Tony Blair and Gordon Brown. Louise Ellman became leader of Lancashire County Council in 1981, standing down upon her election to parliament sixteen years later. Ivan Lewis and Fabian Hamilton served as Labour councillors during the Thatcher years, while Gillian Merron worked as a union official. Barbara Roche, who, like Mrs Merron, would go on to serve as a minister in the Blair government, stood unsuccessfully for Labour in a parliamentary by-election in 1984 and again in 1987, before being elected to Hornsey and Wood Green in 1992. And, perhaps most important of all in terms of the effort to restore Labour's electoral fortunes, Peter Mandelson, a young TV producer whose father had been advertising manager for the *Jewish Chronicle*, was appointed the party's director of communications in 1985.

While many Jews within the Labour Party fought the hard-left takeover, others were ranged on the side of those attempting to storm the moderates' citadels.

Jon Lansman, who was raised in what he described as a 'typical Orthodox family' in north London and spent time on a kibbutz in the Negev, was the youthful driving force behind Tony Benn's near-successful attempt to oust Denis Healey from the party's deputy leadership in 1981.[77] During the campaign, Lansman developed a reputation as a highly capable tactician and masterful organiser. Lansman narrowly lost that battle, although he avenged the loss thirty-four years later when he steered Jeremy Corbyn to victory in the 2015 Labour leadership election.

There were also Jews associated with the hard left who opposed anti-Zionism and were wary of its anti-Semitic undertones. Linda Bellos was emblematic of the new left 'rainbow politics' which dominated London Labour during Mrs Thatcher's time in power. A radical feminist and vocal gay rights activist, Ms Bellos led Lambeth Council in the mid-1980s, clashed with the party leadership over black representation and was reviled by sections of the press – 'Loony Linda' as *The Sun* labelled her.[78] Nonetheless, she resigned as a member of the collective which produced the women's magazine *Spare Rib* after it published a fierce attack on Israel during the Lebanon War headlined 'Women Speak Out Against Zionism' and then refused to print letters from readers questioning the article's thinly veiled anti-Semitism.[79]

Labour's lurch to the left in the early 1980s might have provided an opening for the newly formed SDP to woo left-leaning Jews. Certainly, the SDP managed to attract a number of prominent Jewish Labour defectors, including the MPs David Ginsburg, Edward Lyons (who sat on the new party's National Committee) and Neville Sanderson, as well as the publisher George Weidenfeld, former Cabinet ministers John Diamond and Edmund Dell, and the Cambridge economist Richard Kahn.[80] Another Jewish member of the last Labour government, Harold Lever, was sympathetic and did not join only because he believed it improper after he had accepted a peerage from Callaghan.[81] In 1985, Eric Moonman, a senior vice-president of the Board of Deputies and former Labour MP, also joined the party.[82]

Within four months of the party's launch, an SDP Friends of Israel had been formed with Weidenfeld as its chair and one of the 'Gang of Four' – Bill Rodgers – as its president.[83] Another of the quartet, the former Labour Foreign Secretary, David Owen, promised that the SDP would be 'zealous in the preservation of the State of Israel'.[84] One of the few prominent Conservative parliamentarians to defect, the Duke of Devonshire, was a former president of the Conservative Friends of Israel.[85]

With controversy around Israel stoked by the war in Lebanon, the party made a conscious effort, in contrast to Labour, not to fan the flames. 'The SDP does not want to be known as a party of contention,' reported the *Jewish Chronicle* after witnessing a notably civil debate on Israel at its 1982 conference.[86] Nonetheless, Owen, its foreign affairs spokesman, at times appeared to adopt a more pro-Israeli stance than Mrs Thatcher's government, criticising, for instance, her Foreign Secretary for talking about a Palestinian state without outlining some of the conditions – such as demilitarisation – its creation would need to meet.[87]

The SDP managed to attract the support of some younger Jews who considered themselves on the left but found the Labour Party of the 1980s unpalatable. Sue Slipman, who came from a working-class Jewish family and had been a member of the Communist Party, was president of the National Union of Students in 1977 at the height of the rows over anti-Zionism and anti-Semitism on campuses. Four years later, she joined the SDP, a party committed, she believed, to 'thinking through effective strategies to improve social justice in a way that was economically viable'.[88] Twice an unsuccessful parliamentary candidate for the party, in 1983, she fought Basildon where Moonman had been defeated four years previously. Alongside the barrister Anthony Lester, who had been a special adviser to the former Labour Cabinet minister and now SDP leader, Roy Jenkins, and the then minister of the South London Liberal Synagogue, Rabbi Julia Neuberger, Ms Slipman was one of three Jews to sit on the committee of the SDP's think tank, the Tawney Society.[89] A member of the SDP's National Committee, Rabbi Neuberger was one of the 100 signatories of the party's prototype manifesto and contested Tooting for the SDP in 1983.

Finkelstein, who fought Livingstone in Brent in 1987, joined Labour while he was still at school. Delivering leaflets for the party during a local election campaign, however, he found some SDP leaflets stuck in a letter box. He fished them out, intending to throw them away, but, having read them instead, promptly joined the new party.[90] He rose quickly through its ranks. Two years after the SDP's launch, Finkelstein became chair of the Young Social Democrats. He went on to become a political adviser to Owen and a member of the party's National Committee. At LSE, Finkelstein had witnessed the politics of the hard left up close, and didn't much like what he saw. His family's history – his mother, Mirjam Wiener, survived Belsen, while his father, Ludwik, escaped from a Soviet prisoner of war camp in Siberia – had left Finkelstein with 'quite bland, moderate politics'. 'It's not for nothing that I identify with the politics of Pinner,' he later argued. Having followed Owen into the political wilderness, Finkelstein later joined his mentor in endorsing the Conservatives in the 1992 general election, overcoming his sense that 'the Tory Party was not a hospitable place for an immigrant family'. He later became an adviser to John Major and his successor, William Hague, before being elevated to the House of Lords by David Cameron.[91]

But despite its superficial appeal – the Alliance fielded more Jewish candidates in 1987 than Labour[92] – the SDP's ability to attract the support of significant numbers of Jewish voters was hobbled by the party's decision to form an alliance with the Liberals. 'It damned them,' believed Alderman.[93] The party's problem was succinctly captured by one *Jewish Chronicle* reader who wrote to the paper's letters page soon after the SDP's launch to ask sceptically whether its attitude towards Israel would be 'modelled on the Liberal Party pattern'.[94] Whatever the warm words of its leadership and the civility of its debates, the SDP could not escape the fact that it was the junior partner of a party which, over the previous decade, had come to be viewed by many

Jews as riddled with anti-Israeli sentiment and thus 'virtually non-kosher'.[95] That image was hardly helped when, in 1985, the Liberal leader David Steel resigned from the Liberal Friends of Israel, leading its executive to brand his views on the Middle East 'totally unacceptable and counter to mainstream Liberal thinking in the UK, as well as internationally'.[96] As even his deputy, Alan Beith, recognised Steel was seen as 'leaning towards the Arab view of the Middle East'; he was, indeed, the only party leader to have been willing to meet Yasser Arafat. Thus, for many Jews, calls by Beith – himself a long-standing member of the Liberal Friends of Israel – to rebuild the old ties between the community and the Liberal Party rather fell on deaf ears.[97]

• • •

Like their fellow Britons, many Jews found that the politics of 1980s presented only unpalatable choices: a Labour Party which had moved so far to the left as to strain the loyalties of even many of its traditional supporters, and a centre-ground alternative which was never quite able to convince. But the support Mrs Thatcher attracted was not simply based upon fear or dislike of what else was on offer. Outside Finchley – where her agent asserted that while there was not a specific Jewish vote, 'if there was, it would be for Mrs Thatcher' – other Conservative candidates believed the Prime Minister had a positive appeal.[98] In Hendon South, John Marshall – who in 1987 picked up the Tory baton from the former Cabinet minister, Peter Thomas – suggested that, faced with wavering Jewish voters, he would play up what he called the 'Thatcher factor'.[99] In places, Tory campaigns even came with the imprint of rabbinical approval: as he had done for the first time in 1974, Saul Amias signed John Gorst's nomination papers in Hendon North, while the disgraced former Tory Party chair, Cecil Parkinson, was supported by Alan Plancey, the rabbi at Elstree and Borehamwood (who later became the chair of the Rabbinical Council of the United Synagogue).[100] Perhaps more significantly, by 1987, Mrs Thatcher's revolution appeared to have received the very public backing of Sir Immanuel Jakobovits. The following year, the

Prime Minister would return the compliment sending, for the first time ever, a Chief Rabbi to the House of Lords. The 'milieu' of the Conservative Party which, a decade before, Alfred Sherman had suggested many Jews still found unsympathetic, had undergone a dramatic transformation.

CHAPTER 7

COMRADES IN ARMS: JEWS AND THE THATCHER REVOLUTION

'The number of Jews in her Cabinet?' responded Sir Keith Joseph, 'I don't suppose it ever crosses her mind. I don't know what you're talking about.' When the *Sunday Telegraph* treated its readers to a double-page examination of the relationship between 'the Jews and Mrs Thatcher' in December 1988, the reactions of some of those featured in it to the questions posed by the piece's author (himself Jewish) betrayed the sensitivity of the subject. His religion, protested Mrs Thatcher's Scottish Secretary, Malcolm Rifkind, was simply 'supremely irrelevant'.[1]

But the newspaper's attempt to discover whether a 'peculiarly Jewish flavour' could be detected in 'the affairs of state' was neither malicious nor without interest. Nearly a decade earlier Joseph had been the sole Jewish Cabinet minister in Mrs Thatcher's first government.[2] But by early 1986, nearly one-quarter of the Prime Minister's Cabinet colleagues were Jewish. Alongside Joseph and Rifkind, sat Nigel Lawson, Leon Brittan and Lord Young. It was, as Rifkind suggested thirty years later, 'an extraordinary moment' – albeit a short-lived one: within five months, both Brittan and Joseph had left the government.[3] In her final year in office, by which time Lawson and Young had also departed, Mrs Thatcher appointed the sixth Jew who would serve in her Cabinets, Michael Howard.

While 'extraordinary', Rifkind believed that the moment was also no more than a 'historical aberration, a coincidence'.[4] Lawson, who confessed himself puzzled by the focus on the topic, agreed, believing that it reflected only the fact that Mrs Thatcher displayed 'not the faintest trace of anti-Semitism'. Although he conceded that this, in itself, was an 'unusual attribute'.[5]

Lack of prejudice is, though, not the whole explanation. Chaim Bermant's suggestion that Mrs Thatcher had 'a mystical belief in Jewish abilities' was somewhat of an exaggeration,[6] but the former Prime Minister, discussing her Jewish members of staff and Cabinet, indicated an appreciation for Jewish talent. 'I just wanted a Cabinet of clever, energetic people,' she wrote, 'and frequently that turned out to be the same thing.'[7] Although Howard later wondered if the Prime Minister even knew he was Jewish,[8] Mrs Thatcher was not unaware that the number of Jews at her top table was a topic of comment. In 1985, for instance, her (Jewish) chief of staff, David Wolfson, wrote a memorandum to her on the impending reshuffle, noting in passing that there were 'already enough Jewish members' of the Cabinet.[9]

If the number of Jews in her governments was a historical aberration it was not without historical significance. Throughout the entire post-war period until Mrs Thatcher's accession to power, Joseph had been the only Jew to sit in a Conservative Cabinet. By contrast, Clement Attlee, Harold Wilson and Jim Callaghan's Labour governments had a number of prominent Jewish ministers, including Manny Shinwell, Lewis Silkin, Joel Barnett, John Diamond, Edmund Dell, Sam Silkin, John Silkin, Gerald Kaufman and Harold Lever. However, as we have seen, demographic changes within the Jewish community, Labour's drift towards anti-Zionism and the more meritocratic bent of the Conservative Party, begun under Ted Heath and accelerated by Mrs Thatcher, increased dramatically the number of Jews voting Conservative and sitting on the party's benches in parliament. Mrs Thatcher's Cabinets were thus a reflection of an important shift. As Stephen Sherbourne, Mrs Thatcher's political secretary, who himself is Jewish, suggested shortly after leaving Downing Street: 'The Jews have changed and so has the Conservative Party.'[10]

Perhaps more importantly, in her effort to change the Conservative Party,

Mrs Thatcher would find allies among the now growing ranks of Jewish Conservatives. Joseph, Alfred Sherman and Norman Strauss had been at her side during the battles of opposition. During those of government, Jewish Tories would also play a prominent role. The bond was a natural one and one that was shared with Tories who came from a working-class background who were not Jews, such as Norman Tebbit and Cecil Parkinson. They were similarly attracted by Mrs Thatcher's evident aversion to the exclusive and exclusionary 'grousemoor' Toryism of the past. Moreover, while many of the young Jewish MPs who Mrs Thatcher recruited to her crusade shared her free-market ideology and antipathy towards traditional Tory paternalism, they also had few ties to the Conservative Establishment that she was seeking to overturn.

None of that meant, as the political columnist Alan Watkins claimed in 1984, that Jews were not only 'welcome in the modern Conservative Party, but seem actively to be preferred' by the Prime Minister.[11] Both during her premiership and, indeed, later, the suggestion that Mrs Thatcher's government was dominated by what one of her former ministers, Peter Rees, termed a 'freemasonry' of Jews, exposed a lingering anti-Semitism in some dark corners of the Conservative Party and the Establishment.[12] This was not confined to the political right. The journalist Geoffrey Goodman, for instance, was astounded to have a senior liberal-minded figure in Whitehall suggest to him that Mrs Thatcher's decision 'to surround herself with Jews' reflected 'an odd sense of judgment'.[13]

Such anti-Semitism bubbled to the surface most obviously at the time of the Westland affair in 1986 when, as the Thatcherite minister Alan Clark noted in his diaries, Tory backbenchers discussed whether there were 'too many Jewboys' in the Cabinet.[14] Brittan was not the only target. When there were rumours of Lawson moving from the Treasury to become Foreign Secretary, Clark recorded some Tory MPs questioning whether a Jew could serve in the post.[15]

Edwina Currie, one of the few prominent women in Mrs Thatcher's governments, proved another object of such talk. Born Edwina Cohen, Mrs

Currie renounced her religion when her Orthodox parents disowned her after she married out, while maintaining that she remained 'culturally and genetically' Jewish.[16] Appointed a junior health minister in 1986, her forthright right-wing populism guaranteed a high media profile, the jealousy of many of her colleagues and the disdain of the left. Her tendency to shoot from the lips brought an abrupt end to her ministerial career when she was forced to resign in 1988 after claiming that most of the country's eggs were infected with salmonella.

While few disputed that Mrs Currie was the victim of her own outspokenness, some Tories admitted that, in the words of former MP Anna McCurley, 'the fact that Edwina's a woman and the fact that she's a Jew ... brought out the antagonism of some people in the House'. Mrs McCurley claimed to have heard colleagues refer to Mrs Currie as 'a pushy Jewess', while Melinda Libby, a political adviser to one Cabinet minister, argued that the Tory backbenches were 'riddled with prejudices of every kind' including anti-Semitism. Such prejudices, she said, 'don't emerge unless things are going badly for someone', but when they did, 'they'll pick on anything'.[17] Mrs Currie later acknowledged that she had encountered many instances of anti-Semitism while in parliament. She simply chose to ignore them, she said.[18]

Nor were these necessarily isolated incidents. 'I saw and heard plenty of anti-Semitism in Tory circles in my time as a Member of Parliament,' recalled Michael Latham, a Jewish Conservative MP throughout Mrs Thatcher's time as Prime Minister.[19] His former colleague, Julian Critchley, concurred. The Tory Party, he suggested, was not 'necessarily anti-semitic, simply because it's not a big issue, but if you scratch them you'll find that many of them are anti-semitic'.[20]

Such talk naturally led to a certain wariness on the part of Jewish Cabinet ministers. Asked in an interview to mark his retirement in 1987 about the growth in the number of Jews on the Tory benches during his three decades in parliament – a development which might have occasioned some pride, not least in the woman on whose watch the greatest advances had occurred – Joseph simply responded: 'I wouldn't have any comments at all on that.' Since stepping down as Education Secretary, he continued, he was freer to 'take part as a private citizen in things where my participation might have been misunderstood while I was a minister'. Surprisingly, given the government's stance on the former and the uncontentiousness of the latter, he gave as examples his presence at a demonstration in support of Soviet Jewry and attendance at a Holocaust Day remembrance.[21] In fact, on the rare occasion Joseph was called upon as a minister to involve himself directly in issues which might be said to have a Jewish 'interest' – in 1973 over the Yom Kippur War or when he ruled as Education Secretary against granting voluntary aided status to the Yesodey Hatorah Primary School for Girls in Stamford Hill – his actions provoked the anger of many Jews.[22] Similarly, Lord Young – who noted the 'gratuitous code' by which the media often referred to him as 'the son of Lithuanian parents' – chose not to visit Israel while he was a Cabinet minister. 'I deliberately didn't go because it would have been misinterpreted,' he later explained. 'I'm an Englishman and a Jew, but I didn't want people saying "where do his loyalties lie, here or Israel?"'[23]

There was no 'Jewish coterie' around Mrs Thatcher, as some maliciously suggested, nor was there anything monolithic about 'Mrs Thatcher's Jews' or, as we will discover, their relationships with the Prime Minister. However, from No. 10 insiders – like her chief of staff David Wolfson and political secretary Stephen Sherbourne – to those who sat in her Cabinets to rather more unorthodox characters like Alfred Sherman and David Hart, each of the Jews who served Mrs Thatcher contributed to the story of the longest premiership in modern British history.

David Wolfson: The tough-talking confidant

When Margaret Thatcher moved into No. 10 in May 1979, David Wolfson swiftly nabbed the best piece of real estate in Downing Street: the office next to the Prime Minister's study. For the next six years, as Nigel Lawson sarcastically remarked, Wolfson 'gloried in the title of "Chief of Staff"'.[24] To Kenneth Stowe, her new principal private secretary, Mrs Thatcher regally introduced Wolfson as 'my Pug Ismay' – a reference to Winston Churchill's wartime chief military assistant.[25] Many found his precise role in No. 10 difficult to discern. His title, according to one Downing Street civil servant, seemed 'honorific rather than effective'.[26] Lady Thatcher herself simply suggested that she wanted him to bring his 'charm and business experience on the problems of running No.10'.[27] Wolfson provided little more by way of clarity: his job, he later said, was 'to be aware of the few things that mattered and to make sure that she saw the right people at the right time'.[28]

Wolfson's experience of high-level politics was hardly extensive. His knowledge of direct mail from the family firm, Great Universal Stores, meant that Wolfson had initially been brought into Mrs Thatcher's office after she became Tory leader to help bring some order to the chaos of sorting her huge daily postbag.[29] Coming to appreciate his contacts, insights into the views of business and ability to smooth 'ruffled political feathers', Mrs Thatcher then asked Wolfson to join her team full-time.[30]

In Downing Street, some viewed Wolfson as but an agreeable companion with whom the Prime Minister could swap gossip.[31] Certainly, the Wolfsons and Thatchers, who sometimes holidayed together in Cornwall, enjoyed each other's company. Wolfson's personal assistant, Cynthia Crawford, would also become Mrs Thatcher's personal aide and confidante. 'Crawfie' remained at Lady Thatcher's side for the rest of her life.

But while it is true that her chief of staff's influence waned over time – after her re-election in 1983 the relationship between the two appeared to be based principally on past sentiment – Wolfson's significance in the battles of the early years of her premiership should not be underestimated. Norman Strauss, the brains behind Stepping Stones, who was appointed to the No. 10 Policy Unit after the Tory victory in May 1979, remembered Wolfson as 'a smooth, urbane gentleman with many administrative and organisational skills'. Charming and discreet, Wolfson was 'a wise diplomat when required to be'.[32] Most notably Wolfson, alongside the head of her Policy Unit, John Hoskyns, Strauss, and her economic adviser, Alan Walters, played a significant role in stiffening the Prime Minister's Thatcherite sinews ahead of the critical 1981 Budget.[33]

Wolfson's diplomacy did not, though, eschew plain speaking. Alongside Hoskyns and Ronnie Millar, her favourite speechwriter, he co-authored what became known as the 'blockbuster memorandum'. Ostensibly concerned with her political survival, it accused the Prime Minister of breaking 'every rule of good man-management' and of bullying weaker colleagues.[34] A furious Mrs Thatcher labelled the trio the 'Westwell Three'; a reference to Wolfson's Oxfordshire country home.[35] While the memorandum appeared to have little impact on Mrs Thatcher's management style, she accepted much of its political advice, carrying out the radical reshuffle which purged the Cabinet's 'wets' and brought in rising Thatcherite stars such as Tebbit and Lawson. Perhaps only her husband was able to speak to Mrs Thatcher in the manner that Wolfson did. Writing of an incident during the 1987 election when, as she berated an unfortunate Cabinet colleague, he snapped at her: 'Just shut up and read the bloody brief', Lady Thatcher acknowledged that Wolfson was 'one of the few people who gets away with this sort of thing'.[36] She did not hold a grudge. For, among other things, his willingness to speak truth to power, Mrs Thatcher made Wolfson a peer in her resignation honours' list.

Keith Joseph: The uncertain revolutionary

If Keith Joseph was an improbable revolutionary in opposition, he was an uncertain one in government. Steadfastly loyal to Mrs Thatcher, he nonetheless struggled at times to practise the principles that together they had preached.

Arriving in Downing Street, the new Prime Minister honoured the pledge that Willie Whitelaw had extracted from her in 1975 not to make Joseph Chancellor of the Exchequer.[37] In her memoirs, Lady Thatcher confessed that while she had no doubts about her old mentor's 'unshakeable' commitment to the course they were about to embark upon, she worried that his sensitivity and compassion might be ill-suited to the 'cruel hurly-burly of political life which Chancellors above all must endure'.[38] Despite this concern, however, she dispatched him to the department which, perhaps more than any other, was on the frontlines of the Thatcher revolution. As Industry Secretary, Joseph would be charged with tackling the inefficiencies and over-manning which afflicted Britain's giant nationalised industries.

It was a task to which Joseph was ideologically committed: he issued his civil servants with a reading list of twenty-nine free-market tracts;[39] admitted to the Confederation of British Industry that he did not think his department should exist;[40] and, when asked by an enquiring Cabinet colleague for a brief on his industrial strategy, replied that no such strategy existed.[41] When the government faced its first major confrontation with the trade unions – a strike by steelworkers in early 1980 – Joseph showed the courage of his convictions and refused to intervene.

But Mrs Thatcher was often disappointed in Joseph's performance. 'Really, Keith!' she scribbled on a submission from the Industry Secretary when he recommended continuing a subsidy promised by Labour to one company.[42] Such recommendations were not uncommon. The root of the problem was that Joseph was emotionally ill-suited to his department's work. 'Constantly regaled with tales of woe from industrialists and pleas to be baled [*sic*] out from the state-owned industries,' recalled Jim Prior, a leading Cabinet 'wet', the 'decent, soft-hearted' Joseph found his task 'unbearably difficult'.[43] For the journalist David Lipsey, the Cabinet minister's evident discomfort stemmed 'from a very Jewish sense of personal guilt which makes him absurdly hard on himself'.[44]

Joseph's struggle to reconcile his principles, economic necessity and his instinctive compassion was most graphically demonstrated when the ailing nationalised car manufacturer, British Leyland, requested a further huge infusion of government cash. Paralysed by indecision, Joseph performed several about-faces on the issue before giving in, later reflecting that he 'didn't have the conviction and moral courage' to refuse the bail-out.[45] At the Centre for Policy Studies, an appalled Sherman turned a framed picture of Joseph to the wall.[46]

The gesture was unfair. As unemployment mounted and the government's popularity sank, Joseph proved one of the few voices around the Cabinet table to speak out vigorously in favour of staying the course. He showed, Lady Thatcher later suggested, 'unswerving loyalty' to the economic beliefs he had advanced in opposition. 'Keith never lost heart, never wavered'.[47] It was the highest praise she could offer.

That did not mean, however, that Joseph did not feel the lash of her tongue at times.[48] Joseph responded with a form of gallows humour. On his way to a meeting with the Prime Minister, he was asked by his civil servants whether he needed anything else. Yes, he replied, 'ambulances at three-thirty'.[49] Mrs Thatcher simply believed that 'Keith and I have no toes' – they were such intimates that, even when they argued, they could not offend one another.[50] More often, though, the Prime Minister exhibited strong maternal instincts towards her older colleague. Dispatching Tebbit to become a minister in Joseph's department, Mrs Thatcher told him: 'Norman, I want you to look after Keith – dear Keith, they are so unkind to him and he needs someone to protect him.'[51] Not all of their colleagues viewed the relationship as a healthy one. For Prior, Mrs Thatcher's behaviour towards Joseph was like that of 'a mother who cannot refrain from indulging a favourite son, even though she knows it will do him no good'.[52]

Joseph's unhappy spell as Industry Secretary came to an end in September 1981 when he asked Mrs Thatcher to move him to her old department, Education. At best, it was a sideways move, even if Lady Thatcher later portrayed it as part of an effort to tackle the 'anti-enterprise culture' at its roots.[53] While Joseph spoke warmly of 'my beloved Education Service', he was, once again, frequently buffeted between harsh political realities and his principles.[54] For critics on the left, his commitment to financial rigour meant that he frequently failed to defend the education budget against the Treasury, while his desire that pay should reflect performance meant that he was often at loggerheads with the teaching profession. For Mrs Thatcher and the right, however, Joseph's time at the department proved a wasted opportunity. At his first Tory Party conference as Education Secretary, he had initially raised their hopes, speaking of how he was 'intellectually attracted' to education vouchers as a way of increasing parental choice and driving up standards.

But the complexities of the policy soon overwhelmed him. Two years after marching it up the hill, Joseph marched the Tory Party conference back down again, declaring vouchers, 'at least in the foreseeable future, dead'.[55] In retirement, Joseph characteristically once again blamed his own lack of 'moral courage' for the failure.[56]

When, however, Joseph did display such 'moral courage' in 1984 by proposing that wealthier parents should pay more towards the cost of their children's university education, he found himself unsupported by the Prime Minister. Hitting the pockets of her supporters in middle England was not the kind of bravery she was keen to see her ministers display. Amid uproar on the Tory backbenches, Joseph was forced into a humiliating U-turn. He offered Mrs Thatcher his resignation. She told him not to be ridiculous.[57]

However, Joseph's days at the Education Department were now numbered. The following summer – knowing, she later claimed, that Joseph was contemplating retirement – the Prime Minister offered the job of Education Secretary to the Leader of the House of Lords, Lord Gowrie.[58] Her advisers were keen that she dispatch Joseph to the backbenches. Joseph was 'certainly the nicest person I have met in politics', Wolfson wrote to the Prime Minister. However, if judged by the same standards as other ministers, his 'relative lack of success in office' meant he should go.[59]

She knew that Wolfson was right. 'Dear old Keith is so much governed by his officials,' she confided to her chief journalistic cheerleader, *The Times* and *News of the World* columnist and former Labour MP Woodrow Wyatt. But even as the words left her lips, she reminded herself that Joseph was always 'absolutely reliable and solid'.[60] Thus had Gowrie accepted her offer, she planned to keep Joseph in the Cabinet as Minister without Portfolio.[61] As she well knew, his devotion to her meant that Joseph could always be guaranteed to guard her back when the political waters got rough. For Lawson, who was distantly related to Joseph through his first wife, Vanessa Salmon, the Education Secretary's sole 'profound personal loyalty' was to Mrs Thatcher, the woman he had come 'to admire and adore'.[62]

Joseph, however, was ready to go. Four months after he told his constituency association in January 1986 that he would not fight the next election, he resigned from the Cabinet. The traditional exchange of letters between the Prime Minister and the departing minister went beyond the rote formulations. Joseph's 'integrity, selflessness and thought for others are an example to us all,' she wrote. More than anyone else, he was the 'architect who, starting from first principles ... shaped the policies which led to victory in two elections'.[63] In her memoirs, in which she is frequently critical of her Cabinet colleagues, with the noticeable exception of Whitelaw, Young and Joseph, Lady Thatcher suggested that the departure of 'my oldest political ally and friend, indeed mentor, saddened me'. Joseph was 'irreplaceable ... politics would never be the same again'.[64]

Joseph's loyalty to Mrs Thatcher never faltered. He would write no memoirs lifting the lid on his unique relationship with her and no veiled public criticisms would cross his lips. He was appalled at Michael Heseltine's attempted 'counter-revolution' in November 1990.[65] Shortly after, he encountered the man he regarded as her political assassin. Joseph turned, remembered Sir Geoffrey Howe, 'courteously but firmly away from me', uttering the words: 'I'm sorry, Geoffrey: we're not friends anymore.'[66]

The martyrdom of Alfred Sherman

For Alfred Sherman, Mrs Thatcher and Joseph's outspoken fellow traveller on the long march to Downing Street, the Tories' victory in 1979 proved to be the end of the road. There was to be no post at No. 10 or job as a ministerial special adviser.

Instead, Sherman used his position at the Centre for Policy Studies to position himself as keeper of the revolutionary flame. As always, he turned frequently to ferreting out traitors. The 'Heathites', he warned Mrs Thatcher in early 1980, were 'on the rampage'. 'The animus against the Prime Minister and Keith Joseph on the part of some dissenters,' he reported, 'is so strong as to blind them to the possible consequences for the party and country of what they are doing.' Dissidents needed to be 'exposed' to their constituency associations in order to bring them back into line.[67] A few weeks later, Sherman warned Mrs Thatcher of the apparently baleful influence of the (unnamed) individual – 'violently hostile to the Prime Minister, vulgarly so when in his cups, which is not infrequent' – the Tories had overseeing parliamentary selections.[68]

Sherman was, moreover, ever-watchful for heresy. The government's first crack at the unions in 1980 was, he reported to her, 'worse than useless' (neither Joseph nor the Prime Minister were fans of Employment Secretary Jim Prior's cautious legislation, either),[69] while Howe's second Budget – of which she was rather more enamoured – was not cutting public spending fast enough. He quoted back Joseph's words from 1976 – 'cuts mean cuts, not cutting projected expenditure' – and then helpfully reminded Mrs Thatcher that they had appeared in a pamphlet 'which still carries your imprimatur'.[70] Her government, Sherman wrote Mrs Thatcher several months later, was 'continuing to follow British Socialist Keynesian policies'.[71] The Prime Minister did not appear to mind. 'Alfred's the leader of the awkward squad,' she told aides affectionately.[72] For Ferdinand Mount, who became the head of Mrs Thatcher's Policy Unit in the spring of 1982, it was clear that 'the whole point of Alfred was that he was horrible and licensed to be horrible', even if 'when he went around hissing that "Margaret is surrounded by enemies" in her cabinet, he was speaking nothing less than the truth'.[73]

Few, however, regarded Joseph as one of Mrs Thatcher's enemies. But it was his old comrade-in-arms for whom Sherman reserved a particular animus. Appalled by his decision to 'shore up the costly, failing nationalised British Leyland',[74] Sherman denounced the apostate to Mrs Thatcher. Reminding her of Joseph's record in Ted Heath's government when his department 'swallowed him up so completely that I virtually came to regard meeting him as a waste of time', Sherman cautioned that history was repeating itself. 'I wonder whether I should continue to lend intellectual respectability,' he pompously declared, 'to an enterprise which diametrically contravenes our aspirations'.[75] Nor did Sherman share his concerns only with the Prime Minister: a few months later, he was described in the media as Joseph's 'most virulent "dry" opponent'.[76]

For the time being, Sherman remained a member of the Thatcher court, albeit a semi-detached one. He continued to pen bloodcurdling denunciations of the left for her speeches. 'You made a brilliant contribution. I hope that you realise just how grateful I am,' Mrs Thatcher wrote him sweetly on one occasion.[77] She also found that threatening to call in 'Alfred' was an excellent spur to action for flagging speechwriters.[78] More significantly, Sherman was the driving force behind securing Alan Walters's appointment to the newly created post of Mrs Thatcher's economic adviser.[79] Much to his frustration, though, Sherman's insistence that 'if she were to convert her rhetoric into action', Mrs Thatcher needed to radically reshape the state was largely ignored.[80]

Sherman's departure from the CPS after the 1983 general election – 'I was summarily dismissed ... and blacklisted,' he over-dramatically recorded in his memoirs[81] – resulted in part from a power struggle at the think tank. Ironically, his nemesis was Hugh Thomas, one of the converts from the left Sherman had wooed during the opposition years who had subsequently become its chairman.[82] Thomas had proved less malleable in the role than Joseph and had tired of Sherman's frequent histrionics. 'In some ways he is a genius,' he suggested to Mrs Thatcher's trusted parliamentary aide, Ian Gow. 'But the essence of genius is that there are strange shadows in such a person's soul.'[83]

But the feud had its roots in the more fundamental issue of the nature of Thatcher's project. Sherman believed loyalty was owed to 'Thatcherism' rather than to the party or government Mrs Thatcher led. But his ill-disguised criticisms, sometimes of the Prime Minister herself, often reached the press. 'She has palpably failed to do what we told her,' an anonymous source – described as 'one of her advisers at the arch right-wing think tank the Centre for Policy Studies' – told the *Sunday Times* in May 1981. 'She has come under the influence of the layabouts and the landowners of the party. Her faith is cracking.'[84]

As the general election approached in 1983, Thomas demanded a period of public silence from Sherman and appealed to him to put the 'interests of the

Prime Minister & the party' first.[85] Threatening to resign, Sherman would have none of it: he knew Mrs Thatcher's mind and her best interests. 'Her view,' he wrote to Thomas, 'is that I should be free to express my views.'[86] 'Her view' was, perhaps, less clear-cut than Sherman claimed. On a copy of a memo drawn up by Sherman on the CPS's future, Mrs Thatcher scrawled her distinctive disapproving squiggled line under his suggestion that he be given 'a free hand in the formulation and presentation of policy' and should become 'responsible for the Centre's entire output'.[87] That, barely a month before she called a general election, the Prime Minister should have been concerning herself with his role indicated the special sensitivities around Sherman. 'She was very careful with him as if it was a family thing,' recounted one insider.'[88]

The brutal truth was that Sherman had outlasted his usefulness. When they were launching their insurrection against the 'layabouts and landowners' of the Tory Party in the 1970s or guarding against a counter-revolution in the bleak days of 1981, Sherman was required on the barricades, lobbing his verbal Molotov cocktails. But, with re-election now securing Mrs Thatcher's position, Sherman's rhetorical grenades were beginning to land a little too close to home. He had always been happiest fighting civil wars whether in Spain in 1936 or the 'London Spring' four decades later. But the Prime Minister had little desire to see her second-term raked by friendly fire, especially when dislike of Sherman ran so wide and deep.[89]

Mrs Thatcher tried to soften the blow: seeing Sherman occasionally at No. 10 at his request, awarding him a knighthood, even busying herself with his pension arrangements.[90] Privately, though, he was devastated by his fall from grace. He complained bitterly to Sherbourne about the 'de-Shermanization' of the CPS, but most of all he was perplexed by Mrs Thatcher's attitude. 'I still do not know what Her intentions were, or what information had been given to Her,' he wrote, but he remained 'haunted by the question of whether I could have played my cards better'.[91]

Publicly, he presented himself as a Thatcherite martyr. It was better, he argued in a lecture, for an adviser to face political death than 'to be drawn into competition in courtiership and sycophancy'.[92] He lashed out, too, at the presentation of his relationship with Mrs Thatcher as 'an amalgam of Pere Joseph, Svengali and the Elders of Zion'[93] and argued that the Tories had tired of thinking the unthinkable because 'a complacent government was starting to find [it] irksome'.[94] He became obsessed with the notion that he was being written out of the history of the Thatcher revolution he had helped to create – 'unpersonning', as he termed it.[95] In anger, he even took to saying of Mrs Thatcher: 'I virtually invented her.'[96]

Sherman's worst fears appeared to be realised when Lady Thatcher published the first volume of her memoirs in 1993. *The Downing Street Years* made one cursory reference to him. The damage was somewhat repaired by the second volume, *The Path to Power*, in which she commended Sherman's 'brilliance' and 'the force and clarity of his mind' and offered him due recognition for his role in the opposition years.[97] He, in turn, was rather more generous towards her in his 2005 account of the Thatcher years. 'In retrospect,' he wrote, 'I am bound to marvel at how much she achieved under the circumstances.'[98] Lady Thatcher attended the book's launch, declaring: 'We could never have defeated socialism if it hadn't been for Sir Alfred.'[99]

Radicals old and new: Norman Strauss and Oliver Letwin

By the time of the 1983 election, another of the Jewish advisers who had helped Mrs Thatcher reinvent the Conservative Party in opposition, Norman Strauss, had also left the Prime Minister's side. She had, according to Charles Moore, agreed to the appointment of the somewhat unorthodox Strauss to the Policy Unit in 1979 only on the basis that she never had to see him.[100] This apparent stipulation is rather belied by a brief examination of her appointments diary, but hints, perhaps, at the slight unease Strauss continued to instil in the Prime Minister several years after Sherman had recommended that he take John Hoskyns to his first meeting with her.

Like Hoskyns, Strauss was to find the experience of government a frustrating one. Their criticism – that Mrs Thatcher was too timid in her approach to both institutions and policies – in many ways echoed those of Sherman. By the time he left Downing Street in 1982, Strauss had 'almost written her off'.[101] He found the Prime Minister unwilling to radically reform Whitehall and bemoaned the fact that she was not strategic in her thinking. 'If you wanted to ... discuss strategy,' he recalled, 'she'd put it off as long as possible.'[102] She, in turn, had little interest in the management speak and systems analysis pressed on her by Strauss and Hoskyns.

Like Sherman, Strauss had little patience for the Establishment, whether it be the Tory old guard, or, especially, the civil service, which he viewed as elitist and hostile to profit and the men who made it. Highly unusually for a Prime Minister's adviser,[103] in September 1981 he appeared on *Newsnight* and attacked members of the Cabinet who had voiced public dissent about the government's economic strategy, singling out Foreign Secretary Francis Pym and the departing Tory Party chairman, Lord Thorneycroft, whose complacent comments 'all we can do is our best' had outraged the impatient Strauss.[104] Strauss's attack on the ministers was 'entirely justified', recorded Alan Walters in his diary, while wondering whether he could remain in post.[105] The following week, he appeared on the programme again and lashed out at 'civil service conservatism'.[106] But while Mrs Thatcher's private secretary, Clive Whitmore, warned him that 'after this week no minister will talk to you and after next week no civil servant, there does not seem much point in continuing', the Prime Minister herself never showed any sign of displeasure against Strauss's double-headed broadside.[107] No doubt, she shared some of his sentiments.

Strauss stayed on for a few more months. He departed No. 10 shortly after Hoskyns in 1982, feeling that far from being the revolutionary she presented herself as, Mrs Thatcher was 'an incremental pragmatist with convictions'.[108] 'When isolated with her back against the wall, with survival at stake she leads,' he said of his former boss two years after leaving Downing Street. 'When closeted in comfort, she merely follows.'[109]

• • •

Sherman and Strauss, the Jewish radicals of the opposition years who grew increasingly disenchanted with the timidity of their leader in government, had departed the Prime Minister's inner circle as she embarked upon her second term. But shortly after her triumphant re-election, Mrs Thatcher had a new Jewish adviser in her Policy Unit, Oliver Letwin, who was – if not always to the same degree – also prepared to 'think the unthinkable'.

Letwin was another of Joseph's discoveries. His parents, the American academics, Bill and Shirley Letwin, were friends of Joseph and had later helped Mrs Thatcher with speeches after she became Tory leader. While wearing his Jewishness 'lightly', in the words of one journalist, Letwin came from a long line of rabbis on his mother's side.[110] All four of his grandparents were Ukrainian Jews who fled Soviet persecution.[111] Oliver's childhood was rather more comfortable. The family's home near Regent's Park was 'ludicrously grand', as Letwin later put it,[112] with debates about politics, economics and philosophy echoing through the house. For Letwin, who was 'argumentative by instinct', this was to prove good training for working for Mrs Thatcher, who shared a similar trait.[113]

Formidably bright, Oliver won a scholarship to Eton, studied at Cambridge and became a visiting fellow at Princeton. He had not intended to go into politics, but the offer of a job from his parents' old friend, now the Secretary of State for Education, sounded like 'fun', he decided.[114] One of the areas Letwin was assigned to work on was school vouchers. Neither the complexities surrounding the policy, nor the seemingly endless stream of objections raised by officials, intimidated the young radical in the manner they did Joseph, so much so that when, after the 1983 general election, Letwin went to work for Mrs Thatcher's Policy Unit, he tried to give the issue another push.[115]

But it was as a foot soldier in another of the battles with the left, that against Labour local authorities, which opened up during Mrs Thatcher's second term in which Letwin was to make his mark. For Mrs Thatcher, the results were ultimately to prove politically fatal. As her government fought to rein in high-spending, left-wing local councils, Letwin became the Prime

Minister's principal adviser on local government. She placed, believed David Norgrove, a member of her Private Office, 'a surprising amount of trust' in the young man who had begun working for her government barely two years previously.[116]

Letwin's graphic reports provided Mrs Thatcher with a guide to the forces ranged against her government. From Sheffield, for instance, he reported on the 'extremely impressive ... machinery employed by the Marxists' and the manner in which the local trade unions were 'in the hands of Trotskyists'.[117] With their language of 'counter-attacks', 'one-sided disarmament' and 'revolution',[118] Letwin's memos girded Mrs Thatcher's loins for battle, appealed to her warrior instinct and encouraged her down the path of confrontation with the municipal left. 'The policy is brinkmanship,' he declared. 'It will require nerves of steel; but it stands a real chance of defeating most of the councils.'[119]

Politically, the town hall antics of the hard left were an electoral millstone around the Labour Party's neck. But, with Letwin's encouragement, Mrs Thatcher now waded further into the treacherous waters of local government finance. They would eventually overpower her and sweep her from office. Her 28-year-old adviser was not the father of the poll tax. An orphan by the time of its birth, there are many individuals to whom that label could be attached. Letwin's advice, though, strongly favoured the poll tax and on that advice, Mrs Thatcher made a decision which would come back to haunt her.[120] Get the government's proposals 'through Cabinet and out into the world as soon as possible', he urged her in late 1985, otherwise 'the rats will start nibbling'.[121] Five years later, though, as the newly introduced poll tax dragged down the Tories' popularity, it was Letwin's gung-ho attitude which would come back to bite Mrs Thatcher.

Dame Shirley Porter: the other 'grocer's daughter'

While Mrs Thatcher's government was at war with 'loony left' town halls, one local authority more than any other was seen as the flagship of municipal Thatcherism, Dame Shirley Porter's Westminster. In place of the exotic concerns of Labour's London councils, Dame Shirley concerned herself with good housekeeping: holding local taxes down, privatising services and keeping the streets clean. Much to her delight, her efforts earned her the reputation of 'the Iron Lady of the town halls'.[122]

The daughter of Sir Jack Cohen, the legendary street trader who built the Tesco supermarket chain, Dame Shirley's early hopes for a seat in parliament were frustrated when the panel in charge of vetting potential female candidates for the 1959 general election decided that, in the words of one of its members, she was not 'bright enough'.[123] In anger, Dame Shirley joined the Finchley Liberals and played a role in uncovering the golf club scandal (See Chapter 2). By 1974, however, Dame Shirley was back in the Tory fold and had become a Conservative councillor in Westminster. Five years later, when Westminster's most famous resident moved into Downing Street, Dame Shirley took to referring to herself as the 'other grocer's daughter', venerating her father in a manner similar to Mrs Thatcher, and developing a penchant for power dressing and showmanship akin to the Prime Minister's. Her strident manner – the love of an argument so long as she eventually prevailed – was similar to Mrs Thatcher's, as was her desire to compare her leadership to that of a careful housewife minding the family budget.

But in most respects the two women were hardly alike. The Prime Minister, unlike Dame Shirley, would never, for instance, have referred to herself as having 'a butterfly mind'.[124] Nor, despite calling on the advice of Sherman, did Dame Shirley have any of Mrs Thatcher's interest in winning a battle of ideas. Even allowing for the smaller stage afforded by Westminster City Hall, she had none of the Prime Minister's vision. 'Basically, I was just interested in cleaning things up,' Dame Shirley suggested. 'I wasn't a deep thinker.'[125] Nonetheless, her self-proclaimed 'War Against Reckless Spending' campaign and agitation for the abolition of the alleged chief culprit of profligate expenditure, Ken Livingstone's GLC, were not without impact. Her well-judged opposition to Livingstone was not simply a matter of economy. She correctly identified the GLC's 'thinly disguised attack on Jewish people and Israel', while her vocal support for Soviet Jewry[126] stood in stark contrast to the blind eye turned by the hard left.

Dame Shirley's admiration for the Prime Minister appeared boundless: one local Tory councillor noticed the way the otherwise strong-willed Westminster leader became 'like putty' in her presence.[127] After Mrs Thatcher left office, Dame Shirley was keen to play up the comparisons: 'To put it bluntly', she wrote, 'she was an inspiration … they called us bossy. Autocratic, difficult. They howled if we bypassed second-rate people or challenged old-fashioned methods.'[128]

Her admiration was, however, unrequited. Mrs Thatcher, wrote Andrew Hosken, 'appeared indifferent to Porter and gave the impression that she considered her something of a nuisance'.[129] She was even reported to have described Dame Shirley as 'really scary'.[130] When, desperate to end Porter's reign at City Hall, two senior Westminster Tories met with Mrs Thatcher's parliamentary private secretary and sought to arrange the peerage Dame Shirley coveted, they received short-shrift. 'She can't stand the woman', the Prime Minister's parliamentary aide told them bluntly.[131]

As John Ware, a producer for the BBC's *Panorama* who investigated Dame Shirley's record in Westminster, later suggested: 'I think she experienced quite a lot of subliminal, posh anti-Semitism. When a Tory said "she's ghastly" you knew what they meant.'[132] The novelist Jenny Diski, herself no fan of the former Westminster leader, also detected in some of the criticism directed at Dame Shirley a disdain for 'a working-class Jewish upstart'. 'I've been an English Jew for too many decades not to recognise the echo of something more than simple class snobbery', she wrote.[133]

Much of the criticism of Dame Shirley was, however, utterly justified. As the Law Lords ruled, the gerrymandering 'homes for votes' scandal for which her time in Westminster will for ever be remembered, was 'a deliberate, blatant and dishonest misuse of public power'.[134] From her home in Israel, Dame Shirley presented herself as a political exile. 'I am being hounded for who I am, for my unrepentant Thatcherism, for the sins of the Eighties, real or imagined', she unconvincingly proclaimed.[135]

David Hart: Mrs Thatcher's 'Blue Pimpernel'

Of all the characters in the Thatcher court few were as colourful as David Hart, a man even less conventional than Alfred Sherman. The son of the wealthy merchant banker Louis 'Boy' Hart, David was subject to anti-Semitic bullying at Eton, where he was nicknamed 'Jew Hart'.[136] While this early brush with upper-class anti-Semitism made Hart, in the words of Charles Moore, 'very conscious of his Jewishness',[137] it may also have driven his life-long determination to cock a snook at the Establishment: an attribute which formed the basis of the relationship between Mrs Thatcher and many of her more unorthodox admirers.

As was also the case for others for whom Thatcherite radicalism had a somewhat greater appeal than the Conservative Party, Hart met the Prime Minister through his support for the Centre for Policy Studies. His fierce anti-communism and free-market philosophy proved a comfortable fit: less so, his libertarian instincts and libertine lifestyle. A failed attempt at property development in the mid-1970s had landed him in the bankruptcy court, where, after hearing of his two mistresses, multiple homes and fleet of cars, the official receiver accused him of 'delusions of grandeur'.[138] Only thanks to a large inheritance from his estranged father had Hart's fortunes recovered. Access to the corridors of power did not temper his views or behaviour. At a meeting in No. 10, Mrs Thatcher was horrified when he tried to convince her of the case for legalising drugs.[139] Even less welcome was a drunken late-night pass at the 'incredibly beautiful and sexy' Prime Minister. 'Don't be such a silly boy,' she responded.[140]

Hart's occasional speechwriting contributions, suggestions for holiday reading and torrent of policy ideas were, however, less important to her than the psychological boost she received from his accounts of the view on what he termed 'the street'.[141] Purportedly marshalled from his network of agents, which ranged from retired Welsh policemen to contacts in inner-city Brixton, Hart's reports were, in the words of the former Tory MP Jonathan Aitken, 'suspiciously supportive' of her own opinions. Mrs Thatcher, however, was 'delighted to have her prejudices confirmed by Hart's proletarian voices'.[142] 'Gosh, you do cheer one up,' she told him after one early-morning phone call.[143] The Prime Minister's civil servants, though, were rather less en-amoured. 'She pays far too much attention to him', Sherbourne was warned as he took up his new post at No. 10. 'He's a spiv. Give him a wide-berth.'[144]

As the miners' strike began in early 1984, Hart offered more reassurance to Mrs Thatcher. 'The opposition to police action in this dispute is in Fleet Street and the Labour Party. Emphatically not on the street,' he wrote. It would be 'very foolish' to make any concessions to avoid this necessary and inevitable clash with the union movement. Mrs Thatcher gratefully under-lined Hart's encouraging words.[145] But during this critical period for the Thatcher government, Hart provided the Prime Minister with much more than comforting flattery; instead, suggested Sherbourne, he played 'a very important role' in helping to defeat the strike.[146] Incongruously travelling between the country's coalfields in a chauffeur-driven Mercedes, Hart – who had adopted the alias 'David Lawrence' – began to put together a network of miners who had defied Arthur Scargill's call to strike. Hart laid the ground-work in pubs in Nottinghamshire pit villages where, playing dominoes and taking snuff with disaffected working miners, he began to slowly win their trust.[147] His contacts and cash would eventually lead to the establishment of the National Working Miners' Committee.[148] Mrs Thatcher's speechwriter, Ronnie Millar, christened Hart the 'Blue Pimpernel'.[149]

For the Prime Minister, Hart's accounts of the mood among the working miners – in whose hands the outcome of the strike and her fate ultimately rested – became a vital source of intelligence. [150] He even travelled behind enemy lines: on one occasion, he provided her with a menacing account of a rally held by striking miners in Sheffield. 'I could not escape thoughts of Nuremberg,' he wrote, 'The stink of fascism. Admiration bordering on adoration for their leader.'[151]

Hart also financed and coordinated a legal offensive against the National Union of Mineworkers (NUM) and its leadership. He labelled it the 'Gulliver concept' – tying the union in so many legal and financial knots until it 'woke up one day and couldn't move'.[152] Few things can have given Hart or Mrs

Thatcher greater pleasure than the moment when, in response to a High Court ruling following a case brought by two working Yorkshire miners, he flew a chartered helicopter to Blackpool to ensure that Scargill was served a writ for contempt of court on the floor of the Labour Party conference. This set in motion a chain of events which led to the sequestration of the NUM's assets.

As the strike dragged on, Hart reinforced Mrs Thatcher's determination to give no ground, fed her doubts about her ministers' handling of the dispute and repeatedly urged her to throw her Cabinet colleagues' and advisers' caution to the wind. 'The Street', he told her six months into strike, wanted to see 'its General in the field', 'walking the streets' of the coalfield villages where 'the intimidation is at its worst'.[153] Despite her wish to do more for the working miners who had acquired an elevated status in the pantheon of Thatcherite heroes, even the Prime Minister knew that her open identification with them would do little to help their cause.

Hart's combative stance infuriated the Energy Secretary, Peter Walker, while Mrs Thatcher's staff worried continually that his links to Downing Street would be exposed and thus rebound on the working miners.[154] Visits to No. 10 were banned. Instead, Sherbourne took to taking Hart for 'John le Carré-style' walks around the lake in St James Park and then feeding his reports back to the Prime Minister.[155] When the very link her staff fretted about was revealed in the *Daily Mirror*,[156] Mrs Thatcher warned Hart that he must not talk about his direct access to her. Hart reassured the Prime Minister that he was 'infinitely deniable'.[157]

Nonetheless, as victory came into sight in early 1985, No. 10 began to freeze the Blue Pimpernel out.[158] This was less a case of ingratitude for services in the coalfields which were no longer required, instead, it reflected growing concerns that Hart was 'playing up his No. 10 connection' in a way which risked embarrassing Mrs Thatcher. Beyond fears that he was planning an 'insiders' account' of the strike and was meddling in the talks to end the dispute, Hart, a consultant to British Aerospace, was now attempting to present himself as a 'go-between' between Mrs Thatcher and the Reagan Administration over the Strategic Defence Initiative. It was time, Sherbourne advised the Prime Minister, to 'sever the link' with Hart.[159] Mrs Thatcher was unmoved by Hart's desperate pleas against banishment: six months after Scargill had been vanquished, he was denied a pass to attend the Conservative Party conference.

Like many an ambitious courtier, Hart had overplayed his hand. He had also, argued Sherbourne, developed 'completely inflated ideas' about how he could serve Mrs Thatcher now that the strike was over. He proposed, for instance, that he might become a White House-style press secretary. It was, believed her political secretary, a totally ridiculous notion that Hart, 'a completely unguided missile', was going to be allowed to speak on behalf of the Prime Minister on television.[160]

The key to the somewhat improbable relationship between Mrs Thatcher and Hart was the Prime Minister's keenness to avoid cutting herself off from views outside the political Establishment and civil service which surrounded her. Amid myriad bizarre and politically unfeasible ideas he might come up with, she believed, there might be one worth pursuing.[161] Sir Malcolm Rifkind identified an additional dynamic. Quite simply, he argued, 'she loved buccaneers'.[162]

Hart was down but by no means out. Despite his apparent rejection by Mrs Thatcher, he remained a true believer. In the run-up to the 1987 general election, he founded the Committee for a Free Britain, a right-wing pressure group which attacked Labour, backed red-blooded Thatcherism at home and right-wing causes abroad. Hart remained ever-hopeful of recognition, telling Woodrow Wyatt after her third election victory that Mrs Thatcher needed to 'fill the [House of] Lords with people loyal to her'. He reeled off a few names, Wyatt recorded in his diary, before recommending himself.[163]

Hart also dabbled in fiction writing. The thread which connected his works was that of a Jewish hero who overcomes prejudice and misunderstanding.[164] Unsurprisingly, Hart attracted the attention of fiction writers. In David Peace's novel about the miners' strike, *GB84*, he appears as the vain, 'compellingly creepy' Stephen Sweet, whom his chauffeur, Neil Fontaine – a shady character with links to the secret services – refers to throughout simply as 'The Jew'. For Peace, the phrase was intended to convey the 'peculiar and troubled alliances' behind Thatcherism: both the Prime Minister's admiration for Jews and Jewish culture, and the less wholesome attitudes of some of those who surrounded her.[165]

Lord Young: the rise of 'Finchley man'

In October 1987 Mrs Thatcher travelled to Blackpool to receive the plaudits of the Conservative Party on her historic third consecutive general election victory. Much of the media attention that week focused, however, on a man whose name had never appeared on a ballot paper, Lord Young. Mrs Thatcher had promoted him to become Secretary of State for Trade and Industry the day after her return to Downing Street four months previously, and he was deemed by one journalist as potentially 'the most influential member of the Cabinet'.[166]

But it was the accolade awarded him by the historian John Vincent – 'the Beveridge of Thatcherism' – which no doubt pleased Young the most. As the Prime Minister began to sketch her vision of what pundits termed 'social Thatcherism' – the far-reaching drive to tackle the plight of the decaying inner cities – it was Young, Vincent believed, who was, if not the co-star, then the principal supporting actor as the curtain was raised on Mrs Thatcher's third term. 'Her social policy is Lord Young,' wrote Vincent. 'He has funds and prime ministerial backing such as no other minister enjoys. His politics, far from being New Right, stem from the Jewish ethos of practical charity.'[167] It was her sympathy for that ethos, and her belief that, as she later put it, Young 'understood how to make things happen', which was to make him a Prime Ministerial favourite.[168]

Young's family story embodied the journey many Jews had made which Mrs Thatcher so admired. His father and grandparents had left the village of Yurevitch in what is now Lithuania in 1905. Arriving in Britain, they initially shared a two-room property in the East End with Young's great-grandfather and his wife and three children. Over time, Young's grandfather was able to start a bakery, and then become a flour wholesaler. The family moved out to Stamford Hill. In the 1920s, his father, now running the business, took up golf, married and set up home in Clapton Common. During the war, he moved his wife and two sons to Finchley.[169] (David's brother, Stuart, would later become chairman of the BBC Board of Governors.)

But Young wanted more than the comfortable suburban life his parents had provided for their sons. When an opportunity to work for Great Universal Stores came up, he quit his job as a solicitor and leapt at it. Within months, he was assistant to the chairman, the prominent Jewish businessman, philanthropist and communal leader, Isaac Wolfson.[170] He was soon restless again. Although working in a commercial environment allowed Young to discover his true 'entrepreneurial nature', he began to find the constraints of the corporate world stifling, wanting to get out and 'take the consequences of my own mistakes'.[171] Starting his own property company, Young embarked upon a roller-coaster ride. He made a fortune – he sold his company for £4 million in 1970 – and lost a fortune: when the property market crashed in 1973, he was close to being wiped out. Young survived, however, helping to develop the European subsidiary of America's fourth largest bank.

Unlike many of his future Cabinet colleagues, Young's interest in politics developed late. A Labour voter until 1964, his enthusiasm for the party soured during Harold Wilson's premiership. Having voted Conservative in 1970, Young was dismayed by the Heath government's U-turn: 'Gone went the idea of an entrepreneurial society and in came the corporate state with a vengeance.'[172] While Labour's return to office in 1974 so disheartened him that he considered emigrating, Young held out little hope for the Conservative alternative. He didn't mourn Heath's ousting but thought that by selecting a woman to replace him, the Tories had done little to improve their chances. His feelings began to change, however, when Joseph came to address a fundraiser for ORT, a Jewish charity focused on training and vocational education, with which Young was heavily involved. Joseph's words about the need for more entrepreneurs and a smaller state were music to Young's ears and he volunteered to help with the Centre for Policy Studies.[173] In 1978, he met Mrs Thatcher for the first time when she, too, came to address an ORT lunch. Young told her of his work with Joseph. 'I have no doubt we will meet again,' she said as she left.[174] Within six years, he was sitting around her Cabinet table.

However, ORT held a much deeper significance for Young's relationship with Mrs Thatcher. Like many Jewish parents, his mother and father had impressed upon their sons the need both to study and to give something back. If the first lesson was somewhat lost on him as a schoolboy, Young took the second to heart as an adult. ORT had been started by wealthy Jews in Tsarist Russia to help provide technical education to their poverty-stricken coreligionists. Learning a trade was to prove an escape route for many from the Pale of Settlement. Over the next ninety years, ORT's work spread worldwide: by the time Young became chairman of the UK organisation, it operated in more than twenty-two countries.

A trip to Israel in the 1970s to visit ORT schools proved to be, Young later said, the week that 'changed my life'.[175] He travelled the country from the Lebanon border to the Negev desert, visiting religious schools, Arab schools and schools in huts in newly established settlements. All had one thing in common: their focus on vocational education. What was most striking for Young was the manner in which young people once considered drop-outs by their previous schools now 'walked tall'.[176] His experience in Israel shaped his belief that Britain's low regard for vocational education and training lay at the heart of its economic difficulties. It was that belief which was to rest at the core of the work for which Mrs Thatcher would reward him in government.[177]

Young spent the first three years of Mrs Thatcher's government behind the scenes, working as an unpaid special adviser to Joseph. In 1982, it was time to go front of house when the new Employment Secretary, Norman Tebbit, picked him to become chairman of the Manpower Services Commission, the government body responsible for employment and training services. The appointment was not universally welcomed, but, through a combination of charm, the realisation that he wielded considerable clout in high places, and his occasional willingness to stand up to his friends in the Cabinet, Young was able to win over many sceptical civil servants and trade union officials.

All the while, Young spread the ORT gospel: inviting ministers in key departments and senior civil servants to presentations by the charity to hear about the latest developments in vocational and educational training.[178] At the commission, reported the *Sunday Times*, 'his method was largely a matter of following the principles that have guided his charity work over many years with the Organisation for Rehabilitation and Training'.[179] The 'waste and the moral degradation' of unemployment offended him, Young later wrote. 'An old saying from the Talmud ... continually went through my mind: "Give a man a fish and he will soon be hungry. Teach him to fish and he will never starve".' The government's opponents, he believed, simply wanted to hand out more fish.[180] This, however, offended Young's Jewish sensibilities. It had, he believed, never occurred to his father and grandfather that someone should give them a job when they had arrived in Britain. Instead, 'they knew that, if they did not look after their own, no one else would'.[181]

Young was determined to focus on teaching the unemployed and young people who were not academically gifted to fish. He pushed through what was to become the government's flagship policy to tackle youth unemployment, the Youth Training Scheme, and, with Joseph's blessing, launched the government's initiative to boost vocational training in schools. In two years, suggested *The Observer* – not normally a cheerleader for Tory Cabinet ministers – Young had transformed the commission 'switching [its] emphasis from first aid for the unemployed to the positive regeneration of industrial training'.[182]

Young's work had already caught the eye of the Prime Minister. Despite her landslide re-election in 1983, Mrs Thatcher's advisers worried that rising unemployment endangered her chances of winning a third term.[183] For this problem, Young was to prove the solution. In the spring of 1984, he travelled to Chequers to see the Prime Minister. In a bullish mood, he reeled off his accomplishments. His work at the commission, Young told her, was done.[184] Soon after, the *Financial Times* reported Mrs Thatcher saying: 'Other people come to me with their problems, David Young comes to me with his achievements.' Over time, the word 'achievements' became 'solutions'.[185] Either way, the Prime Minister's alleged words, with their barely concealed contempt for her ministers, did not endear Young to his future colleagues.

Several months later, she summoned him to Downing Street and told him that – as he had 'nearly earned it anyway' – she was going to send him to the House of Lords and appoint him to the Cabinet as Minister without Portfolio. Heading a new enterprise unit, she wanted him to 'take a special interest in job creation'.[186] As the media scrambled to find out more about the sudden elevation of the largely anonymous new Cabinet minister, Downing Street spun Young's appointment as 'Minister for Jobs'.[187] Given the seeming intractability of the problem, one Tory likened the position to 'getting a call from the Vatican and being told you're in charge of the anti-sin drive'.[188] Arriving at his first Cabinet meeting, Young realised that he was not even a member of the Conservative Party.[189] A year later, with unemployment stubbornly refusing to fall, Mrs Thatcher promoted Young again, this time to Employment Secretary. 'I want you to deal with unemployment by the next election,' she ordered him.[190]

Young plunged in enthusiastically. Despite the odd gaffe – he appeared to suggest on one occasion that even the unemployed had never had it so good[191] – the new minister proved a success. With a host of programmes which were all promoted through a national advertising campaign known as 'Action for Jobs', Young's Employment Department exuded energy in the fight against the most pressing political problem facing Mrs Thatcher's government. Most importantly, Young earned the Prime Minister's confidence. He had told her his programmes would see unemployment begin to drop before the likely date of the next election and it did.[192] Young had not, of course, achieved this success alone – the strength of the economy had made a handsome contribution, too – but he had proved to be, believed Hugo Young, 'an unusually competent salesman' for the government's effort to cut the dole queues.[193]

The relationship between Prime Minister and peer was a warm one. Young found his meetings with her left him 'walking on air', he later recalled. 'She was so resolute, so clear sighted in what she wanted to get done.'[194] In turn, believed Charles Moore, her choice of Young proved to be 'one of the few important appointments that she did not partially regret'.[195] In part, this reflected the fact that he was, as the *Sunday Times* put it, a fellow 'self-made outsider with a lowish opinion of Old Guard's competence'.[196] But there was also possibly something else at work. Alan Clark, a junior minister in Young's department, found himself pleasantly surprised by his new boss and understanding of Mrs Thatcher's admiration for him. 'He is pleasant, charming almost, and fresh … I can quite see why the Lady fancies him. He is utterly different from the rest of the Cabinet.'[197] Critically, though, in her eyes, Young was also the author of her final victory. 'I reckon,' Lady Thatcher later suggested, 'he won the '87 election for us because of his employment policies'.[198]

Young was, however, to play a rather more contentious part in the 1987 campaign itself. His status as a favourite of Mrs Thatcher had, unsurprisingly, already provoked the jealousy of some of his Cabinet colleagues.[199] But even those who were better disposed to Young, such as Lawson, baulked at the notion that someone who had never stood for political office or fought an election campaign should have found himself on the frontline of the Tories' battle for a third term.[200] Young's ill-defined role at Central Office – Jonathan Aitken described him simply as Mrs Thatcher's 'personal ferret down every campaign rabbit hole where she suspected failings' – principally arose from her growing distrust of the man in charge of the campaign, Norman Tebbit.[201] Once a close ally, she had come to suspect the party chairman had his eye on her job, while also fearing – with little good reason – that his strategy was leading the Tories to the brink of electoral defeat. That Mrs Thatcher should have alighted upon Young as the answer to her perceived problems was not altogether surprising. As a peer, Young was a self-described 'political eunuch' and automatically excluded in Mrs Thatcher's mind as a potential pretender to her throne.[202] Alongside his ability to bring her 'solutions', this was a key factor in oiling the wheels of their relationship. Moreover, given the Prime Minister's propensity to believe that political problems usually resulted from poor presentation, this left her particularly susceptible to the arguments of Young, a man who, as Lawson suggested, was a 'great believer in the power of advertising'.[203]

The political phoney war ended when Mrs Thatcher halted mounting press speculation and called the general election for 11 June. She had taken care to avoid the previous Thursday, which was a Jewish holiday.[204] Nothing was to be allowed to hinder her Finchley constituents from registering their appreciation for their Member of Parliament. But in the heat of the campaign kitchen – with Labour's slick and professional efforts winning media plaudits – tempers inevitably frayed and none more so than Mrs Thatcher's. Fearing defeat, she lashed out at the campaign high command on the infamous 'Wobbly Thursday', provoking a confrontation later that day between Tebbit and Young. Grabbing him by the lapels, Young told the party chairman: 'Norman, listen to me, we're about to lose this f—king election. You're going to go, I'm going to go, the whole thing is going to go. The entire election depends upon her doing fine performances for the next five days – she has to be happy.'[205]

Trying to make the fretful Prime Minister happy as she cruised towards re-election was thus to be Young's principal task throughout the campaign, and a thankless one at that. Few of his colleagues were sympathetic and some accused him of feeding Mrs Thatcher's anxieties. For Lawson, Young had 'panicked' on 'Wobbly Thursday'. 'There was no wobble,' he later suggested, 'David Young didn't meet any voters.'[206] In reality, as Moore suggested, the ultimate fault lay with Mrs Thatcher who throughout the campaign was 'sure of nothing except that everything was going wrong'. Young, in turn, was right to focus his efforts on keeping her happy in order to 'coax the best performances out of her'.[207] Tellingly, Lady Thatcher, who later had few kind words to say about anyone involved in the national campaign that returned her to Downing Street with a majority of 102, nonetheless praised Young's 'great flair and energy'.[208]

Back in Downing Street, she rewarded Young with the Department of Trade and Industry and set him the task of working out how to fulfil her election-night promise to 'do something about those inner-cities'. He believed that the decision may have been linked in the Prime Minister's mind to her admiration for Lord Jakobovits's trenchant thinking on the subject (see Chapter 9).[209] But another Prime Ministerial ambition – to appoint Young chairman of the Conservative Party – was thwarted by Willie Whitelaw, who was adamant that the Trade and Industry Secretary could not do both jobs. Sensing a split at the top of the government, stories began to appear in the newspapers. Young detected an unpleasant undercurrent to some of the mutterings against him, having been told that 'the word [that was] being put out was against my origins rather than my policies'.[210] Privately, Mrs Thatcher was furious with Young's detractors: 'They should remember how well he did on unemployment and the Manpower Commission [*sic*] and be grateful for it,' she told Woodrow Wyatt.[211]

When, two years later, Young told Mrs Thatcher he wished to leave the Cabinet, she again wanted to make him party chairman but, this time, the man who had helped the Tories secure a third term was not up for the fight. The atmosphere in the party, especially on the backbenches, he felt, made it impossible.[212] As her political problems mounted, this time, David Young could not bring her any solutions.

Stephen Sherbourne: the inside man

On the morning after his wife's third victory at the polls, Denis Thatcher told Stephen Sherbourne: 'You have done as much as anyone else to win the election. We could not have done it without you.'[213] Lord Young may have been one of the public faces of the Tories' electoral hat-trick, but it was another of her Jewish confidantes who, behind the scenes, had played a crucial role.

Sherbourne was, in some regards, an unlikely choice by Mrs Thatcher as her political secretary in 1983. The two had first met in 1974 when he worked for the Conservative Research Department. After a brief spell helping her prepare for Prime Minister's Questions after she became Tory leader, Sherbourne departed to work for Ted Heath on the European referendum campaign. This wasn't the natural path to advancement under the new regime. Eight years later, though, Sherbourne was asked to help Mrs Thatcher prepare for her morning press conferences during the election campaign. She found him 'both quick and methodical' – two supreme virtues in the Prime Minister's eyes – and after winning her second term asked him to become her political secretary.[214] Without a job description, it took Sherbourne about a year to work out the exact nature of his role. As the only political person, apart from her parliamentary private secretary, working in Downing Street, his task, he realised, was 'to make sure Mrs Thatcher remained Prime Minister. Nobody else was thinking about that. So long as she remained leader of the party, so long as she won general elections, I was doing my job.'[215]

Sherbourne proved an able diplomat with a finely tuned political ear. 'I have seldom worked with anyone more capable and self-effacing,' recalled one No. 10 civil servant.[216] During a second term in which, as Lady Thatcher put it, it frequently felt as if it were 'raining all the time', Sherbourne was there to assist with both the downpours and the squalls.[217] As the government hit a rocky mid-term in the summer of 1985, Sherbourne worried that a resurgent Alliance might push the Tories into third place in the opinion polls, sparking panic on the backbenches. He even feared what might happen at a general election if the third party moved into second place in the polls and then 'got a bandwagon rolling'.[218] The government's problems, Sherbourne advised Mrs Thatcher in August 1985, primarily stemmed from 'poor public relations': she needed a new chairman of the Tory Party; a wide-ranging reshuffle with 'fresh new faces', especially good communicators, brought in; and a revamped PR effort.[219]

The extensive 1985 reshuffle – which saw Young's promotion and Leon Brittan's sacking as Home Secretary – was no sooner over, however, when the Westland affair, one of the most perilous moments of Mrs Thatcher's time in office, struck. In its wake, and to both counter accusations of the Prime Minister's high-handed style of government and help ministers better prepare for a general election the following year, Sherbourne proposed an informal political committee of the Cabinet.[220] Dubbed the 'A-Team' by the press, it helped to present an image of unity and purpose which the government had lacked for many months.

At the same time, however, relations between Mrs Thatcher and her new party chairman, Norman Tebbit, were becoming more strained and word of tensions was leaking to the press. Sherbourne played the role of peacemaker, urging the Prime Minister to assuage some of Tebbit's anxieties by holding regular weekly meetings with him. Sherbourne, Lady Thatcher wrote in her memoirs, 'understood politics as well as any Cabinet minister and ... [his] shrewdness never failed me'.[221] When it came to drafting the party's general election manifesto, it was Sherbourne, with what Lady Thatcher termed 'his special kind of tactful ruthlessness', who kept the whole process on track.[222] The resulting document was, she modestly declared, 'the best ever produced by the Conservative Party'.[223]

Indeed, such was Mrs Thatcher's trust of Sherbourne that he could raise with her subjects that few others could. It was her political secretary, for instance, who diplomatically raised what he termed 'the main issue' at the next general election: 'you and your personality'. No one doubted the strength of her convictions, Sherbourne wrote, but, at the back of their mind, many would be asking: 'What is there to be done in this third Parliament that only Mrs Thatcher can do?' In other words, he continued, 'why do we need this strong woman?'[224] He subtly suggested some ways to smooth the Iron Lady's rougher edges: fewer formal political interviews, more with 'Jimmy Young type programmes with Radio 2 type audiences' and fewer visits to factories and more to hospitals.[225]

Sherbourne's time as political secretary helped to ensure that, when the country went to the polls in June 1987, Mrs Thatcher 'remained Prime Minister'. Mission accomplished, Sherbourne stepped down within months of the general election. On the issue which ultimately brought her down three years later, the poll tax, Sherbourne's had been a voice for caution, especially when compared with those of her policy advisers – he likened them to 'clever schoolboys in science laboratories' – who lacked his sharp political antennae.[226] As Mrs Thatcher's ship of state headed into choppy seas, the Prime Minister was to sorely miss her first mate.

Nigel Lawson: the Prince Regent of Thatcherism

Other than the Prime Minister, no face seemed to better encapsulate Thatcherism at its high tide than that of her Chancellor, Nigel Lawson. 'He looks,' wrote the journalist Edward Pearce in 1985, 'like the Prince Regent on a diet.'[227] With a self-confidence which bordered on arrogance, Lawson strode the political stage for six years when, as the economy expanded rapidly, Mrs Thatcher's free-market revolution appeared to have cured the country of 'the British disease'.

Lawson had, as the *Sunday Times*'s Susan Crosland discovered after interviewing him shortly before he delivered his first Budget, 'a distaste for introspection'.[228] His memoirs, which stretch to over 1,000 pages, contain just one paragraph detailing his life before he went to Oxford. Lawson's grandfather, Gustav Leibson, arrived in Britain from Latvia around 1890. While his grandfather's love of casinos did not make him a particularly successful businessman, Lawson's father, Ralph, was an altogether more staid character and built a successful tea merchant firm in the City of London.[229] Lawson's childhood was thus a comfortable one: the family's Hampstead home employed a cook, maid and nanny. His upbringing was, however, not a Jewish one. 'I was not brought up in any Jewish culture but rather in the culture of this country,' he later suggested.[230] For Lawson, like his parents, being Jewish was something he 'took for granted'. He was 'puzzled – not peeved or irritated, simply puzzled' by the focus on it.[231]

Unlike Mrs Thatcher, who began her search for a parliamentary seat almost as soon as she left university, Lawson went first into journalism. However, a short stint as a speechwriter for Harold Macmillan and Sir Alec Douglas-Home gave him a taste for politics. Unsuccessful in 1970, he was elected for a safe Leicestershire seat as the Tories left office in February 1974. Although later sharply critical of Ted Heath's administration, Lawson had been part of the former Prime Minister's inner circle, drafting both the 1974 manifestos and advocating the proposed 'national government' which Mrs Thatcher had found so offensive at the time.[232] Nonetheless, Lawson was instinctively closer to the economic thinking of the new Tory leader and each was impressed by the other when they worked together for the first time between the 1974 elections on her housing policy group.[233]

In opposition, Mrs Thatcher found Lawson one of the 'more solid Shadows'. Nor did he initially disappoint her in government.[234] Sent to the Treasury with Howe, he helped provide intellectual ballast for the new government's radical economic policies and in a speech in Zurich in early 1981 became the first minister to publicly use the term 'Thatcherism'.[235] Despite the efforts of Willie Whitelaw to prevent his promotion – a reflection, as the writer R. W. Johnson suggested, of the strain between 'the old guard and the new'[236] – Lawson joined the Cabinet in the autumn of 1981 as Energy Secretary. Once again, her rising star's performance – readying the gas industry for privatisation and helping prepare for the next inevitable clash with the miners – impressed the Prime Minister. By the time of her re-election in 1983, Lady Thatcher wrote somewhat cuttingly in her memoirs, she had 'come to share Nigel's high opinion of himself'.[237] Basking in her victory, Mrs Thatcher appointed Lawson as her Chancellor, making him the first Jew since Benjamin Disraeli to hold the post.[238]

For much of her second term, Mrs Thatcher delighted in the performance of the man she would publicly laud as 'my brilliant Chancellor' and who in 1986 laid the groundwork for the government's re-election by cutting the basic rate of income tax for the first time since 1979. The following year, he cut it again, and pledged more of the same if the Tories were re-elected. 'The genius of the tax-cut philosophy was that it got the party mood going, it got us all glowing', one happy voter later recalled.[239]

Tax cuts were not Lawson's only contribution to getting the Thatcherite party of the mid-1980s going. Even while Mrs Thatcher herself harboured some doubts in the early years of her time in power, Lawson was an arch-exponent of privatisation. As Chancellor, he was an evangelist for the sale of state-owned industries such as British Telecom and British Gas, hailing the advent of 'people's capitalism'.[240] Again a little more slowly than he, she also came to embrace Lawson's enthusiasm for sweeping away the restrictive practices which governed the City. Together, the October 1986 'Big Bang', sweeping tax cuts and the glittering financial prizes to be gained from privatisation gave the City a hitherto absent allure.[241] 'In a few dramatic years,' wrote Andy McSmith, it 'was transformed from a club run by an old-boy network of public-school alumni to a place where the ambitious sons of working-class families were given free rein to make a great deal of money.'[242] Its 'get-rich-quick' values were, however, very unlike those preached and practised by Alfred Roberts, whose virtues his daughter, as Prime Minister, continued to extol.

The party was, however, about to turn sour and so was the relationship between the Prime Minister and her Chancellor. Lawson's way of working was very different from the more collegiate style of his predecessor. As Lady Thatcher later related, he 'did not generally like to seek or take advice'.[243] The real issue was their respective roles in running the economy. Mrs Thatcher jealously asserted her rights as 'First Lord of the Treasury';[244] Lawson believed there could 'only be one Chancellor'.[245] Her admiration, believed Rifkind, 'turned to intense irritation', a feeling fuelled by her belief that Lawson was someone 'she had created'.[246]

Mrs Thatcher's irritation was exacerbated by the fact that the Chancellor behaved towards her in a manner unlike any of his Cabinet colleagues. On one occasion, as she repeatedly interrupted Joseph, Lawson suddenly let rip: 'Shut up, Prime Minister, just occasionally let someone get a word in edgeways.' As Nicholas Edwards, her former Welsh Secretary recalled, 'for the first and last time, I saw Margaret Thatcher blush and then for twenty minutes she was silent'.[247] Not all encounters between the two were so bruising. Sherbourne believed that Mrs Thatcher enjoyed much of the cut and thrust of her discussions with Lawson. Watching them argue was akin to 'a heavyweight boxer holding his ground and she was like a flyweight' jabbing him with a series of opposing arguments.[248]

Moreover, even when the radicalism of her Chancellor thrilled the Prime Minister, she also worried about his political instincts and presentational abilities.[249] While Mrs Thatcher was always keenly attuned to what 'our people' would stand for, the Chancellor valued intellectual consistency.[250]

As Lawson pointedly suggested in his memoirs 'Thatcherism' did not mean 'whatever Margaret Thatcher herself at any time did or said'.[251]

After the 1987 election, this combustible mix was to produce fireworks in the relationship between the two. She came to believe that he was pursuing 'a personal economic policy without reference to the rest of the Government'.[252] Behind closed doors, the two rowed ferociously: Lawson resented her aggressive manner, Mrs Thatcher his alleged deceptions. He considered resigning, she toyed with firing him.[253] Her anger was compounded by another fear. As early as 1985 she had warned the head of her Policy Unit, Brian Griffiths, that Lawson was 'a gambler'.[254] Now, while in public she lauded his swingeing tax cuts in 1988 as 'the epitaph for socialism',[255] in private, she worried that the economy was already overheating and the government's hard-won reputation for having defeated inflation was at risk.[256]

Those fears were soon realised as inflation rose steeply and interest rates were hiked to try and douse it. In parliament, Mrs Thatcher did little to disguise the differences between the Downing Street neighbours. In May 1989, she nearly pushed him too far when she publicly laid the blame for inflation at his door. Lawson's threat to quit won him a profuse private apology, 'a phenomenon so uncharacteristic,' he recalled, 'as to have been almost unique'.[257] Five months later, however, Lawson was gone. The final provocation was the Prime Minister's decision to recall her former economic adviser, Sir Alan Walters, to No. 10, despite his strident public criticisms of Lawson. Mrs Thatcher failed to appreciate how insulted her intensely proud Chancellor would be. At their final meeting on the day of his resignation, she told Lawson she would miss him. They parted, he recorded, 'in an atmosphere of suppressed emotion'.[258] Whatever their disagreements, believed Sherbourne, 'she respected Nigel in a way that, unfortunately, she never respected Geoffrey Howe'.[259]

If Mrs Thatcher had come to regard Lawson as 'a riverboat gambler',[260] he had come to view her as reckless: both in the way she treated her colleagues and on some policy issues.[261] The prime example was the poll tax, a measure he opposed in Cabinet and warned Mrs Thatcher was 'completely unworkable and politically catastrophic'.[262] In November 1990, Lawson voted for her challenger, Michael Heseltine, in the first ballot of the leadership election which brought about her fall. It was 'impossible not to feel for Margaret', he later wrote, but 'in the true classical tradition' it was she, not those whom she would later accuse of betrayal, who was 'the author of her own misfortune'.[263] In retirement, she laid the blame for the consequences of the 'Lawson boom' squarely at her former Chancellor's door, even while admitting that, whatever their later differences, she could never deny him a leading place on any list of 'Conservative – even Thatcherite – revolutionaries'.[264]

Leon Brittan: the fall guy

As she got into her car to leave No. 10 on Monday 27 January 1986, Mrs Thatcher turned to her Cabinet Secretary, Sir Robert Armstrong, and remarked: 'I may not be Prime Minister by six o'clock tonight.'[265] The spark which lit the powder keg which now threatened to explode under her premiership was the future of the Westland helicopter manufacturer. But the argument within government which had consumed ministers over the preceding months – whether the ailing company should be rescued by an American firm or a European consortium – had long faded from view. Instead, it was questions about her style of government and integrity which had left Mrs Thatcher fighting for her political life.

She survived in large part by sacrificing Leon Brittan, the brilliant young minister she had promoted to the Home Office in 1983, thereby making him, at that time, only the second Jew to hold the post of Home Secretary, and the first to do so in nearly five decades.[266]

Brittan's grandfather had been a doctor in Lithuania and his father had studied medicine in Berlin before emigrating to London in 1927 and establishing a practice in Cricklewood. The prospects for a doctor in Eastern Europe, he had decided, were less good than in Britain. Given the events of the next decade, it was to prove a fateful decision.

Brittan was brought up less as an Orthodox Jew, but in what he termed the 'orthodox Jewish tradition'.[267] His parents spoke Yiddish and his upbringing was infused with what one writer termed 'a strong Jewish atmosphere'.[268] The family avidly followed the birth pangs and early years of Israel, Brittan recalled: 'There could have been no family which followed those events more eagerly, with greater anxiety or keener hope.'[269] Leon was taken to a public meeting to hear Viscount Samuel, the first High Commissioner for Palestine and the man whose former Cleveland constituency Brittan would later represent, and position as Home Secretary he would later hold.

'Prodigiously clever', as *The Observer* noted after his appointment as Home Secretary, Brittan won an exhibition to Cambridge at sixteen, the presidency of the Union and a double first in English and Law.[270] In the university Conservative Association, Michael Howard recalled, Brittan was 'our undoubted leader'. 'He was the cleverest, the most eloquent and much the most formidable debater.'[271] His contemporaries – Howard, Kenneth Clarke, John Gummer, Norman Lamont and Norman Fowler – would serve alongside him in Mrs Thatcher's governments and came to be dubbed the 'Cambridge Mafia'. Like her, they had not attended England's great public schools from which the Tory Party had traditionally selected its elite, but had grown up in middle-class homes and been educated at grammar and direct-grant schools.

At the time he arrived in Cambridge, however, Brittan was not a long-standing Conservative. Growing up, he had supported Labour, but had become disillusioned over the 'really nauseating' attitudes of the left at the time of Suez.[272] Brittan's Judaism – he would later become a member of the same Chelsea Synagogue as Joseph – played a part, too, as he came to believe that 'the narrow-minded collectivism of the Labour Party is anathema to Jewish individualism'.[273]

Nonetheless, like his friend Sir Geoffrey Howe, Brittan's politics were economically dry but socially liberal. That political synthesis was to contribute to his political rise and fall; while Mrs Thatcher shared the former, she had little time for the latter. Brittan first came to her attention shortly after he was elected to parliament in February 1974. Although he was initially unconvinced by her appeal,[274] the new Tory leader was impressed by the 'enormously intelligent and hardworking' young barrister's performance when she appointed him to the shadow front bench.[275]

Eighteen months after she entered Downing Street, with the economy deep in recession and her popularity plunging, Mrs Thatcher began to dispense with her internal Cabinet critics. Brittan was to be the principal beneficiary. Reshuffling her team for the first time in January 1981, she promoted him from a junior ministerial role at the Home Office to become Chief Secretary to the Treasury. At forty-one, Brittan became the youngest member of the Cabinet. The responsibility for making further cuts in public spending was not one designed to enhance Brittan's popularity, but his stock rose where it counted. For Mrs Thatcher, he was to be the best Chief Secretary of her years in office.[276] On 23 July 1981, at arguably the most crucial Cabinet meeting of her premiership, Brittan proved his worth. As her ministers, including some loyalists from whom she had expected support, called for a change of economic direction, Mrs Thatcher felt her 'whole strategy' was under attack.[277] As the leading Cabinet 'wet', Sir Ian Gilmour, noted, the Prime Minister found herself 'alone in a laager' with only Joseph, Whitelaw, Howe and Brittan supporting her efforts to ensure that, less than two years after coming to office, Thatcherism did not become a footnote in history.[278]

Brittan's reward came two years later when Mrs Thatcher decided to deploy his 'keen lawyer's mind and intellectual rigour' at the Home Office as she began her second term.[279] She was to find his performance a source of acute disappointment.[280] From the outset, Brittan was hobbled by the perception that he was, in the words of *The Guardian*'s commentator Hugo Young, 'a complete Thatcher creation',[281] even if he had none of her populist instincts and proved ill-suited in the 'hang 'em and flog 'em' garb which the Tory rank and file traditionally expect of Home Secretaries. Nor, as the Prime Minister was to find, was Brittan a natural in the role of attack dog when she attempted to unleash him on the Trotskyites whom her husband believed ran the BBC.[282] Mrs Thatcher could be forgiving of liberal transgressions on the part of her ministers if she believed them politically adept.[283] But on this count, too, the jury found against Brittan. 'Poor Leon is frightfully bad at public relations,' she told Woodrow Wyatt.[284]

With the government hitting a bout of mid-term turbulence in 1985, neither Mrs Thatcher's knowledge that he would be devastated by the decision, nor her gratitude for his 'tough and competent' performance during the miners' strike, could save the Home Secretary.[285] Not only did the public find him unconvincing, she had decided, but Brittan had proven that, like some other first-class lawyers, he was 'better at mastering and expounding a brief than in drawing up his own'.[286] Summoned to Chequers, a shell-shocked Brittan was told that she wanted him to move to the Department of Trade and Industry. In a rare admission of error, Mrs Thatcher confessed to Wyatt that Brittan had been too young and inexperienced when she had appointed him to one of the Cabinet's most senior posts.[287]

Angry that he had been made the 'fall guy' for the government's wider travails,[288] and with his confidence severely undermined, Brittan retreated to his new posting. There, he swiftly walked into a political turf war with the Defence Secretary, Michael Heseltine, over the fate of Westland. It was a deeply unequal fight, pitting a political 'carnivore against [a] herbivore'.[289] Although Brittan appeared to have triumphed when Heseltine flounced out of the Cabinet in early January 1986, his days were also numbered. As the government became engulfed in a political storm over who had authorised the leaking to the media of a confidential Solicitor-General's letter designed to discredit the former Defence Secretary, a fall guy was once again needed. Seventeen days after Heseltine quit, Brittan took the fall. Mrs Thatcher tried, she later wrote, to talk him out of resigning, hating to 'see the better man lose'.[290]

As Howe later suggested, Brittan's meteoric rise meant that 'jealous critics, some with malodorous streaks of anti-Semitism, were never too far away'.[291] Brittan himself denied that he had been subject to anti-Semitism. He recalled his selection in Cleveland prior to the 1974 election, when a local party member had questioned whether it was wise to select him for a seat where there were 'no Jews and ... a strong Christian tradition'. Another had quickly shut down the conversation: 'We're not choosing a parson, we're choosing an MP.'[292] Nonetheless, he had previously been through fifteen selection contests before Cleveland's Tories picked him. A decade later, when the seat disappeared in boundary changes, *The Independent*'s political commentator, Peter Jenkins, detected 'unpleasant ripples of anti-Semitism' as Brittan, despite being a member of the Cabinet, was forced to hunt for a new constituency.[293]

Whatever the truth about events prior to January 1986, the atmosphere at the time of Brittan's resignation was sulphurous. There was, believed Nigel Lawson, 'an unpleasant whiff of anti-semitism' in the air.[294] One senior Conservative anonymously accused Brittan of 'behaving like a cornered rat'.[295] A crucial meeting of the 1922 Committee, which sealed Brittan's fate by indicating his lack of support on the backbenches, 'resembled a pogrom', suggested the Tory MP Julian Critchley.[296] It was 'poisonous', agreed his colleague, Jonathan Aitken, 'a witch-hunt … tainted by an undercurrent of anti-Semitism. Personally, I felt disgusted by the attacks of several of my colleagues.'[297] One of those attacks by the right-winger John Stokes calling for Brittan's replacement by 'a red-blooded, red-faced Englishman preferably from the landed interests' soon found its way into the media.[298]

Anti-Semitism was not the sole, or even primary, cause of Brittan's fall. He was not an entirely innocent party in the disclosure of the Solicitor-General's letter. His vulnerability was compounded by a shyness which was easily construed as coldness and the fact that, as Howe recognised, he had risen fast without 'a substantial lobby of personal support in the Commons';[299] in part, a result of his aversion to political glad-handing.

Brittan consistently refused to be drawn on whether he had been a victim of anti-Semitism.[300] At the time, however, there were signs of his heightened sensitivity to his Jewish background. When at a meeting with Mrs Thatcher during the Westland drama an official suggested the government had come to resemble 'a warring tribe', Brittan interjected: 'Prime Minister, I must object in the strongest possible terms to the use of such language.'[301] His wife, Diana, felt less constrained in blowing the whistle publicly. Days after he quit, she suggested her husband had been subjected to 'horrible and quite wrong' anti-Semitic innuendo. 'It is difficult for Leon; he could never say it is antisemitism, and there are other elements as well, like jealousy,' she suggested.[302] Her assessment was widely shared in the media. Brittan had 'suffered as a consequence' of his Jewish background and the 'stigma which will always be attached to such a man in some sections of the Conservative Party', wrote James Naughtie in *The Guardian.*[303]

Although he initially bit his tongue, Brittan was later less reticent about blaming Mrs Thatcher for his fall. 'I think this episode showed her at her worst,' he complained. 'She egged me on with fierce support, but refused to argue directly with [Heseltine]. Far from being the Iron Lady, she proved curiously weak and indecisive.'[304] Brittan's bitterness was understandable. As Mrs Thatcher knew, had he chosen at the time to publicly contradict her account of events she, too, may well have been forced from office. Moreover, her response to his resignation letter – 'I hope that it will not be long before you return to high office to continue your ministerial career'[305] – contained within it, Brittan believed, 'an informal understanding' that he would be brought back.[306]

The call, however, never came. After she was re-elected in 1987, and had reinstated to the Cabinet another of her fallen ministers, Cecil Parkinson, the Prime Minister bluntly told Wyatt that Brittan had had his chance. He was 'very loyal', she suggested, but 'not an alert politician'.[307] To assuage her conscience, she eventually appointed him as one of Britain's European Commissioners. Just as she had failed to enquire too closely into his views when she promoted him to the Home Office, so she did again: she ended up sending to Brussels one of the most pro-European of the men who had served her in government.[308]

In her memoirs, Lady Thatcher labelled Brittan a 'civilised but not very streetwise politician'.[309] Her comments, believed Rifkind, a cousin of Brittan's, reflected the fact that 'she felt rather guilty' that she never gave a second chance to the man whose sacrifice had saved her premiership.[310] In January 1986, it was Rifkind, however, who was to get a seat in the Cabinet as a result of the scandal that had consumed that career.

Malcolm Rifkind and Michael Howard: the next generation

In the mini-reshuffle which followed Michael Heseltine's resignation, the appointment of Malcolm Rifkind as Scottish Secretary was one about which Mrs Thatcher had decidedly mixed feelings.[311] Little that happened over the remaining years of her premiership was to convince her that the fifth Jewish member of her Cabinet was 'one of us'. Indeed, she would later deem him 'my sharpest personal critic in the Cabinet'.[312]

Rifkind may not have been a Thatcherite, but his upbringing was one that Alfred Roberts's daughter would have admired and, in some respects, recognised. His grandfather, Charles, travelled to Edinburgh in 1899 aged twenty-two from Mshad, a small town in Lithuania. His wife Emma and the first of their ten children joined him the following year. 'They were what would now be called economic migrants,' suggested Rifkind.[313] Charles became a self-employed draper, selling his wares in the mining villages of Fife. Rifkind's father, Elijah, or Elky as he was universally known, did not go to university, but worked for many years in his mother's drapery shop before becoming a self-employed small businessman, selling clothes, carpets and furniture in working-class towns to low-income families who couldn't get credit. The family was, recalled Rifkind, 'middle-class ... with a very modest background ... We were not wealthy but nor were we short of any of the necessities of life.'[314] Like Alfred Roberts, Elky was 'unimpressed by wealth', remembered his son, instead being 'more interested in achievement'. He sent both of his sons to fee-paying schools.[315]

Edinburgh's Jewish community was a small one, then consisting of only several hundred families. The family was Orthodox and observant – Elky went to the city's sole synagogue every Saturday and Malcolm was expected until his mid-teens to accompany him. But Rifkind's parents were – unlike those of Margaret Roberts – 'never rigid', allowing their son, for instance, to attend his beloved school debating society on Friday evenings after the commencement of the Sabbath.[316]

Like other Jewish families who had entered the ranks of the middle class-es, the Rifkinds were Conservatives (although Ethel hinted to her son that she occasionally voted Liberal), albeit not politically active. When he went to university, Rifkind initially joined the Liberal Club: it was 1963 and the Tories, led by the former Earl of Home, had been in power for over a decade. Rifkind soon tired of the 'lovely but dull as ditchwater' student Liberals: the Tories, he discovered, threw better parties.[317] Moreover, as a liberal Tory he found himself more at home than he had been as a right-wing Liberal.

Politically precocious – in 1970, he was Scotland's youngest parliamentary candidate – he won the marginal seat of Edinburgh Pentlands four years later aged twenty-seven. Both personally and politically, he encountered little by way of anti-Semitism, despite a Labour-supporting uncle warning him as a student: 'You won't get anywhere in the Tory Party if you are Jewish.' Rifkind, however, believed this view was outdated and failed to take into account that, with many in the Jewish community now firmly entrenched in the middle class, 'everything was in a total flux'.[318] When he was seeking selection, his Jewish background had not been a cause for comment, save for when a concerned local association member warned him: 'I don't think there are many synagogues in the Borders.'[319]

Like his fellow Tory MPs, the most important choice facing Rifkind following the party's defeat in the October 1974 election was who should lead it. Out of loyalty rather than affection, Rifkind voted for Heath over Mrs Thatcher in the first ballot. Once Heath withdrew, however, this self-professed liberal Conservative made what he admitted was a surprising choice and voted for Mrs Thatcher. Admiring the combative style she had deployed from the opposition front bench against the Labour government, he decided she was best placed to lead the party to victory.[320] Despite his discomfort with the 'style and some of the substance' of Thatcherism, Rifkind never regretted his choice.[321]

The tensions which would characterise the relationship between the two was apparent almost from the outset when Rifkind resigned as a shadow Scottish minister in December 1976 over the party's decision to vote against the government's devolution proposals. Rifkind, Lady Thatcher believed, was flirting with ideas which were taking the Tories 'well into Labour territory'.[322] The seed of doubt about Rifkind's ideological commitment had been sown. For a time, though, it lay dormant. When the Conservatives were elected in May 1979, Mrs Thatcher ended Rifkind's self-imposed backbench exile and appointed him a Scottish Office minister. Now he had an opportunity to shine, impressing the Prime Minister as he pushed through her flagship policy of council house sales north of the border.

Rifkind's reward came in April 1982, when, in a reshuffle provoked by the Falklands War, Mrs Thatcher promoted him to become a Foreign Office junior minister. She asked him – a question provoked, she said, by recalling an article he had written in the *Jewish Chronicle* – whether Rifkind was Jewish. The Prime Minister was delighted when he confirmed that he was. Although she emphasised that this was not the reason for his appointment, she hoped that it would help to counter the Foreign Office's anti-Israel reputation. She also hinted strongly that a place in the Cabinet as Scottish Secretary awaited him.[323]

Just under four years later, Mrs Thatcher made good on her words of encouragement. In truth, as Rifkind recognised, given the number of Scottish Tory MPs, the Prime Minister was not spoilt for choice.[324] Lady Thatcher's final judgement on her long-serving Scottish Secretary – Rifkind would go on to hold the post for nearly five years until the end of her premiership before rising through the Cabinet ranks to become John Major's Foreign Secretary – was as harsh as it was unfair. He was, she wrote, 'a brilliant and persuasive debater' and she doubted neither his 'intellect [n]or his grasp of ideas'. Nonetheless, she found Rifkind 'sensitive and highly strung' with 'erratic' judgement and 'unpredictable' behaviour. But the most serious charge, in her eyes, was his failure to implement in socialist Scotland a 'radical Thatcherite approach'.[325]

The Tories' poor performance in Scotland at the 1987 general election crystallised Mrs Thatcher's doubts. Rifkind was acutely aware of the government's precarious mandate north of the border. She believed the perfect cure for the ailing Scottish Conservative Party's woes was to 'extend Thatcherism to Scotland' and recoiled at what she saw as Rifkind's 'counter-productive' attempt to cast himself as 'Scotland's defender against Thatcherism'.[326] The division, however, was not as sharp as she cast it. Rifkind similarly believed that, as he put it shortly after the 1987 election, Scotland needed to rid itself of its 'anti-enterprise, paternalistic, quasi-socialist culture'.[327] Nonetheless, he had little time for the Thatcherite notion of 'permanent revolution' without any need for the occasional pause for consolidation.[328] He had also come to believe that it was Mrs Thatcher's 'bossy Englishwoman' style, rather than Thatcherism per se, which was at the root of the Tories' difficulties in Scotland.[329]

Rifkind hoped that Mrs Thatcher might retire gracefully but, when Heseltine launched his leadership bid in November 1990, he recoiled from the notion of deposing her and voted for the Prime Minister on the first ballot. When she met her Cabinet individually the night before her resignation, he cautioned her that her authority in the country had been fatally weakened, 'like a ship being holed below the waterline'.[330] She asked if he would support her in a second ballot. Rifkind indicated he would abstain, assuring her he would never vote against her. 'I thanked God for small mercies,' she later wrote.[331]

Out of office, Lady Thatcher privately gossiped that Rifkind 'really ought to have been in the Labour Party'.[332] It was not the first time that she had let slip her belief that he was 'a socialist'.[333] It was a facetious remark as well as an inaccurate one. Nonetheless, it highlighted Mrs Thatcher's particular brand of conviction politics which saw weakness and ideological heresy in the pragmatic 'One Nation' Toryism which Rifkind, while lacking their patrician backgrounds, shared with the 'wets' whom she had purged from her first Cabinet. Unlike theirs, however, Rifkind's politics was rooted in the 'trauma of the twentieth century' which had befallen the Jewish people: it had shaped his views on the virtues of tolerance and evils of racism,[334] but also ignited a suspicion of politicians, even in democracies, who claimed to have 'ideological solutions or total answers' to societies' problems.[335]

• • •

When Mrs Thatcher appointed Rifkind to a junior Foreign Office post, she dangled before him the prospect of becoming Scottish Secretary. For Michael Howard, she had higher aspirations. She hoped, she told him when giving him his first ministerial job in September 1985, 'you will be sitting where I am sitting one day'. Perhaps, Lord Howard modestly wondered thirty years later, Mrs Thatcher said that to all new junior ministers.[336] She almost certainly did not: instead, she had correctly identified a true believer.

Howard may not have made it to No. 10 but his rise to the highest ranks of British politics – first as Mrs Thatcher's Employment Secretary, later as John Major's Home Secretary and, in 2003, Conservative leader – was, in many regards, a ready-made Thatcherite morality tale. Another of Mrs Thatcher's one-time favourites, Norman Tebbit, famously recalled that during the Depression his unemployed father 'got on his bike' and looked for work. Michael Howard's father had got on a boat. Bernat Hecht had been born in Ruscova, a remote village in northern Transylvania's Carpathian mountains. Ambitious, intelligent and, as the synagogue's cantor, well-respected, it was a desire to better himself, rather than the increasingly perilous situation of Romanian Jews, which led Hecht to travel to Britain in the late 1930s.[337]

After working for a time as a cantor at the Fairclough Street Synagogue in Whitechapel, Bernat chose to settle in Llanelli in South Wales, where he married Hilda Kurshion, a fellow Jewish immigrant. A year after their marriage, their son, Michael, was born. The Kurshions were drapers and, like her widowed mother, Hilda sold clothes door to door or from market stalls in Llanelli and nearby towns. Bernat took up his new wife's trade: by the 1950s the couple had opened two stores, including one selling fashionable women's clothes. A third followed in 1960.

Michael's Orthodox parents were active in Llanelli's small Jewish community, serving on the committee of the synagogue. Their son, remembered his cousin Renée Woolf, was 'very frum': 'He could teach Chumash and he did lots in the schul.'[338] Perhaps reflecting the lack of anti-Semitism experienced by most Jews in Wales, young Michael does not appear to have been bullied for being Jewish.[339] At Cambridge, Howard moved away from Orthodox Judaism. Although he belonged to the University Jewish Society, many of his fellow students later claimed they were unaware he was Jewish.[340] Many years later, his rabbi at the St John's Wood Liberal Jewish synagogue, Dr David Goldberg, suggested that, like many Jews, Howard was 'punctilious about observing the New Year and Day of Atonement but not much else'.[341]

In contrast to Mrs Thatcher, Howard only rarely addressed his religious beliefs in public, venturing little beyond the suggestion he 'accepted those Jewish values I was brought up with. They are still an important guide and influence on my life'.[342] Nor did he often speak about his family background. It clearly still caused him 'much emotional pain', noted a reporter to whom he gave a rare interview about it.[343] The reason was obvious. For while Bernat was bringing up his young family, tragedy befell those he had left behind: Michael's grandmother, Leah, and her brother, his wife and two of their sons all perished in the Holocaust.

Although Howard's parents were interested in politics, they did not, he believed, vote Conservative until after their son began to get involved in the party.[344] Indeed, Michael's mother had, for a time, been a member of the Labour Party's youth wing.[345] One of Howard's reasons for becoming a Conservative echoes that of Brittan and many other Jews of their age: 'It was the Suez crisis in 1956 when I was 15 that first got me interested in politics,' he suggested. 'I strongly supported [Anthony] Eden's invasion and stand against Nasser's dictatorship.'[346]

Like Brittan, Howard's Conservatism was initially socially liberal but economically dry. He was appalled by Enoch Powell's 'Rivers of Blood' speech and as chairman of the Bow Group two years later wrote a paper which, in the words of the journalist Edward Pearce, offered 'sweepingly liberal' immigration terms for the East African Asians.[347] At the same time, the young barrister was already showing traces of proto-Thatcherism. Enthusiastic about the party's right-wing manifesto in 1970 – at a debate at the party's post-election conference he applauded its plans to get tough with the unions – he was disappointed by the Heath's government U-turn.[348] At a Coningsby Club dinner, he tackled Heath's ally, Jim Prior, on how long the measures would last. 'I was prepared to support [them] on the basis that it wasn't going to be the Tory creed forever … and was a crisis reaction to an undoubted crisis,' he recalled.[349] Howard's first meeting with Mrs Thatcher came in December 1973, when the then Education Secretary spoke at another dinner at the club. 'She made a great impression on me; I thought: "This woman is terrific".'[350] Unsurprisingly, he welcomed the new course Mrs Thatcher began to chart after 1975.

But while other members of the 'Cambridge Mafia' were now entering parliament, a winnable seat eluded Howard. Although unconvinced anti-Semitism was at work – 'I was a London barrister and London barristers were not always the flavour of the month'[351] – the aspiring MP was turned down by over forty constituency associations before being selected for Folkestone and Hythe in 1982.[352] In at least one of those cases, there is some evidence to suggest anti-Semitism may have played a part. As the victorious candidate in West Derbyshire, Matthew Parris, later noted, despite Howard having made the best speech at the selection meeting, 'a minority thought that he sounded too much the London lawyer; while a handful (no more) had been muttering about his being Jewish'.[353]

Whatever the obstacles he encountered on his road to Westminster, Howard experienced rather fewer once he finally reached his destination in 1983. Within two years of entering parliament, he had his foot on the first rung of the ministerial ladder – the first of the 100-strong new Tory intake to achieve this feat. The Prime Minister was impressed by her new recruit: 'He is very good. A very acute Silk,' she told Wyatt.[354] But it was as a minister responsible for local government and the environment after the 1987 general election that Howard earned his Thatcherite spurs championing some of the most controversial policies of Mrs Thatcher's final years in office: the poll tax, water privatisation and Section 28. 'I don't think I realised when Margaret Thatcher asked me to do the job quite how poisoned a chalice it would prove to be,' he later said of his role in the introduction of the poll tax.[355]

While the contents of that chalice were to prove fatal for the Prime Minister, it was Section 28, the infamous bar on schools teaching 'the acceptability of homosexuality as a pretended family relationship', which was to do more lasting damage to Howard's reputation and that of his party. Keen to erase perceptions of the Tories as 'the nasty party', David Cameron formally apologised for the law six years after it was repealed in 2003.

Perhaps unimpressed by his handling of the water privatisation issue – as was often her wont, she deemed the policy's deep unpopularity a result of her ministers' failure to convince the public of its intrinsic merits[356] – Mrs Thatcher seemed initially reluctant to promote Howard to the Cabinet when a vacancy arose in January 1990, preferring Michael Portillo.[357] None of those apparent doubts surfaced in her memoirs, however, where she related the eventual appointment of a 'rising star who shared my convictions'.[358] In his new role as Employment Secretary, Howard swiftly attended to some unfinished Thatcherite business: steering through parliament the final round of union reforms of her premiership.

A mark of Lady Thatcher's regard for Howard was evident in the fact that few others escaped so unscathed the score-settling which accompanied her later recounting of the events of November 1990. Howard, she wrote, was 'altogether stronger and more encouraging', than his colleagues, pledging that he would 'campaign vigorously' for her re-election if she chose to contest the second ballot.[359] After her departure from office, his social conservatism, support for a smaller state and Euroscepticism would make Howard one of Thatcherism's most enduring proponents, even if he was unable to convince the country of its virtues when he led the Conservative Party to its third consecutive defeat at the hands of Tony Blair fifteen years later.

CHAPTER 8

HOLY WARS: MARGARET THATCHER, THE BISHOPS AND THE CHIEF RABBI

By the mid-point of her premiership, Margaret Thatcher had vanquished many of those she regarded as proponents of, or collaborators in, the post-war consensus. 'One Nation' Conservatives had been sacked or side-lined within her Cabinet. The Labour Party had been crushed at the ballot box. The trade unions had been neutered, with the evisceration of the NUM a warning to those who refused to buckle to her will, and the universities had seen their budgets slashed and their standing diminished.

But in the autumn of 1985, when the Church of England published a damning report into the condition of urban Britain, Mrs Thatcher's government came under fire from one pillar of the old guard with which she had taken care not to tangle publicly. In the face of criticism, her normal instinct was to fight back. The Established Church was, though, an altogether more perilous opponent than Tory Party 'wets', municipal socialists or union barons. Luckily, however, the Prime Minister was to find the perfect shield against this ecclesiastical attack in the form of the man she had knighted four years previously and would soon send to the House of Lords, the Chief Rabbi, Sir Immanuel Jakobovits. Here was a man who, like her, would have no truck with those who seemed not to appreciate the values of hard work, wealth-creation, personal responsibility and family life. And here was a man who would provide her philosophy with the cloak of ethical justification seemingly denied her by Christian churchmen.

The Tory Party at prayer?

That Mrs Thatcher should find her most potentially dangerous philosophical opponent in the mid-1980s to be the Church of England was a situation which both pained her personally and worried her politically. Like all caricatures, the image of the Church of England as the 'Tory Party at prayer' contained a large measure of truth mixed with a healthy dose of exaggeration. Sixty years previously, for instance, its bishops had opposed the Tory government's handling of the general strike as well as its cuts in the dole.

Even before the publication of 'Faith in the City', tensions between Mrs Thatcher's government and the Church were running high. Just a year after she approved his appointment as Archbishop of Canterbury, her Oxford contemporary Robert Runcie had disappointed the Prime Minister by attacking the government's immigration policy and, as the jobless total soared, accusing it of not caring for the plight of the unemployed.[1] He had compounded his offence the following year, striking what she viewed as a decidedly discordant note at the service at St Paul's to mark Britain's victory in the Falklands by preaching the need for penitence and reconciliation. Then, during the miners' strike, the Church had proved itself worryingly keen to meddle in the dispute and broker a settlement, one which, the Prime Minister no doubt suspected, ran the risk of resulting in precisely the kind of messy compromise which had allowed the unions to ride roughshod over the British economy for far too long.

But in the prime ministerial canon of errors it was 'Faith in the City' which was to have a special place. Four hundred pages long and two years in the making, it proved to be, argued Eliza Filby, 'one of the most incisive and important critiques of Thatcher's Britain'.[2] Among the membership of the Archbishop of Canterbury's Commission on Urban Priority Areas were individuals almost designed to provoke a neuralgic reaction on the part of Mrs Thatcher. Chaired by Sir Richard O'Brien, whom Norman Tebbit had eased out of the Manpower Services Commission, its vice-chair was the Bishop of Liverpool, David Sheppard, a close collaborator of Michael Heseltine in the feared Cabinet minister's urban regeneration efforts on Merseyside, and a self-confessed socialist. Other members included the socialist sociologist A. L. Halsey and Canon Eric James, a left-leaning troublesome urban priest who had publicly denounced the Church for 'retreating to suburbia'.[3]

While pulling no punches in its attacks on the Church itself for being too absent and detached from the inner cities, it was its criticisms of government policy which were to dominate the headlines when the report was published in December 1985. From the outset, it was scathing: 'It is our considered view that the nation is confronted by a *grave and fundamental injustice* [original italics]' in urban areas. 'The situation continues to deteriorate and requires urgent action. No adequate response is being made by government, nation or Church.'[4]

Accusing the government of slashing spending on the inner cities, with the notable exception of the police, it suggested that urban areas could not be expected to 'pull themselves up by their own economic bootstraps'.[5] More money for public sector employment and higher welfare payments were thus required – a stance which flew directly in the face of the policies that had been adopted by Mrs Thatcher's government since it came to office. All twenty-three of its main public policy recommendations involved an increase in public expenditure.[6]

The report went on to denounce the government's flagship policy of council house sales, including mocking references to it as the 'sale of the century';[7] bemoan the 'divisive' impact of private schools;[8] and pronounce – in a chapter provocatively entitled 'Order and Law' – that the solution to inner-city crime was neither to 'intensify policing' nor to deploy former Home Secretary's Willie Whitelaw's 'short, sharp shock' of punishment for young offenders.[9]

It was not simply individual government's policies which 'Faith in the City' attacked, more damagingly it attacked the entire Thatcherite philosophy which underpinned them. The report had warm words to impart about

Christian socialism and 'all forms of collective action for the common good' and explicitly backed the redistribution of wealth. 'The creation of wealth,' it declared, 'must always go hand in hand with just distribution.'[10] It noted Marx's suggestion that evil can be present in 'the very structures of economic and social relationships', suggesting that he may actually have derived this perception from the Old Testament.[11]

In contrast, it was dismissive of some of the key tenets of the Prime Minister's beliefs. 'Individual responsibility and self-reliance are excellent objectives,' it breezily noted. 'The nation cannot do without them. But pursuit of them must not damage a collective obligation and provision for those who have no choice, or whose choices are at best forced ones. *We believe that at present too much emphasis is being given to individualism and not enough to collective obligation* [original italics].'[12] Finally, the report took aim at one of the principal doctrines of Thatcherism – the expansion of choice – and one of its most prized policy achievements, the encouragement of home ownership, and declared them an illusion. 'For most low-income city residents, freedom of choice is a cruel deception,' it argued.[13]

By 1985 the bishops had come to see themselves, believed Filby, as 'one of the main custodians' of the post-war consensus, even if they failed to recognise the degree to which the middle-class discontents of the 1970s, which Mrs Thatcher both shared and was responding to, had already fatally undermined it before she set foot in Downing Street.[14] But while the Prime Minister believed she had her finger on the pulse of the middle classes' political outlook, she understood all too well the potential power of words delivered from pulpits. She knew, too, that the Church of England's flock was her political base; more than six in ten Anglicans were believed to be Tory supporters.[15] The Church may have had fewer people in its pews every week, but it was congregations in the Labour-voting inner cities, not the heavily Tory suburbs and shires, that were shrinking fastest. The bishops were keenly aware of this, as indicated when Sheppard wrote to the Chief Rabbi of the report: '[It] is rightly aimed at suburban Britons, who all too easily blame those who have been left behind.'[16] As Runcie decreed that 'Faith in the City' be debated in every parish, and the public snapped up 60,000 copies of an abridged version, Mrs Thatcher faced a challenge rather more potent than that provided by her opponents across the floor of the House of Commons.

'Faith in the City' did not, however, simply represent a political challenge. As her Political Secretary, Lord Sherbourne, suggested, she was 'hurt' by the report 'not because they criticised [her policy] because she was quite a hardened politician when it came to policy. I think she was hurt [by] ... the idea that she didn't care about these things, didn't care about people'.[17] On reading 'Faith in the City' she had, noted Moore, alighted on one of the submissions it approvingly quoted – that 'the exclusion of the poor is pervasive and not accidental' – and scrawled two large question marks beside it, heavily underlining the words 'not accidental'.[18]

Beyond her injured feelings, though, Mrs Thatcher disagreed both philosophically and theologically with the report. Privately, she complained to one of her ministers, John Selwyn Gummer, a former chairman of the Conservative Party and a member of the General Synod, that 'Faith in the City' was 'unbelievably woolly' and showed a lack of understanding of how the economy worked.[19] To Woodrow Wyatt, she confided: 'There's nothing about self-help or doing anything for yourself in the report.'[20] But ultimately, suspected Sherbourne, Mrs Thatcher also believed – not uniquely among politicians when they're criticised by religious leaders – that the bishops should 'stick to their theological and ecclesiastical issues'. Instead of 'meddling' in government policy, they should be 'saving souls'.[21]

Unusually for a Prime Minister, Mrs Thatcher had repeatedly attempted – both in set-piece speeches at St Lawrence Jewry in 1978 and 1981, and to the General Assembly of the Church of Scotland in 1988, as well as in various media appearances – to demonstrate that, while Christians did not have to be Conservatives, there was 'a deep and providential harmony' between her political philosophy and religious beliefs.[22] The common thread, she sought to show, was the importance of personal responsibility and the freedom to choose. For Mrs Thatcher, Antonio Weiss noted, this had important implications: 'Wealth creation and philanthropy went hand-in-hand with personal responsibility which validated a curtailment of welfare expenditure, and freedom of choice necessitated strong moral leadership from the Churches'.[23]

'Faith in the City' had not simply challenged Mrs Thatcher's policies and philosophy, it had also effectively repudiated the religious underpinnings of them that she had been so careful to spell out. Her advisers were forthright in their criticisms of it. A summary of the report prepared by the head of her Policy Unit, Brian Griffiths, warned the Prime Minister of a 'deep hostility' to the government running through the report and accused it of being underpinned by 'Marxist analysis'.[24] Nonetheless, in response to the gauntlet the bishops had thrown down, they urged caution. Griffiths, an Anglican academic who had lectured on Christian morality and the marketplace, recommended she welcome the report as 'a serious investigation of a real problem', but then go on to 'express surprise that the recommendations of the report lay far more emphasis on central and local government than they do on the family'. 'Kill it with kindness,' recommended another adviser, 'A Church-Government row would keep the Report on the front pages.'[25]

Mrs Thatcher followed the script. She told the BBC diplomatically that she had read the report with 'great interest', before continuing that none of its recommendations concerned individuals and families. 'I must say I was really absolutely shocked at that,' she said, barely biting her tongue.[26] Others were less disciplined. One unnamed Cabinet minister denounced the bishops' 'pure Marxist theology'; another Tory MP suggested it proved that the Church of England was led by a 'load of Communist clerics'.[27] Predictably, the report now found its way to the front pages.

Enter the Chief Rabbi

Mrs Thatcher may have been stung by the Church of England's attack, but she was not required, as Hugo Young argued, to depend upon it for 'spiritual succour'.[28] That role would be played instead by the memory of the Methodism of her Grantham youth and the strong echoes she detected of it in the Judaism she encountered in the streets and synagogues of her Finchley constituency. But while the Methodist Church showed little more approval of

Thatcherism than had the Church of England – in 1988 its conference would condemn the government's supposedly divisive policies – Mrs Thatcher was to find a more sympathetic ear in the Chief Rabbi.

Born in East Prussia in 1921, Immanuel Jakobovits was sent to London to escape the Nazis at the age of fifteen. Alone, as his parents and younger brothers and sisters had remained in Berlin, and unable to speak English, the young man was placed in an overcrowded hostel in Stamford Hill. Despite his unfamiliar surroundings and having previously been a somewhat unimpressive schoolboy, Jakobovits passed his matriculation exam nine months after his arrival. Like Mrs Thatcher, he decided to study science and won a place at Queen Mary's College. But, like Alfred Roberts, Dr Julius Jakobovits, a judge in Berlin's main rabbinical court, was to exert a powerful parental influence. Hailing from a distinguished line of rabbis, he persuaded Immanuel to drop his studies, enrol at Jews' College and a *yeshiva*, and enter the rabbinate. Immanuel's willingness to do so was unsurprising: as Chaim Bermant wrote, he had 'not only been very close to his father, but had almost worshipped him'. Throughout his life, Jakobovits viewed his father – who died when he was only sixty-one – as a 'mentor and guide' and spoke often of him.[29] In these regards – paternal influence and evoked memory – Prime Minister and Chief Rabbi had much in common. Kristallnacht finally persuaded Julius that his family could no longer remain in Berlin. They followed Immanuel to London.

For a time, the family struggled. Julius had lost his job and his status. Living in hardship, they were often forced to accept charity handouts. Eventually, however, their fortunes began to improve. The younger sons found work, so too in time did their father: in 1945, he accepted a post at the London Beth Din rabbinical court similar to that which he had held in Berlin. Immanuel Jakobovits, meanwhile, served in various synagogues in London during the 1940s before succeeding Isaac Herzog as Chief Rabbi of the Jewish communities in Ireland in 1949. A decade later, Jakobovits moved his young family to New York to take up a post at the Fifth Avenue Synagogue.

Despite his love of the United States and its Jewish community, in 1966 Jakobovits accepted the offer to become the Chief Rabbi of the United Hebrew Congregations of the British Commonwealth. He considered the move carefully; he had previously told a colleague that the American Jewish community was the 'First Division of Jewish life', but Jakobovits was unable to resist the lure of a return to Britain. He shared Mrs Thatcher's passion for the country which had saved his immediate family from death in the 1930s – he termed Britain 'a kingdom of righteousness'[30] – and he also shared her lifelong distrust of Germany and deep scepticism about European integration.[31] He never returned to his homeland. When invited to speak at a conference in Aachen, he choose to deliver the lecture just across the Dutch border in, ironically given its later role in furthering the European project, Maastricht. However, the 'Victorian values' of hard work, thrift, clean-living and self-reliance which were so beloved of Alfred Roberts and Mrs Thatcher had a Teutonic tinge. They were derived in part from the Protestant work ethic, itself stemming from the German reformer Martin Luther, as well as the prevailing morality which came with the accession of Victoria to the throne and her later marriage to Prince Albert of Saxe-Coburg and Gotha, with more than a dash of the self-help promulgated by the Scottish writer Samuel Smiles. Continuing to govern Germany's Jewish communities long after others had abandoned them, argued Chaim Bermant, these values heavily influenced Jakobovits's upbringing in Königsberg in East Prussia – as they had Margaret Thatcher's in Grantham. As Bermant concluded: 'Jakobovits was thus not a convert to Victorian values, but a natural Victorian himself.'[32]

Minister of Defence

Jakobovits's principal social concern on becoming Chief Rabbi was the poor state of Jewish education. In 1971 he established the Jewish Educational Development Trust which produced a network of primary and secondary schools supported by public funds. In the same year, he met Mrs Thatcher, then Secretary of State for Education, for the first time. It was to be the first of many meetings. He told her about the importance of education in

Judaism, reminding her that inside the mezuzahs, which are fixed to the doors of Jewish homes, are words from Deuteronomy: 'Teach them to your children.' 'You are really the Minister of Defence,' he told her, underlining the critical role he believed schools played in shoring up the nation's moral fortifications.[33] With her love of martial-sounding and patriotic hymns, it is not hard to see why this analogy would make a lasting impression on Mrs Thatcher. Years later, after she had entered No. 10, the Prime Minister reminded Jakobovits of it.

It was the beginning of a warm friendship and ideological kinship which would span her years as opposition leader, Prime Minister and beyond. Sherbourne compared it to her relationship with Ronald Reagan. 'She felt affinity with people who shared her approach to life and I think she felt that with Reagan. We are not talking about politics here, we are talking about instinct and I think this is what she felt about Jakobovits.'[34]

The key to the friendship – Mrs Thatcher was one of the few people who called Jakobovits by his first name[35] – was his wife, Amèlie. 'She made them friends,' said Shimon Cohen, executive director of the Chief Rabbi's office. 'Immanuel did not have friends, he had intellectual discussions with people who wished to have an intellectual discussion with him.' Without his wife's nurturing of the social side of the relationship, Jakobovits would probably have communicated with the Prime Minister primarily by sending her copies of his speeches.[36] Thanks to Amèlie, Mrs Thatcher and Denis visited the Chief Rabbi and his wife at their home in Hamilton Terrace, St Johns Wood, and the couple dined with the Thatchers in Downing Street. On one occasion, Mrs Thatcher and her husband were dinner guests at the Jakobovits's sukkah, the temporary hut erected during the Jewish festival of Sukkot. Amèlie recalled that both Mrs Thatcher and Denis were 'always full of questions and wanted to know as much as they could from the Chief Rabbi about our rituals, the meaning of Jewish law, the meaning of Jewish ethics and the explanations'.[37]

While Mrs Thatcher and Jakobovits discovered their shared interest in science, Amèlie bonded with Denis, seeing that he exercised the same 'supportive restraint' towards his wife as she offered to her husband.[38] She was often barely able to contain the pride she felt at Mrs Thatcher's evident regard for her husband. 'Look at how Margaret Thatcher is looking at my husband,' she gushed at a Jewish charity function where the Prime Minister was speaking, 'She really admires him.'[39] For Amèlie, who, like the Chief Rabbi, never lost the 'childish excitement' of meeting a member of the Royal Family or a Prime Minister, this admiration was further evidence of her mother's prediction of her husband: 'This man is going to be great.'[40]

At a speech to mark his retirement two months after she was ejected from Downing Street, Mrs Thatcher let the guests into what she termed 'one of the nation's worst kept secrets' – that, through 'his thinking and writing', the Chief Rabbi had had 'a deep effect on me'. Did that, she pondered, make her 'a Jakobovite or him a Thatcherite'?[41] It was a poorly kept secret because the Prime Minister had never tried to maintain it. Instead, she had repeatedly lavished praise on the 'absolutely marvellous' Chief Rabbi who 'always speaks up fearlessly on everything'.[42]

While Jakobovits would no doubt have felt obliged to deny the suggestion that he was a Thatcherite, the admiration was mutual. Certainly, his letters to her went beyond the perfunctory wishes of congratulation or commiseration which might have been expected of a man in his position. The day after she secured a landslide re-election in 1983, for instance, Jakobovits wrote to offer his 'personal felicitations on the resounding endorsement of your resolute leadership'. He hoped, he wrote, that she would 'continue to guide the destinies of our country through these turbulent times on the firm foundations of our moral heritage which you have done so much to uphold and promote'.[43] When Mrs Thatcher survived the IRA's attempt to murder her a year later in Brighton, he expressed his gratitude at her 'miraculous escape … at the hands of a merciful Providence'. 'Your personal example of fortitude,' he wrote, 'will be a source of inspiration and great solace to the entire nation.'[44]

The relationship between the Prime Minister and the Chief Rabbi piqued the interest of the press. In *The Guardian* Hugo Young speculated that Jakobovits had become her 'private counsellor, supplier of spiritual uplift, therapist beyond the walls'.⁴⁵ The *Sunday Telegraph*'s Peregrine Worsthorne awarded the Chief Rabbi the accolade of 'spiritual leader of Thatcherite Britain ... more than amply filling the vacuum created by the blank refusal of the Christian Churches to make any constructive contribution towards her crusade for the regeneration of Britain'.⁴⁶ For the *Daily Telegraph* it was clear that Jakobovits was 'the one prelate whose preaching did not, in the view of Mrs Thatcher, give God a bad name'.⁴⁷

The notion of Jakobovits as the high priest of Thatcherism was, in some respects, something of a misnomer. Certainly, this is not how the Chief Rabbi regarded himself. 'I have never seen myself as right wing. I believe I am a moderate,' he suggested when denying that he was a Conservative. 'Moderation is an article of faith. The willingness to see both sides and always to be concerned about compromise.'⁴⁸ As Mrs Thatcher prepared to mark her tenth year in Downing Street, Jakobovits proclaimed his adherence to another principle which the Prime Minister had publicly scorned. 'I'm concerned,' he told *The Guardian*, to 'preserve the heartland of consensus in a society which becomes increasingly polarised – something that still knits us all together.'⁴⁹

It was true that Jakobovits had little interest in party politics. After his elevation to the Lords, the Chief Rabbi was keen to emphasise his independence and that he had not been the beneficiary of a political appointment. 'I am just not by persuasion of any one political party,' he suggested.⁵⁰ Indeed, when Jakobovits first received his offer of a peerage, he was keen to ensure that it was not designed by the government to either, in the words of Cohen, 'stick one to the Church' or politicise his role. The Chief Rabbi dispatched his aide to consult both the opposition and Runcie's office – who confirmed the government had discussed the matter with them and the Church had offered 'a very fulsome recommendation'. Lord Mishcon, a Jewish grandee who served on Labour's front bench, urged acceptance and, along with the Cabinet minister Lord Young, was one of Jakobovits's two supporters at the Chief Rabbi's introduction ceremony in the House of Lords.⁵¹

As if to drive home the point of his independence, Jakobovits used his maiden speech in 1988 to attack the government's further tightening of immigration controls – a subject on which he had publicly opposed Mrs Thatcher's administration during its first year in office.[52] The Chief Rabbi's maiden speech also touched on another subject – Israel's relationship with the Palestinians – on which he had provoked disquiet in some sections of the Jewish community, but where, as discussed in Chapter 9, he and Mrs Thatcher were broadly in agreement. He would later go on to speak out passionately against cuts in the health service and the Conservatives' NHS reforms.

Jakobovits was also keen not to be seen as abusing his relationship with the Prime Minister. In the late 1980s when *shechita* appeared to come under threat from new regulations, the Agriculture Secretary, John Gummer, who was under pressure from animal welfare groups, suggested to Cohen that only a direct approach from the Chief Rabbi to Mrs Thatcher was likely to break the impasse. Jakobovits, recalled Cohen, was 'hesitant, reluctant to circumvent the formal process' but was persuaded he had little option.[53] Mrs Thatcher was aware of the sensitivities: the issue had been raised locally and the Tories had indicated during the 1987 election that the government would not introduce policies designed to ban *shechita*.[54] At a private meeting in her flat above No. 10, the Chief Rabbi and the Prime Minister struck a deal which saved *shechita*.[55]

Speaking out

Although Jakobovits professed his commitment to consensus, he did not believe he should shy away from expressing strongly held views simply to avoid controversy. 'Only horses,' he believed, 'walk in the middle of the road.'[56] He sometimes appeared surprised by the controversy his forthrightly expressed opinions caused, but he was also conscious that he was redefining the role of Chief Rabbi. His first decade in office had focused very much on the Jewish community; his second was to be very different. 'In the past there has been too much reticence,' he suggested in 1986, 'Jews preferred to be discreet. Deliberately, I have been speaking out on moral issues.'[57] Thus he backed

Victoria Gillick, the Catholic mother who ran a high-profile campaign to prevent doctors prescribing contraception to under-16s without the consent of their parents, and, reflecting his long-standing interest in medical ethics, attacked the Warnock Committee on surrogate motherhood for refusing to limit access to infertility treatment to only married couples. He believed the law should set public standards for what was right and wrong and should be a tool to 'express public abhorrence'. This belief also led him to advocate that 'homosexual acts' and adultery should be criminalised, even if he accepted that no prosecutions would be made.[58]

Mrs Thatcher's voting record suggests these were issues on which she and Jakobovits might part ways. She was an astute enough politician to know there were precious few votes to be gained in attempting to legislate against adultery, nor, indeed, was she particularly personally censorious. 'What's that got to do with anything?' she asked her party chairman, Cecil Parkinson, when on polling day in 1983 he turned down her offer to make him Foreign Secretary because, he confessed to the Prime Minister, he had made his former secretary pregnant.[59] Moreover, while Mrs Thatcher had opposed reform of the divorce laws on the basis that it would make it easier for husbands to abandon their wives, she had also voted to decriminalise both abortion and homosexual acts. As a lawyer and politician, she later wrote, she felt it was important that laws should be 'enforceable and its application fair to those who might run foul of it'. In retirement, however, Lady Thatcher hinted at a greater sympathy for Jakobovits's views. Laws, she argued, had 'a symbolic significance: they are signposts to the way society is developing'. Taken together, the liberal reforms of the 1960s amounted to more than the sum of their parts and provided a 'radically new framework' for the way in which young people were supposed to behave.[60] Those signposts, she clearly now believed, had pointed in the wrong direction.

On perhaps one of the most contentious moral issues of the 1980s – how to respond to Aids – Mrs Thatcher and Jakobovits were similarly in tune. Unusually for a Prime Minister who believed in leading from the front, the fight against Aids was not an issue on which Mrs Thatcher wished to make the running. To her credit, however, she swallowed her initial doubts and allowed her Health Secretary, Norman Fowler, to launch a high-profile campaign to promote safer sex.[61] Jakobovits avoided some of the more intemperate language of social conservatives and the mass media – 'we are never entitled to declare a particular form of suffering as a punishment for a particular manifestation of wrongdoing,' he wrote in *The Times* – and urged compassion for those who were sick.[62] Nonetheless, his stance was uncompromising. Aids was 'the price we pay for the "benefits" of the permissive society', he suggested, while the government's campaign, he wrote to the House of Commons Social Services Committee, 'encourages promiscuity by advertising it. It tells people not what is right, but how to do wrong and get away with it.'[63] Mrs Thatcher recognised the potential huge public health danger posed by Aids and, as a pragmatist, she understood that 'there will be some people who will get together in any event and it is our duty to tell them of the dangers if they do'. But her personal feelings were closer to those of Jakobovits. Should the churches speak out more about the supposed moral laxity which allowed the spread of Aids, she was asked in 1987? 'I feel so, yes,' she replied.[64]

On terrorism, too, the views of the Prime Minister and Chief Rabbi were closely in sync. With IRA terrorism at home and Arab terrorism abroad playing on his mind, Jakobovits wrote to Mrs Thatcher suggesting that terrorists thrive on what he termed 'the oxygen of publicity' and that a way needed to be found to starve them of it.[65] In July 1985, nine months after the Brighton bombing, and following the hijacking of TWA Flight 847 in Beirut the previous month, she adopted the phrase as her own; it would eventually lead to the introduction of an ultimately futile ban on broadcasting the voices of IRA and Sinn Fein spokesmen. She would, on other occasions, appropriate phrases from the Chief Rabbi. In 1986, for instance, she asked to borrow a metaphor Jakobovits used in a Finchley sermon about a man on life's journey leaving some baggage behind in the 'spiritual left-luggage office'. On this occasion, she was less interested in God than Mammon: she wished to apply the phrase to the enterprise culture, which had been similarly misplaced in Britain before her arrival in Downing Street.[66]

Taking on the Bishops

Robert Runcie was another of the select band of people with whom Jakobovits was on first-name terms. When meeting at Lambeth Palace or the Chief Rabbi's residence, the two would often spend time walking and talking together alone. Jakobovits was sensitive to the heavy criticism the Archbishop was frequently under and liked to call him to give him an encouraging word. The two religious leaders often sent each other copies of their speeches in advance. It was, therefore, no surprise when Runcie sent Jakobovits an advance copy of 'Faith in the City', asking for his views.[67]

It took little time for the Chief Rabbi to come to a view. 'When we read it,' recalled Cohen, 'it wasn't Jewish – it wasn't meant to be Jewish – but it didn't have that "get up and go" … It did not resonate with our immigrant experience.'[68] Jakobovits later spoke of his misgivings on reading the report. 'They charged the government with not having taken action on behalf of the underprivileged classes, with emphasis placed mainly on the government's shortcomings,' he argued. 'They said nothing about strengthening the family', nor did they mention the 'intrinsic value of work' or suggest that people needed to take any personal responsibility for improving their condition. Jakobovits's view was that the solution to the plight of urban Britain 'lies primarily in the efforts of the immigrants themselves'.[69]

The Chief Rabbi decided to undertake a short study of his own, spending time at Toynbee Hall and some of the churches and mosques of London's East End, which both had large immigrant communities and had originally been the place in which most Jewish migrants had settled. He proceeded to write Runcie a twenty-page personal reply. The Archbishop responded: he did not agree with all of Jakobovits's analysis but urged him to publish it. It would help provoke an interesting and important debate, Runcie suggested.[70]

In January 1986, the *Jewish Chronicle* cleared three pages and, under the headline 'From Doom to Hope', published the Chief Rabbi's dissection of the bishops' attack on Thatcherism. The Prime Minister could scarcely have hoped for a more thoroughgoing rebuttal. In place of the ill-conceived 'Marxist' analysis they had offered, here was a religious authority taking the fight to her clerical critics and, albeit without explicitly saying so, endorsing much of the basis of her political philosophy and her government's actions.

As the opening paragraphs of his essay made clear, however, Jakobovits's views were long-standing. Their power, and the controversy they provoked, rested on his attempt to draw a sharp contrast between the manner in which immigrant Jews had worked their way out of the ghettos during the early twentieth century and life in Britain's inner cities in the 1980s. With the riots of the summer of 1981 and autumn of 1985 still fresh in his mind, the Chief Rabbi quoted from the farewell address he gave when he left New York in 1966 – a period when urban unrest was similarly sweeping America:

> How did we break out of our ghettos and enter the mainstream of society and its privileges? How did we secure our emancipation and civil rights? Certainly not by riots and demonstrations, by violence and protest-marches … Above all we worked on ourselves, not on others. We gave a better education to our children than anybody else had. We hallowed our home life. We channelled the ambition of our youngsters to academic excellence, not flashy cars. We rooted out crime and indolence from our midst, by making every Jew feel responsible for the fate of all Jews.[71]

Jakobovits then proceeded to provide black Britons with a lecture on law and order. Instead of complaining about alleged 'institutionalised racism' in the police force, he suggested, their leaders should take a leaf out of the book of Jewish immigrants who had 'cultivated trust in and respect for the police, realising that our security as a minority depended on law and order being maintained'.[72] He echoed the words that Alfred Sherman had written to Mrs Thatcher on the eve of the Ilford by-election and noted that Jews had always been 'quite content for Britain to remain "ethnocentrically" British'; they had attempted to preserve their own identity, but hadn't asked for 'public help, nor … changes in official policies' in order to do so.[73] Finally, he counselled patience. Jews had been prepared to 'wait and struggle for several generations' to better themselves. Why, he implied, couldn't more recent immigrants? Indeed, those presently living in hardship should draw comfort from the fact that, as the Jewish experience proved, 'self-reliant efforts and perseverance eventually pay off'.[74]

Having offered the residents of the inner cities a supposedly comforting history lesson, Jakobovits then provided some religious instruction on work, wealth-creation and welfare. The Jewish work ethic, he lectured, was 'rather more positive and demanding' than the Christian one set out in 'Faith in the City'. The report had failed to make clear that work was 'a virtue in itself' and that 'no work is too menial to compromise human dignity and self-respect'. Idleness, the Chief Rabbi contended, was 'a greater evil' than unemployment, while low-paid work was 'more dignified than a free dole'. Contentment, Judaism suggested, came from 'economic self-reliance and self-sufficiency'.[75]

Beside bemoaning the Church's attitude towards work, Jakobovits was also unimpressed by its approach towards welfare and wealth-creation. He disputed the notion that wealth must be justly obtained but also fairly distributed. Judaism, he argued, insisted on the former but did not demand the latter.[76] Jakobovits did not deny that there was a 'collective responsibility' to ensure social justice, but insisted this involved neither 'compensation' nor 'entitlement'. 'The poor cannot be compensated for monies which others earn'; it was the responsibility of those who could to give to those in need, but he dismissed the notion that they had any entitlement to such giving. Philanthropy should be directed, moreover, towards providing a hand up not a hand out.[77]

Finally, Jakobovits outlined what he thought the report lacked. It failed to provide a proper emphasis on both the importance of personal responsibility – 'building up self-respect by encouraging ambition and enterprise' – and the central role of the family in regenerating the inner cities.[78] 'When the family breaks down,' he wrote, 'the most essential conditions for raising happy, law-abiding and creatively ambitious citizens are frustrated'.[79] The Chief Rabbi concluded by suggesting that 'Faith in the City' was 'unduly slanted' against the government's policies and placed too much responsibility on them for the ills of the inner cities. At the same time, he took the trade unions – on whom, he noted, the report had placed no blame – to task for both the 'crippling effects on the economy of strikes which paralyse entire industries' and the 'self-ishness of workers' who attempted to attain better conditions even at the cost of 'rising unemployment and immense public misery'.[80]

Jakobovits was not, as his critics charged, simply spouting Thatcherite mantras. As his reference to his sermon in New York indicated, these were views, however unpalatable some were to find them, which he genuinely held. Two years before Mrs Thatcher arrived in Downing Street, for instance, he spoke publicly of his fear that the welfare state was draining individuals of self-reliance and he disavowed people 'getting things for nothing' from it.[81] As Cohen suggested, the Chief Rabbi's views on social policy were based on his reading of Jewish teaching. It was the fact that Mrs Thatcher believed those teachings echoed her own philosophy which underlay their relation-ship.[82] 'Their friendship,' wrote Bermant as her premiership drew to a close, 'arises not from the fact that one converted the other, but from a coincidence of attitudes, and she is sufficiently religious to cherish the fact that she has at least one man of God on her side.'[83]

Recreating Britain

Despite her preference that churchmen stick to 'saving souls', Mrs Thatch-er was, unsurprisingly, grateful for Jakobovits's intervention, believing, in the words of Sherbourne, that 'the record had been set straight'.[84] But her admiration for the 'wonderful' Chief Rabbi long predated this.[85] When Me-nachem Begin visited No. 10 three weeks after her victory in 1979, she told the Israeli Prime Minister – 'her eyes ablaze with enthusiasm,' recalled one of his staff – of her respect for 'your marvellous chief rabbi here'. He had, she continued, 'an inspiring commitment to the old-fashioned virtues, like com-munity self-help, individual responsibility, and personal accountability – all the things I deeply believe'. Already, it was clear, she was drawing compari-sons with 'her' lily-livered bishops. 'Oh, how I wish our own church leaders would take a leaf out of your chief rabbi's book,' she complained to Begin.[86]

Her comments to Begin encapsulated a key element in the Prime Minister's admiration for the Chief Rabbi. While the Church of England seemed somehow embarrassed by its supposedly old-fashioned teachings, she believed, Jakobovits evinced no such discomfiture. Just as she viewed herself as someone ever-willing to deliver hard truths whether or not they were fashionable or popular, so she saw that same quality in the Chief Rabbi. And it was, Mrs Thatcher was convinced, one that was sadly lacking in many of the bishops of the Church of which she herself was a member. Perhaps, too, she also found in his teachings a forthrightness and moral certainty reminiscent of her father.[87] After all, as she made clear on the steps of Downing Street on the day she became Prime Minister, there would be no place for doubt in Margaret Thatcher's Britain.

Nothing over the next eleven years would change her view: out of office, as we have seen, she bemoaned the fact that Christians and their leaders did not 'take closer note of the Jewish emphasis on self-help and acceptance of personal responsibility'. Lady Thatcher believed these were not just words: she had seen those values in action in Finchley, where she claimed she had never had 'a Jew come in poverty and desperation' to one of her constituency surgeries.[88] 'My, they were good citizens,' she later told Charles Moore.[89]

These were themes which had long animated her, and to which she would repeatedly return when, as she frequently did, she addressed Jewish audiences. In 1978, for instance, Sherman prepared a note for her before she attended a lunch organised by the Jewish education and vocational training charity ORT (see Chapter 7). On it, she underlined points that interested her: that the charity had been established in Tsarist Russia as a form of 'communal self-help', that the minority of Jews who were professionally and economically able 'set out energetically to assist their less fortunate fellows', and that the charity's current work reflected 'the perennial Jewish desire to share with fellow-humans [sic] beyond their own circle'.[90]

Even as Prime Minister, Mrs Thatcher enjoyed reading theological books, including those by the former Archbishop of York, Stuart Blanch, the leader of the Catholic Church in England and Wales, Cardinal Hume, CS Lewis and, of course, the Chief Rabbi.[91] In 1988, she decided to tackle the Old Testament. Her staff received regular updates on her progress. The eager Grantham schoolgirl was, once again, on display. What is the only book in the Bible not to mention God, she asked one day? She was delighted when nobody knew the answer and she could reveal it was the Book of Esther. 'It is a very gory book,' she warned them.[92]

But such study was no mere arid scholarship or simple interest. For there were strains of non-conformity, like that which the young Margaret Roberts had absorbed, that drew from the Old Testament an outlook, a morality and a muscularity, which were not easily discernible within the Catholic and Established churches. How much her attachment to the Old Testament coloured her Christianity and thus her politics may be seen when, referring to the Jews as 'the people of the Old Testament', she asked: '[h]ow can you believe in the New unless you believe in the Old?'[93]

Mrs Thatcher had, as Peregrine Worsthorne argued, chosen to 'revive what might be called the strict parts of the Christian message … [those] which stem from the Hebrew tradition. It is the mode of commandments and, if those commandments are not fulfilled, of punishments.'[94] It was a message which resonated with many, Jew and non-Jew alike, and, perhaps, it contained a cold-eyed understanding of human nature. Others, however, found it hard-hearted and unforgiving of individual weakness or misfortune.

While some parts of the Old Testament, Mrs Thatcher later told the broadcaster David Frost, should not be left in 'untutored hands', in Jewish teachings she saw her own values – those instilled in her by the experience of both the grocery and chapel in Grantham – reflected.[95] 'She had a true sense of religion, and she admired many Jewish values,' believed Jakobovits's successor, Lord Sacks. 'In particular she liked the Jewish emphasis on accountability and responsibility, on entrepreneurial ambition mixed with compassion and on the priority Jews accord to giving back to their community.'[96] Like Jakobovits, he, too, had offered Judaic legitimacy for some of the key tenets of Thatcherism. In 'Wealth And Poverty: A Jewish Analysis',[97] which was published a few months before 'From Doom to Hope', the then-principal of Jews' College argued that, while Judaism placed an 'extreme emphasis' on charity, precisely because it regarded poverty as 'an unmitigated evil', it demanded that 'no-one may relieve the poverty of others at the cost of impoverishing himself' especially if it destroyed one's 'wealth-creating possibilities'.[98]

These values, not the soggy Christianity of 'Faith in the City', offered the route to the regeneration of Britain. At their core was the principle of individual responsibility. The concept of human rights, the Prime Minister told the Technion University dinner in November 1989, derived from Judaism with its emphasis on the dignity of the individual and his accountability for his actions. But, she added, so too did the recognition that with rights come responsibilities. She recited the words of the Chief Rabbi: 'There is no bill of rights in the biblical tradition: there are only ten commandments. The stress is not on what we may claim, but on the debt we owe: the duty to give, the duty to help future generations, the obligation to give back more than we have received.'[99]

She was inspired by the way Jews discharged that obligation through the duty of *gemilat hasadim* or charitable concern. As she described it, it was not difficult to discern the link in her mind between it and her own beliefs. 'The Jewish tradition understands first, the importance of creating wealth through one's own efforts,' she told the Board of Deputies, 'and, second, the importance of sharing one's wealth with others, the recognition that with wealth comes responsibility.' Or, as she had put it to the Conservative Party conference a few months previously: 'Only by creating wealth can you relieve poverty. It's what you do with your wealth that counts.'[100] Nonetheless, as she implicitly suggested, 'sharing one's wealth' was a personal responsibility,[101] to be exercised through charitable giving, not one which, as she had suggested in her speech at St Lawrence Jewry twelve years previously, should become the exclusive responsibility of the state. For her, *gemilat hasadim* was a very practical notion of compassion. Jews, she reflected in retirement, believed in 'not just talking, but doing and giving'.[102] This thus set them apart from those who, as she put in on the eve of the 1987 election, 'drool and drivel they care' while shirking off their responsibilities to 'society' and the state.[103]

But there was something else about the way in which she believed Britain's Jews lived their lives which the Prime Minister had come to so admire. The trait Mrs Thatcher most admired in Jews, believed Lord Young, was that, hailing from immigrant backgrounds, 'they tended to be self-starters'. Being the daughter of a small businessman who worked for himself, 'she understood that ethos'.[104]

The Prime Minister took this as her theme when, accepting an honorary degree in October 1988 from the Hebrew University in Jerusalem, she declared that the 'Jewish people have set an example for the rest of us to follow'. This came in the form of what Mrs Thatcher termed 'the Jewish approach to life'. This was not just about 'the high achievement, the generosity, the sense of community and of helping each other' – important though these were – but also 'the recognition that – as the philosopher Thomas Huxley said – the great end in life is not knowledge but action: the belief that you must always press forward to change and improve'. This was, indeed, the path for Thatcherite Britain to follow. 'That restlessness, that determination always to strive, to build and create', she declared, was something that was now being recreated in the country as a whole: 'More and more of our people are taking the opportunities, welcoming responsibility, showing initiative and enterprise.'[105] As 'Faith in the City' had proved, it was not, however, a vision she would find sanctioned by the Established Church. Jewish teachings, she understood, provided many warmer words for ambition and self-advancement than those of Christianity. This had been her overriding mission all along: national rebirth through instilling a new moral code in the British people. 'Economics are the method,' she had declared in 1981, 'the object is to change the heart and soul.'[106]

Her speech to the Friends of Hebrew University was, though, but one in a plethora of glowing tributes to British Jewry whose contribution to the country, as she put it six months before she left office, was 'so great and so outstanding' precisely because it had 'always been guided by a desire to contribute to the community, and not just to benefit from it'.[107] She recognised, of course, that the values she discerned in the Jewish community – respect for education (Jews, she believed, were 'one of the most scholarly races'[108]), personal responsibility, hard work and giving back to the community – were not unique to Jews. However, she believed that the community practised them in an 'exemplary fashion'.[109]

Mrs Thatcher's admiration for Judaism was fully acknowledged by the Chief Rabbi. She had, he suggested at the time of her resignation, 'a remarkable ... appreciation' for Judaism as 'a source and repository' of many of the ideals to which she was 'uncompromisingly committed' and which sustained her philosophy: industriousness, enterprise, ambition, the value of work for its own sake. No political leader, he continued, had ever acknowledged the debt to Judaism 'as openly or as fully' as Mrs Thatcher. The community and faith she had long championed, the Chief Rabbi concluded, would increasingly acclaim over the passage of time 'the debt owed to her'.[110]

'An awful reactionary: he's well to the right of Thatcher'

Ten months before she was deposed, Mrs Thatcher bathed in the warmth of the applause which greeted her address to the Board of Deputies. While returning the compliment, she paused briefly to speak of her Jewish constituents. 'I am very pleased to note,' she joked, 'that the majority there seem to hold my views on very many things.'[111] As we have seen, she was not wrong in her assessment of Finchley's Jews, whose support for the Prime Minister and her policies reflected more widespread sentiment in the community.

However, as the reaction to Jakobovits's pronouncements on the inner cities proved, many British Jews were keen to dispel the notion that he spoke in their name. This was wholly unsurprising. Formally, of course, Jakobovits was the religious authority of the United Synagogue, the roughly 200 Orthodox congregations – mainly British, but also covering some in the Commonwealth – which elected him and recognised his office as their supreme authority. The Orthodox were, and remain, the largest synagogue group by denomination, with around two-thirds of synagogue members in 1990.[112] By contrast, Progressive Jewish communities – the Reform and smaller Liberal movements – constituted approximately 22 per cent of synagogue members at the time.[113] That said, the Chief Rabbi was also seen by many to act as religious spokesman for Anglo-Jewry as a whole on issues such as Israel, anti-Semitism or Soviet Jewry. In this role, Jakobovits suggested, he was careful to ensure that his pronouncements 'reflect the consensus of opinion'. But he felt, there was no such need when speaking on moral issues, such as Aids, or social issues like 'Faith in the City'. Here his job was to offer views 'not on behalf of the community but on behalf of Judaism'. On such questions, he was acting as 'the authentic interpreter of Judaism'.[114]

Jakobovits's interpretations of Judaism – certainly as they related to the Thatcher government's policies – as well as his retelling of the Jewish experience in Britain proved to be very much open to challenge. His apparent defence of Thatcherism was, in the words of Rabbi David Goldberg of the Liberal St John's Wood Synagogue, a 'totally perverse view of Jewish thinking'.[115] As Goldberg and John Rayner argued, there was, indeed, a strong emphasis in Jewish teaching on the value of work, both as an economic necessity and for the dignity and self-respect it conferred on workers. But, they stressed, society had 'a special responsibility towards its weakest members' and this was not simply a matter for private charity, but also for public policy. Thus while Jakobovits may have found plenty of injunctions in Jewish teachings pointing to the importance of self-help, for Goldberg and Rayner, it was clear that there were others which suggested that:

> The modern concept of the Welfare State is in line with biblical tradition, and that the individual citizen's payment of his taxes, in so far as they provide social security and welfare services, is one way of fulfilling his obligation of *tzedakah* [the moral obligation of charitable giving] towards his fellow citizens.[116]

If Jakobovits's view of Judaism was challenged by some, his reading of Jewish history in Britain was decried by others. The socialist historian Raphael Samuel argued that had the Chief Rabbi consulted east London newspapers from the time of mass immigration in the 1890s, he would have found 'the Jews behaving in quite Caribbean ways', showing little of the respect for law and order for which Jakobovits had lauded them. Indeed, anti-Semitism was stoked in this period by a right-wing 'attack on "criminal" aliens', provoking a moral panic about supposed Jewish criminality.[117] The Jewish Labour MP Leo Abse accused Jakobovits of concocting a 'fairy-tale romance' of Jews escaping the ghettos for St John's Wood which ignored the role of Jewish socialists who fought sweatshop exploitation and whose radicalism antagonised Anglo-Jewry and the then-Chief Rabbi, Hermann Adler, who himself was deeply ambivalent about Jewish immigration at the time.[118]

Many Jews disliked the impression of their community which Jakobovits's intervention had conveyed. Rabbi Sidney Brichto, the director of the Union of Liberal and Progressive Synagogues, warned that the community risked looking 'self-congratulatory and self-righteous'.[119] As an editorial in *Manna*, the journal of the Reform Synagogues of Great Britain, suggested: 'To exhort those trapped by society in appalling social conditions merely to work harder and marry wisely is as out of touch with reality as was Marie Antoinette.'[120] On the letters pages of the *Jewish Chronicle*, many reactions were equally scathing: readers accused the Chief Rabbi of displaying 'smug complacency'; adopting the 'get on your bike' philosophy of Norman Tebbit; and of revealing himself to be simply 'the Chief Rabbi of the Right-wing Tory Jew'.[121] Even Chaim Bermant – who believed that 'Faith in the City' was 'not so much wet as soggy' – felt the need to remind Jakobovits that the Jewish escape from the ghetto was not as clear-cut as he implied. 'Not every Jew in this country is a doctor, lawyer, property developer or Cabinet Minister,' he argued.[122]

Predictably, the Chief Rabbi's homily was not warmly received by black politicians and community leaders. In a speech to the Jewish Social Responsibility Council shortly after the publication of 'From Doom to Hope', Paul Boateng, a prominent member of the GLC whom Labour had selected to fight Brent South at the next general election, argued that those who 'lecture the Black community on self-help, and the need for perseverance' should visit some of London's schools where they would discover that black inner-city residents shared the same aspirations – that their children should

'go on to do the things that they weren't able to do' – as did previous generations of immigrants.[123] Some were less restrained. The black weekly *The Voice*
accused the Chief Rabbi of suggesting that black Britons were 'workshy'.
'Black people have a right to dignity something they [the Jews] claim is taken
away from them by antisemitism,' its editorial angrily warned.[124]

As Greville Janner, the former president of the Board of Deputies, publicly warned, the Chief Rabbi had walked into a 'minefield'.[125] It was one
into which, as Bermant suggested, his American experience – where 'WASPS
could not speak ill – in public at least – of ethnic minorities, but ethnic
minorities could, and often did, speak ill of each other' – had, perhaps,
encouraged him to wander.[126] In the wake of inner-city riots the previous
autumn, the shadow Home Secretary, Gerald Kaufman, had appealed to
his fellow Jews, though not perhaps in a manner best designed to elicit a
positive response, to show solidarity with black Britons. Those failing to do
so, he scolded, should feel 'ashamed' of themselves. 'Any Jew who believes
he or she can opt out of being a religious and ethnic minority is living in a
dreamworld,' he told the *Jewish Chronicle*. 'It is true that some Jews, though
by no means all, have managed to become affluent. But that is not a matter
of merit, and it doesn't give you the right to sneer at people who are in a more
difficult economic position than you are.'[127]

After the publication of 'From Doom to Hope', Jews on the left were
appalled by what Louise Ellman, the then-leader of Lancashire County
Council and a future MP, termed the Chief Rabbi's attempt to 'identify Jews
and Judaism with the cruellest Conservative Government since the war'. It
would be tragic, she suggested, if Jakobovits's statement led some to conclude that Jews had abandoned 'the battle for economic and social justice'.[128]
For Ian Mikardo, it was clear that the Chief Rabbi was 'an awful reactionary'
and 'well to the right' of Mrs Thatcher. Branding his reaction to 'Faith in the
City' as 'absolutely disgraceful', the veteran Labour MP questioned the very
basis of Jakobovits's remarks. 'I don't know,' he said, 'what sources of Jewish
teaching and tradition provide him with material for disputing that what the
inner cities of Great Britain need is an influx of resources.'[129]

If, in the eyes of his critics, Jakobovits had become the 'Chief Rabbi of the Right-wing Tory Jew', Rabbi Julia Neuberger represented a very different image of British Jewry and a very different interpretation of Judaism. In her mid-30s, she was only the second female rabbi to be ordained in Britain. Her prominent media profile – shortly after Jakobovits's attack on 'Faith in the City', the BBC chose Rabbi Neuberger to present its new Sunday evening programme *Choices* and she remained a leading figure in the SDP – made her one of the most prominent rabbinical figures. While her behaviour at times was a little too unorthodox for many Jews – reportedly, one member of her Liberal congregation was shocked to find the rabbi eating bacon sandwiches in the synagogue[130] – her outspoken advocacy of liberal values reflected the view of many in the Jewish community. While the Chief Rabbi advocated putting the 'offence of homosexual acts' back on the statute books,[131] Rabbi Neuberger was president of the Social Democrats for Gay Rights. As Jakobovits excoriated the government's advertising campaign promoting safer sex, Rabbi Neuberger used the high holy day of Yom Kippur to ask her congregation to atone for their attitudes towards those with Aids. And when she pronounced on surrogate motherhood, the Chief Rabbi spluttered his condemnation of her 'obscene perversion of Jewish values'.[132]

Thus while Jakobovits's office let it be known that the Chief Rabbi 'did not regard her beliefs as authentic Judaism', Rabbi Neuberger made it clear she did not view his defence of Thatcherism as authentic Judaism either.[133] His response to 'Faith in the City', she declared, was 'outrageous and offensive'.[134] There was, she suggested, no doubt that the Chief Rabbi was a 'total Thatcherite' and it was, therefore, 'plainly wrong' for him to present himself as the spokesman for the community.[134] This concern was one that was widely shared among Progressive Jews. They may, as Goldberg argued, have afforded 'an unspoken primacy' to the Chief Rabbi but Jakobovits's move to the right caused both concern and resentment.[136]

Nonetheless, even some of those who shared that resentment accepted that Jakobovits's response to 'Faith in the City' reflected a powerful seam of thinking among many Jews. Geoffrey Alderman, who publicly accused the Chief Rabbi of 'lamentable ignorance' of the very different experiences of black and Jewish immigrants and urged him to 'seek an early and discreet retirement',[137] later agreed that Jakobovits was reflecting and not leading opinion in the community. Even among working-class, Labour-supporting Jews, he believed, there had long been a certain antipathy towards a welfare state which did not appear to reflect the contributory principles which underpinned the 'mini-welfare state' of the pre-war Jewish friendly society movement.[138] Many Jews, agreed Bermant, felt ill-at-ease with a Labour Party which 'seeks to limit the scope of individual initiative and ease the weight of individual responsibility'. A Jew may readily accept he was his brother's keeper, 'so long as his brother does not expect to be eternally kept'.[139]

Jakobovits found the hostile reaction to 'From Doom to Hope' in some parts of the community 'baffling and quite disturbing', he wrote shortly afterwards. 'One wonders whether it derives from gross political bias among Jews, an undue sense of insecurity, or a wide Jewish divergence from public opinion at large'.[140] In reality, as Shimon Cohen suggested, Jakobovits, 'was not a political animal at all' and had not expected the Tories 'to do with it what they did'.[141] The Chief Rabbi's reaction suggested a degree of naivety. Given the assault from the bishops the previous autumn, he swiftly became the toast of the Conservative backbenches. Over 150 Tory MPs signed a parliamentary motion congratulating him on his 'excellent paper'.[142] Jakobovits's staff scrambled to get a handful of helpful Labour MPs, including former Prime Minister James Callaghan, to sign the motion 'so we could say: "it's not all Tories"'.[143] The Cabinet minister responsible for the inner cities, Environment Secretary Kenneth Baker, met with Jakobovits and endorsed his view that there was much to learn from the Jewish experience and its emphasis on 'individual enterprise within the framework of support for the family and for law and order'.[144] For Cohen, it was less the content of the report, than the feeling that the Chief Rabbi had been 'politicised' which provoked much of the unease in the community.[145]

Jakobovits was, however, undeterred. Six months after the publication of 'From Doom to Hope', he offered a pithy summary of his views, although not, maybe, one which reflected 'authentic Jewish teaching': 'The point is many people in this country are work-shy: the British just don't like to work,' he told *The Guardian*.[146] And when, two years later, the Bishop of Durham suggested that some elements of Thatcherism were evil, the Chief Rabbi again rushed to Mrs Thatcher's defence: there was, he suggested, 'a big element of caring' in the government's policies. Jakobovits's words could have come from the Prime Minister's mouth: the government's approach might differ from that of the left, he argued, but that did not make it morally inferior. 'They believe that if this country isn't prosperous and creating wealth then we can't look after the disadvantaged ... Making the rich less rich doesn't make the poor less poor.'[147] As Jakobovits's time as Chief Rabbi drew to a close, a packed meeting in north-west London debated the motion 'This House believes that the United Synagogue is the "Tory Party at prayer"' – an event which would have been unthinkable when he took up his post a quarter of a century before.[148]

CHAPTER 9

ISRAEL'S FRIEND
IN DOWNING STREET:
MRS THATCHER AND
THE JEWISH STATE

W hen Margaret Thatcher's plane touched down at Ben Gurion airport
on the evening of 24 May 1986, she became the first serving Prime
Minister to visit Israel. She came, she declared, as 'a friend. Indeed, an old
friend'.[1] But, although treated as such, Mrs Thatcher's relationship with the
Jewish state was more complex than the praise she heaped upon the country
and the adulation she received in return.

Her three days in Israel, Anthony Elliott, the British ambassador, later
cabled the Foreign Office, were 'a personal triumph';[2] she would later remember it as the most memorable of her overseas trips.[3] Even those who
normally viewed the Prime Minister with a more critical eye agreed. After a
bruising six months at home, *The Guardian*'s James Naughtie suggested that
the tour was 'a glittering success'.[4] From her tears at the Holocaust memorial
at Yad Vashem to the scenes of her dancing with her Israeli counterpart,
Shimon Peres, at a state banquet at the Knesset, Mrs Thatcher's emotional connection to Israel was readily apparent. She lauded the 'miracles' the
country had performed and the 'greatest miracle of all, the spirit of ... [its]
wonderful people'.[5]

The Prime Minister's warmth was richly reciprocated. When she arrived
in Ramat Gan, the Tel Aviv suburb twinned with Finchley, 25,000 people

turned out to greet her. In a dusty field in Ashkelon, where she had gone to lay the foundation stone of an ORT school, the crowd cheered as the Prime Minister was told she was the biggest thing to hit the ancient port city since Samson slew several dozen of the Israelites' enemies.[6] At times, the apparent adoration of much of the Israeli public took even stranger turns. On a bus in Jerusalem, where union flags fluttered in sun-kissed skies for the first time since the bloody end of the British Mandate, a man claimed he had stood 'almost next' to the Prime Minister. What was she like, his fellow passengers enquired. 'She's a *chaticha*,' the man replied.[7] Mrs Thatcher was rarely described as 'a piece of skirt' on the London public transport system.

The hand of friendship

There was nothing contrived about Mrs Thatcher's professions of admiration for the Jewish state; her foreign affairs private secretary, Charles Powell, believed that it ranked alongside America and Singapore as one of her three favourite countries.[8] Nor was she a stranger to the country. Her first trip had occurred two decades earlier in 1965. Given her strong faith, she was unsurprisingly affected on that occasion by being able to visit places whose names will have rung in her ears in the Finkin Street Chapel forty years earlier. Criss-crossing the country, she journeyed north to Nazareth and the ancient Biblical city of Tiberias. She later recalled telling her children about her experiences of standing on the shores of the Sea of Galilee: being able to 'relive the Bible stories ... seeing where Jesus had been born, where he grew up and where he preached', had left an 'indelible impression'.[9] Moreover, although she was already keenly aware of them, her visit reinforced in her mind the links between her constituency and Israel: swimming in the pool of her hotel in Eilat, she encountered Alan Cohen, one of the Finchley Liberals who had caused her some political trouble at home.[10]

But it was the young country's vulnerability which struck her most. Staying at Jerusalem's magnificent pink limestone King David Hotel, which stood guard over the 'no man's land' that split the city between Jews and Arabs, Mrs Thatcher saw at first hand the close proximity between the Jewish state and its enemies. As Prime Minister, she frequently compared managing the economy to a housewife overseeing the family budget. On returning from Israel for the first time, she reached for a similarly domestic analogy. 'It was like having another country on the other side of your own garden wall at home,' she told an audience in Finchley.[11] She had little doubt, too, about the rights and wrongs of the conflict: 'Israel holds out the hand of friendship to all who will accept.'[12]

For Mrs Thatcher, Israel's virtues were heightened by the nature of the threat it faced: she viewed the Jewish state, believed Powell, as 'a lone bulwark of democracy in a pretty unpleasant area'.[13] As Yehuda Avner, Israel's ambassador to Britain for five years of Mrs Thatcher's premiership, later put it, she admired 'the old fashioned patriotism of Israelis and [the country's] "grit and guts"'.[14] After her visit, she talked of Israelis' 'sense of purpose and complete dedication, their pioneer spirit, and their realism'[15] and paid tribute to the 'tremendous courage and self-reliance' which its people displayed 'in the face of the threat which is ever present'.[16]

Self-reliance, of course, ranked high on the list of Thatcherite virtues. Recalling a conversation she had had with an Israeli Labour Exchange official, she told her constituents: 'They don't pay people for being idle in Israel.' 'The few who are unemployed are set to work five hours a day on government projects. Perhaps that was why in Israel there was a comparatively small amount of juvenile delinquency, and the rate of crime was very low.'[17] Once again, Alderman Roberts's belief in the moral imperative of work shone through in his daughter's words. Writing after her first visit to the country as Tory leader, Malcolm Rifkind suggested that, in many ways, Israel encapsulated many of Mrs Thatcher's own values and persona: 'Self-help, hard work and an interesting combination of stubbornness and enterprise.'[18]

There was, perhaps, one final factor at work. Mrs Thatcher's attachment to Zionism, and her admiration for Israel and the Jewish people, mirrored that of Winston Churchill, the Prime Minister in whose footsteps she most wished to tread. Like Mrs Thatcher, Churchill represented a constituency with a large Jewish population for a time: while still a Liberal MP, he sat for

Manchester North West. Losing the seat in 1908, he still won the support of an estimated 95 per cent of its Jewish voters.[19]

Like Mrs Thatcher, he too exhibited throughout his career both what he described in 1946 as 'the strongest abhorrence of the idea of anti-Semitic lines of prejudice' and a sympathy for the Jewish people's right to self-determination.[20] In the aftermath of the Balfour Declaration, he urged support for the 'inspiring movement' of Zionism[21] and, from the backbenches in the 1930s, opposed what he viewed as attempts to backslide from the pledges Britain had made in 1917. In opposition after 1945, and in the face of much hostility from within his own party, he urged that Britain honour the Zionist policy which he viewed as a 'condition of the Mandate'[22] and lauded the eventual establishment of the State of Israel as 'an event in world history'.[23] While he never visited the state he had helped to establish, he admired the achievements of 'this tiny colony of Jews' and, in retirement, pledged to its ambassador to London that he would 'continue to see to it that no evil befalls Israel'.[24]

•   •   •

There was, of course, an irony in the fact that, led for its first three decades by Mapai (the forerunner of the Israeli Labor Party) and its allies, the fledgling Israeli state had a distinctly socialist hue. Nonetheless, at the time this did not appear to attract Mrs Thatcher's attention or ire, although she was not enamoured by her first experience of a kibbutz – 'this rather unnerving and unnatural collectivist social experiment' – on her 1965 trip.[25] Mrs Thatcher's teenage daughter, however, took a different view. Carol, her mother later recalled, had developed some 'left-wing leanings' and told her parents she wanted to spend some time on a kibbutz. Although unimpressed with their daughter's request, the Thatchers eventually gave way. Carol's stay, it seems, was not an unqualified success. 'Life there was extremely hard and … rudimentary,' wrote Lady Thatcher, as her daughter struggled with tasks such as inoculating young chickens. Carol returned with 'an unromantic view' of the kibbutzim. Denis, however, was pleased that while his daughter might not have been very good at inoculating chickens, she had returned 'inoculated against socialism'.[26]

Mrs Thatcher's second visit to Israel in 1971 left her with a less romanticised view. Like other Western countries, she complained on her return, Israel was afflicted by strikes, pollution, crime and hippies, perhaps indicating, she suggested, that 'the pioneer spirit is ending'. She was also concerned about the country's building programme in areas of historical interest. 'How far in the opening up of beauty spots', she mused, 'do you destroy that which you wish to preserve?' And she struck what, in retrospect, seems a distinctly un-Thatcherite note: 'A degree of commercialism shakes you a bit and it needs a great deal of careful control.'[27]

Five years later, the new Leader of the Opposition returned to Israel once again. She now had rather more to concern her than whether the country was overrun by hippies and commercialism. She was already sensitive to how the politics of the Middle East could reverberate on the doorsteps of Finchley. The wounds inflicted on the Tory Party's reputation from the actions of Heath's government during the Yom Kippur War were still raw. One attempt to salve them, mirroring the launch of Labour Friends of Israel in 1957 in the wake of Suez, was the establishment of Conservative Friends of Israel in January 1975. The brainchild of former Tory MP Michael Fidler, CFI immediately succeeded in signing up nearly ninety Conservative MPs, prominent among them Mrs Thatcher, Jim Prior and Peter Thomas from the shadow Cabinet.[28]

But, even with Mrs Thatcher now at the helm, the path to rebuilding bridges the Tories had burned in 1973 was not smooth. While Israel now had many friends on the Conservative benches,[29] most of Mrs Thatcher's shadow Cabinet were, in her words, 'traditional Tory "Arabists"'.[30] Almost immediately, their actions were to cause Mrs Thatcher some discomfort. While she remained tight-lipped about the decision of Lord Carrington, the shadow Leader of the House of Lords, to meet with the PLO leader, Yasser Arafat, on a trip to Damascus in March 1975 – the visit was passed off as something that had been agreed on Ted Heath's watch – she could less easily escape responsibility for the actions of the man she had appointed as shadow Foreign Secretary.[31] Reginald Maudling's close business connections and political sympathies with the Arab world were sufficiently well known to cause anxiety among some in the Jewish community when Mrs Thatcher, aware that her own lack of experience in foreign affairs was being contrasted unfavourably with Heath's, chose him for the post.[32] She soon came to regret her decision, as Maudling proved himself singularly cack-handed. In a move that could barely have been less well timed, he chose the week the UN General Assembly passed its controversial resolution equating Zionism with racism to announce that the Tories backed a Palestinian state and supported recognition of the PLO as the voice of the Palestinians.[33]

Under fire, and aware of the divisions in her party that Maudling's words threatened to open, Mrs Thatcher was forced to step in and deny she had authorised any shift in the Tories' stance.[34] Instead, she told a dinner in Finchley, the Conservatives remained committed to a settlement based on UN Resolution 242: Israeli withdrawal from occupied territory and 'the right of every State in the area to live in peace within secure and recognised boundaries free from threats or acts of force'. Moreover, Mrs Thatcher's condemnation of terrorism 'in whatever form, and whatever cause it purports to serve' left little doubt about her attitude towards the PLO.[35] Such pronouncements, however, masked a series of choices – ones with which, in government, she and her ministers would wrestle and, at times, come to rather different conclusions. As for Maudling, he somewhat contemptuously wrote to Mrs Thatcher to apologise for the fact she was having 'trouble with your Jewish Community', but warned her that 'from time to time, this is unavoidable'.[36] She was, though, already tiring of a man whose performance she regarded as embarrassing and lazy; the following year, Maudling was sacked.[37]

Mrs Thatcher was acutely aware of where her own sympathies were seen to lie. While even her political opponents conceded her support for Israel was deep-felt and not simply driven by what some in the Foreign Office derisively called the 'Finchley factor',[38] the new Leader of the Opposition wanted to project an image of even-handedness. Thus when one of her shadow

Cabinet, Lord Hailsham, wrote to her asking for advice on whether he should join CFI, she scribbled back that while she was a member, he should 'keep out – otherwise if too many of us join we shall have "Arab" problems'.[39] Her response may have been prompted by a conversation with Carrington. In Jordan, as part of the trip on which he met with Arafat, he discussed with the British ambassador how the Arab capitals viewed Mrs Thatcher's pro-Israel sympathies and her involvement with groups such as the Finchley Anglo-Israel Friendship League and CFI. The ambassador suggested all such links 'should if at all practicable be severed', it being in the 'national interest'; his embassy later cabled the Foreign Office, 'to counter Arab fears and suspicion that the leader of HM opposition is already a prisoner of the Zionists'. Sympathetic to the ambassador's concerns, Carrington promised to raise the issue with Mrs Thatcher on his return to London. A postscript appended to the account of the meeting sent from Amman to London sarcastically asked: 'Why can't you advise her to swap Finchley for Westminster? Christopher [Tugendhat, the sitting Tory MP] might prefer such a change.'[40] In response, the Foreign Office assured its men in Amman that 'Central Office is well aware of the problems these links might pose' now that Mrs Thatcher was party leader.[41] However, despite her advice to Hailsham, Mrs Thatcher did not sever her ties with either CFI or the Finchley Anglo-Israel Friendship League – of which she was still president when it celebrated its twenty-fifth anniversary nine years after she first entered No. 10.

Two months before Mrs Thatcher arrived in Israel in March 1976, she had journeyed to Egypt and Syria. But while her visit to a Palestinian refugee camp in Syria angered the Israelis, their irritation was not long-lasting. Before leaving Damascus, she rowed with Arab journalists at a press conference when they questioned her on Britain's refusal to recognise the PLO.[42] Her political courage thus guaranteed her a warm reception when she arrived in Israel two months later. As Anthony Elliott relayed back to London, Mrs Thatcher's visit received 'considerably more attention' from the public and press than those of most VIPs and media reports were 'universally favourable'.[43] She met with old acquaintances, including former Prime Minister

Golda Meir, a woman whose 'strange blend of hardness and softness', Lady Thatcher later wrote, 'made her alternately motherly and commanding'.[44] She also forged new friendships, which were to prove of later significance; among these new friends was Defence Minister Shimon Peres. Mrs Thatcher's personality, suggested an evidently impressed Elliott, 'produced remarkable results' throughout the trip, most obviously during her meeting with the famously taciturn Prime Minister, Yitzhak Rabin, who appeared to the ambassador 'much more relaxed than I have seen him on other occasions' and 'unusually expansive'.[45]

Before she set off for Israel, Mrs Thatcher's staff were warned by a nervous Foreign Office of the delicacy of making statements which might seem to 'endorse either Israeli claims to Arab-occupied territory or the nature of the occupation regime'.[46] While Elliott noted the 'great caution' with which she had responded to journalists' questions, as Mrs Thatcher well knew, a picture was often worth a thousand words. Having ignored the efforts of staff at the Tel Aviv embassy to persuade her to take an overcoat on her visit to the Golan Heights, Mrs Thatcher allowed herself to be photographed on a hilltop lookout post wearing an Israeli general's anorak.[47]

Beginning with Begin

It would not, however, be Golda Meir, Yitzhak Rabin or Shimon Peres with whom Mrs Thatcher would deal when she entered Downing Street in May 1979, but Menachem Begin. He was not a man with whom she was keen to do business. Regarding the former Irgun leader as a terrorist for his role in ordering the 1946 bombing of the King David Hotel, Mrs Thatcher had vowed never to shake the Israeli Prime Minister's hand.[48] 'She hated Begin,' recalled Mrs Thatcher's principal private secretary, Clive Whitmore.[49] Memories of the violence which had accompanied the end of the Mandate appeared to affect her deeply: in 1981, she reportedly wept when recounting the brutal murder of two kidnapped British soldiers by the Irgun in July 1947 to the Canadian Prime Minister, Pierre Trudeau. She declared that she could never forgive Begin for ordering the act.[50] She also later dispatched her chief of staff, David Wolfson, to request the Israeli leader not appoint one of his old Irgun comrades as ambassador to Britain.[51]

Begin, however, was to be one of Mrs Thatcher's first foreign visitors to Downing Street. They were joined by her new Foreign Secretary, Lord Carrington, a man Mrs Thatcher relied upon and trusted. He, in turn, was able to gently exploit her inexperience and exercise a greater degree of influence over foreign affairs than any of his successors.[52] Even before he set foot in the Foreign Office, though, Carrington had form in the eyes of Israel: not only as the man who had met Yasser Arafat in 1975, but as the Defence Secretary in the Heath government who had enforced the arms embargo in October 1973. Little he said or did over the next three years would convince Israel that Carrington was any kind of friend.

While a Downing Street note of Begin's visit suggested 'a most friendly atmosphere', in reality it was anything but.[53] Things began well enough. Over drinks, Mrs Thatcher talked about her support for Soviet Jewry and her admiration for Jews in general and the Chief Rabbi in particular. But the atmosphere soon soured. Carrington assailed what he termed Israel's 'bag and baggage approach toward settlements', accusing it of pursuing a policy which was expansionist, illegal and a barrier to peace: robbing the Palestinians of their land and arousing the anger of moderate Arab states. The Foreign Secretary spoke for the government, the Prime Minister interjected supportively.[54] Viewing them as illegal – and placing a high premium on the importance of legality – Mrs Thatcher would always take a firm line with Israeli leaders on the question of settlement-building.[55]

Begin, though, defended the settlements as an assertion of his country's historic rights and vital to its national security. 'Whenever we Jews are threatened or attacked we are always alone,' he continued. 'Remember in 1944, how we came begging for our lives – begging at this very door?' While Mrs Thatcher attempted to engage with Begin's reference to the Allies' refusal to bomb the rail lines to Auschwitz, Carrington did little to calm the by-now fraught exchanges. 'And what does this have to do with the settlements?' he asked, provoking a further eruption from Begin. Placing her hand on his arm, Mrs Thatcher suggested gently: 'Please do not allow yourself to get upset. You are truly among friends here. In my constituency, I go to synagogue more often than I go to church.'[56]

While Mrs Thatcher showed a greater sensitivity to Begin, she proved no more able than Carrington to persuade him to shift his ground. She urged the Israeli leader to help his partner in the Camp David peace process, Egyptian president Anwar Sadat, by making progress in negotiations about the West Bank. Given the circumstances surrounding his murder by Islamic militants in October 1981 – an event which bolstered a view shared by Mrs Thatcher and her Foreign Office that extremists would thrive in an atmosphere in which moderates were seen to have failed[57] – her concerns about Sadat's well-being proved prophetic.[58]

She tried, too, to frame her arguments around Israel's self-interest: the Islamic revolution in Iran six months previously had shown the instability of the region. 'The whole thing could blow up and you would be at the centre of it,' she cautioned Begin.[59] Then, appealing to their shared hatred of communism, the Prime Minister reminded Begin that a wider deal was not only in Israel's interests, but also of those of the West as a whole. 'The tyranny of the Soviet Union,' she argued, 'thrived on disunity and dissension'. Begin had an answer for that: the PLO were Russian stooges and a Palestinian state would become 'a Soviet base in the heart of the Middle East'.[60]

Mrs Thatcher was soon complaining to fellow world leaders about what she described to US President Jimmy Carter as her 'profoundly disheartening' meeting with Begin.[61] As Azriel Bermant argued, Mrs Thatcher's first encounter with Begin and his 'Greater Israel' ideology, which resisted any form of territorial concessions, 'instilled in her a strong distaste' for the policies of Likud – the party whose leaders were to occupy Israel's premiership for all but two of her eleven years in Downing Street.[62]

The three interlocking issues on display at the meeting – Britain's concern that settlement-building in the occupied territories endangered the prospects of a comprehensive peace agreement; the need to bolster the stability of moderate Arab states against the radicalism which had felled the Shah in

Iran; and the importance of resisting Soviet meddling in the region – would dominate much of the Thatcher government's approach to Israel.[63] On these fundamental concerns, moreover, Mrs Thatcher and her Foreign Office agreed rather more than many assumed that they did.[64]

But although discouraged by her meeting with Begin, Mrs Thatcher was unconvinced by the approach advanced by Carrington and the Foreign Office on how to proceed. There were thus disagreements between the Prime Minister and her Foreign Secretary from the outset. Shortly after Begin's visit, Carrington proposed that Britain support a UN Security Council resolution backing Palestinian self-determination and closer contacts with the PLO. 'I will leave Lord Carrington a free hand in this,' she wrote in response, but 'I remain concerned at the proposed course of action.' Her reservations were two-fold. First, she continued to view Israel as the West's only truly reliable ally in the Middle East: if the Arab oil states were to fall under Soviet control, she noted, there was 'only one nation there that would really stand & fight and that is Israel'. Second, she was unconvinced that anyone had 'really thought through a new Palestinian "homeland"'.[65] In private, she gave Carrington a dressing down about concerns rather closer to home. 'Your foreign policy is going to lose me the next election,' she barked at him several months later, 'and it's going to lose me Finchley!'[66]

For the Foreign Secretary, however, the Soviet invasion of Afghanistan in December 1979 simply increased the urgency of the situation. It had, he wrote to Cabinet colleagues two months later, created a 'unique opportunity' to capitalise on the anger of the Islamic world to encourage it to work with the West to counter Soviet expansionism. The principal obstacle to realising this opportunity, though, was US policy towards Israel and the West's wider perceived failure to resolve the Arab–Israel conflict. With Jimmy Carter both preoccupied by his uphill struggle for re-election and attached to the Camp David process, to which – Egypt aside – most Arab countries were bitterly opposed, Carrington proposed that Britain and its European allies launch a new effort at the UN Security Council. Carrington's draft resolution reaffirmed Resolution 242 but supplemented it with a call for Palestinian self-determination.[67]

Mrs Thatcher shared much of Carrington's analysis and, in a letter to the US president in January 1980, suggested that, in the eyes of moderate Arab states, 'the whole Western position in the area was undermined by the Arab/Israel conflict and the failure to solve the Palestinian problem'.[68] In adopting this view, she was influenced not only by Carrington, but also by King Hussein of Jordan, a frequent visitor to Britain who regarded London as his 'second home'.[69] Beyond the traditionally close ties between Britain and Jordan, Mrs Thatcher had come to trust and respect the charming Hashemite monarch who had been educated at Harrow and Sandhurst. 'She had a soft spot for kings,' believed Powell.[70]

Nonetheless, she was deeply sceptical of the Foreign Secretary's proposals. Her view was best captured by the Lord Chancellor, Lord Hailsham. Responding to Carrington's note, Hailsham suggested that, with the exception of Egypt and, potentially, Jordan, there was little indication that any of the other Arab states would abandon their 'wholly illegal stance' and accept Israel's right to exist. Nor should the government overlook Jewish opinion, which was 'fanatically involved in the fate of Israel', at home. Constituencies in Manchester, Leeds and north London, Hailsham dramatically predicted, could be 'profoundly affected'. 'Have we not enough on our plate just now not to consider leaving this hot potato alone?' Hailsham concluded. On an accompanying note from the Cabinet Secretary, Sir Robert Armstrong, Mrs Thatcher simply wrote: 'I agree with the Lord Chancellor.'[71]

As Armstrong suggested to the Prime Minister, the central issue at stake was when and how the proposed new initiative might involve a 'direct approach' to the PLO and what the political implications of such a move would be. Of course, the Cabinet Secretary continued, 'the realities of the present and the needs of the future' sometimes allowed the 'misdeeds of the past' to be overridden. Britain had come to such accommodations with the Kenyan leader Jomo Kenyatta, Cyprus's Archbishop Makarios and, indeed, Begin himself, Armstrong concluded.[72]

Intellectually, Mrs Thatcher knew this was the case and, on occasion, she was prepared to say so. Three months earlier, in a meeting with leaders of the Board of Deputies, she admitted she could not say that she would 'never, never deal with the PLO' and drew a parallel with the recent negotiations over the future of Rhodesia involving Robert Mugabe and Joshua Nkomo, which had forced her to 'derogate from her absolute stand on terrorism to pursue peace'.[73]

But her instincts and political interests led her to resist strongly the logic of this argument with regard to the PLO, thus bringing her into conflict with the Foreign Office. Just days after her meeting with the Board, she wrote to her old comrades in the Finchley Anglo-Israel Friendship League reassuring them that the government would not recognise the PLO.[74] She 'recoiled somewhat', she told Hussein around the same time, at the idea that the PLO should be accepted as the sole representative of the Palestinians. Were there no spokesmen who were not terrorists? she asked.[75] When in September 1979 Carrington recommended 'a modest advance in our contacts with the PLO' and suggested that 'if a suitable opportunity arose for an informal Ministerial meeting, we should take it', Mrs Thatcher wrote an angry 'NO' in the margin.[76] Her aversion to a group which continued to engage in terrorism, refused to recognise Israel's right to exist, and had warm relations with the Soviets was coupled with a strong personal dislike of Arafat. 'He looks like a terrorist,' she would say of the PLO leader[77] and was appalled when, having initially failed to recognise him, she inadvertently shook hands with Arafat at Marshal Tito's funeral in May 1980.

Eventually recognising that US opposition made a push for a new UN Security Council resolution futile, Carrington decided, with the strong encouragement of Hussein, to focus instead on a European initiative. The resulting Venice Declaration in June 1980 saw Britain and its eight EEC allies reaffirm Israel's right to exist and to security, but also call for an end to its 'territorial occupation' of the lands seized in 1967, condemn settlements as 'a serious obstacle to the peace process in the Middle East' and urge that the Palestinian people be able to 'exercise fully their right to self-determination'. The PLO, the declaration suggested, would have to be 'associated' with the negotiations it was calling for.[78] The Foreign Office had been pushing internally since 1976 for Britain to harmonise its position with the rest of the EEC – fearing that, as the author of the Balfour Declaration, it bore a unique responsibility for its supposed baleful consequences in the eyes of the Arab world – and adopt a more publicly sympathetic line on the rights of the Palestinians.[79] The men in King Charles Street had thus scored a small but significant victory.

In her memoirs, Lady Thatcher implied that she regarded the Venice Declaration as ineffectual and pointless. It seemed to strike the right balance, she grudgingly conceded, but in doing so 'it pleased no one'.[80] Her scepticism was evident in the sarcastic commentary she appended to the draft communiqué sent to her by Carrington before they departed for Venice. Next to the suggestion that any peace settlement should be guaranteed by the United Nations, she scribbled: 'Not a happy example in this region', while she scoffed at European participation in such guarantees: 'Not much use in this region'. She went on to place disapproving square brackets around a suggested reference to 'the establishment of a homeland for the Palestinian people' – something which did not, in the end, make the final statement – as well as the reference to the PLO's involvement in any negotiations.[81]

She had told King Hussein the previous autumn that she believed it 'far better' that any 'Palestinian political entity ... be tied to another state. Confederation with Jordan would be the best outcome'.[82] She was also determined that, as long as the PLO refused to renounce terrorism or accept Israel's right to exist, there could be no suggestion of Arafat participating directly in talks.[83] Mrs Thatcher's resistance to an independent Palestinian state and the rear-guard action she fought against Foreign Office attempts to upgrade contacts with the PLO would characterise much of the rest of her premiership.

Understandably, she was also sensitive to the political ramifications. At the top of the letter from Carrington, she wrote irritably: 'The Chief Whip must see the draft communiqué. I fear it will cause a lot of trouble and be unacceptable to quite a lot of our MPs.'[84] She was right to be concerned, especially given the Foreign Secretary's own political tin ear. Two months before Venice, he had caused consternation by denying in parliament – in contradiction to previous statements made by Mrs Thatcher – that the PLO was a terrorist organisation.[85] In a sign of growing unease within the Conservative Party about Carrington's position, CFI passed a hard-hitting resolution suggesting that any 'deviation from the Conservative Party's traditional support of Israel' would be 'mostly strongly resisted'.[86]

Mrs Thatcher's attempt to dampen the row – in a letter to a local rabbi, she denied there had been any change in the government's attitude to the PLO, condemned its links with terrorism and reiterated her 'total commitment to Israel's future' – were largely unsuccessful.[87] In what must have appeared in Downing Street like an unpleasant echo of the autumn of 1973, the spring and summer of 1980 brought the sounds of protests throughout north London. The launch of the Committee for True Peace in the Middle East at Hendon Synagogue attracted 400 people. Its minister, Leslie Hardman, a strong supporter of Begin who nonetheless had a friendly relationship with Mrs Thatcher, urged the audience – especially those living in Finchley – to write to their MPs warning them 'you cannot vote for a Conservative Party adopting the present stand' on the Middle East.[88]

In Finchley, there was also a rumble of anger: old allies of Mrs Thatcher such as Queenie Weber of the Finchley Anglo-Israel Friendship League and Councillor Frank Gibson, a former mayor of Barnet and stalwart of the local Conservative Party, organised a rally attended by 1,000 people. The message to Mrs Thatcher was unmistakable. After the speakers – appearing under a banner adorned with the words 'Maggie! Do you know who your proposed friends really are?' – had concluded, the text of a message to be sent to their local MP was passed. It warned: 'Your policy is fraught with dangerous inconsistencies' and pleaded with her not to repeat 'the horrendous consequences of appeasement'.[89] Thirty of Barnet's Tory councillors issued a statement reaffirming support for Israel and urged the government not to recognise the PLO.[90] In the national press, stories began to appear suggesting the government's policy was causing a 'Finchley problem' for Mrs Thatcher.[91] Such was the concern locally that Jewish members of Mrs Thatcher's

Finchley party later confided to Geoffrey Alderman that there had even been discussions on whether the Prime Minister should be moved to Hendon South, an adjacent and potentially safer constituency.[92]

When Mrs Thatcher returned from Venice, the fires continued to burn. As in 1973, her constituency neighbour, Hendon North's John Gorst, was at the forefront of stoking them, attacking Carrington's policy as 'lamentable and misguided', accusing the government of having stooped to 'back street morality' and vowing to resist 'a policy of surrender to violence'. Speaking alongside him in the Edgware United Synagogue, Gorst's old ally, Saul Amias, proclaimed: 'If Mrs Thatcher meets with the terrorists, she must know that, North-West of Baker Street, there are many voters in Barnet who will think twice about re-electing her.'[93] It was Carrington, though, who bore the brunt of the community's anger. The Foreign Secretary later recalled addressing a Jewish audience at Caxton Hall in London where he was, 'heartily booed; interrupted incessantly; and barely given a hearing. People refused to shake hands with me'.[94] Some Israelis, however, believed the buck stopped at No. 10. 'Once again,' wrote Israeli ambassador Shlomo Argov after Mrs Thatcher had strenuously defended Venice in parliament, 'Israel's "friend in Downing Street" has made it clear that she was no more or less friendly than Carrington.'[95]

Predictably, Begin's reaction was one of fury. In a letter to Mrs Thatcher, he noted the PLO's adoption of a resolution just days before Venice pledging to 'liberate Palestine completely' and to 'liquidate the Zionist entity'. 'Madam Prime Minister,' he asked, 'did anybody since the days of Hitler and Goebels [sic], Goering, Rosenberg and Streicher ever declare more plainly and more precisely that the endeavour is to destroy both our people and our State?'[96] He went on to ask the Prime Minister to reconsider Britain's refusal to sell Israel the defence equipment it had requested. He didn't get his weapons or a reply.[97]

Antagonism between the two governments increased: the following month, Carrington summoned Argov and carpeted him for a speech in which he had suggested that the EEC had sold out Israel's security for its oil needs. The charge was not without justification: in the very month the Prime Minister went to Venice, the Foreign Office was explicitly suggesting that rising oil prices necessitated a more pro-Palestinian line.[98]

Israel was also right to bridle against the fact that, while arms sales to it were highly restricted (and banned altogether in 1982),[99] Mrs Thatcher enthusiastically hawked Britain's military hardware to Jordan, Saudi Arabia and Iraq, and repeatedly refused to sell the Jewish state North Sea oil.[100] At the same time, Britain continued to help maintain the Arab boycott of Israel. It was not until 1986 that the shameful practice was ended by which the Foreign Office authenticated the documentation, which showed they had no dealings with Israel, that companies were required to produce when exporting to Arab states.[101]

Given the constituency she represented, Mrs Thatcher was keen not to antagonise needlessly Jewish public opinion. However, she was also a sensitive enough reader of it to recognise the undercurrents which existed beneath the broad-based support for Israel. As Colin Schindler has argued, throughout much of the Jewish state's first three decades, British Jews were expected to give unquestioning support to Israeli governments as they attempted to stave off the country's many enemies. The election of Begin shook that consensus.[102] Thus while Mrs Thatcher correctly understood that, given its commitment to the destruction of Israel, steps towards the recognition of the PLO were liable to arouse strong passions, she also knew that many Jews shared her dislike of Begin's policies. As she told Hussein shortly after she returned from Venice, the Jewish community in Britain 'disapproved' of Begin's settlement-building.[103] This message was reinforced by those within the community to whom she was especially close. The Chief Rabbi, Immanuel Jakobovits, suggested in February 1980 that Israel should consider an eventual agreement including a demilitarised Palestinian state in the West Bank and Gaza and some form of shared sovereignty for Muslim holy sites in Jerusalem and believed the 'silent majority' of British Jews shared his views.[104]

Within the Jewish community, the notion that Mrs Thatcher was somehow being led astray by Foreign Office 'Arabists' was a recurring theme. It resurfaced again during the difficult year which commenced with Israel's bombing of the Iraqi nuclear reactor at Osirak in June 1981 and concluded with its invasion of Lebanon the following June. Israel's friends in Britain and the new American president, Mrs Thatcher's ideological soulmate Ronald Reagan, appeared willing to accept Begin's justification of the Osirak raid as a preemptive strike on a facility that Saddam Hussein was planning to use to build nuclear weapons to attack it. Mrs Thatcher was, however, less understanding.[105] 'Had there been an attack on Israel of the kind that there has just been on Iraq,' she told parliament, 'I should totally and utterly have condemned it. I, therefore, totally and utterly condemn the attack in Iraq.'[106] In a tense interview with the *Jewish Chronicle*, she was bluntly asked whether she hadn't simply 'handed over conduct of our Middle East policies to Lord Carrington and the old Arabists in the Foreign Office'.[107]

Osirak was unfortunate for another reason from Mrs Thatcher's point of view: buoyed by polls which had shown it strongly ahead, the Prime Minister and her Foreign Secretary were hoping Peres's Labor Party would win the general election Begin had called for June 1981. The popularity of the bombing raid, just three weeks before polling day, allowed Begin to eke out a narrow victory.

One of the consequences of that victory was felt six months later when Israel formally annexed the Golan Heights the night before Mrs Thatcher prepared to address the Board of Deputies. The speech had already caused much anxiety within Downing Street, with David Wolfson warning that, given the tensions between Israel, the British government and the Jewish community, the Prime Minister should steer clear of 'a political defence of Government policy in the Middle East'.[108] In the end the speech was what Neill Lochery described as 'vintage Thatcher'. The strong attack which she personally penned condemning the annexation – 'contrary to international law ... [and] harmful to the search for peace' – was wrapped up in 'long passages outlining her emotional and political connection to Israel'.[109] While she escaped the rough treatment meted out on Carrington, Mrs Thatcher did suffer the indignity of having the president of CFI, the

Duke of Devonshire, denounce her comments on the Golan Heights before the audience.[110]

Unbeknown to all, however, Carrington's tenure at the Foreign Office was about to come to a dramatic end. Ironically, it was while on a bridge-building visit to Israel in March 1982 that the Foreign Secretary learned of reports that the Argentinians were preparing to invade the Falkland Islands. Cutting short his trip, he dashed back to London and resigned as the islands fell. The appointment as Mrs Thatcher's foreign policy adviser shortly afterwards of Sir Anthony Parsons, a Foreign Office diplomat who had long argued that UK's national interest was better served by a less supportive stance towards Israel, ensured that many of Carrington's inclinations continued to be voiced in discussions about Britain's approach to the Middle East.[111] However, the high-profile Foreign Secretary's departure began the process of healing some of the rifts between Anglo-Jewry and the Conservative Party which had opened up during the Prime Minister's first three years in office.

First, however, they would take another knock. As British forces prepared for the decisive battle to retake Port Stanley in June 1982, Israel invaded Lebanon; an event sparked in part by the attempted assassination of Shlomo Argov on a London street. Mrs Thatcher's response to 'Operation Peace for Galilee' – she compared Israel's supposed aggression to that of the Argentinians – was shaped by the war she was waging in the South Atlantic and drew a stinging rebuke from Begin.[112] If Britain could send its forces thousands of miles to defend its territory, why could Israel not send its troops a few kilometres to protect its citizens in the north of the country from PLO terrorism?[113]

Although Mrs Thatcher's anger at Israel was fuelled by allegations that it had supplied arms to the Argentinians, it also reflected her wider fears about the perception in Arab capitals of American one-sidedness in the conflict.[114] Exasperated, Mrs Thatcher wrote to Reagan, bluntly cautioning him that 'Arab opinion is running violently against the United States since the impression has been given, rightly or wrongly, that you condone rather than condemn the recent Israeli action'. The loss of life, she continued, was 'horrifying' and she feared that even friendly Arab regimes would increasingly look to the Soviets 'unless they see some move in their direction'. Beyond the immediate crisis in Lebanon, there was 'an urgent need for a balanced policy towards the Arab-Israel conflict' and to tackle the Palestinian issue 'which lies at the heart of the dispute'.[115] Mrs Thatcher was not simply concerned about the impact of the bloodshed in Lebanon on the West's friends in the Middle East. She was also worried, as she wrote Reagan shortly afterwards, that the PLO's withdrawal from the country needed to be conducted in a way that increased the chances of the Palestinian leadership pursuing 'moderate and sensible policies in the future'.[116]

Her desire to strengthen the forces of moderation – in the Arab world, among the Palestinians and in Israel – would become an increasing preoccupation and one for which she was willing to take political risks in her second term. Mrs Thatcher's disapproval of Begin's actions did not, however, prevent her from bridling at the recommendation of her new Foreign Secretary, Francis Pym, that a British minister – contacts had hitherto been limited to officials – meet the head of the PLO Political Bureau, Farouk Kaddoumi. 'No – not a minister. The PLO will continue their terrorist activities – possibly in London,' Mrs Thatcher wrote in response. Hinting at her awareness of the potential domestic repercussions, she continued: 'Such a meeting would have far-reaching effects here.'[117] Days later, the Arab League announced that it was sending a delegation, including Kaddoumi, to European capitals to discuss the situation in Lebanon and requested a meeting with the Prime Minister. Mrs Thatcher agreed to meet the delegation but she would not – she underlined the word – meet the PLO representative.[118] From Belgrade, Pym sent a cable urging her to reconsider, suggesting that he or a junior Foreign Office minister, Douglas Hurd, meet the delegation, and warning that a refusal to do so would be seen as 'a snub to moderation and to our friends in the Arab world'. Mrs Thatcher gave way, but was furious at having to do so. 'ARGOV. Shot in London by Arab terrorists' she scribbled on Pym's message.[119] As Hurd later wrote in his diary, his subsequent meeting represented 'a shift in policy only dragged out of a reluctant Prime Minister'.[120] Israel reacted angrily to news of the meeting, justifiably unconvinced by the government's insistence that Britain's policy towards the PLO had not changed.[121]

Although there was initial support among many British Jews for the invasion of Lebanon, the manner in which Begin and his Defence Secretary, Ariel Sharon, soon began to exceed their stated aims, led to sharp divisions within the community, reflecting those in Israel itself.[122] At the same time, Hurd's encounter with Kaddoumi confirmed a perception among many that there was a double-standard at work in Britain's attitude towards Israel and little recognition of the havoc that the PLO's presence had caused both within Lebanon and on Israel's northern border. The *Jewish Chronicle* angrily accused Mrs Thatcher's government of fast becoming 'the most anti-Israel administration this country has known since that in which Ernest Bevin was Foreign Secretary'.[123] Such hyperbole was somewhat unfair: even as fighting raged in Lebanon, Mrs Thatcher responded to a request from CFI to become its patron by overruling civil service objections and suggesting her inclination was to accept. 'I started the first Friends of Israel,' she proudly wrote, referring to her role in establishing the Finchley Anglo-Israel Friendship League.[124] Concerned also about the rhetoric coming out of the Foreign Office, she ordered it to cease its public condemnations of Israel.[125]

The mood shifted, however, with what Mrs Thatcher termed the 'savage massacre' at the Sabra and Shatila refugee camps in September 1982,[126] which provoked a furious reaction among British Jews. Lord Mishcon, a former vice-president of the Board of Deputies and a highly respected communal figure, spoke for many when he charged that Begin and his government had 'tarnished the proud name of the Jewish people and ... breached the fundamental principles of our great faith. Many of us ... will never forgive you'.[127]

The rocky relationship between Israel and the Thatcher government during its first term led the *Jewish Chronicle* to conclude on the eve of the 1983 general election that there was 'nothing to choose between the three main parties', with regard to Middle East policy, a somewhat curious assessment given the levels of anti-Zionism infecting the Labour Party.[128] But it was clearly a view shared by some: while Mrs Thatcher was comfortably re-elected in Finchley, her support among Jewish voters took a knock: the 'abnormal degree of support for Labour', Geoffrey Alderman argued, being a reflection of 'short-term antipathy' to her government's approach towards Israel, specifically the PLO.[129]

Seizing the moment: the Peres interlude

By early 1984, Mrs Thatcher was heartily sick of the policies of Begin and the man who had succeeded him the previous autumn, Yitzhak Shamir. He may have been less 'fanatical' than Begin, she told Reagan's recently appointed special envoy to the Middle East, Donald Rumsfeld, but there was little basic difference between the two.[130] Frustrated, Mrs Thatcher warned the US Defence Secretary, Caspar Weinberger, in February 1984 that it was time for 'a reappraisal of Israeli policy'; the problem, in her eyes, was that Israel simply seemed to annex whatever it wanted.[131]

However, a general election in Israel five months later provided Mrs Thatcher with an opportunity to turn a page on the bad-tempered relations with its governments which had hitherto marked her premiership. Recognising that the moment might potentially be fleeting – a stalemate at the polls had produced a coalition between Labor and Likud, with Peres serving as Prime Minister for the first two years of the government's term, before the premiership rotated back to Shamir – she was nonetheless determined to seize it. After her government's re-election, Mrs Thatcher and her ministers had met at Chequers and decided that a major objective of their policy towards Israel should be to strengthen those within the country who, in the words of Bermant, 'shared Britain's approach to a negotiated settlement based upon territorial compromise'.[132] Peres, believed Mrs Thatcher, was such a man. She now sought to bolster his position and to encourage the Americans to do likewise. Meeting Reagan at Camp David in December 1984, she tried to impress upon the president the narrow window of opportunity if the United States was to make any progress in the region. Her efforts over the next year – relentless, brave but ultimately fruitless – were to be scuppered in large part by Reagan's failure to act upon his ally's insights.

While retaining her sense of scepticism about whether a peace settlement in the Middle East was indeed attainable,[133] Mrs Thatcher saw a potential opening in the signing in Amman of an accord between King Hussein and Arafat in which, for the first time, the PLO agreed to work with Jordan toward 'a just and peaceful settlement' of the Israeli–Palestinian conflict.[134] Mrs Thatcher welcomed the agreement and, at Hussein's request, furiously lobbied Reagan to support it.[135] Within the Israeli government, opinion on Hussein's initiative was divided. Despite reservations, Peres diplomatically abstained from criticising it; Shamir, now serving as Foreign Minister, disliked not simply the premise of a complete Israeli withdrawal from the territories but also feared that the idea of PLO participation in a joint Jordanian–Palestinian negotiating team would legitimise the organisation.[136] Unsurprisingly, a tense meeting between Mrs Thatcher and Shamir when he visited London in June 1985 produced little by way of agreement between the two. He insisted Israel would have nothing to do with the PLO; she tried to persuade him that sometimes – as she herself had done – it was necessary to deal with people whose terrorist backgrounds one found repugnant.[137] Meeting with CFI MPs, Mrs Thatcher happily admitted that she had been blunt with Shamir, tellingly suggesting that nothing she had said to the Israeli Foreign Minister would not have been welcome to Peres.[138]

But her MPs' primary concern was that ministers might meet with a joint Jordanian–Palestinian delegation, which would include representatives of the PLO, that King Hussein was planning to dispatch to Europe.[139] With both the Prime Minister and her trusted adviser, Powell, 'very reluctant' to agree to the meeting,[140] Mrs Thatcher wrote to the monarch, telling him she would authorise a meeting between the delegation and Sir Geoffrey Howe, who had replaced Pym after the 1983 election, but she had a non-negotiable condition. She had been assured by the Jordanians that the two PLO representatives travelling to Europe, Mohammed Milhem and Bishop Elias Khoury, were moderates who had renounced violence and had not belonged to a terrorist organisation.[141] Mrs Thatcher now wanted them to demonstrate these credentials: in London, they must publicly state their rejection of violence and acceptance of Resolutions 242 and 338, which called for Israel to withdraw to its pre-1967 borders but also spoke of the 'secure and recognised boundaries' of all states in the region.

Meanwhile, however, the Reagan administration, under pressure domestically, toughened its stance: in order for its proposed meeting with the delegation to go ahead, it must not only be free of PLO members; Jordan was now required to show 'prompt and tangible movement towards direct negotiations with Israel'.[142] The US ultimatum angered Hussein and placed him in an impossible position. Meeting in Amman with the King – her visit to Jordan, the first by a serving British Prime Minister, had been deliberately timed to underline her support for his efforts – Mrs Thatcher now prepared to step into the breach. She wanted others to take 'risks for peace', she told the monarch, so Britain must do so, too.[143] Thus, after an agreement was secured around the statements that Milhem and Khoury would make in London, Mrs Thatcher told Hussein that she would announce while she was in Jordan that Britain would receive the delegation.

Agreeing that her Foreign Secretary should meet representatives of the PLO was, as Powell later suggested, 'a big concession' on Mrs Thatcher's part: not simply an apparent U-turn by a woman who prided herself on not executing such moves, but one for which she was likely to receive precious little political benefit domestically; in fact, quite the reverse.[144] The Prime Minister soon found herself under fire from the Board of Deputies, the Zionist Federation and Poale Zion.[145] Old allies, such as CFI and the Finchley Anglo-Israel Friendship League, expressed their unease.[146] Newspapers that were normally among her staunchest supporters weighed in, with both *The Sun* and the *Daily Telegraph* comparing unfavourably her apparent willingness to treat with the PLO with her vociferous condemnations of the IRA.[147]

Israel, already seething at the announcement of a £3 billion arms deal with Saudi Arabia,[148] summoned the British ambassador to the Ministry of Foreign Affairs to express its 'deep displeasure', while Peres poured public scorn on Mrs Thatcher's suggestion that the two PLO men she had agreed could meet Howe were 'men of peace'.[149]

Her efforts soon began to look ill-fated. On Yom Kippur, Palestinian terrorists murdered three Israeli tourists aboard a yacht off the coast of Larnaca. Days later, Peres ordered the bombing of the PLO's headquarters in Tunis, killing seventy-one people and narrowly missing Arafat. Unlike the Reagan administration, Mrs Thatcher's government condemned the raid, the Prime Minister asking Irish Prime Minister Garret Fitzgerald to imagine what the US would say if Britain had 'bombed the Provos in Dundalk'.[150] The following week, a PLO offshoot, the Palestinian Liberation Front, hijacked the Achille Lauro cruise ship as it sailed from Alexandria to Port Said and murdered a disabled American Jewish tourist, Leon Klinghoffer. As the media ramped up its attacks on the 'delegates of terrorism' now in London,[151] Wolfson warned that if the government believed 'Arafat's "wing"' of the PLF had not been involved in the Achille Lauro attack 'we may well be proved very wrong. Or very naive, or both'.[152] Lord Young, recently promoted in the Cabinet reshuffle, told Mrs Thatcher privately that, following so soon after the Achille Lauro, the meeting might suggest to the public that she was appeasing Palestinian terrorists. Thirty years on, Young claimed to still have 'the scars from [her] handbag' after his encounter with the Prime Minister.[153]

In the end, however, she had no choice but to cancel it. With the delegation already in London, Milhem now sought to remove any reference to Israel from his public statement. Powell believed that Mrs Thatcher was neither particularly angry nor surprised by the outcome. 'I don't think that, in her heart, she thought they'd ever bring themselves to do it.'[154] Her critics, however, could not resist crowing. The British government, declared the *Jewish Chronicle*, had learned the hard way what Israel had known all along, that while 'willing to resort to semantic exercises to display their "moderation"', the PLO would never allow its representatives to sign away the fundamentals of its Covenant: that the territory of the state of Israel belongs to the Arabs and that the 'armed struggle' is the only way to 'liberate' it.[155] While true, this was also harsh: believing the cause of peace was best furthered by supporting the forces of moderation, Mrs Thatcher had taken a calculated gamble. She deserved more credit for her willingness, in the face of considerable opposition, to do so.

Against Shamir

In May 1986, just over six months after the failure of her efforts in London, Mrs Thatcher arrived in Israel. The Jewish community had long been keen for her to make the trip. However, it was the electorate in Israel, not voters at home, that was foremost in her mind. Quite consciously, she sought to bolster Peres domestically. She was well-placed to do so: her popularity in the country had surged following her support the previous month for the American bombing of Libya.[156]

Her speech at the Knesset was perfectly judged for this purpose. While lavishing praise on Israel's achievements and the 'outstanding contribution' made by British Jews to their country, and pledging that 'we are at one with you in fighting for the rights of Jews in the Soviet Union', she also addressed the plight of the Palestinians. She was determined, she later suggested, to use her long record of staunch support to deliver some home truths, confident in the fact she could do so 'without too much fear of being misunderstood'.[157] Thus, she warned her audience:

> Because of your own high standards, more is expected of Israel than of other countries, and that is why the world looks to Israel to safeguard the rights of Arabs in the occupied territories, in accordance with the principles which Israel respects and demands should be respected elsewhere. A future in which two classes of people have to co-exist with different rights and different standards is surely not one which Israel can accept, nor one which Israel's reputation allows.[158]

With the exception of her call for mayoral elections in the West Bank and Gaza, suggested the British ambassador, William Squire, it was a speech which was closely aligned with the views of Peres.[159] It was, however, a good degree less palatable to Shamir, the man who would succeed him in just a few months.

But, as she compared herself to Golda Meir and, over the following days, paid tribute to those other heroes of the Labor Zionist movement, David Ben-Gurion and Chaim Weizmann, such diplomatic niceties did not appear to bother Mrs Thatcher unduly. She regarded Peres, she later wrote, as 'sincere, intelligent and reasonable'. She had few kind words for Shamir. It was 'impossible to imagine anyone more different', she later wrote of this 'hard man ... whose past had left scars on his personality'.[160] She regarded Shamir – a former leader of the Lehi paramilitary group which fought British rule – like Begin as a man with Mandate-era blood on his hands.[161] She even went so far as to question Peres on whether there was any way he could not remain Prime Minister, rather than handing over to Shamir.[162] In turn, Peres's adviser, Nimrod Novik, believed that his relationship with Mrs Thatcher was 'unique'; their discussions 'more intimate than those he held with [Helmut] Kohl, [Francois] Mitterrand or anyone else'.[163] Certainly, Mrs Thatcher was the object of Peres's legendary charm. The warmth of their relationship, already apparent when Peres had visited London earlier in the year, was clearly evident as the two Prime Ministers travelled together by road and helicopter across the south of the country. As they drove back from the Negev towards Tel Aviv, Powell recalled catching a glimpse of Mrs Thatcher and Peres sat beside one another on the back seat: 'They were both sound asleep with their heads on each other's shoulders.'[164]

Despite her experiences of the previous autumn, Mrs Thatcher had not entirely given up hope of encouraging the growth of a moderate Palestinian leadership.[165] She was thus the first Western leader to use a visit to Israel to meet with Palestinian leaders, holding a dinner for mayors from the West Bank and Gaza, as well as lawyers, businessmen and journalists. They appreciated the symbolism of Mrs Thatcher's meeting with them, as well as the words she had delivered at the Knesset. But she believed that the 'miserable conditions' of life in the West Bank and Gaza which they described – she had already twice seen for herself Palestinian refugee camps, finding them 'utterly hopeless' – hampered efforts to 'push aside the PLO extremists'. She promised to take up their case with Peres.[166]

Reflecting her own long-held antipathy to the PLO and Hussein's renewed frustration with Arafat, she spoke at her final press conference in
Israel of the need to 'consider an alternative' as to who should represent the
Palestinian people.[167] She made clear, too, her continuing scepticism about
the notion of an independent Palestinian state.[168] While her parting remarks
angered the PLO, the Prime Minister had trod the diplomatic tightrope in
Israel with care, conveying empathy for the Jewish state, as well as delivering
pointed words of warning to its leaders. The Foreign Office, believed Powell,
was simply relieved that the visit hadn't turned into a 'pure and simple
love fest'.[169]

While basking in her popularity among the Israeli public, Mrs Thatcher
departed for London without any real sense of optimism. Peres grasped the
need for compromise but, trapped in a coalition with Likud, had precious
little room for manoeuvre. Moreover, as the weeks ticked down to his replacement by Shamir, she knew that the 'few shafts of light' would soon be
extinguished.[170]

Mrs Thatcher's pessimism was well-founded and proved an accurate prediction of the course that events would take over her remaining four years
in office. For so long as Peres, now Foreign Minister, remained in office
she continued to do what she could to assist him. A year after her return
from Israel, she helped to arrange a meeting between Peres and Hussein in
London. Its result, the London Agreement, envisaged an international peace
conference between Israel and its Arab enemies, with a joint Jordanian–
Palestinian delegation which would not include members of the PLO.
Believing such a conference 'imperilled Israel', Shamir immediately opposed
the agreement.[171]

Both Mrs Thatcher – who, suggested Peres, had played a crucial part
in securing the deal by acting as 'the real bridge' between the two sides –
and the Israeli Foreign Minister now turned to the Americans to pressure
Shamir.[172] Much to her anger, their efforts were to prove unsuccessful. For
the Americans, any intervention on their part represented interference in
Israeli domestic politics. 'The Foreign Minister of Israel's government,' wrote

US Secretary of State George Shultz, 'was asking me to sell to Israel's Prime Minister, the head of a rival party, the substance of an agreement with a foreign head of state, an agreement revealed to me before it had been revealed to the Israeli government itself.'[173] Mrs Thatcher, however, was uninterested in such arguments, meeting with Peres in Downing Street to underline to the Israeli public international support for their Foreign Minister's diplomacy.[174] At the same time, she agreed with both Peres and Hussein that she would impress on Reagan that 'time was running out' and that the US should not leave the two courageous men 'in the lurch', especially as the Soviets were expending much effort on wooing moderate Arab states.[175] When she travelled to Washington in July 1987 and in later correspondence with the president in the autumn, she honoured her pledge, her efforts fuelled by the belief that Shamir was 'incorrigible' and would never agree to an international conference until real pressure was exerted by the US.[176] Later, when the US belatedly proposed inviting Shamir and Hussein to a meeting in Washington, which it planned to host with the Soviets, Mrs Thatcher enthusiastically responded: 'It's putting a stiletto to Yitzhak Shamir's throat. I like that!'[177]

But the American initiative ultimately ran into the ground. In its dying months in office, the Reagan administration held little fear for Shamir who remained resolutely opposed to any international conference. The failure of the London Agreement, the outbreak of the Palestinian Intifada in December 1987 and the opposition of its leaders to a Jordanian role in the occupied territories led Hussein to sever formally his kingdom's legal and administrative ties to the West Bank the following summer. The move dismayed Mrs Thatcher and, as she warned Hussein it would, weakened Peres as Israel prepared to go to the polls, allowing Shamir to narrowly edge ahead of him and retain the premiership.[178] The events of 1988 left Mrs Thatcher's policy in tatters. Although no longer Foreign Minister, Peres soldiered on in coalition with Likud for another eighteen months. The other moderate in whom she had invested much hope, Hussein, was now also removed from the centre of the diplomatic stage. With his exit, Arafat could no longer be consigned to the wings if an end to the Arab–Israeli conflict were to be realised.

For her remaining two years in office, Mrs Thatcher accommodated these new realities. In December 1988, following the PLO's acceptance of Israel's right to exist and renunciation of terrorism, she authorised Foreign Office minister William Waldegrave to meet a senior Arafat adviser during his visit to London on the condition he meet the conditions she had laid down for the ill-fated meeting with Milhem and Khoury in October 1985. With the Prime Minister, recalled Waldegrave, 'watching the wording very closely', this time, things went to plan.[179] Days later, Arafat, too, made a similar public declaration, opening the door for Waldegrave to visit Tunis and meet the PLO leader in January 1989. The meeting provoked anger at the Board of Deputies and in Israel, especially when Waldegrave noted that many of the 'founding fathers of Israel', including Shamir himself, had once been viewed as terrorists.[180] Although she defended her minister's meeting, Mrs Thatcher was privately dismissive, regarding it as little more than a 'Foreign Office ploy',[181] while making clear publicly that she continued to oppose an independent Palestinian state, preferring 'some kind of confederate state'.[182] She also couldn't resist suggesting to Hussein that he advise Arafat to 'clean up his appearance' before a scheduled address to the UN.[183]

Mrs Thatcher had avoided inviting Shamir to London for four years; something which had not gone unnoticed by the Israelis.[184] However, an announcement by the Israeli Prime Minister of a plan to allow elections among the Palestinians as part of a transition to self-rule led her to agree to a meeting with him in May 1989. 'Domineering and self-important', in Shamir's words, Mrs Thatcher proved to be more interested in offering her views than soliciting his.[185] She probably did not miss much: Shamir remained doggedly opposed to any notion of 'land for peace' and even his modest proposals died in the face of internal opposition within his own party.

Despite her exasperation with Shamir's policies, Mrs Thatcher continued to come to Israel's aid at critical moments. In her final weeks as Prime Minister, she fought efforts to diffuse the situation in the Gulf by, as she saw it, appeasing Saddam Hussein's attempt to link Iraqi withdrawal from Kuwait to a resolution of the Israeli–Palestinian conflict. At the same time, she accepted that the West had a 'duty' to return to the issue once Kuwait had been liberated.[186] In Madrid, in the wake of the US victory in the Gulf War and nearly a year after Mrs Thatcher left office, Shamir was forced to attend the international conference she had supported and he had resisted for so long. The Bush administration had exerted the kind of pressure on the recalcitrant Israeli leader that she had often, but unsuccessfully, urged on Reagan. The PLO, with whom Britain had cut off talks because of its support for Saddam, was not present. Mrs Thatcher was probably unsurprised by the actions of an organisation of which she had never held a high opinion. By contrast, her belief that King Hussein had tried to 'excuse the Iraqi action' led to a breakdown in their once-close relationship.[187]

Much to her regret, Mrs Thatcher was unable to slay the final dragon – that of Saddam Hussein – to emerge during her premiership. Her time in Downing Street had been marked by a series of battles, both domestic and foreign, which showed her Manichean view of the world. However, as she herself understood, her policy towards the Israeli–Palestinian conflict recognised the shades of grey she rarely saw elsewhere. 'Throughout my political life,' she wrote in 2002, 'I have usually sought to avoid compromise, because it more often than not turns out to involve an abdication of principle. In international affairs, it is often symptomatic of muddle and weakness. But over the years I have been forced to conclude that the Arab-Israeli conflict is an exception. Here a historic compromise is, indeed, necessary.'[188]

LAST DAYS: SOVIET JEWRY AND NAZI WAR CRIMES

Mrs Thatcher's last speech as Prime Minister to the Board of Deputies in February 1990 contained her usual mix of rhetorical praise for Israel combined with criticism of 'the tragic situation in the occupied territories'. But there was a new, almost melancholic, twist. Referencing the fact that Israel was settling Jews who had been allowed to emigrate from the Soviet Union in the West Bank, she remarked: 'It would be a very ironic and unjust reward for all our efforts if their freedom were to be at the expense of the rights, the homes and the land of the people of the occupied territories.'[1]

Her support for Soviet Jewry had been long and consistent. As a Cabinet minister in the early 1970s, she had met delegations concerned about the issue.[2] As Leader of the Opposition, the persecution of Jews in the Soviet Union had formed a central part of her critique of détente and the Helsinki Accords.[3] And as Prime Minister, she tackled Mikhail Gorbachev on the constraints placed on Jewish emigration to Israel at her first meeting with him in December 1984. The Soviets had to know, she later suggested, that their treatment of the refuseniks would be 'thrown back at them' every time she met with them.[4] This was not mere grandstanding. As Rita Eker, the co-chair of The 35s, the women's campaign for Soviet Jewry, recalled, Mrs Thatcher also quietly made personal appeals to the Soviet authorities about numerous individual cases of injustice perpetrated against Jews.[5]

When she visited Moscow in April 1987, the Prime Minister was determined that, despite the thaw in relations between the Soviet Union and the West, the continuing discrimination suffered by the Jews in the era of glasnost should not be forgotten. Briefed by the Chief Rabbi before she departed, she preceded to grill Gorbachev on human rights in general, and the treatment of the Jews in particular, when they met at the Kremlin. The following morning, a group of refuseniks had breakfast with her at the British Embassy. She found their tale – one of 'heroism under mainly petty but continual persecution' – a disturbing one. One of the group's leaders gave her a tiny Star of David which he had carved out of horn in prison. She kept and treasured the gift.[6]

But as her comments about the settling of Soviet Jews in the West Bank indicated, the seeming double-standards of the Israeli right rankled Mrs Thatcher. Out of office, she wrote of her wish that Israel's emphasis on the human rights of the refuseniks had been matched by a 'proper appreciation of the plight of landless and stateless Palestinians'.[7]

It was a view many Israelis and British Jews shared. There was, though, another reminder in her address to the Board of Deputies as to why – whatever the intermittent disagreements over the years between it and her government over policy in the Middle East – Mrs Thatcher continued to command the respect and support of large sections of the Jewish community. It concerned the question of whether the government should introduce legislation allowing for the prosecution of war criminals who had slipped into Britain after 1945.

Nearly four years previously, the Simon Wiesenthal Centre in Los Angeles had provided the government with a list of seventeen alleged Nazi war criminals living in Britain.[8] Pressure in Parliament and the media eventually led the government to establish an inquiry which recommended a change in the law with a free vote in the House of Commons supporting the principle of legislation. During her speech, the Prime Minister declared herself shocked by the idea that 'people who had committed the most terrible of atrocities might have been living amongst us, unpunished, for fifty years', and reminded the audience of her own vote backing the introduction of a War Crimes'

Bill. She then proceeded to drop a heavy hint that the government was about to do just that.[9]

Over the coming months, in the face of opposition from senior ministers within her Cabinet and backbench Tory attacks on a 'lobby whose main motivations are hatred and revenge',[10] Mrs Thatcher doggedly supported the Bill. When it suffered a heavy defeat in the House of Lords, she took the unprecedented step for a Conservative government of invoking the Parliament Act to overrule the upper house. Without her determination, it is doubtful that the War Crimes Act, which became law several months after she left office, would have reached the statute books. Only one person, Anthony Sawoniuk, who received a life sentence for murdering Jews in Nazi-occupied Belarus, was successfully prosecuted under the Act. But while producing justice, however belatedly, for his victims, the Act also served to atone symbolically for the fact that, as one of its proponents, the historian David Cesarani, suggested, many British officials and politicians knew there were a significant number of war criminals among the East Europeans admitted to the UK in the immediate post-war years.[11]

Sir Geoffrey Howe, by 1990 the Leader of the House of Commons and an opponent of the Bill, dismissed the idea that Mrs Thatcher's support for war crimes' legislation was driven by what he termed the 'Finchley factor'.[12] Instead, he believed a recent visit to Babi Yar may have prompted the Prime Minister's determination to bend the House of Lords to her will. Perhaps, as she looked out over the ravine outside Kiev where the Nazis murdered 30,000 Jews in two days in September 1941, the image of Edith Mühlbauer staring from a bedroom window in North Parade had briefly crossed Mrs Thatcher's mind.

NOTES

Prologue

1   Cited in Arnold D. Richards (ed.), *The Jewish World of Sigmund Freud: Essays on Cultural Roots and the Problem of Religious Identity* (Jefferson, NC: McFarland & Co, 2010), p. 35

2   Edith Mühlbauer, Letter to Alfred Roberts, 21 January 1939, Thatcher Archives, Churchill College Archives Centre (THCR). Correspondence from the Roberts family to the Mühlbauers does not survive.

3   William Shirer, *The Nightmare Years 1930–1940* (New York: Bantam Press, 1984), p. 314

4   http://www.holocaustresearchproject.org/nazioccupation/anschluss.html

5   Margaret Thatcher, *The Path to Power* (London: HarperCollins, 2011), p. 27

6   Jonathan Aitken, *Margaret Thatcher: Power and Personality* (London: Bloomsbury, 2014), p. 28

7   Edith Mühlbauer, Letter to Alfred Roberts, 23 March 1939, THCR

8   Margaret Thatcher, Speech to the General Assembly of the Church of Scotland, 21 May 1988, http://www.margaretthatcher.org/document/107246

9   Peregrine Worsthorne, 'Judaism is the new creed of Thatcherite Britain', *Sunday Telegraph*, 10 January 1988

10 Hugo Young, 'When Mrs Thatcher sings of Jerusalem', *The Guardian*, 27 May 1986

11 Eliza Filby, *God and Mrs Thatcher: The Battle for Britain's Soul* (London: Biteback, 2015), p. 253

12 Margaret Thatcher, *The Downing Street Years* (London: HarperCollins, 2011), pp. 509–10

13 Margaret Thatcher, Remarks on becoming Prime Minister, http://www.margaretthatcher.org/document/104078

14 Thatcher, *Path*, p. 5

15 Charles Dellheim, 'More Estonians Than Etonians: Mrs Thatcher and the Jews', in Stanislao Pugliese (ed.), *The Political Legacy of Margaret Thatcher* (London: Politicos, 2003), p. 255

16 Cited in D. W. Bebbington, *The Nonconformist Conscience: Chapel and Politics 1870–1914* (London: Routledge Library Editions: Political Science Volume 19, 2014), p. 10

17 Bebbington, pp. 8–11

18 See Filby, p. 11

19 Cited in John Campbell, *Margaret Thatcher: The Grocer's Daughter* (London: Vintage, 2007), p. 16

20 Bebbington, p. 8

21 Cited in Antonio E. Weiss, *The Religious Mind of Mrs Thatcher*, http://www.margaret-thatcher.org/document/112748, 2011, p. 15

22 For a full discussion, see Filby, pp. 24–7

23 Cited in Campbell, *Grocer's Daughter*, p. 12

24 Cited in Campbell, *Grocer's Daughter*, p. 2

25 Cited in Filby, p. 21

26 Interview with Miriam Stoppard, 2 October 1985, http://www.margaretthatcher.org/document/105830

27 Filby, p. 21

28 Cited in Bruce Anderson, 'Call them British, not "boo-jhwa"', *Sunday Telegraph*, 28 June 1987

29 Cited in Campbell, *Grocer's Daughter*, p. 18

30 Cited in Campbell, *Grocer's Daughter*, p. 17

31 Cited in Filby, p. 23, although his time as Grantham's mayor in 1945 indicated a sympathy for social reforms he rhetorically decried. See Hugo Young, *One of Us* (London: Pan Books, 1990), p. 10

32 Campbell, *Grocer's Daughter*, p. 16

33 Thatcher, *Path*, pp. 23–4

34 Campbell, *Grocer's Daughter*, p. 17

35 Campbell, *Grocer's Daughter*, p. 16

36 Weiss, pp. 20–1

37 Charles Moore, *Margaret Thatcher: The Authorised Biography Volume One: Not For Turning* (London: Penguin Books, 2014), pp. 7–8

38 Cited in Weiss, p. 22

39 Thatcher, *Path*, p. 105

40 Weiss, p. 24

41 Young, 'When Mrs Thatcher'

42 Dellheim, p. 254. When Charles Moore's authorised biography appeared, Lady Thatcher's early private letters revealed a couple of instances of what he terms the 'mild, unthinking anti-Semitism' which was sadly prevalent at the time. She refers on one occasion to someone being 'a smart woman but she looked a Jewess. She was dark with a fair complexion and the typical long nose.' In another, she speaks of fellow guests on a foreign holiday. 'Some are rather "tatty" tourists: Jews and novo [*sic*] riche.' (Moore, *Not For Turning*, p. 59 and p. 116)

43 Cited in Tim Rayment, 'Found: the Jewish refugee saved by Thatcher's family', *Sunday Times*, 28 May 1995

44 Margaret Thatcher, Speech to Friends of Hebrew University of Jerusalem dinner, 27 October 1988, http://www.margaretthatcher.org/document/107361

45 Cited in Yehuda Avner, *The Prime Ministers: An Intimate Narrative of Israeli Leadership* (New Milford, Connecticut: The Toby Press, 2010), p. 504

46 Interview with Lord Young

47 Thatcher, *Downing Street*, p. 509

48 Campbell, *Grocer's Daughter*, p. 1

49 Cited in Moore, *Not For Turning*, p. 384

50 Alfred Sherman, Letter to Alan Howarth, 7 December 1977, THCR

51 Cited in 'Diary: Macsim', *The Times*, 3 April 1986. It should be noted that Macmillan, along with Churchill, had opposed the 1939 White Paper setting limits to Jewish

immigration to Palestine and, in the immediate post-war years leading up to the creation of Israel, they were in a minority in their party in backing Zionism. See Alastair Horne, *Harold Macmillan 1894–1956* (London: Macmillan, 1988, pp. 308–9)

52 Filby, *God and Mrs Thatcher*, p. 249

53 Immanuel Jakobovits, 'From Doom to Hope': A Jewish View on 'Faith In The City', the Report of the Archbishop of Canterbury's Commission on Urban Priority Areas (London: Office of the Chief Rabbi, 1986), p. 14

54 Young, *One of Us*, p. 423

Chapter 1: In the Beginning

1 Cited in Campbell, *Grocer's Daughter*, p. 3

2 Campbell, *Grocer's Daughter*, p. 22

3 Rayment

4 Young, *One of Us*, p. 12

5 Cited in Moore, *Not For Turning*, p. 11. Those positive views were not, however, universal. See Moore, *Not For Turning*, p. 11

6 Cited in Rayment

7 Filby, p. 39

8 Cited in Campbell, *Grocer's Daughter*, p. 18

9 Thatcher, *Path*, p. 5; Campbell, *Grocer's Daughter*, p. 8

10 Thatcher, *Path*, p. 3

11 Thatcher, *Path*, p. 19

12 Ibid.

13 Cited in Aitken, p. 12

14 Thatcher, *Path*, p. 19

15 Campbell, *Grocer's Daughter*, p. 11

16 Cited in Campbell, *Grocer's Daughter*, p. 12

17 Thatcher, *Path*, p. 21

18 Cited in Aitken, p. 22

19 Thatcher, *Path*, p. 6

20 Cited in Moore, *Not For Turning*, p. 7

21 Cited in Moore, *Not For Turning*, p. 9

22 Interview with Miriam Stoppard

23 Ibid.

24 Campbell, *Grocer's Daughter*, p. 24

25 Interview with Miriam Stoppard

26 Cited in Young, *One of Us*, p. 5

27 Campbell, *Grocer's Daughter*, p. 8

28 Thatcher, *Path*, p. 5

29 Cited in Moore, *Not For Turning*, p. 21

30 Ibid.

31 Rayment

32 Cited in Rayment

33 Ibid.

34 Thatcher, *Path*, p. 11

35 Cited in Moore, *Not For Turning*, p. 21

36 Cited in Moore, *Not For Turning*, p. 20

37   Cited in Moore, *Not For Turning*, p. 20

38   Ibid.

39   Edith Mühlbauer, Letter to Muriel Roberts, 16 May 1939, THCR

40   Ibid.

41   Cited in Rayment

42   Moore, *Not For Turning*, p. 21

43   Thatcher, *Path*, p. 27

44   Thatcher, *Path*, p. 27

45   Interview with Sir Laurens van der Post, 30 December 1982, http://www.margaretthatch-er.org/document/104849. This is not the first reference to Edith. She features briefly in a *Jewish Chronicle* diary item about Mrs Thatcher in November 1971. See 'A friend', *JC*, 12 November 1971, p. 29

46   Thatcher, *Downing Street*, p. 509

47   Young, *One of Us*, p. 20

48   Thatcher, *Path*, p. 19

49   Thatcher, *Path*, p. 22

50   Thatcher, *Path*, p. 28

51   Douglas Reed, *Insanity Fair* (London: Jonathan Cape, 1938) p. 53

52   Reed, p. 84. Reed's work is also littered with examples of anti-Semitism. For examples see pp. 84, 86–8, 234. While opposed to the Nazis, his anti-Semitism grew during the war. See Tony Kushner, 'The Impact Of British Anti-Semitism, 1918–1945' in David Cesarani (ed.), *The Making Of Modern Anglo-Jewry* (Oxford: Basil Blackwell, 1990), pp. 196–7

53   Thatcher, *Path*, p. 29

54   Ibid.

55   Thatcher, *Path*, p. 22

56   Tom Hopkinson (ed.), *Picture Post 1938–1950* (Harmondsworth, Middlesex: Penguin Books, 1970), pp. 32–8

57   Thatcher, *Path*, p. 24

58   Ibid.

59   Cited in Filby, p. 40

60   Ibid.

61   Cited in Campbell, *Grocer's Daughter*, p. 39

62   Moore, *Not For Turning*, p. 18

63   Martin Pugh, *Hurrah for the Fascists: Fascists and Fascism in Britain Between the Wars* (London: Pimlico, 2006), p. 141

64   Pugh, p. 140

65   Gisela C. Lebzelter, *Political Anti-Semitism in England 1918–1939* (London: Macmillan, 1978), p. 31

66   Lebzelter, pp. 32–3

67   Ibid.

68   Lebzelter, pp. 30–31

69   Cited in Richard Griffiths, *Fellow Travellers of the Right: British Enthusiasts for Nazi Germany, 1933–1939* (London: Constable, 1980), pp. 81–2

70   Thatcher, *Path*, p. 26

71   Ibid.

72   Moore, *Not For Turning*, p. 17

73   Thatcher, *Path*, p. 26

74 Ibid.

75 Cited in 'Rotary fellowship that will lead to peace', *Grantham Journal*, 28 January 1939

76 James Callaghan, *Time And Chance* (London: Fontana, 1988), pp. 51–2

77 Cited in 'Rotary fellowship'

78 J. A. Thompson, 'The Peace Ballot and the public', *Albion: A Quarterly Journal Concerned with British Studies*, Vol. 13, No. 4 (Winter, 1981), pp. 381–92

79 Thatcher, *Path*, pp. 10–11. As Moore, *Not For Turning* (p. 16) suggests, however, the results of the ballot may have been misinterpreted by history

80 Thatcher, *Path*, p. 31

81 Thatcher, *Path*, p. 26

Chapter 2: Finchley and Beyond

1 Cited in Campbell, *Grocer's Daughter*, p. 113

2 Cited in Campbell, *Grocer's Daughter*, p. 112

3 Cited in Charles Moore, *Margaret Thatcher: The Authorised Biography Volume Two: Everything She Wants* (London: Allen Lane, 2015), p. 659

4 Thatcher, *Path*, p. 59

5 Thatcher, *Path*, p. 39

6 Cited in Filby, p. 46

7 Thatcher, *Path*, p. 42

8 Campbell, *Grocer's Daughter*, p. 51

9 Cited in Moore, *Not For Turning*, p. 41

10 Cited in Campbell, *Grocer's Daughter*, p. 56

11 Cited in Moore, *Not For Turning*, p. 41

12 Thatcher, *Path*, p. 42

13 Campbell, *Grocer's Daughter*, p. 57

14 Campbell, *Grocer's Daughter*, p. 50

15 Cited in Campbell, *Grocer's Daughter*, p. 50

16 Thatcher, *Downing Street*, p. 129

17 Cited in Aitken, pp. 102–3

18 Interview with Lord Young

19 Avner, pp. 512–13

20 Interview with Lord Howard; Interview with Lord Sherbourne. See also Nigel Lawson's comments in John Ranelagh, *Thatcher's People: An Insider's Account of the Politics, the Power and the Personalities* (London: HarperCollins, 1991), p. 56

21 Thatcher, *Path*, p. 48; Campbell, *Grocer's Daughter*, p. 64

22 Thatcher, *Path*, p. 47

23 Moore, *Not For Turning*, p. 55

24 Cited in Filby, p. 49

25 Both her future Cabinet colleagues, Sir Keith Joseph and Nigel Lawson, had family connections to J Lyons and Co.

26 Thatcher, *Path*, p. 48

27 Filby, p. 61

28 Campbell, *Grocer's Daughter*, p. 78

29 Campbell, *Grocer's Daughter*, p. 97

30 Thatcher, *Path*, p. 94

31 Cited in Campbell, *Grocer's Daughter*, p. 113. The initial shortlist was three, but one of

those on it was selected elsewhere and it was decided, rather than giving people a choice of just two, to add the two next-placed candidates

32 Cited in Campbell, *Grocer's Daughter*, p. 113

33 Cited in Moore, *Not For Turning*, p. 134

34 Interview with Derek Phillips

35 Cited in Moore, *Not For Turning*, p. 135

36 Interview with Neville King

37 Cited in Clive Page, 'King of the fortune hunters', *Kentish Times*, 19 January 1989, p. 5

38 Margaret Thatcher, Letter to Syd King, 30 October 1989, provided to author by Neville King

39 Thatcher, *Path*, p. 98

40 Bernard Donoughue, 'Four Constituency Campaigns', in David Butler and Anthony King, *The British General Election of 1964* (London: MacMillan & Co, 1965), p. 241. Donoughue suggested it may have been 'exaggeratedly estimated at one-fifth'. Mrs Thatcher reported it as 'nearly 25 per cent'. See Campbell, *Grocer's Daughter*, p. 116

41 Geoffrey Alderman, *The Jewish Vote In Great Britain Since 1945* (Glasgow: Centre for the Study of Public Policy, University of Strathclyde, 1980), p. 4

42 David Cesarani, 'British Jews' in Rainer Liedtke and Stephan Wendehorst (ed.), *The Emancipation of Catholics, Jews and Protestants: Minorities and the Nation State in Nineteenth-century Europe* (Manchester: Manchester University Press, 1999), p. 49

43 Cesarani, p. 49

44 Alderman, *Jewish Vote*, p. 5

45 The historian V. D. Lipman suggests that in the early 1880s, 14.6 per cent of the Jewish population of London were upper or upper-middle class; 42.2 per cent were middle class; 19.5 per cent were 'lower class'; and 23.6 per cent were 'in receipt of at least casual relief, on poor lists and in institutions'. Cited in Stephen Brook, *The Club: The Jews of Modern Britain* (London: Constable, 1989) pp. 21–2

46 Alice Nathan, 'Immigration: the Jewish experience', *JC*, 21 April 1978, p. 23

47 See Geoffrey Alderman, *London Jewry and London Politics* (London: Routledge, 1989), pp. 55–81

48 Alderman, *Jewish Vote*, p. 6

49 Alderman, *London Jewry*, p. 79

50 Cited in Alderman, *London Jewry*, p. 80

51 Brook, p. 335

52 Geoffrey Alderman, *The Jewish Community In British Politics* (Oxford: Clarendon Press, 1983), p. 115

53 'Labour's promises and – the performance', *JC*, 16 November 1945

54 For a full description see Harry Defries, *Conservative Party Attitudes to Jews 1900–1950* (London: Routledge, 2001), p. 199

55 Cited in Defries, p. 5

56 Cited in Stuart Ball, *Portrait Of A Party: The Conservative Party In Britain 1918–1945* (Oxford: Oxford University Press, 2013), p. 66

57 Cited in http://spartacus-educational.com/CRIballJ.htm

58 Ball, p. 65

59 See Defries, p. 202

60 Alderman, *Jewish Community*, p. 118

61 The mixed response of Anglo-Jewry to immigration is explored by Brook, pp. 22–3

62 Geoffrey Alderman, 'The Political Conservatism of the Jews in Britain', in Peter Y. Medding (ed.), *Values, Interests and Identity: Jews and Politics in a Changing World*, Studies In Contemporary Jewry XI (Oxford: Oxford University Press, 1995), p. 104

63 Alderman, *Political Conservatism*, p. 104

64 Cited in Alderman, *Jewish Community*, p. 134

65 These were the two Bethnal Green seats, three in Hackney, two of the three in Stepney, Stoke Newington, South Tottenham, Hendon North, the two Ilford Walthamstow, Willesden and Wembley seats, Central and North East Leeds, North Salford, and Glasgow Gorbals (Alderman, *Jewish Community*, p. 127)

66 Aside from the twenty-six Labour MPs and Lipson, there was a Jewish Communist MP, Phil Piratin

67 Chaim Bermant, 'On the other hand', *JC*, 15 July 1983

68 'Party politics', *JC*, 10 October 1947

69 Alderman, *Jewish Community*, p. 134

70 Cited in Alderman, *Jewish Community*, p. 134

71 Defries, p. 206

72 Todd M. Endelman, *The Jews of Britain 1656–2000* (Berkeley: University of California Press, 2002), p. 197

73 Endelman, p. 230

74 Alderman, *Jewish Community*, p. 136

75 Alderman, *Jewish Community*, p. 137

76 Alderman, *Political Conservatism*, p. 105

77 Geoffrey Alderman, 'Jewish Political Attitudes and Voting Patterns in England 1945–1987', in Robert Wistrich (ed.), *Terms Of Survival: The Jewish World Since 1945* (London: Routledge, 1998), p. 254

78 Alderman, *Political Conservatism*, p. 114

79 Harold Wilson, *The Chariot of Israel: Britain, America and the State of Israel* (London: Weidenfeld & Nicolson, 1981), p. 125

80 Cited in John Callaghan, *The Labour Party And Foreign Policy: A History* (Abingdon: Routledge, 2007), p. 231

81 Cited in Alderman, *Jewish Political*, p. 256

82 Alderman, *Jewish Community*, pp. 132–3

83 Cited in Anthony Blond, 'The Jews and Mrs Thatcher', *Sunday Telegraph*, 11 December 1988, p. 14

84 Alderman, *Jewish Community*, p. 134

85 Cited in 'Mrs MH Thatcher adopted by Conservatives', *Finchley Times*, 1 August 1958. Lady Thatcher later admitted her misgivings over Suez, Thatcher, *Path*, pp. 88–9

86 David Dee, 'There is no discrimination here, but the Committee never elects Jews': Antisemitism in British golf, 1894–1970', *Patterns of Prejudice*, 47 (2), p. 4

87 Anthony Howard, 'Foothold in Finchley', *New Statesman*, 16 August 1963

88 Andrew Hosken, *Nothing Like A Dame: The Scandals of Shirley Porter* (London: Granta, 2006), pp. 18–19. See also investigation in the *Jewish Chronicle* in March 1960. See 'Golf clubs and Jews – 1', *JC*, 18 March 1960

89 Interview with Alan Cohen. The Finchley constituency covered two local government authorities, the municipal borough of Finchley and Friern Barnet urban district council. In the London local government reorganisation of 1965, the two local authorities, along with others, were merged into the new London borough of Barnet

90 Howard
91 Cited in 'Antisemitism at golf club', *JC*, 3 May 1957; 'Jews and golf', *Finchley Times*, 3 May 1957. The Board of Deputies Defence Committee informed Davis of its concern at the Liberal campaign, which, they believed, violated its view that Jews should not be appealed to as Jews in election campaigns. See Alderman, *London Jewry*, p. 144
92 'Finchley fragments: the elections', *Finchley Times*, 17 May 1957
93 John Irwin and David Crawford, 'The Finchley story', *New Outlook*, August 1963
94 'Liberals say golf club barred Jews', *Finchley Press*, 31 May 1957
95 Cited in 'Finchley golf club cuts out query on religion', *Finchley Times*, 31 May 1957
96 'Finchley golf club discrimination clause deleted', *JC*, 31 May 1957
97 Cited in Campbell, *Grocer's Daughter*, p. 116
98 Campbell, *Grocer's Daughter*, p. 112
99 Moore, *Not For Turning*, p. 136
100 Thatcher, *Path*, p. 98
101 Thatcher, *Path*, p. 99
102 Campbell, *Grocer's Daughter*, p. 117
103 Thatcher, *Path*, p. 98
104 Cited in 'Life is a private affair', *Finchley Press*, 27 February 1959
105 Campbell, *Grocer's Daughter*, p. 117
106 Moore, *Not For Turning*, p. 139
107 Campbell, *Grocer's Daughter*, p. 119
108 Thatcher, *Path*, p. 109
109 Thatcher, *Path*, p. 111
110 'A safeguard for local democracy', *Yorkshire Post*, 30 January 1960
111 Cited in Andrew Denham and Mark Garnett, *Keith Joseph* (Chesham, Bucks: Acumen Publishing, 2001), p. 90
112 Cited in 'Excluding the press', *The Guardian*, 27 February 1960
113 'Public – keep out', *The Star*, 26 February 1960
114 Moore, *Not For Turning*, p. 148
115 'In a few lines', *JC*, 11 November 1960
116 Cited in 'Fighting prejudice in Finchley', *JC*, 9 February 1962
117 'Towards friendship with Israel', *JC*, 30 November 1962
118 Cited in 'Skilled workers are Israel's need', *JC*, 25 January 1963
119 Interview with Tessa Phillips
120 Margaret Thatcher, Speech at Finchley Synagogue Golden Jubilee, 18 December 1976, http://www.margaretthatcher.org/document/103174
121 Margaret Thatcher, Remarks at Finchley Progressive Synagogue, 3 May 1975, http://www.margaretthatcher.org/document/102684
122 Donoughue, p. 250
123 Campbell, *Grocer's Daughter*, p. 113. Goldman, whose family were Jewish converts to Anglicanism, suffered from anti-Semitism in Orpington. See Chris Cook and John Ramsden, *By-Elections In British Politics* (London: Routledge, 2013), p. 166
124 Irwin and Crawford, p. 28
125 Cited in Howard
126 Cited in Donoughue, p. 247
127 Donoughue, p. 243
128 'Liberal Hopeful', *Evening Standard*, 24 July 1964,

129 Donoughue, p. 242

130 Cited in Howard, p. 186

131 Thatcher, *Path*, p. 131

132 Howard

133 Cited in Howard

134 Interview with Laurence Brass

135 Interview with Alan Cohen

136 Donoughue, p. 251

137 'Frontpage news', *JC*, 3 August 1962

138 'No ban on Trafalgar Square meetings', *JC*, 27 July 1962; 'Anti-fascist bill gets first reading', *JC*, 3 August 1962; 'Ajex advise on how to stamp out fascism', *JC*, 27 July 1962

139 Cited in Moore, *Not For Turning*, p. 167

140 Cited in 'Mrs Thatcher clears the air', *Finchley Press*, 17 August 1962

141 'Liberals in eclipse', *Finchley Press*, 15 May 1964

142 Cited in Donoughue, p. 251

143 'Liberals cheer Israeli', *JC*, 11 September 1964

144 'Finchley Liberals are set to win', *Finchley Times*, 4 September 1964

145 Donoughue, p. 243

146 'Party broadcast', *Finchley Press*, 1 May 1964; 'Borough tour by Liberal chief', *Finchley Times*, 2 October 1964

147 'Borough tour by Liberal chief', *Finchley Times*, 2 October 1964

148 Thatcher, *Path*, p. 131

149 Donoughue, p. 245

150 Cited in Campbell, *Grocer's Daughter*, p. 154

151 Donoughue, p. 249

152 Donoughue, p. 250

153 Cited in 'X-Day – and the fight is tense', *Finchley Press*, 16 October 1964

154 Donoughue, p. 253

155 Donoughue, p. 251

156 Donoughue, p. 252

157 'Little chance of women being elected', *JC*, 25 March 1966

158 Interview with Alan Cohen

159 See Chapter 9

160 Cited in 'United support for Israel', *Finchley Press*, 23 June 1967

161 Azriel Bermant, *Margaret Thatcher And The Middle East* (Cambridge: Cambridge University Press, 2016), p. 9

162 See Philip Ziegler, *Edward Heath: The Authorised Biography* (London: HarperCollins, 2010), pp. 382–6 and John Campbell, *Edward Heath: A Biography* (London: Pimlico, 1993), pp. 348–50

163 Edward Heath, *The Course Of My Life* (London: Hodder & Stoughton, 1998), p. 501

164 Cited in Ziegler, *Heath*, p. 386

165 Cited in Wilson, p. 365

166 Wilson, p. 369–72

167 Adley later converted to Christianity

168 Alderman, *Jewish Community*, p. 142

169 Thatcher, *Path*, p. 230

170 Interview with Geoffrey Alderman

171 'The money rolls in', *Finchley Times*, 19 October 1973

172 'Massive response', *JC*, 26 October 1973

173 'Public back Israel', *JC*, 26 October 1973

174 Cited in 'Jewish councillors condemn embargo', *Finchley Times*, 26 October 1973

175 'Israel letter starts storm', *Finchley Times*, 2 November 1973

176 Cited in '"This oily blackmail": Gorst attacks arms ban', *Finchley Times*, 19 October 1973

177 Ibid.

178 'Cavalier thinking', *Finchley Times*, 19 October 1973

179 Cited in 'Gorst cracks the whip', *Finchley Times*, 2 November 1973

180 'Israel and the election', *Finchley Times*, 26 October 1973

181 'Young Tory on wrong lines', *Finchley Times*, 2 November 1973; 'Israel letter starts storm', *Finchley Times*, 2 November 1973; 'Israel letter – YC quits', *Finchley Times*, 9 November 1973

182 '"This oily blackmail": Gorst attacks arms ban', *Finchley Times*, 19 October 1973

183 Interview with Alan Cohen

184 Cited in 'The money rolls in', *Finchley Times*, 19 October 1973

185 Cited in 'Minister lobbied over arms embargo', *Finchley Press*, 19 October 1973

186 Thatcher, *Path*, p. 230

187 Minutes of Cabinet meeting, 16 October 1973, http://www.margaretthatcher.org/document/111931. Cabinet minutes do not record the names of those who spoke in discussion, but Mrs Thatcher indicated to the editor of the Thatcher Foundation website in 1994 where her contribution fell

188 Minutes of Cabinet meeting, 16 October 1973

189 Minutes of Cabinet meeting, 16 October 1973

190 Cited in Moore, *Not For Turning*, p. 237

191 Thatcher, *Path*, p. 230

192 Alderman, *Jewish Community*, p. 143

193 See Chapter 6 for further detail; Cited in 'Liberals attack government', *JC*, 2 November 1973

194 Cited in 'Candidate's plea', *JC*, 2 November 1973

195 See Chaim Raphael, 'Rock Of Brighton', *The Jewish Chronicle Colour Magazine*, 24 May 1974

196 Cited in Alderman, *Jewish Community*, p. 143

197 'Second attempt', *JC*, 2 August 1974

198 Cited in 'This is not a one-issue election, says Liberal', *Finchley Press*, 15 February 1974

199 Interview with Laurence Brass

200 Interview with Laurence Brass; 'Barnet Liberal resigns over antisemitism', *JC*, 13 November 1970; 'Liberals attack "hysteria"', *JC*, 27 November 1970; 'Davis quits Liberals', *JC*, 7 April 1972

201 Cited in 'Mrs Thatcher shimmers through the hustings', *The Times Higher Educational Supplement*, 22 February 1974

202 Moore, *Not For Turning*, p. 246

203 Campbell, *Grocer's Daughter*, p. 254

204 Thatcher, *Path*, p. 237

205 Interview with Laurence Brass

206 In October 1974's general election, Mrs Thatcher fared still worse. As the non-Conservative vote in the seat solidified around Labour, her majority fell to just under 4,000

207 Interview with Laurence Brass

208 'Champion: don't repeat 1970 error', *Finchley Times*, 22 February 1974; 'Jewish Swing To Tories', *Finchley Times*, 22 February 1974

209 'Terrorist bomb warning', *Finchley Times*, 15 February 1974

210 'Times team tells the story', *Finchley Times*, 8 March 1974

211 Alderman, *Jewish Community*, p. 145

212 Ibid.

213 Alderman, *Jewish Community*, p. 142

214 Alderman, *Jewish Community*, p. 144

215 'Women have fair chance', *JC*, 4 October 1974, p. 6

Chapter 3: The Junior Partner

1 Morrison Halcrow, *Keith Joseph: A Single Mind* (London: Macmillan, 1989), p. 3. Sir Samuel may have confined himself to the politics of the City of London, but close relatives did not. In 1929, three Joseph family members stood as Conservative candidates; two of them – Isidore Salmon, who was first elected to represent Harrow in 1924, and Louis Gluckstein, who was elected in Nottingham East in 1931 – making it to Westminster

2 Alfred Sherman, *Paradoxes Of Power: Reflections on the Thatcher Interlude* (Exeter: Imprint Academic, 2005), p. 96

3 Cited in Ranelagh, p. 138

4 John Biffen, 'Keith Joseph: Power behind the throne', *The Guardian*, 12 December 1994

5 Geoffrey Howe, *Conflict Of Loyalty* (London: Macmillan, 1994), p. 39

6 Cited in Ranelagh, p. 127

7 Thatcher, *Path*, p. 251

8 Thatcher, *Path*, p. xiv

9 Young, *One of Us*, p. 43; Halcrow, p. ix

10 Denham and Garnett, p. 56

11 Denham and Garnett, p. 33

12 Thatcher, *Path*, p. 28

13 Denham and Garnett, p. 56

14 Cited in Anthony Seldon, 'Escaping the chrysalis of statism', *Contemporary Record*, Vol No. 1, Spring 1987, p. 26

15 Halcrow, pp. 3–5

16 Thatcher, *Path*, p. 135

17 Margaret Thatcher, 1950 General Election Address, http://www.margaretthatcher.org/document/100858; Margaret Thatcher, Speech to Dartford Young Conservatives, http://www.margaretthatcher.org/document/100831

18 Cited in Moore, *Not For Turning*, p. 255

19 Biffen

20 Cited in Halcrow, p. 1

21 Halcrow, p. 4

22 Cited in Griffiths, p. 82

23 Cited in Denham and Garnett, p. 57

24 Halcrow, p. 11

25 Cited in Patrick Cosgrave, 'Obituary: Lord Joseph', *The Independent*, 12 December 1994

26 Cited in Denham and Garnett, p. 61 and p. 65

27 Cited in Halcrow, p. 21

28 Cited in Denham and Garnett, p. 119

29 Cited in Halcrow, p. 14
30 Ranelagh, p. 121
31 Cited in Vernon Bogdanor, 'Mad monk's new creed', *The Times Higher Educational Supplement*, 24 May 2002
32 Cited in Seldon, p. 26
33 Geoffrey Alderman, 'Converts to the vision in true blue', *The Times Higher Educational Supplement*, 10 July 1987
34 Cited in 'Profile: Sir Keith Joseph', *JC*, 13 September 1974
35 Cited in Halcrow, p. 2
36 Denham and Garnett, p. 12
37 Leo Abse, *Margaret, Daughter of Beatrice: A Politician's Psycho-Biography of Margaret Thatcher* (London: Jonathan Cape, 1989), p. 160
38 'Profile: Sir Keith Joseph'
39 Denham and Garnett, p. 13
40 Halcrow, p. 14; Denham and Garnett, p. 233
41 Cited in Denham and Garnett, p. 172
42 Alfred Sherman, 'A man of conscience and compassion', *JC*, 16 December 1994
43 Sherman, *Paradoxes*, p. 44
44 Cited in Brian Harrison, 'Joseph, Keith Sinjohn, Baron Joseph (1918–1994), *Oxford Dictionary of National Biography*, Oxford University Press, 2004; online edn, May 2011
45 Cited in Halcrow, p. 36
46 Harrison, ODNB
47 Halcrow, p. 18
48 'Profile: Sir Keith Joseph'
49 Cited in Denham and Garnett, p. 158
50 Sherman, *Paradoxes*, p. 44
51 Cited in 'Sir Keith – A man who talks true Tory policy, *Time And Tide*, 29 January 1970
52 Nicholas Faith, 'How many votes in enterprise?', *Sunday Times*, 8 March 1970
53 'Selsdon Meeting transcript (Morning Session)', 31 January 1970, http://www.margaret-thatcher.org/document/109512
54 Thatcher, *Path*, p. 135
55 Ferdinand Mount, *Cold Cream: My Life and Other Mistakes* (London: Bloomsbury, 2008), p. 270
56 Cited in Campbell, *Grocer's Daughter*, p. 80
57 Margaret Thatcher, 'Conservative Political Centre (CPC) Lecture: "What's wrong with politics?"', Friday 11 October 1968, http://www.margaretthatcher.org/document/101632
58 Thatcher, *Path*, p. 150
59 'What's wrong with politics?'
60 Thatcher, *Path*, p. 200
61 Sherman, *Paradoxes*, pp. 45–6
62 Cited in Nicholas Timmins, *The Five Giants: A Biography Of The Welfare State* (London: Fontana, 1996), p. 293
63 Thatcher, *Path*, p. 200
64 Cited in Halcrow, p. 52
65 Cited in Denham and Garnett, p. 231
66 Cited in Moore, *Not For Turning*, p. 221
67 Cited in Thatcher, *Path*, p. 188

68 Cited in Hugo Young and Anne Sloman, *The Thatcher Phenomenon* (London: BBC, 1986), p. 27
69 Cited in Moore, *Not For Turning*, p. 232
70 Cited in Seldon, p. 27
71 Sherman, *Paradoxes*, p. 11
72 Thatcher, *Path*, p. 221
73 Cited in Campbell, *Grocer's Daughter*, p. 245
74 See Campbell, *Grocer's Daughter*, pp. 245–6
75 State Department Record of Conversation with Margaret Thatcher, 22 May 1973, http://www.margaretthatcher.org/document/110554
76 Lord Hailsham Election Diary, 1 March 1974, http://www.margaretthatcher.org/document/111117
77 Cited in Moore, *Not For Turning*, p. 248
78 Cited in Ranelagh, p. 129. Heath's Chancellor of the Exchequer, Anthony Barber, decided to leave politics after the Tories' defeat in February 1974, leaving the post of shadow Chancellor vacant
79 Howe, p. 86
80 Cited in 'Obituary: Sir Alfred Sherman', *The Times*, 29 August 2006
81 Sherman, *Paradoxes*, p. 34
82 Cited in 'Obituary: Sir Alfred Sherman'
83 Sherman, *Paradoxes*, p. 35
84 Interview with Geoffrey Alderman
85 Halcrow, p. 61
86 Denham and Garnett, p. 182
87 Will Ellsworth-Jones, 'Introducing "The eminence grise behind the eminence grise" of Mrs Thatcher', *Sunday Times*, 4 June 1978
88 Sherman, *Paradoxes*, p. 45
89 Sherman, *Paradoxes*, p. 49
90 Cited in Sherman, 'A man of compassion'
91 Moore, *Not For Turning*, p. 256
92 Thatcher, *Path*, p. 251
93 Halcrow, p. 62
94 Thatcher, *Path*, p. 251
95 Interview with Norman Strauss
96 Interview with Lord Young
97 Sherman, *Paradoxes*, p. 38
98 Halcrow, p. 106
99 Private information
100 Cited in Ranelagh, p. 174
101 Cited in Halcrow, p. 62
102 Cited in Ranelagh, p. 174
103 Halcrow, p. 66
104 Sherman, *Paradoxes*, pp. 71–5
105 Cited in Ranelagh, p. 177
106 Cited in Halcrow, p. 56
107 Halcrow, p. 62
108 Thatcher, *Path*, p. 251
109 For Joseph's interest in the social market, see Denham and Garnett, pp. 240–43

110 Thatcher, *Path*, p. 252

111 Cited in 'Obituary: Sir Alfred Sherman'. Sherman appeared to suggest (*Paradoxes*, p. 48) that the idea of the CPS had been Heath's, but this both seems unlikely and has been disputed by others (see Moore, *Not For Turning*, p. 252)

112 Alfred Sherman, Memorandum to CPS Colleagues, 18 November 1974, http://www.margaretthatcher.org/document/111907

113 Alfred Sherman, 'Why we asked the unasked questions', *The Times*, 1 September 1984

114 Sherman, *Paradoxes*, p. 79

115 Cited in Halcrow, p. 108

116 Ben Jackson, 'The think-tank archipelago: Thatcherism and neoliberalism', in Ben Jackson and Robert Saunders (eds.), *Making Thatcher's Britain* (Cambridge: Cambridge University Press, 2012), p. 52

117 Sherman, *Paradoxes*, p. 51. Sherman's ability to rub people, including potential donors, up the wrong way may also have been a factor (Halcrow, p. 109)

118 Sherman, *Paradoxes*, p. 50

119 Cited in 'Obituary: Sir Alfred Sherman'

120 Cited in Abse, p. 161

121 Keith Joseph, Speech at Upminster, 22 June 1974, http://www.margaretthatcher.org/document/110604

122 John Campbell, *Edward Heath*, p. 637

123 Thatcher, *Path*, p. 253

124 Halcrow, p. 71

125 Thatcher, *Path*, p. 255. See also Howe, p. 87

126 Keith Joseph, Speech at Preston, 5 September 1974, http://www.margaretthatcher.org/document/110607

127 'The sharp shock of truth', *The Times*, 6 September 1974

128 Cited in Dominic Sandbrook, *Seasons In The Sun: The Battle for Britain 1974–1979* (London: Allen Lane, 2012), p. 232

129 Eric J. Evans, *Thatcher And Thatcherism: The Making Of The Contemporary World* (Routledge: Abingdon, 2013), p. 9

130 Thatcher, *Path*, p. 255

131 Sherman, *Paradoxes*, p. 53

132 Howe, p. 87

133 Thatcher, *Path*, p. 243

134 Cited in Campbell, *Grocer's Daughter*, p. 272

135 Moore, *Not For Turning*, p. 259

136 Cited in Moore, *Not For Turning*, p. 259

137 Cited in Campbell, *Grocer's Daughter*, p. 267

138 Thatcher, *Path*, p. 252

139 Cited in Moore, *Not For Turning*, p. 255

140 Cited in Young and Sloman, p. 29

141 Cited in Campbell, *Grocer's Daughter*, p. 269

142 Thatcher, *Path*, p. 257

143 Cited in Campbell, *Grocer's Daughter*, p. 278

144 Cited in Moore, *Not For Turning*, p. 264

145 Thatcher, *Downing Street*, p. 14

146 Cited in Seldon, p. 29

147 Sherman, *Paradoxes*, p. 25

148 Cited in Young, *One of Us*, p. 406

149 Cited in Brian Harrison, 'Mrs Thatcher and the intellectuals', *Twentieth Century British History*, Vol 5, No. 2, 1994, p. 224

150 Keith Joseph, 'We did not go far enough; we failed her', *The Independent*, 23 November 1990

151 Thatcher, *Path,* p. 254

152 Cited in Young and Sloman, p. 30

153 Cited in Denham and Garnett, p. 238

154 Cited in Jackson, p. 58

155 Cited in Moore, *Not For Turning*, p. 254

156 Cited in 'Arthur Seldon, Economist, is dead at 89', *New York Times*, 15 October 2005

157 Thatcher, *Path*, p. 254

158 Cited in Moore, *Not For Turning*, p. 255

159 Cited in Ranelagh, p. 143

160 Cited in Moore, *Not For Turning*, p. 268

161 Cited in Ranelagh, p. 133

162 Thatcher, *Path*, p. 261

163 Young, *One of Us*, p. 93

164 Thatcher, *Path*, p. 261

165 Cited in Halcrow, p. 89

166 Cited in Halcrow, p. 79

167 Cited in Seldon, p. 30

168 Cited in Halcrow, p. 79

169 Denham and Garnett, p. 265; Halcrow, p. 79

170 Cited in Denham and Garnett, p. 266

171 Keith Joseph, Speech at Edgbaston, 19 October 1974, http://www.margaretthatcher.org/document/101830

172 Joseph repeatedly claimed the phrase was his own but in 2010 the barrister Jonathan Sumption took responsibility, Sandbrook, p. 234

173 Cited in Moore, *Not For Turning*, p. 271

174 Thatcher, *Path*, p. 262

175 Cited in Denham and Garnett, p. 268

176 Sandbrook, p. 234

177 Thatcher, *Path*, p. 263

178 'Politicians and prophets', *JC*, 25 October 1974

179 'Law of the jungle', *JC*, 1 November 1974; 'Sir Keith's Speech', *JC*, 25 October 1974

180 'Politicians and prophets', *JC*, 1 November 1974

181 Thatcher, *Path*, p. 263, p. 262

182 Thatcher, *Path*, p. 262

183 Thatcher, *Path*, p. 263

184 See Filby, pp. 96–7

185 Thatcher, *Path*, p. 262

186 Ibid.

187 Ibid.

188 Cited in Thatcher, *Path*, p. 263

189 Moore, *Not For Turning*, p. 272

190 Filby, p. 103
191 Cited in Halcrow, p. 91
192 Samuel Brittan, 'Samuel Brittan', in Roger Backhouse and Roger Middleton (eds.), *Exemplary Economists: Vol II Europe, Asia and Australasia* (Cheltenham: Edward Elgar, 2000)
193 Cited in Halcrow, p. 87
194 Sherman, *Paradoxes*, p. 61
195 Sherman, *Paradoxes*, p. 56
196 Sherman, *Paradoxes*, p. 63
197 Howe, p. 90
198 Thatcher, *Path*, p. 266
199 Cited in Halcrow, p. 93
200 Cited in Philip Kleinman, 'The press', *JC*, 20 September 1974
201 Colin Chapman, 'The richest man in the world', *The Observer*, 6 April 1975
202 Sherman, 'A man of compassion'
203 Thatcher, *Path*, p. 266
204 Cited in Moore, *Not For Turning*, p. 273
205 Thatcher, *Path*, p. 266
206 Thatcher, *Path*, p. 267
207 Howe, p. 93
208 Young, *One of Us*, p. 96
209 Cited in Young, *One of Us*, p. 98
210 Cited in Ranelagh, p. 141
211 Cited in Evans, p. 14
212 Margaret Thatcher, 'My kind of Tory party', *Daily Telegraph*, 30 January 1975
213 Howe, p. 93
214 Margaret Thatcher, Speech of tribute to Keith Joseph, 3 June 1995, http://www.margaret-thatcher.org/document/108343
215 Denham and Garnett, p. 279
216 Thatcher, *Path*, p. 269
217 Campbell, *Grocer's Daughter*, pp. 288–9
218 Thatcher, *Path,* p. 263
219 Cited in Moore, *Not For Turning*, p. 274

Chapter 4: The Senior Partner

1   Cited in Young, *One of Us*, p. 331
2   Cited in Campbell, *Grocer's Daughter*, p. 317
3   Moore, *Not For Turning*, p. 298
4   Thatcher, *Path*, p. 285; Moore, *Not For Turning*, p. 298
5   Moore, *Not For Turning*, p. 298
6   Thatcher, *Path*, p. 286
7   Interview with, *Jimmy Young Programme*, 19 February 1975, http://www.margaretthatcher.org/document/102500
8   Cited in Campbell, *Grocer's Daughter*, p. 366
9   Thatcher, *Path*, p. 286
10   Ibid.
11   Cited in Moore, *Not For Turning*, p. 272
12   Cited in Moore, *Not For Turning*, p. 352

13   Cited in Philip Short, *Mitterrand: A Study In Ambiguity* (London: Vintage, 2014) p. 570

14   'Prophet without honour', *New Statesman*, 29 October 1976

15   Sherman, *Paradoxes*, p. 87

16   Keith Joseph, Letter to Margaret Thatcher, 16 May 1978, http://www.margaretthatcher.org/document/111833

17   Interview with ITN News At Ten, 11 February 1975, http://www.margaretthatcher.org/document/102618

18   Speech to Federation of Conservative Students Conference, 24 March 1975, http://www.margaretthatcher.org/document/102663

19   Cited in Moore, *Not For Turning*, p. 302

20   Cited in Moore, *Not For Turning*, p. 351

21   Cited in Denham and Garnett, p. 298

22   Keith Joseph, Shadow Cabinet Paper, 4 April 1975, http://www.margaretthatcher.org/document/110098

23   Moore, *Not For Turning*, p. 303

24   Cited in Denham and Garnett, p. 288

25   Lord Hailsham Diary, 11 April 1975, http://www.margaretthatcher.org/document/111134

26   Lord Hailsham Diary, 6 October 1977, http://www.margaretthatcher.org/document/111187

27   Lord Hailsham Diary, 29 March 1977, http://www.margaretthatcher.org/document/111182

28   Cited in Moore, *Not For Turning*, p. 298

29   Alfred Sherman, Memorandum to Sir Keith Joseph, 22 April 1975, http://www.margaretthatcher.org/document/111908

30   Cited in Moore, *Not for Turning*, p. 342; Ranelagh, p. ix

31   David Wood, '"Mystery" man behind Tory new thought', *The Times*, 12 June 1978

32   Sherman, *Paradoxes*, p. 82

33   Cited in Moore, *Not For Turning*, p. 309

34   'The making of Tory policy, 1978', *The Economist*, 15 April 1978

35   Alfred Sherman, 'Our second birthday party: Two candles to shed light', 20 May 1976, http://www.margaretthatcher.org/document/111927

36   Sherman, *Paradoxes*, p. 85

37   See Geoffrey Fry, 'An uneasy coalition: the Conservatives in opposition 1975–1979', POLIS Working Papers, May 2015, p. 6

38   Sherman, *Paradoxes*, p. 85, p. 83

39   Cited in Young, *One of Us*, p. 113

40   Hugo Young, *The Hugo Young Papers: Thirty Years of British Politics – Off the Record*, (London: Allen Lane, 2008), p. 114

41   Cited in Adrian Williamson, *Conservative Economic Policymaking And The Birth Of Thatcherism 1964–1979* (Basingstoke: Palgrave Macmillan, 2015), p. 47

42   'Loyalty and leadership', *The Times*, 30 May 1978; Mark Garnett, 'Editor's Foreword', in Sherman, *Paradoxes*, p. 16

43   Young, *One of Us*, p. 87

44   Interview with Norman Strauss

45   Alfred Sherman, Memorandum to Margaret Thatcher, 'A programme for all seasons', 18 September 1978, THCR 2-6-1-225

46   Alfred Sherman, Memorandum to Keith Joseph, 9 July 1975, http://www.margaretthatcher.org/document/111912

47   Cited in Halcrow, p. 102

48 Although, as Denham and Garnett noted, the notion of 'the ratchet of nationalisation' had been coined by Enoch Powell in 1966, p. 296

49 Cited in Denham and Garnett, p. 296

50 Alfred Sherman, 'Note on populism', 3 May 1978, THCR 2-6-1-226

51 Alfred Sherman, Memorandum to Margaret Thatcher, 'A programme for all seasons', 18 September 1978, THCR 2-6-1-225

52 Alfred Sherman, Memorandum to Keith Joseph, 17 February 1976, http://www.margaret-thatcher.org/document/111925

53 Alfred Sherman, Letter to Margaret Thatcher, 25 October 1977, http://www.margaret-thatcher.org/document/111990

54 Alfred Sherman, Memorandum to Margaret Thatcher, 7 March 1979, THCR 2-6-1-225

55 Max Beloff, *A Historian in the Twentieth Century* (New Haven and London: Yale University Press, 1992), p. 5

56 Max Beloff, 'Facing the world', in Patrick Cormack (ed.), *Right Turn: Eight Men Who Changed Their Minds* (London: Leo Cooper, 1978), p. 27

57 Beloff, 1978, pp. 27–9

58 Lord Young, *The Enterprise Years: A Businessman In The Cabinet* (London: Headline, 1990), p. 29

59 Alfred Sherman, Memorandum to Joseph, 27 October 1975, http://www.margaretthatcher.org/document/111972

60 Alfred Sherman, Memorandum to Keith Joseph, 9 November 1977, http://www.margaretthatcher.org/document/111992

61 Thatcher, *Path*, p. 409

62 Alfred Sherman, Memorandum to Margaret Thatcher, 20 July 1978, http://www.margaretthatcher.org/document/111998

63 Alfred Sherman, Memorandum to Margaret Thatcher, 1 June 1978, http://www.margaret-thatcher.org/document/111993

64 Alfred Sherman, Memorandum to Margaret Thatcher, 11 December 1978, http://www.margaretthatcher.org/document/112002

65 Alfred Sherman, Letter to Margaret Thatcher, 2 June 1978, http://www.margaretthatcher.org/document/111994

66 Alfred Sherman, Memorandum to Keith Joseph, 13 July 1977, http://www.margaret-thatcher.org/document/111985

67 Alfred Sherman, Memorandum to Keith Joseph, 6 July 1976, http://www.margaret-thatcher.org/document/111934

68 Alfred Sherman, Memorandum to Keith Joseph, 13 July 1977, http://www.margaret-thatcher.org/document/111985

69 Alfred Sherman, Memorandum to Keith Joseph, 6 July 1976, http://www.margaret-thatcher.org/document/111934

70 Keith Joseph, Letter to Margaret Thatcher, 23 December 1976, THCR 1/18/4

71 Halcrow, p. 130

72 Alfred Sherman, Memorandum to Margaret Thatcher, 20 November 1978, http://www.margaretthatcher.org/document/112001

73 Brittan, p. 290

74 Moore, *Not For Turning*, p. 347

75 Brittan, p. 273

76 Murray Friedman, *The Neoconservative Revolution: Jewish Intellectuals and the Shaping of Public Policy* (New York: Cambridge University Press, 2005), p. 51

77 Cited in Moore, *Not For Turning*, p. 342

78 Friedman, p. 52

79 Cited in Godfrey Hodgson, *The World Turned Rightside Up: A History of the Conservative Ascendancy in America* (New York: Houghton Mifflin, 1996), p. 197

80 Charles Robinson, *Arthur Seldon: A Life For Liberty* (London: Profile Books, 2009), p. 65

81 Denham and Garnett, p. 180, p. 245

82 Campbell, *Grocer's Daughter*, p. 372

83 Milton Friedman, Letter to Ralph Harris, 4 December 1978, http://www.margaretthatcher.org/document/117139

84 Cited in Campbell, *Grocer's Daughter*, p. 366

85 Cited in Subroto Roy and John Clarke (eds.), *Margaret Thatcher's Revolution: How It Happened and What It Meant* (London: Continuum, 2005), p. 66

86 Thatcher, *Path*, p. 567

87 Cited in Ranelagh, p. 182

88 Thatcher, *Path*, p. 567

89 Margaret Thatcher, 'My debt to Keith's intellect – and corner shop wisdom', *Sunday Times*, 18 June 1995

90 Cited in John Hoskyns, *Just In Time: Inside The Thatcher Revolution* (London: Aurum Press, 2000), p. 404

91 Keith Joseph, Stockton Lecture, 5 April 1976, http://www.margaretthatcher.org/document/110796

92 Thatcher, *Path*, p. 318

93 Cited in Fry, p. 11

94 Cited in Halcrow, p. 104

95 Cited in Harrison, p. 212

96 Denham and Garnett, p. 295

97 Cited in Harrison, ODNB

98 Joseph, Stockton Lecture

99 Cited in Harrison, ODNB

100 Cited in Halcrow, p. 194

101 Cited in Halcrow, p. 97

102 Young, *One of Us*, p. 103

103 Margaret Thatcher, Speech to the Zurich Economic Society, 14 March 1977, http://www.margaretthatcher.org/document/103336

104 Cited in Moore, *Not For Turning*, p. 349

105 Alfred Sherman, First Draft of Iain Macleod Memorial Lecture, THCR 5/1/2/142; Margaret Thatcher, Iain Macleod Memorial Lecture, 4 July 1977, http://www.margaretthatcher.org/document/103411

106 Sherman, *Paradoxes*, p. 41

107 Margaret Thatcher, Speech at St Lawrence Jewry, 30 March 1978, http://www.margaretthatcher.org/document/103522

108 Thatcher, *Path*, p. 298

109 Cited in Denham and Garnett, p. 304

110 Young, *One of Us*, p. 107

111 Sherman, *Paradoxes*, p. 87

112 Denham and Garnett, p. 305

113 Thatcher, *Path*, p. 317

114 Thatcher, *Path*, p. 404

115 Cited in Moore, *Not For Turning*, p. 356

116 Thatcher, *Path*, p. 289

117 Keith Joseph, 'Our tone of voice and our tasks', 7 December 1976, http://www.margaret-thatcher.org/document/110178

118 Cited in Campbell, *Grocer's Daughter*, p. 393

119 Keith Joseph, Speech at Doncaster Racecourse, 24 June 1977, http://www.margaret-thatcher.org/document/111944

120 Sherman, *Paradoxes*, p. 100

121 Thatcher, *Path*, p. 402; 'Tory leader denies split in party over closed shop', *The Times*, 14 September 1977

122 Thatcher, *Path*, p. 402

123 Cited in Denham and Garnett, p. 310

124 Cited in Halcrow, p. 125

125 Hoskyns, p. 20

126 Interview with Norman Strauss

127 Ibid.

128 Thatcher, *Path*, p. 420

129 Ibid.

130 Ranelagh, p.12

131 John Hoskyns and Norman Strauss, Stepping Stones, 14 November 1977, http://www.margaretthatcher.org/document/111771

132 Interview with Norman Strauss

133 Thatcher, *Path*, p. 421

134 Meeting of Leader's Steering Committee, 30 January 1978, http://www.margaretthatcher.org/document/109832

135 Thatcher, *Path*, p. 421

136 Hoskyns, p. 67

137 Thatcher, *Path*, p. 422

138 Alfred Sherman, Memorandum to Margaret Thatcher, 11 December 1978, http://www.margaretthatcher.org/document/112002

139 Keith Joseph, Letter to Geoffrey Howe, 9 October 1978, http://www.margaretthatcher.org/document/111868

140 Thatcher, *Path*, p. 422

141 Thatcher, *Path*, p. 436; Moore, *Not For Turning*, p. 405

Chapter 5: Changing the Equation: The 'Jewish Vote' and the Shift to the Right

1 David Leigh, 'Where it's no longer taboo to talk about "the coloureds",' *The Guardian*, 17 February 1978

2 David Leigh, 'Ex-MP fights byelection', *The Guardian*, 17 February 1978

3 Alderman, *Jewish Community*, p. 148

4 The future Labour Cabinet minister had joined Labour Friends of Israel. Although not Jewish, her first husband, Roger Jowell, was.

5 Alderman, *Jewish Community*, p. 147

6 Interview with *World in Action*, 30 January 1978, http://www.margaretthatcher.org/document/103485

7 Campbell, *Grocer's Daughter*, p. 399

8 Ibid.

9   Campbell, *Grocer's Daughter*, p. 184

10   Interview with *World in Action*, 30 January 1978

11   Keith Joseph, Letter to Margaret Thatcher, 22 July 1976, http://www.margaretthatcher.org/document/111233

12   Keith Joseph, Shadow Cabinet Paper, 7 December 1976, http://www.margaretthatcher.org/document/110178

13   Cited in Denham and Garnett, p. 314

14   Alfred Sherman, 'Notes on Immigration-Speeches Strategy', 8 February 1978, THCR 2-6-1-225

15   Note of James Callaghan meeting with Labour whips, 8 March 1978, http://www.margaretthatcher.org/document/111718; cited in Campbell, *Grocer's Daughter*, p. 400

16   Cited in Sandbrook, p. 594; 'A quiver of innuendo', *The Economist*, 4 February 1978

17   Sandbrook, p. 594

18   Cited in Moore, *Not For Turning*, p. 382

19   Will Ellsworth-Jones, 'Introducing "the eminence grise"'

20   'NF march ban', *JC*, 24 February 1978

21   David Leigh, 'Where it's no longer'

22   Alfred Sherman, Memorandum to Margaret Thatcher, 26 January 1978, THCR, 2-6-1-225

23   Interview with Geoffrey Alderman

24   See Alderman, *Jewish Community*, p. 140

25   Alfred Sherman, Letter to Alan Howarth, 7 December 1977, THCR 2-6-1-226

26   Alderman, *Jewish Community*, p. 146. Alderman lists Hendon North, Hampstead, Ilford North, Hove, Finchley, and Middleton & Prestwich

27   '"Jewish vote" row', *JC*, 24 February 1978

28   Interview with Geoffrey Alderman

29   Cited in Denham and Garnett, p. 316

30   Philip Kleinman, 'The press', *JC*, 3 March 1978

31   'Misguided advice', *JC*, 24 February 1978

32   Cited in Alderman, *Jewish Vote*, pp. 2–3. The policy was partially relaxed in time for the 1979 general election, Alderman, *Jewish Community*, p. 152

33   Cited in 'Storm over "Jewish vote"', *JC*, 24 February 1978

34   Cited in 'Warning by Kaufman', *JC*, 24 February 1978

35   Sherman, *Paradoxes*, p. 98

36   Cited in 'Sir Keith's counterblast', *JC*, 3 March 1978

37   Cited in 'Dual standards', *JC*, 17 March 1978

38   'Was Sir Keith right?', *JC*, 3 March 1978

39   'Jews, race and immigration', *JC*, 17 March 1978

40   'Support for Sir Keith', *JC*, 17 March 1978

41   George Clark, 'Labour take heart from Ilford swing and attack spreading of "fear and prejudice"', *The Times*, 4 March 1978

42   'How many votes swung by race?', *The Economist*, 11 March 1978

43   Fred Emery, 'Counting up the Ilford percentages', *The Times*, 4 March 1978

44   Alfred Sherman, 'Ilford and the Jewish vote', *Sunday Telegraph*, 26 February 1978

45   Alderman, *Jewish Community*, p. 149. Alderman conducted a series of polls in seats with a large Jewish population between 1974 and 1992. Unless stated otherwise, all references are from Alderman's extensive polling during this period. The best summary of it is contained in Alderman, *Jewish Political*, p. 261

46   Cited in Alderman, *Jewish Vote*, p. 22

47   Alfred Sherman, Memorandum to Margaret Thatcher, 28 April 1983, http://www.marga-
      retthatcher.org/document/131248
48   Alfred Sherman, Memorandum to Richard Ryder, 23 March 1978, THCR 2-6-1-225
49   Correspondence with Alan Howarth
50   Cited in Alderman, *London Jewry*, p. 119
51   Cited in Alderman, *Jewish Vote*, p. 26
52   'Proliferation of racial hatred', *JC*, 3 March 1978
53   Yona Ginzberg, 'Sympathy and resentment: Jews and coloureds in London's East End',
      Patterns Of Prejudice, Vol. 13, No. 2–3, March–June 1979, p. 39
54   Cited in Barry Kosmin, 'Jewish voters in the United Kingdom', *Research Report* (London:
      Institute of Jewish Affairs, August 1980), p. 6. Small numbers of Jews joined the National
      Front, standing as local and parliamentary election candidates. For a discussion of this see
      Alderman, *Jewish Community*, pp. 165–8
55   Alderman, *Jewish Vote*, p. 28
56   'Jews, race and immigration', *JC*, 10 March 1978
57   According to Mori, concern about immigration during the 1970s peaked in August 1978,
      when it was seen – after unemployment and inflation – as the third most important issue
      facing the country. See https://www.ipsos-mori.com/researchpublications/researchar-
      chive/poll.aspx?oItemId=2439&view=wide
58   Alderman, *Jewish Community*, p. 154
59   Alderman, *Jewish Community*, pp. 156–8 explains his methodology
60   Alderman, *Jewish Vote*, p. 23. Hackney's ultra-Orthodox community has long been sup-
      portive of the Conservatives. This was true of other areas of London with ultra-Orthodox
      communities such as Golders Green and Hendon. See Alderman, *Jewish Political*, p. 261 and
      research by Dr Ofira Seliktar cited in 'Ultra-Orthodox mainly Tory', *JC*, 7 February 1975
61   Geoffrey Alderman, 'Anglo-Jewry: The Politics of An Image', *Parliamentary Affairs*, Vol.
      37, No. 2, Spring 1984, p. 178
62   Alderman, *Political Conservatism*, p. 111
63   Alderman, *Anglo-Jewry*, p. 180
64   Alderman, *Jewish Community*, p. 153
65   Alderman, *Political Conservatism*, p. 111
66   Alderman, *Jewish Political*, p. 265
67   Alderman, *London Jewry*, p. 140
68   Alderman, *Anglo-Jewry*, p. 178
69   Alderman, *Political Conservatism*, p. 111
70   Alderman, *Jewish Political*, p. 257
71   Alderman, *Jewish Political*, p. 258
72   Alderman, *Political Conservatism*, p. 107
73   Kosmin, p. 4
74   Alderman, *Political Conservatism*, p. 112. Labour support among Jews in the constituency
      was also higher, a reflection of the SDP–Liberal Alliance's lack of appeal
75   Cited in 'Key campaigners speak out', *JC*, 29 May 1987
76   Abse, pp. 205–11

Chapter 6: David Becomes Goliath: How the Left Turned on Israel
1   Alderman, *Jewish Political*, p. 258
2   W. D. Rubinstein, *The Left, The Right and the Jews* (London: Croom Helm, 1982), p. 139

3   For a discussion of anti-Semitism within the Labour movement in late Victorian and Edwardian times, when some of the worst culprits were revered figures like John Burns, Robert Blatchford, Harry Quelch and Ben Tillett, see Anthony Julius, *Trials of the Diaspora. A History of Anti-Semitism* (Oxford: Oxford University Press, 2010), especially p. 280–81

4   Joshua Muravchik, *Making David Into Goliath: How The World Turned Against Israel* (New York: Encounter Books, 2014), p. 20

5   Dave Rich's *The Left's Jewish Problem: Jeremy Corbyn, Israel and Anti-Semitism* (London: Biteback, 2016) provides an excellent guide to this subject on which I have drawn

6   Cited in Rich, p. 29

7   See Michael Bloch, *Jeremy Thorpe* (London: Little, Brown, 2014), p. 264, p. 368

8   Cited in Rich, p. 56; 'Pro-Arab Liberals split party', *JC*, 20 November 1970

9   Cited in Rich, p. 59

10   Bloch, p. 302

11   Cited in Rich, p. 61

12   Cited in 'Young Liberals lose public support', *JC*, 24 September 1971

13   Cited in 'Liberal views on Israel', *JC*, 12 September 1975; '"Destroy Israel" call by Arabs', *JC*, 5 September 1975

14   'Lack of guts', *JC*, 5 September 1975

15   'A birthday bonus for Mrs Thatcher', *Finchley Times*, 18 October 1974; Alderman, *Jewish Community*, p. 160

16   Alderman, *Jewish Political*, p. 261

17   Rich, p. 11

18   'Anti-Zionism at British campuses', *Research Report* (London: Institute of Jewish Affairs, July 1977); Eric Breindel, 'The End of the affair? Campus anti-Semitism in Britain', *The New Leader*, 16 January 1978, pp. 10–11

19   See Colin Schindler, *Israel and the European Left: Between Solidarity and Delegitimisation* (New York: Continuum, 2012), pp. 254–6

20   Philip Ziegler, *Wilson: The Authorised Life* (London: Weidenfeld & Nicolson, 1993), p. 76

21   Denis Healey, *The Time Of My Life* (London: Penguin Books, 1990), p. 368

22   Ziegler, *Wilson*, p. 496

23   Cited in Stewart Jones, *British Policy in the Middle East 1966–74* (lulu.com, 2009), p. 69

24   Ziegler, *Wilson*, p. 510

25   Cited in Ziegler, *Wilson*, p. 340

26   Wilson, Preface

27   Ziegler, *Wilson*, p. 388

28   Brook, pp. 336–7

29   Cited in Brook, pp. 337–8

30   Cited in 'Labour bid to revise "Pro-Zionist" line', *JC*, 7 June 1975. For the strength of support for Israel in the parliamentary party, see also Rubenstein, p. 153

31   Paul Rose, 'Labour and Israel', *JC*, 29 June 1979

32   Milton Friedman, Lecture to Mont Pelerin Society, 1972, https://fee.org/articles/capitalism-and-the-jews/

33   Rich, p. 142

34   'Hackney row on Zionism', *JC*, 12 October 1979; Alderman, *London Jewry*, p. 125

35   'Anti-Israel move condemned', *JC*, 19 October 1979; 'Zionists hit back at Hackney', *JC*, 16 November 1979

36 Cited in 'MP Denies Accusation Of Racism', *Hackney Gazette*, 14 October 1980
37 Rudy Narayan, *Black England* (London: Doscarla Publications, 1977), p. 68
38 'Move to oust Hackney MP', *JC*, 21 August 1981
39 'Lebor lashes Labour', *JC*, London Extra, 30 April 1982
40 Alderman, *London Jewry*, p. 126
41 Cited in 'Red faces over Labour motion', *JC*, 31 July 1981
42 'Labour to unravel Middle East policy jumble', *JC*, 8 October 1982
43 'Blackpool Knights', *JC*, 8 October 1982
44 Colin Schindler, *Israel and the European Left*, p. 250
45 Cited in 'Labour man attacks Israel', *JC*, London Extra, 3 December 1982
46 Cited in 'Israel is defended by MPs and peers', *JC*, 12 November 1982
47 'Only Jewish voters', *JC*, 3 June 1983
48 'Fewer Jewish MPs are returned', *JC*, 17 June 1983
49 Philip Kleinman, 'The press', *JC*, 17 June 1983
50 Interview with Geoffrey Alderman
51 Schindler, *Israel and the European Left*, p. 249
52 Cited in Alderman, *London Jewry*, p. 133
53 Cited in Alderman, *London Jewry*, p. 134
54 Ibid.
55 'Beyond our Ken', *JC*, 21 December 1984
56 Cited in 'GLC funds for Pro-Arab group', *JC*, 17 August 1984
57 Cited in 'Livingstone-Brass in public clash', *JC*, London Extra, 8 March 1985
58 Alderman, *London Jewry*, p. 135
59 Cited in 'Livingstone whip resigns', *JC*, 1 March 1985
60 Alderman, *London Jewry*, p. 137
61 Cited in 'Hattersley condemns antisemitism of left', *JC*, 14 October 1983
62 'Labour assurance on Israel', *JC*, 28 October 1983
63 June Edmunds, 'The British Labour Party In The 1980s: The Battle Over the Palestinian/Israeli Conflict', *Politics*, 1998, 18(2), p. 114
64 'Labour will not invite PLO men', *JC*, 2 August 1985
65 Edmunds, p. 115
66 'Kinnock aids refuseniks', *JC*, 14 December 1984
67 Cited in 'Labour's Zionist pledge', *JC*, 27 September 1985
68 'Hostility by women', *JC*, 21 June 1985
69 Edmunds, p. 114
70 Cited in 'Rabbi attacks Ken Livingstone', *JC*, London Extra, 6 May 1983
71 Cited in 'Freeson defiant', *JC*, 3 May 1985
72 Cited in 'Brent East', *JC*, London Extra, 5 June 1987
73 Cited in 'Brent East'
74 Cited in Greville Janner and Derek Taylor, *Jewish Parliamentarians* (London: Vallentine Mitchell, 2008), p. 165
75 Illytd Harrington, 'Obituary: Ellis Hillman', *The Independent*, 24 January 1996
76 Interview with Geoffrey Alderman
77 Cited in 'Ex-kibbutznik who is Corbyn's left-hand man', *JC*, 29 January 2016
78 Cited in 'Bad press', *Inside Housing*, 31 May 2013
79 'Sisters in despair', *JC*, 20 May 1983
80 'Ginsburg joins SDP', *JC*, 16 October 1981; 'Fighting the SDP's battles', *JC*, London

Extra, 8 October 1982; 'Labour peers defect to new party', *JC*, 3 April 1981; 'Manny rejects the Labour whip', *JC*, 26 March 1982

81   Edmund Dell, 'Lever (Norman) Harold, Baron Lever of Manchester (1914–1995)', *Oxford Dictionary of National Biography*, Oxford University Press, 2004, online edn. May 2005

82   'Moonman joins SDP', *JC*, 22 November 1985

83   'SDP friends of Israel', *JC*, 17 July 1981

84   Cited in 'SDP offers support for Israel', *JC*, 31 July 1981

85   'SDP friends campaign', *JC*, 8 October 1982

86   'SDP is meek and mild on the Middle East', *JC*, 22 October 1982

87   'Israel is defended by MPs and peers', *JC*, 12 November 1982

88   Cited in John Carvel, 'Recovery position', *The Guardian*, 26 October 2005

89   'Think tank', *JC*, 5 February 1982

90   John Rentoul, 'Spinning across the spectrum', *The Independent*, 25 August 1995

91   Cited in Alex Zatman, 'Shoah memories spur writer Daniel to seek truth and courage', *Jewish Telegraph*

92   Alderman, *Jewish Political*, p. 265

93   Interview with Geoffrey Alderman

94   'What's the SDP's Israel policy?', *JC*, 10 April 1981

95   'A problem for all three parties', *JC*, 12 December 1980

96   Cited in 'Liberals castigate David Steel', *JC*, 1 March 1985

97   'Liberals stress their friendship', *JC*, 27 September 1985

98   Cited in 'Finchley', *JC*, London Extra, 5 June 1987

99   Cited in 'Hendon South', *JC*, London Extra, 5 June 1987

100 Alderman, *Jewish Political*, p. 265

Chapter 7: Comrades in Arms: Jews and the Thatcher Revolution

1   Cited in Blond

2   Reflecting Thatcher's generally poor record in appointing women, Sally Oppenheim, the other Jewish member of her shadow Cabinet, was effectively demoted and had to settle for a junior ministerial appointment

3   Interview with Sir Malcolm Rifkind

4   Ibid.

5   Nigel Lawson, *The View From No.11: Memoirs Of A Tory Radical* (London: Bantam Press, 1992), p. 256

6   Chaim Bermant, 'More and more Jews are singing the blues', *JC*, 2 July 1993

7   Thatcher, *Downing Street*, p. 509

8   Interview with Lord Howard

9   David Wolfson, Memorandum to Margaret Thatcher, 22 August 1985, http://www.margaretthatcher.org/document/142280

10   Cited in Blond

11   Alan Watkins, 'Diary', *The Spectator*, 24 November 1984

12   Cited in Moore, *Everything She Wants*, p. 70

13   Geoffrey Goodman, 'Keys to the Cabinet', *JC*, 14 February 1997

14   Alan Clark, *Diaries: In Power 1983–1992* (London: Phoenix, 1994), p. 133

15   Cited in Clark, p. 185

16   Cited in William Rubinstein, Michael Jolles, Hilary Rubinstein (eds.), *The Palgrave Dictionary of Anglo-Jewish History* (London: Palgrave Macmillan, 2011), p. 189

17 Cited in 'Tearoom tattle spells prejudice', *JC*, 10 November 1989

18 'Currie talks of Commons prejudice', *JC*, 14 November 1997

19 Cited in 'Anti-Jewish talk at the dinner table', *The Tablet*, 12 June 1993

20 Cited in Naim Attallah, 'Sir Julian Critchley', *The Oldie*, February, 1998

21 Cited in 'Sir Keith and Mik bow out', *JC*, 8 May 1987

22 'Rebuke For Sir Keith', *JC* London Extra, 20 April 1984

23 Cited in 'Young, gifted and back', *JC Magazine*, 28 June 1991

24 Lawson, p. 479

25 Cited in John Campbell, *Margaret Thatcher: Iron Lady* (London: Vintage, 2008), p. 25

26 Private information

27 Thatcher, *Downing Street*, p. 25

28 Cited in Moore, *Not For Turning*, p. 432

29 Thatcher, *Path*, p. 293

30 Ibid.

31 Private information

32 Interview with Norman Strauss

33 Thatcher, *Downing Street*, p. 135

34 Cited in Moore, *Everything She Wants*, pp. 641–2

35 Cited in Aitken, p. 316

36 Cited in Moore, *Everything She Wants*, p. 698; Thatcher, *Downing Street*, p. 584

37 Cited in Moore, *Not For Turning*, p. 427

38 Thatcher, *Downing Street*, p. 26

39 Halcrow, p. 136

40 Cited in Denham and Garnett, p. 336

41 Cited in Halcrow, p. 136

42 Cited in Denham and Garnett, p. 343

43 Jim Prior, *A Balance of Power* (London: Hamish Hamilton, 1986), p. 125

44 David Lipsey, 'Why Sir Keith can only blame himself', *Sunday Times*, 31 May 1981

45 Cited in Seldon, p. 30

46 Moore, *Not For Turning*, p. 518

47 Cited in Halcrow, p. 133

48 See, for example, Campbell, *Iron Lady*, p. 15

49 Cited in Moore, *Not For Turning*, p. 517

50 Cited in Harrison, ODNB

51 Cited in Moore, *Not For Turning*, p. 517

52 Cited in Prior, p. 125

53 Thatcher, *Downing Street*, p. 151

54 Cited in Denham and Garnett, p. 367

55 Cited in Denham and Garnett, pp. 369–70

56 Cited in Seldon, p. 31

57 Cited in Halcrow, p. 183

58 Thatcher, *Downing Street*, p. 420

59 David Wolfson, Memorandum, 22 August 1985

60 Cited in Sarah Curtis (ed.), *The Journals of Woodrow Wyatt* Vol I (London: Pan Books, 1999), p. 124

61 Thatcher, *Downing Street*, p. 420

62 Lawson, p. 600

63 'Text of letters about Sir Keith's resignation', *The Times*, 22 May 1986

64 Thatcher, *Downing Street*, p. 562

65 Keith Joseph, 'Implications of the Tory challenge', *The Times*, 20 November 1990

66 Cited in Howe, p. 676

67 Alfred Sherman, Memorandum to Margaret Thatcher, 29 February 1980, http://www.margaretthatcher.org/document/115119

68 Alfred Sherman, Memorandum to Margaret Thatcher, 10 April 1980, http://www.margaretthatcher.org/document/119483

69 Alfred Sherman, Memorandum to Margaret Thatcher, 11 April 1980, http://www.margaretthatcher.org/document/115130

70 Alfred Sherman, Memorandum to Margaret Thatcher, 28 March 1980, http://www.margaretthatcher.org/document/119482

71 Alfred Sherman, Memorandum to Margaret Thatcher, 10 August 1980, http://www.margaretthatcher.org/document/119487. Sherman's lobbying on economic policy was not without influence. A paper he commissioned by the Swiss monetarist Jorg Niehans led to a change in direction ahead of the pivotal 1981 budget. See Thatcher, *Downing Street*, pp. 133–4

72 Cited in Mount, p. 304

73 Mount, p. 303

74 Sherman, *Paradoxes*, p. 100

75 Cited in Halcrow, p. 157

76 Lipsey

77 Margaret Thatcher, Letter to Alfred Sherman, 13 October 1980, http://www.margaretthatcher.org/document/112656

78 Bruce Anderson, 'Rottweiler that gave a lead to Mrs T', *The Times*, 31 August 2006

79 Young, *One of Us*, p. 213

80 Sherman, *Paradoxes*, p. 103

81 Sherman, *Paradoxes*, p. 119

82 Alfred Sherman, Memorandum to Ian Gow, 1 March 1983, http://www.margaretthatcher.org/document/131222

83 Hugh Thomas, Letter to Ian Gow, 25 April 1983, http://www.margaretthatcher.org/document/131242

84 Cited in Simon Winchester, 'You see before you a rebel', *Sunday Times*, 3 May 1981. The quotes were a 'malicious invention', Sherman wrote Gow, suggesting, implausibly, that the source of the quotes attributed to the CPS were Conservative Party sources (Alfred Sherman, Letter to Ian Gow, 6 May 1981, http://www.margaretthatcher.org/document/121411)

85 Hugh Thomas, Letter to Alfred Sherman, 1 March 1983, http://www.margaretthatcher.org/document/131223; Hugh Thomas, Letter to Alfred Sherman, 11 March 1983, http://www.margaretthatcher.org/document/131226

86 Alfred Sherman, Letter to Hugh Thomas, 12 March 1983, http://www.margaretthatcher.org/document/131226

87 Alfred Sherman, Letter to Ian Gow, 26 March 1983, http://www.margaretthatcher.org/document/131235

88 Private information

89 See, for instance, Young, *Papers*, p. 132, p. 194, p. 219

90 Private information; Young, *One of Us*, p. 339

91   Alfred Sherman, Letter to Stephen Sherbourne, 21 August 1984, http://www.margaret-thatcher.org/document/137642

92   Cited in Peter Hennessy, 'Sherman view on loyalties', *The Times*, 2 May 1984

93   Alfred Sherman, 'Why we asked the unasked questions', *The Times*, 1 September 1984

94   Cited in 'Obituary: Sir Alfred Sherman', *The Times*, 29 August 2006

95   Sherman, *Paradoxes*, p. 121

96   Cited in 'Off the record', *Sunday Times*, 9 October 1994

97   Thatcher, *Path*, p. 251

98   Sherman, *Paradoxes*, pp. 126–7

99   Cited in Dennis Kavanagh, 'Sherman, Sir Alfred (1919–2006)', *Oxford Dictionary of National Biography*, Oxford University Press, Jan. 2010; online edn, Jan. 2011

100 Moore, *Not For Turning*, p. 425

101 Interview with Norman Strauss

102 Ibid.

103 Strauss was no longer working as a civil servant but as a consultant part-time at the Policy Unit

104 Peter Hennessy, 'Unions see Prior removal as direct challenge', *The Times*, 15 September 1981

105 Alan Walters Diary, 16 September 1981, http://www.margaretthatcher.org/document/140942

106 Cited in Peter Hennessy, 'Ministers delayed by mandarins', *The Times*, 21 September 1981

107 Interview with Norman Strauss

108 Norman Strauss, 'Civil servants must catch up with modern times', *Daily Telegraph*, 3 August 1988

109 Cited in Peter Hennessy, 'Call for Thatcher to lead in isolation, *The Times*, 28 April 1984

110 'High society', *JC*, 1 February 2002. In 2013, Letwin removed the reference to 'Judaism' as his religion from his Wikipedia profile saying he was an atheist. 'Letwin's no minyan man', *JC*, 7 June 2013

111 See Oliver Letwin, 'An Englishman of Jewish origin', *JC*, 13 September 1991 for Letwin on his Jewishness

112 Cited in Andy Beckett, 'More Mr Niceguy', *The Guardian*, 7 October 2003

113 Cited in Letwin, 'An Englishman'

114 Cited in 'High society'

115 Halcrow, p. 186

116 Moore, *Everything She Wants*, p. 349

117 Oliver Letwin, Memorandum to Margaret Thatcher, 20 December 1984, http://www.margaretthatcher.org/document/136335

118 Oliver Letwin, Memorandum to Margaret Thatcher, 15 January 1985, http://www.margaretthatcher.org/document/143632

119 Oliver Letwin, Memorandum to Andrew Turnbull, 15 November 1984, http://www.margaretthatcher.org/document/137675

120 Alan Travis, 'Downing Street files reveal how Oliver Letwin kept poll tax plans alive', *The Guardian*, 1 January 2015

121 Oliver Letwin, Memorandum to Margaret Thatcher, 30 December 1985, http://www.margaretthatcher.org/document/141593

122 Robert Medick, 'Shirley Porter? Oh, she's really scary, said Maggie', *Evening Standard*, 7 August 2006

123 Hosken, p. 18

124 Cited in 'At war with Livingstone and litter', *JC*, 15 July 1983
125 Cited in Jay Rayner, 'Dame Shirley of Tel Aviv', *The Observer*, 28 February 1999
126 Cited in 'Has the cleaning Lady been swept aside?', *JC*, 17 May 1996
127 Cited in Hosken, p. 74
128 Cited in Hosken, p. 75
129 Hosken, p. 75
130 Cited in Medick
131 Cited in Hosken, p. 91
132 Cited in Rayner
133 Jenny Diski, 'Be mean and nasty', *London Review of Books*, Vol. 28, No. 10, 25 May 2006
134 Cited in Diski
135 Cited in Rayner
136 David Hart's mother, Elsie Rosewell, was not Jewish but an Irish Protestant
137 Moore, *Everything She Wants*, p. 153
138 Cited in Simon Heffer, 'Hart, David (1944–2011)', *Oxford Dictionary of National Biography*, Oxford University Press, Jan. 2015
139 Interview with Lord Sherbourne
140 Cited in Aitken, p. 452
141 David Hart, Letter to Margaret Thatcher, 4 October 1983, http://www.margaretthatcher.org/document/130959
142 Aitken, p. 449
143 Cited in Aitken, p. 449
144 Ibid.
145 David Hart, Memorandum to Margaret Thatcher, 16 April 1984, http://www.margaretthatcher.org/document/136361
146 Interview with Lord Sherbourne
147 Hart had started taking snuff to get around the rules against smoking at Eton. Many miners were users because of the ban on smoking down the pit
148 See Seumas Milne, *The Enemy Within: The Secret War Against The Miners* (London: Verso Books, 2014), p. 324
149 Cited in Aitken, p. 450
150 Thatcher, *Downing Street*, p. 365
151 David Hart, Memorandum to Margaret Thatcher, 26 April 1984, http://www.margaretthatcher.org/document/136217
152 Cited in Milne, p. 325
153 David Hart, Memorandum to Margaret Thatcher, 18 September 1984, http://www.margaretthatcher.org/document/136219
154 Stephen Sherbourne, Memorandum to Margaret Thatcher, 28 September 1984, http://www.margaretthatcher.org/document/136253
155 Interview with Lord Sherbourne
156 Paul Foot, 'Hart in the right place', *Daily Mirror*, 18 October 1984
157 Charles Powell, Memorandum to Robin Butler, 20 October 1984, http://www.margaretthatcher.org/document/133948
158 Stephen Sherbourne to Charles Powell, 15 February 1985, http://www.margaretthatcher.org/document/138180
159 Stephen Sherbourne, Memorandum to Margaret Thatcher, 27 February 1985, http://www.margaretthatcher.org/document/138185

160 Interview with Lord Sherbourne
161 Ibid.
162 Interview with Sir Malcolm Rifkind
163 Curtis, Vol. I, p. 437
164 Heffer, ODNB
165 Cited in Mike Marqusee, 'No redemption', *Red Pepper*, March 2009
166 James Naughtie, 'Lord without peer in the Tory hierarchy', *The Guardian*, 8 October 1987
167 John Vincent, 'Thatcher: The reality', *The Times*, 10 October 1987
168 Thatcher, *Downing Street*, p. 421
169 Young, *Enterprise Years*, pp. 4–5
170 Young's cousin had married Isaac Wolfson's son, Leonard. David Wolfson was a nephew of Isaac
171 Young, *Enterprise Years*, pp. 9–11
172 Young, *Enterprise Years*, p. 15
173 Young, *Enterprise Years*, p. 29
174 Cited in Young, *Enterprise Years*, p. 32
175 Young, *Enterprise Years*, p. 23
176 Ibid.
177 Interview with Lord Young
178 'ORT aids new skill training scheme', *JC*, 19 November 1982
179 Patrick Bishop, 'The elevation of Finchley man', *Sunday Times*, 16 September 1984
180 Young, *Enterprise Years*, p. 59
181 Young, *Enterprise Years*, p. 174
182 'Super-guru for the dole queue', *The Observer*, 16 September 1984
183 Moore, *Everything She Wants*, pp. 92–3
184 Young, *Enterprise Years*, p. 111
185 Young, *Enterprise Years*, p. 112
186 Young, *Enterprise Years*, p. 115
187 Campbell, *Iron Lady*, p. 219
188 Cited in Bishop
189 Interview with Lord Young
190 Cited in Moore, *Everything She Wants*, p. 440
191 Young, *Enterprise Years*, p. 178
192 Young, *Enterprise Years*, p. 164
193 Young, *One of Us*, p. 516
194 Cited in Aitken, p. 399
195 Moore, *Everything She Wants*, p. 440
196 Bishop
197 Clark, p. 119
198 Cited in Moore, *Everything She Wants*, p. 440
199 See Clark, p. 109
200 Lawson, p. 698
201 Aitken, p. 525
202 Interview with Lord Young. See also Moore's discussion on whether Young entertained the idea of becoming Prime Minister, *Everything She Wants*, p. 691
203 Lawson p. 698
204 Moore, *Everything She Wants*, p. 688

205 Young, *Enterprise Years*, p. 222

206 Cited in Moore, *Everything She Wants*, p. 704

207 Moore, *Everything She Wants*, p. 705

208 Thatcher, *Downing Street*, p. 573

209 Interview with Lord Young

210 Young, *Enterprise Years*, p. 256

211 Curtis, Vol. I, p. 432

212 Sarah Curtis (ed.), *The Journals Of Woodrow Wyatt* Vol II (London: Pan Books, 1999), p. 134

213 Thatcher, *Downing Street*, p. 588

214 Thatcher, *Downing Street*, p. 291

215 Interview with Lord Sherbourne

216 Private information

217 Thatcher, *Downing Street*, p. 416

218 Cited in Moore, *Everything She Wants*, p. 427

219 Stephen Sherbourne, Memorandum to Margaret Thatcher, 22 August 1985, http://www.margaretthatcher.org/document/142279

220 Moore, *Everything She Wants*, p. 525. The idea was taken up by John Wakeham, the Chief Whip, who wrote to Mrs Thatcher proposing it

221 Thatcher, *Downing Street*, p. 564

222 Thatcher, *Downing Street*, p. 572

223 Ibid.

224 Cited in Moore, *Everything She Wants*, p. 526

225 Stephen Sherbourne, Memorandum to Margaret Thatcher, 22 August 1985

226 Cited in Moore, *Everything She Wants*, p. 375

227 Cited in Lawson, p. 250

228 Susan Crosland, *Looking Out, Looking In: Profiles Of Others and Myself* (London: Weidenfeld & Nicolson, 1987), p. 49

229 Ibid.

230 Cited in 'Cameron's got it so easy, says Thatcher's chancellor', *JC*, 19 November 2010

231 Lawson, pp. 256

232 See Ziegler, *Heath*, p. 364; Ziegler, *Heath*, p. 463

233 Lawson, p. 11; Thatcher, *Path*, p. 242

234 Thatcher, *Path*, p. 421

235 Lawson, pp. 64–5

236 R. W. Johnson, 'Is this successful management?', *London Review of Books*, Vol. 11, No. 8, 20 April 1989, pp. 3–6

237 Thatcher, *Downing Street*, p. 309

238 Thatcher, *Downing Street*, p. 308

239 Cited in Campbell, *Iron Lady*, p. 246

240 Cited in Moore, *Everything She Wants*, p. 198

241 Campbell, *Iron Lady*, p. 244

242 Andy McSmith, *No Such Thing As Society: A History Of Britain In The 1980s* (London: Constable, 2011), p. 188

243 Thatcher, *Downing Street*, p. 672

244 Ibid.

245 Cited in Aitken, p. 540

246 Interview with Sir Malcolm Rifkind
247 Cited in Campbell, *Iron Lady*, p. 217
248 Interview with Lord Sherbourne
249 Cited in Moore, *Everything She Wants*, p. 435
250 See Campbell, *Iron Lady*, p. 222
251 Lawson, p. 64
252 Thatcher, *Downing Street*, p. 701
253 Aitken, pp. 545–6
254 Cited in Moore, *Everything She Wants*, p. 410
255 Cited in Aitken, p. 547
256 Thatcher, *Downing Street*, p. 674
257 Lawson, p. 920
258 Lawson, p. 964
259 Interview with Lord Sherbourne
260 Cited in Aitken, p. 549
261 Lawson, p. 936
262 Cited in Lawson, p. 574
263 Lawson, p. 1000
264 Thatcher, *Downing Street*, p. 308
265 Cited in Moore, *Everything She Wants*, p. 485
266 Herbert Samuel had held the post of Home Secretary in 1916 and 1931–32
267 Cited in Terry Coleman, 'Kindly man at the cutting edge of the Cabinet', 30 November 1981, *The Guardian*
268 'Two Jews at the top', *JC*, 17 June 1983
269 Cited in 'East land, Westland', *JC*, 16 January 1987
270 'New Tory who made it on his own', *The Observer*, 19 June 1983
271 Michael Howard, 'Leon was the best of our generation', *JC*, 30 January 2015
272 'Two Jews at the top'; cited in Brook, p. 343
273 Cited in Brook, p. 341
274 Aitken, p. 185
275 Thatcher, *Downing Street*, p. 131
276 Thatcher, *Downing Street*, p. 308
277 Thatcher, *Downing Street*, p. 149
278 Cited in Kwasi Kwarteng, *Thatcher's Trial: Six Months That Defined A Leader* (London: Bloomsbury, 2015), p. 158
279 Thatcher, *Downing Street*, p. 308
280 Interview with Lord Sherbourne
281 Young, *One of Us*, p. 335
282 Campbell, *Iron Lady*, p. 401; see Moore, *Everything She Wants*, p. 437
283 Moore, *Everything She Wants*, p. 438
284 Cited in Curtis, Vol. I, p. 46
285 Thatcher, *Downing Street*, p. 419, p. 308
286 Ibid.
287 Curtis, Vol. I, p. 125
288 Cited in Moore, *Everything She Wants*, p. 437
289 Young, *One of Us*, p. 436
290 Thatcher, *Downing Street*, p. 435

291 Howe, p. 469

292 Cited in 'East land, Westland'

293 Robin Oakley, 'The fall guy bites back', *The Times*, 19 August 1987; Peter Jenkins, *Mrs Thatcher's Revolution: The Ending Of The Socialist Era* (London: Jonathan Cape, 1987), p. 201

294 Lawson, p. 679

295 Cited in Jenkins, p. 201

296 Cited in A. J. Davies, *We The Nation: The Conservative Party And The Pursuit Of Power* (London: Little, Brown 1995), p. 158

297 Aitken, p. 514

298 Cited in 'Obituary: Sir John Stokes', *The Daily Telegraph*, 30 June 2003. Stokes denied to the *Jewish Chronicle* that this remark was a reference to Brittan's Jewish or East European background ('Red-blooded denial', *JC*, 31 January 1986)

299 Howe, p. 469

300 'East land, Westland'

301 Cited in Young, *One of Us*, p. 448

302 Cited in 'Mrs Brittan accuses', *JC*, 31 January 1986

303 James Naughtie, 'A man cursed by cleverness', *The Guardian*, 25 January 1986. See also Philip Kleinman, 'Worries over a fall guy', *JC*, 31 January 1986

304 Cited in Aitken, p. 509

305 Cited in Young, *One of Us*, p. 454

306 Cited in Moore, *Everything She Wants*, p. 482

307 Cited in Curtis, Vol. I, p. 386

308 Moore, *Everything She Wants*, p. 393

309 Thatcher, *Downing Street*, p. 419

310 Interview with Sir Malcolm Rifkind

311 Thatcher, *Downing Street*, p. 620

312 Thatcher, *Downing Street*, p. 852

313 Malcolm Rifkind, *Power and Pragmatism: The Memoirs Of Malcolm Rifkind* (London: Biteback, 2016), p. 9

314 Interview with Sir Malcolm Rifkind

315 Rifkind, p. 17

316 Rifkind, p. 5

317 Interview with Sir Malcolm Rifkind

318 Ibid.

319 Rifkind, p. 7

320 Rifkind, p. 129

321 Rifkind, p. xvii

322 Cited in Thatcher, *Path*, p. 323

323 Interview with Sir Malcolm Rifkind. Rifkind wrote a regular column for the *JC* when he was first elected. As MP for Finchley, Mrs Thatcher frequently read the weekly newspaper

324 Ibid.

325 Thatcher, *Downing Street*, p. 620

326 Thatcher, *Downing Street*, p. 622

327 Rifkind, p. 236

328 Rifkind, p. 243

329 Interview with Sir Malcolm Rifkind

330 Rifkind, p. 257; Thatcher, *Downing Street*, p. 852 suggested Rifkind's advice was rather harsher

331 Thatcher, *Downing Street*, p. 852

332 Curtis, Vol. II, p. 588

333 'A flying Scotsman on the right track', *JC*, 15 February 1991

334 Interview with Sir Malcolm Rifkind

335 Rifkind, p. xiv

336 Interview with Lord Howard

337 Ibid.

338 Cited in 'Friends recall Howard's rock'n'roll childhood', *JC*, 7 November 2003

339 Michael Crick, *In Search Of Michael Howard* (London: Simon & Schuster, 2005), p. 42

340 Crick, p. 64

341 David Goldberg, 'I don't agree with Michael's views on asylum – but he's much better than shambolic Labour', *Mail On Sunday*, 2 November 2003

342 Cited in 'Hard man's comeback', *JC*, 26 September 2003

343 Frances Hardy, 'My grandad the "illegal" immigrant', *Daily Mail*, 12 February 2005

344 Interview with Lord Howard

345 Crick, p. 29

346 Cited in Rae Lewis, 'I was such a rebel I became a Conservative', *Evening Standard*, 14 January 1996

347 Crick, p. 146; Edward Pearce, 'Climbing on to the poll tax gallows', *Sunday Times*, 26 July 1987

348 Crick, p. 148

349 Interview with Lord Howard

350 Interview with Lord Howard. Lord Howard could not recall the precise date or whether Mrs Thatcher was then Education or shadow Education Secretary. Mrs Thatcher addressed a dinner of the club on 11 December 1973, so it seems likely to have been then. Ruth Winstone (ed.), *Events, Dear Boy, Events: A Political Diary of Britain From Woolf To Campbell* (London: Profile Books, 2012), p. 355

351 Interview with Lord Howard

352 Jonathan Freedland, 'The trailblazer', *The Guardian*, 31 October 2003

353 Matthew Parris, *Chance Witness: An Outsider's Life in Politics* (London: Penguin Books, 2003), p. 222. When he became Tory leader in 2003, there were undercurrents of anti-Semitism in some of the media coverage. See Freedland

354 Cited in Curtis, Vol. I, p. 257

355 Cited in Crick, p. 194

356 Curtis, Vol. II, p. 79

357 Norman Fowler, *A Political Suicide: The Conservatives' Voyage Into The Wilderness* (London: Politico's, 2008), p. 57

358 Thatcher, *Downing Street*, p. 852

359 Ibid.

Chapter 8: Holy Wars: Margaret Thatcher, the Bishops and the Chief Rabbi

1 Cited in Campbell, *Iron Lady*, p. 389

2 Filby, p. 172

3 Ibid.

4 'Faith in the City': A Call for Action by Church and Nation (London: Church House Publishing, 1985), p. xv

5   Faith, p. 191, p. 205

6   Moore, *Everything She Wants*, p. 446

7   Faith, p. 245

8   Faith, p. 313

9   Faith, pp. 326–7

10 Faith, p. 56, p. 53

11 Faith, p. 51

12 Faith, p. 208

13 Faith, p. 231

14 Filby, p. 195

15 Cited in Filby, p. 182

16 Cited in Filby, p. 178

17 Interview with Lord Sherbourne

18 Cited in Moore, *Everything She Wants*, p. 445. In 2016, the Church of England unofficially acknowledged that 'Faith in the City' had 'failed to see the moral vision that informed Margaret Thatcher's administrations, and therefore failed to engage coherently with that vision'. Cited in Kaya Burgess, 'Perhaps Thatcher was right after all, Church admits', *The Times*, 9 June 2016

19 Cited in Moore, *Everything She Wants*, p. 447

20 Cited in Curtis, Vol. 1, p. 22

21 Interview with Lord Sherbourne

22 Thatcher, *Path*, p. 554.

23 Weiss, p. 28

24 Cited in Tim Wyatt, '"Faith In The City": a "Marxist analysis"', *Church Times*, 8 January 2016

25 Cited in Moore, *Everything She Wants*, p. 446

26 Cited in Young, *One of Us*, p. 417

27 Cited in Campbell, *Iron Lady*, p. 390

28 Young, *One of Us*, p. 422

29 Chaim Bermant, *Lord Jakobovits: The Authorised Biography of the Chief Rabbi* (London: Weidenfeld & Nicolson, 1990), p. 28

30 Cited in Albert Friedlander, 'Jakobovits, Immanuel, Baron Jakobovits (1921–1999)', *Oxford Dictionary of National Biography*, Oxford University Press, 2004, online edn, Jan. 2014

31 Cited in Michael Shashar, *Lord Jakobovits In Conversation* (London: Vallentine Mitchell, 2000), p. 193

32 Bermant, p. 4

33 Cited in Shashar, p. 91

34 Interview with Lord Sherbourne

35 Interview with Shimon Cohen

36 Ibid.

37 Cited in Gloria Tessler, *Amelie: The Story of Lady Jakobovits* (London: Vallentine Mitchell, 1999), p. 225

38 Tessler, p. 226

39 Cited in Tessler, p. 226

40 Interview with Shimon Cohen

41 Margaret Thatcher, Speech at Lord Jakobovits Retirement Dinner, 21 February 1991, http://www.margaretthatcher.org/document/108261

42 Margaret Thatcher, Speech to the Board of Deputies of British Jews, 18 February 1990, http://www.margaretthatcher.org/document/108017

43 Immanuel Jakobovits, Letter to Margaret Thatcher, 10 June 1983, http://www.margaret-thatcher.org/document/131130

44 Immanuel Jakobovits, Letter to Margaret Thatcher, 13 October 1984, http://www.margaretthatcher.org/document/136291

45 Young, 'When Mrs Thatcher sings'

46 Worsthorne, 'Judaism is the new creed'

47 Cited in Friedlander, ODNB

48 Cited in Tessler, pp. 292–3. Despite these denials about his political allegiances, a hint as to the Jakobovits' support for the Tories was evident when Lady Jakobovits signed the nomination papers of John Marshall, the Conservative candidate in Hendon South in 1992, Alderman, *Political Conservatism*, p. 110

49 Cited in Walter Schwarz, 'A firm believer in the profit of work', *The Guardian*, 29 December 1988

50 Cited in Brook, p. 205

51 Interview with Shimon Cohen

52 Bermant, p. 179

53 Shimon Cohen, 'Her bond with Lord Jakobovits was profound – and it helped save shechita', *JC*, 11 April 2013

54 Geoffrey Alderman, 'London Jews and the 1987 general election', *The Jewish Quarterly*, Vol. 34, No. 3, 1987, p. 16

55 Cohen, 'Her bond with Lord Jakobovits'

56 Cited in Brook, p. 95

57 Cited in Walter Schwarz, 'Tidings of anti-Zion', *The Guardian*, 20 June 1986

58 Cited in Brook, p. 203

59 Cited in Moore, *Everything She Wants*, p. 61

60 Thatcher, *Path*, p. 153

61 Owen Bowcott, 'Thatcher tried to block "bad taste" public health warnings about Aids', *The Guardian*, 1 January 2016

62 Cited in Brook, p. 202

63 Ibid.

64 Interview with *Woman's Own*, 23 September 1987, http://www.margaretthatcher.org/document/106689

65 Cited in Shashar, p. 91

66 Young, *One of Us*, p. 423

67 Interview with Shimon Cohen

68 Ibid.

69 Cited in Shashar, pp. 92–3

70 Interview with Shimon Cohen

71 Jakobovits, Doom, p. 5

72 Jakobovits, Doom, p. 6

73 Jakobovits, Doom, p. 7

74 Ibid.

75 Jakobovits, Doom, pp. 9–10

76 Jakobovits, Doom, p. 11

77 Jakobovits, Doom, p. 13

78 Jakobovits, Doom, p. 14

79   Ibid.
80   Jakobovits, Doom, p. 15
81   Cited in 'The welfare state', *Jewish Tribune*, 17 June 1977
82   Interview with Shimon Cohen
83   Chaim Bermant, 'Is the Chief the true rabbi blue?', *JC*, 26 May 1989
84   Interview with Lord Sherbourne
85   Thatcher, *Downing Street*, p. 510
86   Avner, p. 505
87   Campbell, *Iron Lady*, p. 394
88   Thatcher, *Downing Street*, pp. 509–510
89   Cited in Moore, *Not For Turning*, p. 137
90   Alfred Sherman, 'Notes on the ORT Luncheon', 12 May 1978, THCR 2-6-1-225
91   Interview with David Frost, 30 December 1988, http://www.margaretthatcher.org/document/107022
92   Cited in Young, *One of Us*, p. 426
93   Cited in Moore, *Not For Turning*, p. 137
94   Worsthorne, 'Judaism is the new creed'
95   Interview with David Frost
96   Cited in Aitken, p. 103
97   Jonathan Sacks, *Wealth And Poverty: A Jewish Analysis* (London: Social Affairs Unit, 1985), p. 16
98   Sacks, pp. 5–6
99   Margaret Thatcher, Speech to Technion University Dinner, 2 November 1989, http://www.margaretthatcher.org/document/107814
100 Cited in Campbell, *Iron Lady*, p. 250
101 Margaret Thatcher, Speech to the Board of Deputies of British Jews, 18 February 1990, http://www.margaretthatcher.org/document/108017
102 Cited in Moore, *Not For Turning*, p. 137
103 Interview with David Dimbleby, 10 June 1987, http://www.margaretthatcher.org/document/106649
104 Interview with Lord Young
105 Margaret Thatcher, Speech to Friends of Hebrew University of Jerusalem dinner, 27 October 1988, http://www.margaretthatcher.org/document/107361
106 Interview with the *Sunday Times*, 3 May 1981, http://www.margaretthatcher.org/document/104475
107 Margaret Thatcher, Speech at Women's International Zionist Organisation Centenary Lunch, 2 May 1990, http://www.margaretthatcher.org/document/108078
108 Cited in Moore, *Not For Turning*, p. 137
109 Margaret Thatcher, Speech at Lord Jakobovits Retirement Dinner
110 Immanuel Jakobovits, 'First line of defence', *JC*, 30 November 1990
111 Margaret Thatcher, Speech to the Board of Deputies of British Jews, 18 February 1990
112 Although it should be noted that, as Rabbi Sidney Brichto, executive vice-president of the Union of Liberal and Progressive Synagogue, has argued, approximately 75 per cent of Anglo-Jewry is secular, Progressive or non-believing, non-practising members of Orthodox synagogues. Sidney Brichto, 'Speaking with the one voice but whose?', *JC*, 14 June 1991, p. 20
113 Brook, p. 126
114 Cited in Brook, p. 198
115 Cited in Schwarz, 'Tidings of anti-Zion'

116   David Goldberg and John D. Rayner, *The Jewish People: Their History and their Religion* (London: Penguin, 1989), pp. 307–9

117   Raphael Samuel, 'A reminder for the rabbi', *The Guardian*, 27 January 1986

118   Leo Abse, 'When the bishops and rabbis swap sides', *The Guardian*, 31 January 1986

119   Cited in 'Communal approach to inner cities', *JC*, 31 January 1986

120   Cited in Brook, p. 201

121   'Communal approach', 'Plight of inner cities', *JC*, 14 February 1986

122   Chaim Bermant, 'Not every Jew in Britain is a Cabinet minister', *JC*, 21 February 1986

123   Cited in 'Black leader's warning', *JC*, 31 January 1986

124   Cited in 'Work-shy charge angers Blacks', *JC*, 28 February 1986

125   Ibid.

126   Bermant, p. 177

127   Cited in 'Kaufman attack on race "blindness"', *JC*, 15 November 1985

128   Cited in 'Deprivation in the inner cities', *JC*, 7 February 1986

129   Cited in Brook, p. 208

130   'Rabbinical star in the limelight', *The Observer*, 22 June 1986

131   Cited in Brook, p. 203

132   Cited in 'Rabbinical star in the limelight'

133   Ibid.

134   Ibid.

135   Cited in Brook, p. 205

136   Cited in Brook, p. 206

137   Geoffrey Alderman, *London Jews*; cited in Bermant, p. 178

138   Interview with Geoffrey Alderman

139   Chaim Bermant, 'How to make friends and join a Tory Cabinet', *JC*, 21 September 1984

140   'Chief Rabbi replies to his critics', *JC*, 14 March 1986

141   Interview with Shimon Cohen

142   'Tories back Chief', *JC*, 14 February 1986

143   Interview with Shimon Cohen

144   Cited in 'Chief's report praised', *JC*, 7 March 1986

145   Interview with Shimon Cohen

146   Cited in Schwarz, 'Tidings of anti-Zion'

147   Cited in Schwarz, 'A firm believer'

148   'Leaders deny "Tory Party at prayer" jibe', *JC*, 9 November 1990

Chapter 9: Israel's Friend in Downing Street: Mrs Thatcher and the Jewish State

1   Margaret Thatcher, Speech at Ben Gurion Airport, 24 May 1986, http://www.margaret-thatcher.org/document/106401

2   Moore, *Everything She Wants*, p. 281

3   Interview with Lord Young

4   James Naughtie, 'Shalom and goodbye from a Finchley twin', *The Guardian*, 28 May 1986

5   Margaret Thatcher, Speech at King David hotel, 26 May 1986, http://www.margaret-thatcher.org/document/106406

6   Naughtie, 'Shalom and goodbye'

7   Cited in Chaim Bermant, 'How Margaret Thatcher conquered Israel', *JC*, 6 June 1986

8   Interview with Lord Powell

9   Cited in 'My visit to Israel', *Finchley Press*, 25 June 1965; Thatcher, *Downing Street*, p. 509

10   Interview with Alan Cohen

11   Cited in 'What I saw in Israel', *Finchley Times*, 2 July 1965

12   Cited in 'Large audience for Israel talk', *Finchley Press*, 2 July 1965

13   Interview with Lord Powell

14   Cited in Danna Harman, 'Israel leaders, British immigrants remember Margaret Thatcher as admirer of country's "grit and guts"', *Haaretz*, 10 April 2013

15   Cited in 'Large audience'

16   Margaret Thatcher, Remarks visiting 'Israel 22' exhibition, 11 May 1970, http://www.margaretthatcher.org/document/101747

17   Cited in 'Large audience'

18   Malcolm Rifkind, 'Where the Tories stand on Middle East', *JC*, 9 April 1976

19   Martin Gilbert, *Churchill And The Jews* (London: Simon and Schuster, 2008), p. 18

20   Cited in Gilbert, p. 308

21   Cited in Gilbert, p. 42

22   Cited in Gilbert, p. 254

23   Cited in Gilbert, p. 275

24   Cited in Gilbert, p. 295, p. 293

25   Thatcher, *Path*, p. 379

26   Thatcher, *Path*, pp. 379–801

27   Cited in 'Mrs Meir – by Mrs Thatcher', *Finchley Times*, 14 January 1972

28   'Tory friends get off the ground', *JC*, 31 January 1975

29   'Survey shows most MPs back Israel', *JC*, 31 March 1976

30   Thatcher, *Path*, p. 373

31   'Tories are surprised by Israeli rebuke', *JC*, 7 March 1975; 'Mrs Thatcher misses cue', *JC*, 23 March 1975

32   Philip Kleinman, 'Maudling as a risk', *JC*, 28 February 1975

33   'Tories advocate Arab Palestinian state', *JC*, 14 November 1975

34   Thatcher, *Path*, p. 374; 'Tories divided on Maudling', *JC*, 21 November 1975

35   Margaret Thatcher, Speech to Finchley Association of Jewish Ex-Servicemen and Women, 27 November 1975, http://www.margaretthatcher.org/document/102814

36   Cited in Bermant, *Margaret Thatcher*, p. 21

37   Thatcher, *Path*, p. 319

38   Interview with Laurence Brass; interview with Alan Cohen

39   Lord Hailsham, Letter to Margaret Thatcher, 17 February 1975, http://www.margaretthatcher.org/document/111128

40   Letter from British Embassy in Amman to FCO, 28 February 1975, http://www.margaretthatcher.org/document/110906

41   Letter from FCO to British Embassy in Amman, 5 March 1975, http://www.margaretthatcher.org/document/110907

42   'Mrs Thatcher shocks Arab audience', *JC*, 16 January 1976

43   Anthony Elliott, Letter to FCO, 30 March 1976, http://www.margaretthatcher.org/document/111177

44   Thatcher, *Path*, p. 378

45   Anthony Elliott, Letter to FCO, 30 March 1976, http://www.margaretthatcher.org/document/111178; http://www.margaretthatcher.org/document/111177

46   A. B. Urwick, Letter to Anthony Elliott, 30 January 1976, http://www.margaretthatcher.org/document/111179

47   Anthony Elliott, Letter to FCO, 30 March 1976; Neill Lochery, 'Debunking the Myths: Margaret Thatcher, the Foreign Office and Israel, 1979–1990', *Diplomacy & Statecraft*, 21:4, p. 691

48   Campbell, *Iron Lady*, p. 335

49   Cited in Moore, *Everything She Wants*, p. 271

50   Bermant, *Margaret Thatcher*, p. 67

51   Moore, *Everything She Wants*, p. 272

52   Bermant, *Margaret Thatcher*, p. 23

53   No.10 Minute of Meeting with Menachem Begin, 23 May 1981, http://www.margaretthatcher.org/document/117934

54   Avner, pp. 506–9

55   Interview with Lord Powell

56   Cited in Avner, p. 508

57   Peter Carrington, *Reflecting On Things Past* (New York: Harper & Row, 1988), p. 340

58   No.10 Minute, 23 May 1981

59   Cited in Azriel Bermant, 'The impact of the Cold War on the Thatcher government's Middle East policy', *Israel Affairs*, 19:4, p. 625

60   No.10 Minute, 23 May 1981

61   Margaret Thatcher, Letter to Jimmy Carter, 15 June 1979, http://www.margaretthatcher.org/document/118925

62   Bermant, 'The impact', p. 625

63   These themes are discussed in detail in Bermant, 'The impact', pp. 623–39. The FCO's views are described in Bermant, *Margaret Thatcher*, pp. 34–6

64   See Young, 'Mrs Thatcher Sings'

65   Cited in Moore, *Everything She Wants*, p. 270

66   Cited in Bermant, *Margaret Thatcher*, p. 84

67   Peter Carrington, Memorandum to Margaret Thatcher, 13 February 1980, http://www.margaretthatcher.org/document/120543

68   Margaret Thatcher, Letter to Jimmy Carter, 26 January 1980, http://www.margaretthatcher.org/document/112686

69   Cited in Nigel Ashton, 'Love Labour's lost: Margaret Thatcher, King Hussein and Anglo-Jordanian relations, 1979–1990', *Diplomacy & Statecraft*, p. 654

70   Interview with Lord Powell

71   Lord Hailsham, Memorandum to Margaret Thatcher, 14 February 1980, http://www.margaretthatcher.org/document/120544

72   Robert Armstrong, Memorandum to Margaret Thatcher, 20 February 1980, http://www.margaretthatcher.org/document/120545

73   No. 10 Minute of Meeting with Board of Deputies of British Jews, 27 November 1979, http://www.margaretthatcher.org/document/120539

74   'Anglo Israeli link to stay', *Finchley Times*, 6 December 1979

75   No.10 Minute of Meeting with King Hussein, 20 September 1979, http://www.margaretthatcher.org/document/142034

76   Peter Carrington, Memorandum to Margaret Thatcher, 11 September 1979, http://www.margaretthatcher.org/document/117951

77   Cited in Moore, *Everything She Wants*, p. 270

78   Meeting of the European Council, 12–13 June 1980, http://www.margaretthatcher.org/document/114098

79 Lochery, p. 694

80 Thatcher, *Downing Street*, p. 91

81 Peter Carrington, Memorandum to Margaret Thatcher, 6 June 1980, http://www.margaretthatcher.org/document/120554

82 Cited in Ashton, p. 655

83 Thatcher, *Downing Street*, p. 90

84 Peter Carrington, Memorandum to Margaret Thatcher, 6 June 1980

85 'Minister defends PLO', *JC*, 21 March 1980

86 Cited in 'Friends warn Carrington', *JC*, 13 June 1980

87 Cited in 'Reassuring Barnet's Jewish voters', *Hendon Times*, 3 April 1980

88 Cited in Alderman, *Jewish Community*, p. 170

89 Cited in '1000 voters voice protest', *JC*, 13 June 1980

90 Alderman, *Jewish Community*, p. 171

91 Ian Bradley, 'A Finchley problem for Mrs Thatcher', *The Times*, 29 October 1981

92 Interview with Geoffrey Alderman

93 Cited in 'Change course! Local Jews urge government not to deal with terrorists', *Hendon Times*, 17 July 1980

94 Carrington, p. 345

95 Cited in Bermant, *Margaret Thatcher*, p. 46

96 Menachem Begin, Letter to Margaret Thatcher, 17 June 1980, http://www.margaretthatcher.org/document/119707

97 Margaret Thatcher, Unsent letter to Menachem Begin, 14 July 1980, http://www.margaretthatcher.org/document/120568

98 Bermant, *Margaret Thatcher*, p. 51

99 Although the ban, imposed after the invasion of Lebanon, was eased over time, it was not completely lifted until 1994. See Bermant, *Margaret Thatcher*, p. 90, p. 113

100 Bermant, *Margaret Thatcher*, p. 215

101 'Britain lifts Arab boycott barrier', *JC*, 31 January 1986

102 Colin Schindler, 'The Reflection Of Israel Within British Jewry', in Danny Ben-Moshe and Zohar Segev (eds.), *Israel, The Diaspora And Jewish Identity* (Brighton: Sussex Academic, 2007), p. 229

103 No.10 Minute of Meeting with King Hussein, 24 June 1980, http://www.margaretthatcher.org/document/120565

104 Bermant, *Lord Jakobovits*, p. 148

105 Margaret Thatcher, Letter to Michael Latham, 20 November 1981, http://www.margaretthatcher.org/document/121719

106 Cited in Bermant, *Margaret Thatcher*, p. 62

107 Interview with *Jewish Chronicle*, http://www.margaretthatcher.org/document/104476

108 David Wolfson, Memorandum to John Coles, 11 December 1981, http://www.margaretthatcher.org/document/121882

109 Lochery, p. 696; Margaret Thatcher, Notes on Speech to Board of Deputies of British Jews, 15 December 1981, http://www.margaretthatcher.org/document/121884

110 'Thatcher in a clash over Golan Heights', *JC*, 18 December 1981

111 See for instance Anthony Parsons, Minute for Douglas Hurd, 8 August 1979, http://www.margaretthatcher.org/document/136387

112 Interview with IRN, 10 June 1982, http://www.margaretthatcher.org/document/104965

113 Cited in Bermant, *Margaret Thatcher*, p. 88

114 Bermant, *Margaret Thatcher*, p. 99
115 Margaret Thatcher, Message to Ronald Reagan, 15 June 1982, http://www.margaretthatcher.org/document/123364
116 Margaret Thatcher, Message to Ronald Reagan, 29 July 1982, http://www.margaretthatcher.org/document/123430
117 John Coles, Memorandum to Margaret Thatcher, 30 June 1982, http://www.margaretthatcher.org/document/124658
118 UK Embassy Tunis, Cable to FCO, 2 July 1982, http://www.margaretthatcher.org/document/124660
119 Francis Pym, Message to Margaret Thatcher, 6 July 1982, http://www.margaretthatcher.org/document/124665
120 Cited in Campbell, *Iron Lady*, p. 335
121 'Protest at Hurd talks', *JC*, 16 July 1982
122 Schindler, p. 229
123 'Bevin's mantle', *JC*, 9 July 1982
124 John Coles, Memorandum to Margaret Thatcher, 12 July 1982, http://www.margaretthatcher.org/document/142665
125 Bermant, *Margaret Thatcher*, p. 104
126 Margaret Thatcher, Speech at Japan Press Club, 21 September 1982, http://www.margaretthatcher.org/document/105020
127 Cited in 'British Jews are appalled', *JC*, 24 September 1982
128 'How to vote', *JC*, 3 June 1983
129 Alderman, *Jewish Political*, p. 260
130 No.10 Minute of Meeting with Donald Rumsfeld, 20 January 1984, http://www.margaretthatcher.org/document/146427
131 Cited in Lochery, p. 698
132 Bermant, *Margaret Thatcher*, p. 110
133 Interview with Lord Powell
134 Cited in Moore, *Everything She Wants*, p. 277
135 Moore, *Everything She Wants*, p. 277
136 Bermant, *Margaret Thatcher*, p. 117
137 Bermant, *Margaret Thatcher*, pp. 118–19
138 No.10 Minute of Meeting with CFI, 20 June 1985, http://www.margaretthatcher.org/document/145427
139 No.10 Minute of Meeting with CFI, 20 June 1985
140 Interview with Lord Powell
141 Bermant, *Margaret Thatcher*, p. 121
142 Cited in Moore, *Everything She Wants*, p. 278
143 Cited in Moore, *Everything She Wants*, p. 279
144 Ibid.
145 'Israel rebukes Britain, *JC*, 27 September
146 'Thatcher attacked by rabbi', *JC*, 4 October 1985
147 Cited in Philip Kleinman, 'Maggie wakes up to the PLO', *JC*, 4 October 1985
148 'Israeli anger at arms deal', *JC*, 20 September 1985
149 Cited in 'Israel rebukes'
150 Cited in Campbell, *Iron Lady*, p. 280
151 Cited in Philip Kleinman, 'Opinion turns against PLO', *JC*, 18 October 1985

152 Cited in Moore, *Everything She Wants*, p. 280

153 Interview with Lord Young

154 Interview with Lord Powell

155 'No other way', *JC*, 18 October 1985

156 Cited in Bermant, *Margaret Thatcher*, p. 142

157 Thatcher, *Downing Street*, p. 510

158 Margaret Thatcher, Speech at Knesset, 25 May 1986, http://www.margaretthatcher.org/document/106402

159 Cited in Bermant, *Margaret Thatcher*, p. 144

160 Thatcher, *Downing Street*, p. 511

161 Interview with Lord Powell

162 Bermant, *Margaret Thatcher*, p. 149

163 Cited in Moore, *Everything She Wants*, p. 281

164 Interview with Lord Powell

165 Thatcher, *Downing Street*, p. 511

166 Thatcher, *Downing Street*, p. 509; Thatcher, *Downing Street*, p. 511

167 Margaret Thatcher, Press Conference At King David Hotel, 27 May 1986, http://www.margaretthatcher.org/document/106407

168 Margaret Thatcher, Remarks at Ramat Gan, 27 May 1986, http://www.margaretthatcher.org/document/106410

169 Interview with Lord Powell

170 Thatcher, *Downing Street*, p. 512

171 Yitzhak Shamir, *Summing Up: An Autobiography* (London: Weidenfeld & Nicolson, 1994), p. 167

172 Cited in Bermant, *Margaret Thatcher*, p. 157

173 Cited in Ashton, p. 663

174 Bermant, *Margaret Thatcher*, p. 159

175 Cited in Ashton, p. 664

176 Cited in Bermant, *Margaret Thatcher*, p. 162

177 Cited in Bermant, *Margaret Thatcher*, p. 167

178 Ashton, p. 665

179 William Waldegrave, *A Different Kind Of Weather: A Memoir* (London: Constable, 2016), p. 205

180 Cited in 'Britain strives to reassure Israelis', *JC*, 20 January 1989; 'Waldegrave angers Board', *JC*, 20 January 1989

181 Interview with Lord Powell

182 'Britain strives to reassure Israelis'

183 Cited in Ashton, p. 665

184 Bermant, *Margaret Thatcher*, p. 168

185 Shamir, p. 188

186 Thatcher, *Downing Street*, p. 827

187 Thatcher, *Downing Street*, p. 816

188 Margaret Thatcher, *Statecraft: Strategies For A Changing World* (London: HarperCollins, 2011), p. 243

Epilogue: Last Days: Soviet Jewry and Nazi War Crimes

1 Margaret Thatcher, Speech to the Board of Deputies of British Jews, 18 February 1990, http://www.margaretthatcher.org/document/108017

2   'Minister sees delegation', *JC*, 30 July 1971
3   Margaret Thatcher, Speech to Conservative Party rally, 31 July 1976, http://www.marga-retthatcher.org/document/103086; Margaret Thatcher, Speech to Board of Deputies of British Jews, 15 December 1981
4   Thatcher, *Downing Street*, p. 460
5   Rita Eker, 'Mrs Thatcher and human rights', *The Norrice Leader*, June/July 2013, p. 6
6   Thatcher, *Downing Street*, p. 484
7   Thatcher, *Downing Street*, p. 510
8   Cited in Guy Walters, *Hunting Evil: The Nazi War Criminals Who Escaped And The Quest To Bring Them To Justice* (London: Bantam Books, 2009), p. 563
9   Margaret Thatcher, Speech to the Board of Deputies of British Jews, 18 February 1990
10 Cited in Walters, *Hunting Evil*, p. 563
11 Cited in 'War crimes trial could be first and last', 1 April 1999, http://news.bbc.co.uk/1/hi/uk/309814.stm
12 Howe, p. 627

BIBLIOGRAPHY

Those embarking on a study of Margaret Thatcher are well-served by a number of well-researched and highly readable biographies. Charles Moore's two-volume authorised biography, *Not for Turning* and *Everything She Wants*; John Campbell's *Margaret Thatcher: The Grocer's Daughter* and *Margaret Thatcher: Iron Lady*; Hugo Young's *One of Us* and Jonathan Aitken's *Margaret Thatcher: Power and Personality* were invaluable in writing this book. So too were Geoffrey Alderman's excellent studies of the history and political attitudes of Britain's Jews, including *The Jewish Community in British Politics* and *London Jewry and London Politics* and Stephen Brook's *The Club: The Jews of Modern Britain*. Eliza Filby's *God and Mrs Thatcher* provided much useful background on Mrs Thatcher's religious beliefs and their impact on her politics.

Although his significance warrants rather more attention from potential biographers, Sir Keith Joseph's life and career is brilliantly chronicled by Andrew Denham and Mark Garnett in *Keith Joseph*. Mark Garnett also edited Alfred Sherman's memoirs, *Paradoxes of Power: Reflections on the Thatcher Interlude*. These two books, together with Morrison Halcrow's *Keith Joseph: A Single Mind* (the closest Joseph left to an autobiography) and John Ranelagh's fascinating *Thatcher's People*, did much to inform my understanding of the somewhat odd couple who did so much to bring about 'Thatcherism'.

My knowledge of Margaret Thatcher's dealings with Israel was aided greatly by Azriel Bermant's *Margaret Thatcher and the Middle East*, which offers new, and perhaps sometimes surprising, perspectives on her relationship with the Jewish state. The late Chaim Bermant, a great Jewish journalist and writer, wrote the authorised (but by no means uncritical) biography of Lord Jakobovits. *Lord Jakobovits: The Authorised Biography of the Chief Rabbi* provided much insight into Lady Thatcher's favourite religious leader.

I am grateful to the following for permission to quote extensively from their books: Jonathan Aitken, Geoffrey Alderman, Stephen Brook, Azriel Bermant, Andrew Denham and Mark Garnett, Eliza Filby, Charles Moore, John Ranelagh and Lord Young. I am also grateful to the copyright estate of Lady Thatcher; the Church of England for permission to quote from 'Faith in the City'; the estate of Lord Jakobovits for 'Doom to Hope'; the Toby Press for Yehuda Avner's *The Prime Ministers: An Intimate Narrative of Israeli Leadership* and Imprint Academic for Alfred Sherman, *Paradoxes of Power: Reflections on the Thatcher Interlude.*

Prologue and Chapter 1: In the Beginning

Jonathan Aitken, *Margaret Thatcher: Power and Personality* (London: Bloomsbury, 2014)

Yehuda Avner, *The Prime Ministers: An Intimate Narrative of Israeli Leadership* (New Milford, Connecticut: The Toby Press, 2010)

D. W. Bebbington, *The Nonconformist Conscience: Chapel and Politics 1870–1914* (London: Routledge Library Editions: Political Science Volume 19, 2014)

John Campbell, *Margaret Thatcher: The Grocer's Daughter* (London: Vintage, 2007)

James Callaghan, *Time and Chance* (London: Fontana, 1988)

Charles Dellheim, 'More Estonians than Etonians: Mrs Thatcher and the Jews', in Stanislao Pugliese (ed.), *The Political Legacy of Margaret Thatcher* (London: Politico's, 2003)

Eliza Filby, *God and Mrs Thatcher: The Battle for Britain's Soul* (London: Biteback, 2015)

Richard Griffiths, *Fellow Travellers of the Right: British Enthusiasts for Nazi Germany, 1933–1939* (London: Constable, 1980)

Tom Hopkinson (ed.), *Picture Post 1938–1950* (Harmondsworth, Middlesex: Penguin Books, 1970)

Tony Kushner, 'The Impact Of British Anti-Semitism, 1918–1945' in David Cesarani (ed.), *The Making of Modern Anglo-Jewry* (Oxford: Basil Blackwell, 1990)

Gisela C. Lebzelter, *Political Anti-Semitism in England 1918–1939* (London: Macmillan, 1978)

Charles Moore, *Margaret Thatcher: The Authorised Biography Volume One: Not For Turning* (London: Penguin Books, 2014)

Martin Pugh, *Hurrah for the Fascists: Fascists and Fascism in Britain Between the Wars* (London: Pimlico, 2006)

Douglas Reed, *Insanity Fair* (London: Jonathan Cape, 1938)

Arnold D. Richards (ed.), *The Jewish World of Sigmund Freud: Essays on Cultural Roots and the Problem of Religious Identity* (Jefferson, NC: McFarland & Co, 2010)

William Shirer, *The Nightmare Years 1930–1940* (New York: Bantam Press, 1984)

Margaret Thatcher, *The Downing Street Years* (London: HarperCollins, 2011)

Margaret Thatcher, *The Path to Power* (London: HarperCollins, 2011)

Hugo Young, *One of Us* (London: Pan Books, 1990)

Chapter 2: Finchley and Beyond

Geoffrey Alderman, *London Jewry and London Politics* (London: Routledge, 1989).

—, 'Jewish Political Attitudes and Voting Patterns in England 1945–1987', in Robert Wistrich (ed.), *Terms of Survival: The Jewish World Since 1945*, (London: Routledge, 1998).

Stuart Ball, *Portrait of a Party: The Conservative Party in Britain 1918–1945* (Oxford: Oxford University Press, 2013)

Azriel Bermant, *Margaret Thatcher and the Middle East* (Cambridge: Cambridge University Press, 2016)

Stephen Brook, *The Club: The Jews of Modern Britain* (London: Constable, 1989)

John Callaghan, *The Labour Party and Foreign Policy: A History* (Abingdon: Routledge, 2007)

John Campbell, *Edward Heath: A Biography* (London: Pimlico, 1993)

David Cesarani, 'British Jews' in Rainer Liedtke and Stephan Wendehorst (ed.), *The Emancipation of Catholics, Jews and Protestants: Minorities and the Nation State in Nineteenth-century Europe* (Manchester: Manchester University Press, 1999)

Chris Cook and John Ramsden, *By-Elections in British Politics* (London: Routledge, 2013)

Harry Defries, *Conservative Party Attitudes to Jews 1900–1950* (London: Routledge, 2001)

Andrew Denham and Mark Garnett, *Keith Joseph* (Chesham, Bucks: Acumen Publishing, 2001)

Bernard Donoughue, 'Four Constituency Campaigns', in David Butler and Anthony King, *The British General Election of 1964* (London: MacMillan & Co., 1965)

Todd M. Endelman, *The Jews of Britain 1656–2000* (Berkeley: University of California Press, 2002)

Edward Heath, *The Course of My Life* (London: Hodder & Stoughton, 1998)

Andrew Hosken, *Nothing Like a Dame: The Scandals of Shirley Porter* (London: Granta, 2006)

Charles Moore, *Margaret Thatcher: The Authorised Biography Volume Two: Everything She Wants* (London: Allen Lane, 2015)

John Ranelagh, *Thatcher's People: An Insider's Account of the Politics, the Power and the Personalities* (London: HarperCollins, 1991)

Harold Wilson, *The Chariot of Israel: Britain, America and the State of Israel* (London: Weidenfeld & Nicolson, 1981)

Philip Ziegler, *Edward Heath: The Authorised Biography* (London: HarperCollins, 2010)

Chapter 3: The Junior Partner

Leo Abse, *Margaret, Daughter of Beatrice: A Politician's Psycho-biography of Margaret Thatcher* (London: Jonathan Cape, 1989)

Samuel Brittan, 'Samuel Brittan', in Roger Backhouse and Roger Middleton (eds.), *Exemplary Economists: Vol II Europe, Asia and Australasia* (Cheltenham: Edward Elgar, 2000)

Eric J. Evans, *Thatcher and Thatcherism: The Making of the Contemporary World* (Routledge: Abingdon, 2013)

Morrison Halcrow, *Keith Joseph: A Single Mind* (London: Macmillan, 1989)

Geoffrey Howe, *Conflict of Loyalty* (London: Macmillan, 1994)

Ben Jackson, 'The think-tank archipelago: Thatcherism and neoliberalism', in Ben Jackson and Robert Saunders (eds.), *Making Thatcher's Britain* (Cambridge: Cambridge University Press, 2012)

Ferdinand Mount, *Cold Cream: My Life and Other Mistakes* (London: Bloomsbury, 2008)

Dominic Sandbrook, *Seasons in the Sun: The Battle for Britain 1974–1979* (London: Allen Lane, 2012)

Anthony Seldon, 'Escaping the chrysalis of statism', Contemporary Record, Vol. No. 1, Spring 1987, p. 26

Alfred Sherman, *Paradoxes of Power: Reflections on the Thatcher Interlude* (Exeter: Imprint Academic, 2005)

Nicholas Timmins, *The Five Giants: A Biography of the Welfare State* (London: Fontana, 1996)

Hugo Young and Anne Sloman, *The Thatcher Phenomenon* (London: British Broadcasting Corporation, 1986)

Chapter 4: The Senior Partner

Max Beloff, *A Historian in the Twentieth Century* (New Haven and London: Yale University Press, 1992)

—, 'Facing the world', in Patrick Cormack (ed.), *Right Turn: Eight Men Who Changed Their Minds* (London: Leo Cooper, 1978)

Murray Friedman, *The Neoconservative Revolution: Jewish Intellectuals and the Shaping of Public Policy* (New York: Cambridge University Press, 2005)

Godfrey Hodgson, *The World Turned Right Side Up: A History of the Conservative Ascendancy in America* (New York: Houghton Mifflin, 1996)

John Hoskyns, *Just in Time: Inside the Thatcher Revolution* (London: Aurum Press, 2000)

Colin Robinson, *Arthur Seldon: A Life for Liberty* (London: Profile Books, 2009)

Subroto Roy and John Clarke (eds.), *Margaret Thatcher's Revolution: How It Happened and What It Meant* (London: Continuum, 2005)

Philip Short, *Mitterrand: A Study in Ambiguity* (London: Vintage, 2014)

Adrian Williamson, *Conservative Economic Policymaking and the Birth of Thatcherism 1964–1979* (Basingstoke: Palgrave Macmillan, 2015)

Hugo Young, *The Hugo Young Papers: Thirty Years of British Politics – Off the Record* (London: Allen Lane, 2008)

Lord Young, *The Enterprise Years: A Businessman in the Cabinet* (London: Headline, 1990)

Chapter 6: David Becomes Goliath: How the Left Turned on Israel

Michael Bloch, *Jeremy Thorpe* (London: Little, Brown, 2014)

Denis Healey, *The Time of My Life* (London: Penguin Books, 1990)

Greville Janner and Derek Taylor, *Jewish Parliamentarians* (London: Vallentine Mitchell, 2008)

Stewart Jones, *British Policy in the Middle East 1966–74* (lulu.com, 2009)

Anthony Julius, *Trials of the Diaspora: A History of Anti-Semitism* (Oxford: Oxford University Press, 2010)

Joshua Muravchik, *Making David into Goliath: How the World Turned Against Israel* (New York: Encounter Books, 2014)

Rudy Narayan, *Black England* (London: Doscarla Publications, 1977)

Dave Rich, *The Left's Jewish Problem: Jeremy Corbyn, Israel and Anti-Semitism* (London: Biteback, 2016)

W. D. Rubinstein, *The Left, the Right and the Jews* (London: Croom Helm, 1982)

Colin Schindler, *Israel and the European Left: Between Solidarity and Delegitimisation* (New York: Continuum, 2012)

Philip Ziegler, *Wilson: The Authorised Life* (London: Weidenfeld & Nicolson, 1993)

Chapter 7: Comrades in Arms: Jews and the Thatcher Revolution

John Campbell, *Margaret Thatcher: Iron Lady* (London: Vintage, 2008)

Alan Clark, *Diaries: In Power 1983–1992* (London: Phoenix, 1994)

Michael Crick, *In Search of Michael Howard* (London: Simon & Schuster, 2005)

Susan Crosland, *Looking Out, Looking In: Profiles of Others and Myself* (London: Weidenfeld & Nicolson, 1987)

Sarah Curtis (ed.), *The Journals of Woodrow Wyatt Vol I* (London: Pan Books, 1999)

A. J. Davies, *We, The Nation: The Conservative Party and the Pursuit of Power* (London: Little, Brown 1995)

Norman Fowler, *A Political Suicide: The Conservatives' Voyage into the Wilderness* (London: Politico's, 2008)

Peter Jenkins, *Mrs Thatcher's Revolution: The Ending of the Socialist Era* (London: Jonathan Cape, 1987)

Kwasi Kwarteng, *Thatcher's Trial: Six Months That Defined a Leader* (London: Bloomsbury, 2015)

Nigel Lawson, *The View from No.11: Memoirs of a Tory Radical* (London: Bantam Press, 1992)

Andy McSmith, *No Such Thing as Society: A History of Britain in the 1980s* (London: Constable, 2011)

Seamus Milne, *The Enemy Within: The Secret War Against the Miners* (London: Verso Books, 2014)

Matthew Parris, *Chance Witness: An Outsider's Life in Politics* (London: Penguin Books, 2003)

Jim Prior, *A Balance of Power* (London: Hamish Hamilton, 1986)

Malcolm Rifkind, *Power and Pragmatism: The Memoirs of Malcolm Rifkind* (London: Biteback, 2016)

William Rubinstein, Michael Jolles and Hilary Rubinstein (eds.), *The Palgrave Dictionary of Anglo-Jewish History* (London: Palgrave Macmillan, 2011)

Ruth Winstone (ed.), *Events, Dear Boy, Events: A Political Diary of Britain from Woolf to Campbell* (London: Profile Books, 2012)

Chapter 8: Holy Wars: Margaret Thatcher, the Bishops and the Chief Rabbi

Chaim Bermant, *Lord Jakobovits: The Authorised Biography of the Chief Rabbi* (London: Weidenfeld & Nicolson, 1990)

David Goldberg and John D. Rayner, *The Jewish People: Their History and Their Religion* (London: Penguin, 1989)

Michael Shashar, *Lord Jakobovits in Conversation* (London: Vallentine Mitchell, 2000)

Gloria Tessler, *Amelie: The Story of Lady Jakobovits* (London: Vallentine Mitchell, 1999)

Chapter 9: Israel's Friend in Downing Street: Mrs Thatcher and the Jewish State and Epilogue

Peter Carrington, *Reflecting on Things Past* (New York: Harper & Row, 1988)

Martin Gilbert, *Churchill and the Jews* (London: Simon and Schuster, 2008)

Yitzhak Shamir, *Summing Up: An Autobiography* (London: Weidenfeld & Nicolson, 1994)

Margaret Thatcher, *Statecraft: Strategies for a Changing World* (London: HarperCollins, 2011)

William Waldegrave, *A Different Kind of Weather: A Memoir* (London: Constable, 2016)

Guy Walters, *Hunting Evil: The Nazi War Criminals Who Escaped and the Quest to Bring Them to Justice* (London: Bantam Books, 2009),

ACKNOWLEDGEMENTS

My earliest political memory concerns Margaret Thatcher. On the eve of the 1979 general election, I remember asking my parents whether it would be good to have a woman Prime Minister. I was told it would indeed be a good thing – but just not 'that woman'. Like many Britons of my age, 'that woman' dominated my childhood. I tagged along on demonstrations against her; helped deliver Labour Party leaflets and collect Christmas presents for the children of striking miners (both somewhat thankless tasks in Surrey); and – a sign of my teenage political innocence – was utterly shocked when she was re-elected in 1987, so confident and hopeful was I that Neil Kinnock was going to become Prime Minister.

Perhaps that dominance helps explain why, twenty-five years after Mrs Thatcher left office, I decided to write a book about her. My purpose was to examine a rather neglected element of Mrs Thatcher's remarkable story: her relationship with Britain's Jewish community and its impact on her beliefs and policies. In so doing, I discovered that she was a more complex and, in some regards, sympathetic figure than I had allowed myself to believe. Her abhorrence of anti-Semitism and high regard for all that the Jewish community contributes to Britain – together with the simple truth of her recognition of Israel as a bulwark of democracy in the Middle East – are great virtues sadly missing from some parts of the country's political discourse.

I am grateful to Iain Dale, James Stephens and their colleagues at Biteback for giving me the opportunity to write this book. Olivia Beattie provided support and guidance throughout the process, while Bernadette Marron proved an excellent editor and meticulous fact-checker. All errors are, of course, my own.

I would like to thank, too, those who agreed to be interviewed for this project for sharing their time and recollections with me: Geoffrey Alderman, Laurence Brass, Alan Cohen, Shimon Cohen, Lord Howard, Neville King, Tessa and Derek Phillips, Lord Powell, Sir Malcolm Rifkind, Lord Sherbourne, Norman Strauss and Lord Young.

Geoffrey Alderman, Shimon Cohen, Jennifer Gerber and Nick Laitner read sections of the book and I am grateful for their comments and feedback. I have been fortunate to have worked, and been friends with, Jennifer for nearly fifteen years. I have learned a lot about both Israel and the Jewish community in Britain from her and this book reflects the interest she has helped to spark. Jo Tanner gave me my first job in journalism and taught me the ropes. For that, and much else besides, I am grateful.

The idea for this book stemmed from researching a piece for the *Jewish Chronicle*. I began writing for the paper three years ago and have much appreciated the opportunities provided by its editor, Stephen Pollard, and the staff of the *JC*. I am also grateful to Stephen for providing me with access to the *JC*'s archives.

During the process of writing the book, I was awarded a grant by the Society of Authors, which allowed me to have more space and time than I otherwise would have had.

Andrew Riley of the Thatcher Archives at Churchill College, Cambridge provided much-valued guidance and help, allowing me to tap into his unsurpassed knowledge of the resources available to those researching aspects of Lady Thatcher's life and premiership. The Margaret Thatcher Foundation has an excellent online trove of original documents (www.margaretthatcher.org) from which I have drawn heavily. Richard Goldstein of the Institute for Jewish Policy Research helped me to track down some hitherto elusive publications.

As well as giving me the happiest of childhoods, my mum and dad imparted and encouraged a love of history and politics in their (slightly precocious) schoolboy son. Our many happy family holidays included one to Israel when I was aged eight. Although I have returned to Israel on a number of occasions since, I cannot but think there is some connection between that holiday and this book. For all of this, and all that I continue to owe them, I am always grateful. During my writing of this book, my dad acted as indefatigable researcher and editor and, most importantly, unfailing enthusiast. Both of our names should really be on the cover. For Paul Lantsbury's love, support, limitless good humour and patience, I am ever appreciative. This book is dedicated to the three most important people in my life.

INDEX